THE ONE YEAR

DAILY ACTS

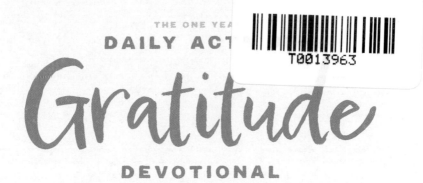

Gratitude

DEVOTIONAL

365 INSPIRATIONS TO ENCOURAGE A
LIFE OF THANKFULNESS

JULIE FISK | KENDRA ROEHL | KRISTIN DEMERY

TYNDALE
MOMENTUM®

A Tyndale nonfiction imprint

Visit Tyndale online at tyndale.com.

Visit Tyndale Momentum online at tyndalemomentum.com.

Tyndale, Tyndale's quill logo, *Tyndale Momentum*, and the Tyndale Momentum logo are registered trademarks of Tyndale House Ministries. Tyndale Momentum is a nonfiction imprint of Tyndale House Publishers, Carol Stream, Illinois.

The One Year is a registered trademark of Tyndale House Ministries. *One Year* is a trademark of Tyndale House Ministries.

The One Year® Daily Acts of Gratitude Devotional: 365 Inspirations to Encourage a Life of Thankfulness

Published in association with the literary agency of Books & Such Literary Management, 52 Mission Circle, Suite 122, PMB 170, Santa Rosa, CA 95409

Designed by Eva M. Winters

Edited by Donna L. Berg

For information about special discounts for bulk purchases, please contact Tyndale House Publishers at csresponse@tyndale.com, or call 1-855-277-9400.

ISBN 978-1-4964-6232-9

Printed in the United States of America

29	28	27	26	25	24	23
7	6	5	4	3	2	

To our wildest cheerleaders:
Aaron, Kyle, and Tim.

Your unwavering support, vision for what could be,
and superior math skills are why anything we've ever written
has had the chance to be published. We love you.

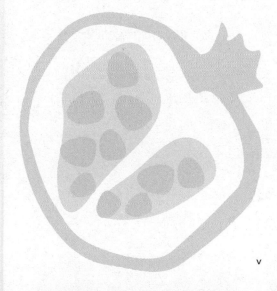

Introduction

I (Kendra) looked down the row at my children. We'd just listened to a sermon on the importance of gratitude, and although I fully agreed with everything the impassioned pastor said, I couldn't help but wonder: *Gratitude? Sure, that sounds good, but how do I incorporate those ideas on a practical level? How can I be more grateful for every part of my real, messy life? How might an increase in gratitude change me, my family, and my community?*

Over the years, Kristin, Julie, and I have written about kindness, friendship, and the power of words, sharing our own efforts to intentionally incorporate those principles into our lives. And though we have experienced peace and purpose, we knew there was still work to be done in our hearts. We felt anxious, tired, and a little stressed out, but the hope of "more"—more Jesus, more peace, more appreciation for the people and things in our lives that often go overlooked—tugged at us.

The benefits of having a grateful spirit are undeniable. We will suffer fewer aches and pains and less stress, and we won't experience toxic emotions like envy, resentment, and regret quite as often. Gratitude has been shown to increase happiness, reduce depression, and foster resilience, and it can even help us to overcome trauma. On top of that, grateful people tend to be more empathetic and to have healthier self-esteem and improved sleep. They are even better equipped to resist making social comparisons and instead can appreciate other people's accomplishments.[*] I don't know about you, but these are all things I want more of in my life.

We know that creating any new habit can be challenging, and developing a

---

*Amy Morin, "7 Scientifically Proven Benefits of Gratitude," *Psychology Today*, April 3, 2015, https://www.psychology today.com/us/blog/what-mentally-strong-people-dont-do/201504/7-scientifically-proven-benefits-gratitude.

habit of gratitude is no different. In the busyness of friend and family activities, work commitments, social obligations, and a never-ending to-do list, making and finding the time to help ourselves and our families become more grateful, loving, and kind feels overwhelming.

Yet Kristin, Julie, and I often realize that when we are struggling with something—in this instance, finding ways to be thankful—it's time to pay attention. We wrote this book as we began imperfectly incorporating a habit of gratitude into our own everyday lives. As we intentionally began looking for opportunities to be thankful, our perspectives shifted and our eyes were open to see all of the good God is doing every day.

One of the most beautiful gifts of practicing gratitude and living out thankfulness is that we get to stop focusing only on ourselves. Instead, we become better equipped to see the needs of others while still being thankful for what we have at the same time.

Throughout our gratefulness journey, we rediscovered the excitement of being on mission with God in a million ordinary ways. We learned that once we were intentional in expressing gratitude, it began to spill out onto those around us in the most humbling and beautiful ways.

So, in the pages of this book, we invite you to take the first steps toward incorporating gratitude into your daily life. While it may be challenging at first, we promise you won't regret it.

Kendra, Kristin, and Julie

January

Why Be Grateful?

"You must love the LORD your God with all your heart, all your soul, all your mind, and all your strength." The second is equally important: "Love your neighbor as yourself." No other commandment is greater than these.

MARK 12:30-31

"Why be grateful?" my husband asked one morning as we talked about writing a devotional on gratitude.

I thought for a moment, surprisingly stumped.

"I'm not sure," I said with a laugh. "I think there are lots of reasons—God asks us to, it's good for us, I *really* want our kids to have a good example of being grateful. Just to list a few."

He nodded in agreement. "That's for sure." We both chuckled.

As we finished our devotions and I went about my day, I kept pondering his question. *Why should we be grateful?* I prayerfully thought, bringing my question to God.

And as I listened for an answer, I realized thankfulness pulls me out of myself and away from focusing on my life and problems. It frees me up to love others without strings attached. It shifts my focus so I can see another person's needs and have empathy for what they may be going through in life. And it reminds me to appreciate all I have, even the simplest of things.

Jesus' two greatest commandments were to love God and to love others. Everything else we do as Christians hinges on these two things. When we go throughout our days with an attitude of gratitude for the things we have, the people we love, and the simple joys in our lives, we will be more inclined to show love to God and others because we won't be jealous or angry about what others have or stingy with our own possessions. With a grateful heart, we're able to recognize that there is abundance in the Kingdom of God, leaving us free to share all that we have.

Kendra

Today's Act of Gratitude

What might God be inviting you into as you consider gratitude this year? Think about three ways thankfulness could change your perspective and how you love God and those around you.

Embracing Feedback

People who accept discipline are on the pathway to life,
but those who ignore correction will go astray.

PROVERBS 10:17

Ping.

The gentle chime heralded the arrival of an email I was slightly dreading: my student evaluations had come in and were available via a single mouse click.

My cursor hovered over the link to instantaneous statistics in bar graphs and percentages, comparing my teaching to that of other faculty on campus. At a granular level, they would measure student outcomes and my ability to engage learners in the day-to-day grind through the material.

I hate the seemingly long moments between receiving these emails and clicking the link. As a classic overachiever with tendencies toward people-pleasing, I simultaneously long for and dread feedback. My heart races as old insecurities and questions of worth flood my brain, and persistent lies try to resurrect themselves, insisting that I entertain them yet again.

I've learned to pray over feedback (teaching or otherwise), asking first that Jesus would help me filter it through the lens of scriptural truth, but also that I'd receive it with an open heart and mind, without taking offense or becoming defensive.

And as much as I hate receiving anything but the highest ratings, I'm grateful for harder feedback—information that reveals blind spots or shortcomings, suggestions for what I've learned to call growth opportunities. Truthful feedback highlighting a weak spot means someone was brave enough to risk offending or angering me because they see my potential and care enough about my future growth to speak up.

As a woman who loves and follows Jesus, I am continually being refined in my faith and other areas of life—whether that be professionally or in my relationships. If I'm not actively growing—listening to those who love me enough to offer correction—then I'm stagnant, at risk of going astray from the best God has for me and what he's called me to do. Admittedly, this is hard. But the resulting growth and improvement are so worth it.

Julie

Today's Act of Gratitude

As we start this new year, take a moment to gratefully consider a piece of honest feedback given in good faith. What change do you need to make?

The Morning Shift

The faithful love of the LORD never ends! His mercies never cease.
Great is his faithfulness; his mercies begin afresh each morning.

LAMENTATIONS 3:22-23

My friend Andy told me that he begins each day with gratitude. For the last several years, he's made it his practice: before he emerges from bed each morning, he sits on the edge and thinks about what he's grateful for. By the time his feet touch the floor, he's already listed several items, including his wife and young children, his business and clients, and his health.

Starting the morning with gratitude focuses him on what matters. He's not grumbling that his preschooler woke him up after a night terror, or that he has a lot to accomplish, or that his alarm sounded too early. Instead of focusing on what has gone wrong, he focuses on what is right.

If I'm honest, the first thing I usually do in the morning is reach for my phone, if only to check the time. Intrigued by my friend's idea, I decided to try it for myself. The night before my experiment began, I wrote GRATEFUL in capital letters on a sticky note and placed it on my phone.

When I woke up, the little reminder was just the push I needed to find reasons to be grateful instead of focusing on my to-do list. Instead of complaining to myself about how chilly the room was in the predawn hours, I was thankful for the fuzzy slippers next to the bed. Instead of becoming impatient with how long my coffee took to brew, I spent those few minutes switching on a heating pad and starting up the fireplace so I'd have a cozy nook to sit in once the coffee was finished. Instead of wishing my daughter had slept just a little bit longer so that I could complete my early morning tasks, I curled her into my side and pulled up a fuzzy blanket as we admired the pink and purple hues of the rising sun.

Within a few days of incorporating my sticky note system, I found myself looking forward to the peaceful daybreaks. The morning shift was just what I needed to refocus my day.

Kristin

Today's Act of Gratitude

Place the word "grateful" on your phone or mirror so that you see it first thing in the morning. Then, list three things for which you're grateful.

Honest Emotions

Be happy with those who are happy, and
weep with those who weep.

ROMANS 12:15

"I'm so sad," a dear friend admitted to me recently over the phone. We had been discussing a dream we were pursuing together, and things weren't working out as we'd hoped.

"I am too," I admitted, feeling relieved by her honesty that allowed me the opportunity to express the heaviness in my heart as well. "What should we do?" I asked.

"I have a few ideas," she answered.

We spent the next hour brainstorming ways to keep pursuing our goals together while adjusting and shifting our next steps. I hung up, encouraged and grateful for a friend that I could be truthful with, not having to hide or diminish my feelings. And although nothing had changed—not yet anyway—simply being able to vent and then look for ways to improve our approach felt good because I knew I wasn't alone in my discouragement.

Hiding harder emotions, especially disappointments, is something we often feel pressure to do. Statements like "It's no big deal," "I wasn't that interested," or "I'm fine" are all ways we try to dismiss letting others know when we're sad or discouraged.

But God gave us our emotions, all of them. And to deny our feelings, especially the more troubling ones, is to deny what God has given us to feel as human beings. We've all had disappointment, pain, and sadness, and when we share it with others, they can help us carry our burden. It is what God wants us to do. We are to "be happy with those who are happy, and weep with those who weep." To do that, we have to be honest with one another about our joys but also our sorrows and disappointments. It's not always comfortable, but once we take a chance and let others know how we're feeling, it allows them the opportunity to show us support and offer comfort. And I am thankful that this is God's heart for all of us.

Kendra

Today's Act of Gratitude

Share a recent disappointment with a trusted friend and ask for their prayers. Express your gratitude to God for providing such a friend.

No Such Thing as Bad Weather

Blessed be the name of God forever and ever, to whom belong wisdom and might. He changes times and seasons; he removes kings and sets up kings; he gives wisdom to the wise and knowledge to those who have understanding; he reveals deep and hidden things; he knows what is in the darkness, and the light dwells with him.

DANIEL 2:20–22, ESV

Surveying the sled tracks that skirted the playground and led directly to the trees edging the bottom of the backyard, I hesitated. I'm more of a read-books-in-front-of-a-cozy-fire mom than a go-sledding-in-freezing-temperatures mom.

But my kids had been begging me to go sledding, and in a weak moment, I'd finally said the magic words: "Okay, I'll go sledding tomorrow."

Well, tomorrow had arrived, and I planned to make good on my promise.

All three of my children came to life when I started to layer up indoors, and they raced to get on their own gear. By the time I finished adding dry-wicking clothes, a heavy coat and snow pants, and cozy boots and gloves, I was overheated. As I made my way to the backyard, I was reminded of a Scandinavian saying: "There's no such thing as bad weather, only bad clothes." And as I zoomed down our backyard hill, I couldn't help but agree.

Because I'd forgotten how magical it all was: the sparkling snow, the joy on my kids' faces, the excellent workout of trudging up a hill again and again. Taking a moment to breathe in the crisp air, I flopped into the snow and surveyed my surroundings. I took note of the swaying trees, the flitting birds, and the whispering wind. The world felt reverently still, almost holy, the silence broken only by my kids' happy shouts.

There is beauty to be seen in all seasons—in nature and life—if only we're willing to look for it. Yet our preparation is vital. Just like I need to put on the proper layers of clothing for sledding downhill, I need to store God's Word in my heart. That way, when storms or hard seasons come, I'll be ready to thank God for preparing the way.

Kristin

Today's Act of Gratitude

Spend time outside. Take notice of five things you usually wouldn't pay attention to, thanking God for them.

The Heart of Worship

With all my heart I will praise you, O Lord my God. I will give glory to your name forever, for your love for me is very great. You have rescued me from the depths of death.

PSALM 86:12-13

Having plugged my destination into the navigation system, I readjusted my seat, turned on the seat warmers, and took a deep breath. I had a ninety-minute drive before me on twisty country roads, and I was alone, a relatively rare occurrence for such a long drive.

What to do with myself? I mentally ran through several podcasts and novels I had been listening to before deciding on a favorite playlist. And as I pulled out of the parking lot, having turned my car toward home, I cranked the volume to levels no mother would approve of and began belting out the lyrics in all of my tone-deaf and off-key glory.

When I tell people I cannot sing, they assume I'm being falsely modest or, at the very least, exaggerating the utter woefulness of my singing voice. And I'm too embarrassed to prove to them just how honest I am when I confess that I. Cannot. Sing. I'm awful. You don't want to stand next to me at church because I'll pull you out of key and off the beat if I sing above a whisper.

Despite all of this, I love singing. I have a deep, desperate, lifelong desire to sing beautifully, especially to God. And I know it's something I won't accomplish this side of heaven.

But this is the thing: it is my heart that God will find beautiful when I loudly croak along to worship songs. He is not put off by my inability to find the key or the beat. He cares more about my thoughts, motivations, and intentions. These are the things that reveal my love and awe for him. When I pause amid busy days to acknowledge the enormity of what God has done for me, that is what he finds pleasing, no matter the sound of my voice.

Julie

Today's Act of Gratitude

Sing a song of worship to God, turning off all distractions so that your heart is fully engaged. "Amazing Grace" is a lovely choice if you don't have a favorite.

Secure in God's Love

I am convinced that nothing can ever separate us from God's love. Neither death nor life, neither angels nor demons, neither our fears for today nor our worries about tomorrow—not even the powers of hell can separate us from God's love.

ROMANS 8:38

As we were driving home from school, my daughter Jasmine exclaimed, "Mom, Sara is so boy crazy. I feel bad. She has a different boyfriend every week. She's always talking about a new boy that she likes, and she's only in sixth grade."

I nodded, understanding. "And why do you think that is?" I asked.

Jasmine shrugged. "I'm not sure. Why do you think?"

"Well," I responded, "Sara only has her mom. Her dad was an alcoholic and doesn't have much to do with her, and her sister died last year. She's been through a lot in her life. Sometimes when people are looking for love, they think romantic love will fill them up when really, they're probably just missing those other people and relationships."

"That makes sense," Jasmine said.

"Just be a good friend to her," I advised. "Encourage her that she doesn't need a boyfriend to know that she's loved and valued. Let her know that you are there for her."

"Okay. I will," Jasmine responded.

It can be easy to look at the surface of someone's life and make judgments about them based on their behavior or choices, but often if we take a step back, we can see a trail of pain or hurt that led them there.

Everyone wants to be loved. God put that desire in us, and it is good. But sometimes that desire gets twisted when we experience pain or hurt from those around us, and we can go looking to gain love in ways that aren't healthy. The good news is, whether the people in our lives love us or not, God's love for us never changes. It never ceases. And there is nothing in all creation that can separate us from his love! We are always and forever secure in him and his love for us.

Kendra

Today's Act of Gratitude

Thank God for all the ways that he's shown his love to you.

Special Deliveries

*Now, just as you accepted Christ Jesus as your Lord, you must
continue to follow him. Let your roots grow down into him, and
let your lives be built on him. Then your faith will grow strong in
the truth you were taught, and you will overflow with thankfulness.*

COLOSSIANS 2:6-7

"Did you take a trip out to Napa again?" the UPS driver asked. I shook my head, laughing a bit as he held out a device for me to sign electronically for the wine at his feet.

"Some kind of sale, I think," I said ruefully.

Over the last couple of years, we've struck up a friendly relationship with our delivery driver, getting to know him in bits and pieces. He's always gracious and smiling, even when it's the hottest of summer days or the coldest of winter ones. One time, he even looped back later to deliver an item he knew we were expecting but hadn't been home to receive earlier in the day.

I'm grateful for him because I know how hard he works. And over time, the job has gotten harder. Long days, overtime, grumpy customers. He still enjoys his career, but the work is tiring.

So while I'm grateful that items can be delivered to my door, I'm even more thankful for the folks who make the deliveries.

I recently put together a little care package as a small way to say thanks: a cooler full of bottled water and other drinks, along with a variety of sweet and salty snacks. A note taped to the top—decorated by my six-year-old—read, "Thank you! Please take what you'd like," along with the names of delivery companies. We left it out for a couple of weeks and replaced items each day. By the time we finished, we had given out a couple of dozen items.

Sometimes practicing gratitude simply requires us to notice—to look for someone who might be overlooked, to thank someone who may go unthanked. We love others because Christ first loved us, and the way we treat others is an outpouring of that love. By following his lead, we will overflow with thankfulness for the many blessings we've received—and when we do, we'll begin to notice the many people who are worthy of our gratitude.

Kristin

Today's Act of Gratitude

Go out of your way to thank someone who delivers mail or packages.

That's Just the Way We Like It

Now to Him who is able to do exceedingly abundantly above all that we ask or think, according to the power that works in us, to Him be glory in the church by Christ Jesus to all generations, forever and ever. Amen.

EPHESIANS 3:20-21, NKJV

"Carol, I think we have a problem." The panicked tone of voice spoke volumes; we indeed had a problem amid the ten other problems all vying for our fearless leader's attention moments before three thousand women descended upon the convention center for a two-day conference.

I've learned so much about faith-filled leadership from Carol Lund, but her intentional calm in uncertainty and complete chaos ranks at the top of my list. Anyone privileged to volunteer under Carol for any length of time has heard her calm statement in the face of panic: "And that's just the way we like it."

For as long as I've known Carol, that has been her response—after a pause and with a wry smile—before launching into problem-solving mode, and we've all adopted it. Anytime the unexpected happens, you'll hear a collective pause before we all simultaneously chime in with "And that's just the way we like it." Then we draw a deep breath, remember that our event has been prayed over for months, and find a solution. It breaks the tension, allowing us to move quickly past disappointment and frustration, and propels us into grace-filled solution finding rather than leaving us to assign blame or wallow in dismay over what was supposed to happen.

Isn't it amazing how eight little words can trigger an immediate attitude readjustment, shifting the atmosphere for an entire group of people from chaos and frustration to peace and mercy? I am so grateful for Carol's example of intentionally resetting the tone in a room without diminishing the issue.

"And that's just the way I like it" has become my version of this phrase, a shortcut I whisper over situations and people, remembering that God is not surprised by the turn of events I'm facing and that he is both good and trustworthy.

Julie

Today's Act of Gratitude

Develop your own version of Carol's motto, trying it out as a way to reset your attitude when faced with difficulty.

Sharing the Burden

*Share each other's burdens, and
in this way obey the law of Christ.*

GALATIANS 6:2

Our son was in the hospital after getting his appendix removed. I was sitting alone with him in a room. We were unable to have visitors, but I posted a request for prayer on social media and sent a few texts to close friends.

Once family and friends saw my messages, my phone began to light up with offers to take our other kids or bring meals to our house, along with prayers for a quick recovery.

"How can we help?" The words came across my screen from several concerned friends.

I smiled as I read each one of their notes, grateful for their support and feeling more than willing to accept their offers of help. I let my husband know. "April will be by to pick up the girls for a bit. Don't worry about lunch; she'll feed them." A little while later: "Krista is bringing a meal over for supper."

I clicked my phone off and laid my head back on the chair, letting out a big sigh. I turned to look at my son resting comfortably in the bed, and I was overwhelmed with gratitude for the people around us.

A little while earlier, I had felt helpless to meet all of my family's needs. The messages from loved ones reminded me that we were not alone. I could feel the prayers and love even though we were physically separated.

As Christians, we are meant to share one another's burdens. God made us to be in community with others. Sharing honestly when we have needs is part of what brings us together. It's a give-and-take. Sometimes we offer help, and other times we receive it. Being on both sides of giving and accepting help is essential and needed. And I am learning to feel gratitude when I am placed in either position.

Kendra

Today's Act of Gratitude

Who has been giving to you lately? Send a note or message
to say how much you appreciate their support.

The Joy of Working

*Work willingly at whatever you do, as though you
were working for the Lord rather than for people.*

COLOSSIANS 3:23

It took me a while to find a job in college. My one requirement was that it needed to be flexible enough to accommodate my class schedule. The problem was that every student was looking for those kinds of flexible jobs, and openings were few and far between.

I remember wishing I could simply write potential employers a personal note each time I filled out an application: I am a good worker. I will be on time and work hard. You will not regret hiring me!

When I was finally hired at a clothing store, I loved it. The camaraderie among the workers was fun; we even spent time together outside of work. I enjoyed helping customers feel beautiful by finding the perfect fit. I learned how to fold a shirt expertly. And I became really good at figuring out what my 40 percent off discount would be for an item.

Of course, there were challenges as well. Occasionally there was drama or cattiness among the employees. My feet ached after hours of standing. Customers could be unkind, and busy Saturdays could be stressful.

Initially, I was excited to get hired. But over time, the excitement waned. The truth is that no matter the job, we can always find reasons to be grateful—if we look for them.

Rarely is a job 100 percent negative or 100 percent positive. The decision to be grateful need not be based on circumstances that ebb and flow. Instead, when we willingly view our work as yet another way to honor God in all we do, we will recognize the more significant implications it has for building our character and providing opportunities to influence those around us. Asking questions—*Who am I influencing for the better in this position? How do people see me praising God in the way I treat others?*—can help us reframe our attitude. When we look for the good, we'll find it. And when we do, we will be more likely to praise God for giving us the work of our hands to accomplish.

Kristin

Today's Act of Gratitude

List a few reasons you're grateful for a job or other work you pursue.

An Invaluable Gift

*Listen to advice and accept discipline, and
at the end you will be counted among the wise.*

PROVERBS 19:20, NIV

"I can't do it. I'm dropping out of law school." My melodramatic declaration on an inhaled sob clearly caught my mom off guard.

Classes for my first semester had ended, finals week was a few days away, and the pressure cooker of law school culture had finally gotten to me. In a moment of panic, I'd packed a bag and driven home. And here I stood, a teary mess, outside the classroom where Mom taught as a paraprofessional.

My mom is steady and calm in the midst of chaos, and once she got over the shock of finding me outside her door, she hugged me close, told me we'd figure it out together, and sent me to my childhood home to get a snack and rest until she arrived.

"What's your plan B?" she asked hours later after dinner, as the two of us sat at the kitchen counter over cups of coffee.

"My plan B?" I replied. "I don't know. Do I need one?"

"You do. You can quit, but you need to plan for what you will do instead. And, while you think about that, why don't you stay here and study for finals instead of driving back to campus?"

Stumped and slightly flummoxed, I did exactly what Mom suggested. I stayed with my parents, and in the end, passed my finals, decided law school could be endured, and never did think of a suitable alternative plan.

Mom kept me from making a rash decision in a moment of intense pressure, and I've been forever grateful for her objective wisdom and love when my emotions prevented me from seeing the situation clearly.

Scripture has a lot to say about wisdom, including calling it "more precious than rubies" (Proverbs 3:15) and promising that when we pray for wisdom, God—who is generous—will freely give it to us without reproach (see James 1:5). Godly wisdom is ours; we merely need to ask. Other than salvation, I'm hard-pressed to think of a more valuable gift.

Julie

Today's Act of Gratitude

Who has been a wise influence in your life? Reach out
with a thank-you even as you consider how you might pay
it forward by sharing wisdom with someone else.

Experience Is Evidence

Taste and see that the LORD is good.
Oh, the joys of those who take refuge in him!

PSALM 34:8

"Can you read that letter?" the optometrist asked.

Staring across the room, I tried hard to make out the black shape on a white background. It looked fuzzy. Sighing, I admitted the truth. "Only if I squint."

The fact that I could barely see a letter the size of my palm felt a little disheartening. Having worn glasses for thirty years, I'm no stranger to having my eyes checked. But the longer I sat there, staring at the visible proof of just how much I rely on the lenses I wear each day, I couldn't help but blurt out what I was thinking.

"It's amazing how much I take being able to see for granted," I told the optometrist as she typed up her notes.

She nodded wryly, fingers still tapping on keys. "We definitely do."

When I put my contact lenses back in my eyes, I couldn't help but marvel at the crispness of the colors and the beauty of the world around me. My temporary loss had reminded me of the great privilege I have in using all five senses. Without my glasses, I wouldn't be able to drive safely. The horizon would be blurred, my depth perception would be off, and I wouldn't be able to read any of the signs.

Our eyeballs are only about an inch in diameter, but they have an outsize impact on our daily lives. So, too, do our other senses. The smell of lilacs or woodsmoke, the sound of croaking frogs or our favorite song, the taste of coffee or chocolate, the feel of a cozy blanket or a piping hot bath—all of these small experiences add up to the sum of our lives. As Christians, we're called to "taste and see that the LORD is good"—in other words, experience is what teaches us how good God is. Experience is evidence, and our experience of the world is a reminder of the many gifts God has given to us through his creation.

Kristin

Today's Act of Gratitude

Choose one of your senses to focus on. Spend time
considering all of the ways you use it each day.

In God's Image

This is how God loved the world: He gave his one and only Son,
so that everyone who believes in him will not perish but have eternal life.

JOHN 3:16

"Way to clear the goal, Omar!" As Jon's teammate booted the soccer ball down the field and away from our goalie, I sighed in relief. I smiled softly as two languages—English and Somali—filled the sidelines where we collectively cheered on our middle schoolers. Our two coaches, one fluent in Somali, strode up and down our side of the field, pulling players aside shoulder to shoulder as they leaned close with advice.

I'm on the constant hunt for opportunities to build community across cultures, and I'd stumbled upon this one with our middle school soccer league. In my eyes, the teamwork skills Jon learned on a culturally diverse team was the true win, regardless of games won and lost.

Echo chambers are dangerously easy to slip into with social media algorithms and cable news pundits. We will find ourselves surrounded almost entirely by people with similar backgrounds unless we intentionally choose a different path.

Aaron and I love people from Ireland, Kenya, Iraq, China, Taiwan, Somalia, Afghanistan, and beyond. Our friends' willingness to share parts of their culture and perspective has been one of the greatest blessings of our lives. We've repeatedly discovered—firsthand—that our wildly different friends are created in God's image, just as we are.

We can unintentionally adopt and perpetuate harmful stereotypes and assumptions about those "not from here" or "from here but not like us." The best way to sift fact from fiction is to draw near, share meals, and most importantly, listen carefully when someone feels safe enough to share about challenging circumstances, even if what they've walked through is different than your interactions or experience.

God loves the world, and he doesn't play favorites. Jesus is the sacrificial lamb for every last one of us if we'll accept him. As news stories and quotes from Martin Luther King Jr. trend, let's recognize that our fellow image-bearers of God may have struggled in ways we have not, and those struggles may be more recent than we'd care to admit. We can love God with our whole, thankful hearts and acknowledge when the church has fallen short, determined to do better going forward.

Julie

Today's Act of Gratitude

As you hear the difficult stories of others, prayerfully
ask God to break your heart for what breaks his, asking
him what he might call you to do about it.

God Is in the Small Answers

*Faith shows the reality of what we hope for;
it is the evidence of things we cannot see.*

HEBREWS 11:1

I sat one morning flipping through my journal. Having a few extra moments, I decided to skim back over the past year, reminding myself of all that we had gone through as a family. As I looked through the pages, I was unexpectedly reminded of all the little ways God had shown up for our family and other loved ones throughout those months.

Prayers for family members facing illness, a friend needing wisdom regarding buying a new house, a child desiring a good friend—all things I would easily have forgotten about had I not jotted down just a few sentences each day, unintentionally charting the course of our lives through its ebbs and flows.

As I read back through each answered prayer, my heart filled with gratitude to God for his faithfulness in so many little details of our lives. I was also struck by how easily I could forget all he had done. I decided to take just a moment to thank God for the answers I hadn't even remembered, and I determined to continue writing down even the smallest of things, so as never to forget.

Keeping a record of our lives and prayers is one way to see how our faith is lived out in what we hope for and yet do not see. When we can look back and remember all the ways God has been faithful to us, our faith will continue to grow, and our gratitude will increase. We will be encouraged to continue bringing all things we currently face to God in prayer because we can see how he has shown up in the past. Don't dismiss the small prayers that God answers; they add up to a whole lot of faith.

Kendra

Today's Act of Gratitude

Begin to record the small and large prayer requests
you bring to God daily, weekly, or even monthly. Look
back and thank him for what he has done.

Sun Dog Surprise

God said, "I am giving you a sign of my covenant with you and with all living creatures, for all generations to come. I have placed my rainbow in the clouds. It is the sign of my covenant with you and with all the earth."

GENESIS 9:12–13

Teeth chattering, I leaned over and turned the heat up to full blast. It was cold, so cold that I hadn't wanted my kids to wait at the bus stop and had decided to drive them to school instead. Though my car said it was minus twelve degrees, I knew from checking the weather online that it felt like a chilly minus twenty-four degrees.

I adore Minnesota, but this cold? Not so much. As we headed toward school, the girls chattered away in the back seat while I hunched over in my coat, seeking warmth.

Suddenly, I gasped. Since I was leaning over, I was perfectly positioned to notice the rainbow-like halos shimmering in the sky.

"Girls, do you see those sun dogs?" I asked, pointing to the patches of light that looked like parentheses on each side of the sun. "They look kind of like mini rainbows. We see them mostly when it's really cold."

"Yes!" they said excitedly, craning their necks to see the effect caused by the refraction of sunlight through ice crystals in the atmosphere. As we pulled to the curb at the school and the girls exited the car, I could still see them pointing to the sky, stopping to take a better look.

As I drove away, I was reminded of another shimmering vision in the sky: the rainbow mentioned in Genesis. After the great Flood that Noah, his family, and two of each animal survived in the ark, God promised Noah that he would never again flood the earth. As a sign of his promise, he sent a rainbow to arch through the sky.

And on a wintry day with no rain in sight, thinking of Noah's rainbow is a reminder to me that even now, God's love is evident in his creation. His promise to Noah endures—if only we'll look for it.

Kristin

Today's Act of Gratitude

Look to the skies. Thank God for the cloudless blue sky, the falling snow, the nourishing rain, the soaring birds, or the glowing sunset as it dips over the horizon.

Seasons of Life

For everything there is a season,
a time for every activity under heaven.

ECCLESIASTES 3:1

Julie and I had just finished sharing all about kindness and kind acts at a MOPS group when a young mom approached us. She had all these wonderful ideas for ways she wanted to help in her community, but she felt frustrated. "My kids are so young. I can't get out to volunteer at these places and do as much as I want to."

"Of course, you can't," Julie said with a smile. "You've got a three-year-old and a newborn. But that's okay. This is just a season. Hang on to your dreams. There will come another season soon, and you'll have more flexibility to get out. In the meantime, think of things you might be able to do from home to support these places."

The woman nodded, grateful for the insight and permission to do what she could now while looking forward to a season in which she could do more.

"You can do all that you want in life; you just can't do it all right now. And that's okay," I reminded her as we hugged, and she left to get her small children from childcare.

It seems obvious, but sometimes when we are in the midst of a challenging season, it's hard to see that someday things will change. But if we take a step back, we can see that we have walked through several seasons in life, and there will be many more to come. Being mindful of the stage of life we're in and grateful for all the good in it is so important, even while we're facing difficulties.

Soon enough, we'll be in a new phase that will have its joys but also its unique challenges to overcome. Scripture encourages us that there is a certain season for everything, and a particular time for each activity. Sometimes we have to wait on a dream or goal, but rest assured, if God has given it to you, he will be faithful to bring it to fruition. It just may have to wait until a better season.

Kendra

Today's Act of Gratitude

Thank God for something you are grateful for in your current season
of life and something you are looking forward to in the next.

Beauty for Ordinary Days

You are worthy, O Lord our God, to receive glory and honor and power. For you created all things, and they exist because you created what you pleased.

REVELATION 4:11

"Mom, why did you buy flowers?"

Reaching for the last grocery bag in the trunk, I peered over my shoulder at my son as he approached from around the corner of the house, "Because I have an empty vase."

"That's not a reason to buy flowers," Jon scoffed as he took two bags so I could balance my bouquet and the last bag and still close the trunk.

"Honey, that's a perfect reason to buy flowers. Now, tell me about guitar practice," I said as we both turned to lug the groceries to the house.

I'd bought the blooms on a whim, pausing on my way through the grocery store floral department to breathe in the wafting scent of dozens of bouquets. Looking past roses and lilies, my eyes snagged on the small bunch of mini carnations as I thought of the trio of milk glass bud vases tucked away in my cupboard, waiting to be used.

It was an ordinary day in an ordinary week. And a younger version of me would have scoffed—both at the mundaneness of carnations and at the waste of money to have fresh flowers on my kitchen island. But this version of me is learning to slow down, to use the pretty vases kept hidden away, to notice the beauty of God's creation surrounding us, even on regular days.

It's easy to race through our days, weeks, or seasons, intent on tasks, obligations, and chores, so focused on accomplishing our to-do lists that we forgo little pleasures, believing either that they are a waste of energy or that we don't deserve them. Searching out beauty on ordinary days is an act of worship when we pause to acknowledge and appreciate God's handiwork. It can bring our thoughts back to God and help us recognize his sovereignty and his creative genius.

Julie

Today's Act of Gratitude

Search for beauty as you go about your tasks, pausing
to acknowledge God's authority and thanking him for
creating both the practical and the beautiful.

Support through Prayer

*All the believers devoted themselves to the apostles'
teaching, and to fellowship, and to sharing in meals
(including the Lord's Supper), and to prayer.*

ACTS 2:42

"How can we pray for you?"

It's the question asked at the end of every one of our church community gatherings, and it's probably my favorite part of our meetings together. Of course, I love the Bible reading and discussion—I'm always challenged and encouraged—but sharing needs and offering support and prayer is the most cherished time for me.

As I listen to others' needs and joys, I feel encouraged in what I am facing in my own life. Knowing others have their own burdens yet are willing to walk with me through mine reminds me that overcoming difficulties together is better than doing it alone.

Sometimes people have requests regarding jobs and finances; other times, they need prayer for children going through challenging seasons. Someone else may share about a family we all know is struggling and offer ways to work together to help. Others have pregnancy concerns or health issues. Nothing is too big or too small to be mentioned.

Throughout my week, I'll whisper prayers for the requests I heard, trusting that God is with our group no matter what they face that day, and knowing that they are praying the same for me.

Scripture tells us that the early church devoted themselves to teaching, fellowship, sharing meals, and prayer. And our lives today should look very similar to this. We need the same things the first Jesus followers did—community, teaching, support, and prayer. Although many things have changed over time, these things have remained, and they are essential for all Jesus followers.

Kendra

Today's Act of Gratitude

Who do you know who needs prayer? Reach out to let
them know that you are thinking of them, and see if there
is anything specific you can be praying about.

Making the Most of Every Moment

Be careful how you live. Don't live like fools, but like those who are wise. Make the most of every opportunity in these evil days. Don't act thoughtlessly, but understand what the Lord wants you to do.

EPHESIANS 5:15-17

Unthinkingly, I reached my hand out to hold my daughter's, but she pretended not to notice. We were leaving Target, and the parking lot was busy. For more than ten years, I'd held a small hand in my own while navigating noisy trucks and fast cars. It felt natural for me to grab a child's hand. I'd forgotten that at age twelve my daughter was "too old" for that, according to her.

Quickly realizing my faux pas, I let the moment pass. But in the car on the way home, I reached my hand into the back seat, toward her. Now that no one else was around, she grabbed it and held it between her own, and I savored the moment.

I've been reminding myself to be more present in moments like these, not only because the people around me deserve my full attention, but also because this time of my life is slipping away. Two of my children will already be grown and gone within ten years. I'll know them as adults much longer than I will have known them as children.

I don't want to miss these precious times. So I hug my littlest daughter close and breathe her in as she clings, arms and legs wound around my neck and waist, as I carry her from her bed to the living room couch each morning before school. I kiss her squishy cheeks as often as I can, smile at misspoken words, and listen to a million made-up songs about her stuffed animals. When we go to Target, I tuck her tiny hand into my own, knowing that soon, like her sister, she'll be too old to want me to do so.

Though this moment in life is temporary, the effects can last a lifetime. Whether it's parenting children, being a good friend, working hard at our job, or loving well, wisdom requires us to make the most of every opportunity. When we do, we honor how God wants us to live. And we value the temporary, grateful that we have been given a chance to appreciate it.

Kristin

Today's Act of Gratitude

List five things in your life that are temporary.
Spend time thanking God for them.

Who's in Charge?

*If your sinful old self is the boss over your mind, it leads to death. But if
the Holy Spirit is the boss over your mind, it leads to life and peace.*

ROMANS 8:6, NLV

Well, next time I'll just . . . Shaking my head in an attempt to hush my angry internal tirade, I sighed as I reached for my second cup of coffee.

I was frustrated. Frustrated with the mad scramble to find a missing notebook just as we were supposed to be out the door for school, frustrated with the tension in the car as my kids scrambled out to beat the first bell, frustrated with the small argument I'd had with Aaron even before we were missing the notebook or were late to school.

Everything about the morning had gone awry, and the little voice in my head desperately wanted to continue picking fights with my kids and Aaron, despite their being in other places and unable to respond.

Taking a deep, calming breath, I determined I'd had enough. I sent my husband a text prayer, praying a specific blessing over his busy day filled with meetings and a big presentation. I finished by reminding him of my love for him, for us, for our family.

And as I set the phone back down, I prayed for myself: *Lord, help me let this go. Help me have grace for him, our kids, and myself. Give me peace to go about my day. Help me to release this frustration. Help me redeem today.*

Living in community with others—parents, siblings, a spouse, kids, roommates, neighbors, church family, friends, coworkers—brings moments of frustration, misunderstanding, irritation, and anger. It also brings laughter, joy, contentment, peace, support, and love.

The beautiful thing is that we have control. We choose who gets to be boss in our mind: our old, sinful nature or the Holy Spirit. Isn't that a refreshing revelation? Regardless of what the world tries to tell us, we decide which emotions we feed and which we starve. We are not victims of our negative feelings. Our decision to follow Jesus provided a new way, and in that way lies peace, redemption, and life.

Julie

Today's Act of Gratitude

Be intentional about starving negative emotions.

Simplifying Gratitude

*Your love has given me much joy and comfort, my brother, for
your kindness has often refreshed the hearts of God's people.*

PHILEMON 1:7

I'm embarrassed to admit it, but I'm terrible at sending thank-you notes. It's not that I'm ungrateful or haven't tried in the past. On many occasions I've cleaned out a dresser drawer or a shelf in the mudroom and found half-finished notes I started and discarded: notes for baby showers, birthdays, gifts for my children—all written out but never sent.

It's not that I don't feel gratitude. I do. The problem is that I fail to prioritize getting those notes in the mail. I stress out about what the card should say, feel awkward, and fool myself into thinking I'll return to it later. *I don't have time to hunt for an address label or a stamp*, I reason. Saying thank you in person I can do, but a note? That feels extra. And who has time for extra?

The truth is that I have plenty of time to read books or go out for coffee with a friend. I make time for plenty of other activities, but expressing gratitude can sometimes get lost in the shuffle of daily life. Yet we know that it matters when we go out of our way to say thank you to another person. Like dropping off a cozy drink on a cold day, it both heartens and comforts the recipient, reminding them that they are worthy and loved.

I think I've sometimes made gratitude too difficult, and I wonder if perhaps you've done the same. If so, maybe we need to simplify things. Let's stick a note on the mirror listing people to thank so we have a visual reminder each time we brush our teeth. Perhaps we could slot in a calendar reminder for five minutes each day to send text messages to thank others. Maybe we need to spend a few minutes prepping a stack of envelopes with a stamp and return address so they're ready when we need them.

Thankfulness is an outward expression of the internal change in our lives, a reflection of God's love for us, but it doesn't need to be complicated. Let's simplify it so that we can focus on truly living it.

Kristin

Today's Act of Gratitude

Write an overdue thank-you note. Send it right away.

Jesus Is Here

The church is his body; it is made full and complete by Christ, who fills all things everywhere with himself.

EPHESIANS 1:23

We try to make it a habit to spend a little time reading through Scripture with our kids every week. Our attempts are not perfect, and sometimes in busy seasons they don't happen as often as we'd like, but over the years, we've come back to this goal again and again.

One day as we were reading through the first chapter of Ephesians, I asked my kids what stood out to them. One child commented that they felt grateful God had adopted us, another marveled that Paul wrote about thanksgiving while in prison himself, and the third child was struck by the idea that Jesus "fills all things everywhere with himself."

We pondered that together as I asked them to imagine Jesus being in every space we find ourselves—school, work, activities, everywhere—and to consider what a comfort it is to know that he not only goes with us but goes before us. I told the kids that maybe this is one reason Paul was grateful, even while in prison. The Holy Spirit was there, encouraging, ministering to, and reminding Paul of what was true, no matter his surroundings. And then I told them, "And Jesus is still doing this today through his Spirit. Still giving peace and joy amid our everyday lives, even in the hard seasons, he fills everything with himself." My children nodded understanding as we closed our time in prayer.

There is no place on earth that is void of God's presence, no space too dark for him to occupy. We get to be his body, made complete in Christ, who "fills all things everywhere with himself." What hope this should give us as we go throughout our days and face both good and challenging times! We are not alone; Jesus is here.

Kendra

Today's Act of Gratitude

Write down and then share with someone else a time recently when you were grateful God was with you.

Work Smarter, Not Harder

Trust God from the bottom of your heart; don't try to figure out everything on your own. Listen for God's voice in everything you do, everywhere you go; he's the one who will keep you on track.

PROVERBS 3:5-6, MSG

"ARGH! What's with the streaks?" I whisper-shouted to no one in particular as I stood in my sunroom, hands on hips, lip curled in disgust, glaring as the late afternoon sun revealed the smudges in the windows I'd spent all day washing.

I'd tried everything I knew to prevent streaks, including lots of old-fashioned elbow grease and a special concoction my friend swears works miracles. Yet my best efforts hadn't been good enough. Muttering to no one in particular, I picked up my rags and cleaner, ready to return to work now that I could see the problem well enough to tackle it properly.

As I cleaned with purpose, my arm already aching from having blindly wiped for hours, I pondered the spiritual significance of working hard but blindly versus working with precision because I could see clearly.

How often do I race through life, trying to do what I think Jesus wants me to do before finally pausing halfway through to prayerfully ask if I'm on the right track?

How much unnecessary time and energy do I expend and what emotional toll do I subject myself to by not asking God to direct my steps before I jump into a situation?

My thoughts were gently convicting as I stood on sore feet, redoing work already done, silently praying: *Lord, forgive my perennial attempts to run ahead of you. Thank you for your guidance, your promise to direct my steps. Help me to wait patiently on you; your way is always better. Amen.*

God promises to direct our paths, to guide our steps, to make the way clear, but we have to trust him, listen for the Holy Spirit's voice through Scripture and prayer, and wait on God's plan. While waiting may feel hard in the moment, it almost always brings about better results with less striving. His plan is far superior to ours, and he's willing to share it—if we'll listen.

Julie

Today's Act of Gratitude

Ask God for clear direction on a big decision through prayer and Scripture, thanking him in advance for showing you the correct path.

You're More than a Label

We know that God causes everything to work together for the good of those who love God and are called according to his purpose for them.

ROMANS 8:28

"My sister didn't ask for the label of cancer. She didn't want it to be a part of her identity," I said as I looked around the room of women gathered for a retreat meant to encourage and revive them. "And yet, she told God, 'if you're going to allow this, I want to see how you will use it for your glory, even now.'"

I noticed a woman near the front brush a tear from her eye.

"And that's just what he did. God used that part of her identity to bring others to himself, healing and wholeness to people she came in contact with. And he will do the same for you."

Julie and I finished our time with prayer and walked off the stage. As we made our way back to our table, a woman gently touched my arm. She wanted to share with me her own label that she hadn't asked to receive. As I listened, my heart broke for the pain she'd faced. We prayed together and embraced before she went back to her seat. I quietly prayed that God would continue to encourage her as she left to go home.

Spouse. Parent. Student. Employee. Volunteer. We are all more than the labels that we, others, and society at large have given us over the years. Although most of our labels may be good or positive, far too many of us carry labels that can feel like heavy burdens and that we try to hide from others. Labels like failure, mess-up, incompetent, unlovable, divorced, abused, physically or mentally ill. Labels we never asked for and didn't want.

Yet God says that he can cause everything to work together for the good of those of us who love him. Does that mean he's okay with the pain we've experienced? No. But God often has a way of taking the hard things and using them to build our faith and the faith of those around us if we let him.

Kendra

Today's Act of Gratitude

Spend some time writing down the labels you've carried in life. Thank God for using even the negative labels for good in your life. Ask him how you can use one of those labels to bless or encourage someone else.

The Dishwasher Fiasco

Don't worry about anything; instead, pray about everything.
Tell God what you need, and thank him for all he has done.

PHILIPPIANS 4:6

I woke up to a strange groaning noise, rhythmic and awful. Instantly, I knew what it was.

The dishwasher was broken, and it was all my fault.

Earlier that night, I had reached under the sink for the detergent and accidentally grabbed the dish soap refill. The bottles had about the same height and heft. I realized my mistake almost immediately and wiped out the dispenser, replaced the dish soap with a small amount of the correct detergent, and started the cycle.

Thirty minutes later, I noticed water and bubbles on the floor. Uh-oh. I wiped up the spill and went to bed.

But when I heard the groaning, I knew. I launched out of bed and ran downstairs, filled with dread. At 3:17 a.m., the cycle should have finished hours ago. Instead, the motor was trying and failing, again and again. Cutting the power to the dishwasher, I headed back upstairs.

I can't believe I did that, I berated myself. *What a mess.* Instantly, the worries began: *What if it's expensive to fix? What if we need to get a new dishwasher?* My anxiety spiked as the negative thoughts circled.

The next morning, I sheepishly told my husband what had happened. Calmly, he said he'd contact a general contractor friend. By the time the morning was over, our friend had fixed the problem. What a relief!

Although I was happy my dishwasher was back in working condition, I was ashamed about my initial response. I hadn't bothered to pray. I hadn't asked God for his peace or comfort as I tried to sleep. I hadn't remembered all the times in the past when he's demonstrated his unchanging faithfulness to me. No, my worries and self-blaming hadn't fixed the situation—if anything, they had made it worse.

I love how straightforward Paul's words to the church of Philippi are when addressing their concerns: *Don't worry. Instead, pray. Tell God what you need. Thank him for what he's done.* You and I don't have to figure out everything in this life independently. Instead, let's seek God first, knowing that his ways are better than ours.

Kristin

Today's Act of Gratitude

Identify one situation that is troubling you. Follow Paul's advice to the Philippians: *Don't worry. Instead, pray. Tell God what you need. Thank him for what he's done.*

His Good Gifts

Whatever is good and perfect is a gift coming down to us from God our Father, who created all the lights in the heavens. He never changes or casts a shifting shadow.

JAMES 1:17

"I hope you are okay with this office; I know it's busy near the elevator."

The rest of his words were lost on me as I stared at what was going to be my very own office. Brick walls and an entire wall of windows stretching from the floor to the impossibly tall ceiling had me grinning from ear to ear. The trees just outside framed a beautiful view of the college campus where I'd be teaching. It was better than I could ever have imagined.

And the busy hallway with an elevator and stairwell just steps from my door was the perfect location for this extrovert who keeps a bowl of chocolates on the corner of her desk and leaves her door open, hoping to lure in passing faculty and students alike.

The very features that bothered other faculty members, marking my new office as the least desirable on the second floor of our historic building, were the same features I loved most about it. Every time I step into that beautiful space, I thank God for his goodness and for the gift of a beautiful place to write and work after years without a dedicated space.

And isn't that the amazing thing about gifts from God? He knows what delights us, what makes us laugh, and how our hearts are encouraged and comforted, and he sends those gifts to us. They might be as significant as a lovely office of our very own or as simple as a funny note from a friend we've been missing on a harder-than-average day. God's gifts are good and perfect and a reminder that we have a heavenly Father who sees us, knows us, loves us.

Julie

Today's Act of Gratitude

List three good gifts (big or small) that you've received this month.
And keep your eyes open for more gifts God sends your way.

Choosing to Love

I have loved you even as the Father has loved me. Remain in my love.
When you obey my commandments, you remain in my love, just as I obey
my Father's commandments and remain in his love. I have told you these
things so that you will be filled with my joy. Yes, your joy will overflow!

JOHN 15:9-11

My first car was a grandma car. Literally: it was my Grandma Jo's car—a white 1986 Olds 88 that she drove out of town once a week to play bingo. She had it for thirteen years, and when she no longer needed it and I began driving, it was still in pristine condition. It had a plush red interior that caused my young niece to exclaim, "Auntie, it's like a big couch!"

Of course, it wasn't sporty or anything that excited me as a sixteen-year-old girl—except that it was mine. That was thrilling. I can still remember the exhilaration of driving in our small town, music turned up, windows rolled down. I reveled in that freedom. Even now, a little time spent driving on an open road can bring peace on a stressful day.

But as with any new item, the glamour eventually wore off. Instead of being thankful that I had a car, I focused on what I didn't like. I wished I had a newer model that had heated seats and didn't need to be plugged in to a battery warmer every night to make sure it started in the winter. The shine had faded. I'd lost my first love.

If I'm honest, there have been times when the newness of living for Jesus has faded too. In John 15, Jesus talks about remaining in him. He compares himself to a grapevine, with the Father as the gardener and his followers as branches. He reminds us that we will continue to produce fruit only when rooted in him. He tells us that we must remain in his love for our joy to overflow. Remaining—making the ongoing decision to live out his commandments in our daily life—is what sparks joy and spurs gratitude to overflow.

Just like my first car, our love for Jesus isn't something to take for granted. The decision to love someone or something doesn't happen only once. We need to continually remember his blessings. His mercies are new every morning—what a delight! What a reason to be grateful. Let's thank him for his constant, abiding presence.

Kristin

Today's Act of Gratitude

In what ways have you been taking God's love for granted?
Spend time thanking God for his love for you.

A Change in Perspective

Since everything God created is good,
we should not reject any of it but receive it with thanks.

1 TIMOTHY 4:4

I've lived my entire life in Minnesota, and although I've appreciated the change of seasons, I have always disliked winter. There weren't any winter activities I liked, and I hate being cold, so most years I simply found myself suffering through winter, counting down the days until spring.

As an adult, I realized I didn't like half the year because of winter. And since my mood was starting to be affected, I decided that one of two things needed to happen: either we needed to move to a new location without winter (or at least with one that was much milder) or I needed to find a way to enjoy it.

One holiday season, my family decided to spend a few days at a nearby resort. There were so many outside activities for us to enjoy—bonfires, sleigh rides, and cross-country skiing. I got out with my kids and husband and enjoyed the outdoors more than I had in a long time.

When we got home, my husband suggested that we get some cross-country skis since it was an activity that we could do together. We purchased a pair for each of us, and for the rest of the winter, we went out several times on specially groomed trails around our community. And I thoroughly enjoyed it.

Now, a few years later, I've noticed I don't mind winter that much anymore. I have something I look forward to doing, and although I'm still not crazy about the cold, I no longer dread the season.

Have you ever had a shift in perspective in which something you disliked became something you enjoyed? Maybe you needed to get in shape for your health, and now you enjoy exercise, or you knew vegetables would be good for you, and now you enjoy them. Whatever it is, our preferences can grow and change over time. Scripture reminds us that everything God created is good, and we should receive it with thanks. Maybe we just need a change in perspective to do it.

Kendra

Today's Act of Gratitude

What is one thing you've changed your opinion about and can now say you are grateful to God for? What else might you need to change your perspective on?

Buddies

*Love is patient and kind. Love is not jealous or boastful or
proud or rude. It does not demand its own way. It is not
irritable, and it keeps no record of being wronged.*

1 CORINTHIANS 13:4-5

Glancing into the bleachers as she passed the basketball to a teammate, Carrie did a quick double take. "Jack came to my game?" Her mind whirled as she raced up and down the court, processing that her mom's fiancé was at her basketball game solo. With her mom needing to work full time, Carrie wasn't accustomed to having anyone in the stands to cheer specifically for her. And yet there Jack was, and there he would continue to be, throughout her junior high and high school sports career.

Carrie first met her stepdad, Jack, at the awkward age of twelve. A man with an observant, gentle heart, he asked if they could be buddies—a role meant to be carved out and defined by the two of them without intruding on parental or other traditionally defined relationships. Jack's steady presence, patient love, and gentle ways were a gift Carrie didn't know she needed but now credits as the best present she's ever received.

His arrival in her life was perfectly timed, and he remained a quiet, loving influence even as Carrie got married, became a pharmacist, and raised her children with all of the highs and lows that go into navigating life.

I had the privilege of knowing Jack, and he was just as Carrie describes him: unassuming and kindhearted, with an unexpected twist of funny. The love described in today's verses was the kind Jack epitomized. His influence was no less potent for being quiet, and his legacy is one any of us would be proud to have.

We can have a similar legacy—no special degrees, fancy titles, or particular skill sets required. It's as simple (and as difficult) as routinely and intentionally showering the love defined in 1 Corinthians 13 onto those around us. As we do that, even imperfectly, we'll transform situations and relationships in ways that will have an impact long after we've gone home to heaven.

Julie

Today's Act of Gratitude

Who has been a Jack in your life? Let them know how much
they've meant to you. Prayerfully consider who in your
circles needs a Jack and how you might respond.

What's Your Focus?

*Dear brothers and sisters, when troubles of any kind come
your way, consider it an opportunity for great joy.*

JAMES 1:2

"Here's why Minnesota has the best weather in the United States," I hear my husband say, his voice carrying from across the room. I look over with a smile, having heard this reasoning before. His audience looks skeptical, but he continues.

"January? Fresh year. Who's not excited about a new year? Everyone is setting goals and resolutions. February is equally cold, but it's the shortest month of the year. March is a coin flip—we've had Marches in the seventies, although we might get a storm or two. April is pretty and not as cold, and then our amazing weather starts in May or June," he says. His audience is fully engaged by now and listening intently, curious as to how he'll finish his pitch. "By the time it gets cold again, it's Thanksgiving and Christmas, and there's excitement around the holidays."

He pauses for breath, then finishes with a flourish: "We knock out our bad weather at the beginning of the year and get it out of the way—and that's why Minnesota has the best weather."

At this point, his listeners usually laugh or shrug. A Minnesota transplant, Tim could spend his time bemoaning our below zero temperatures or the fact that we have fewer sunny days than his home state of Colorado. Instead, he's chosen to embrace the weather—both the good and the harsh.

Our decision to be grateful doesn't mean we ignore or negate the hard things in life; it just means they aren't our focus. The choice to dwell instead on the joy we get out of having four seasons doesn't mean that we disregard the extreme cold and snow. It simply means we recognize that no temporary season should define our overall response. In the same way that our troubles are often opportunities for joy, our experience in life is not based on our circumstances alone—it's based on what we choose to pay attention to.

Kristin

Today's Act of Gratitude

Each time you are tempted to complain about
something, choose to find the good instead.

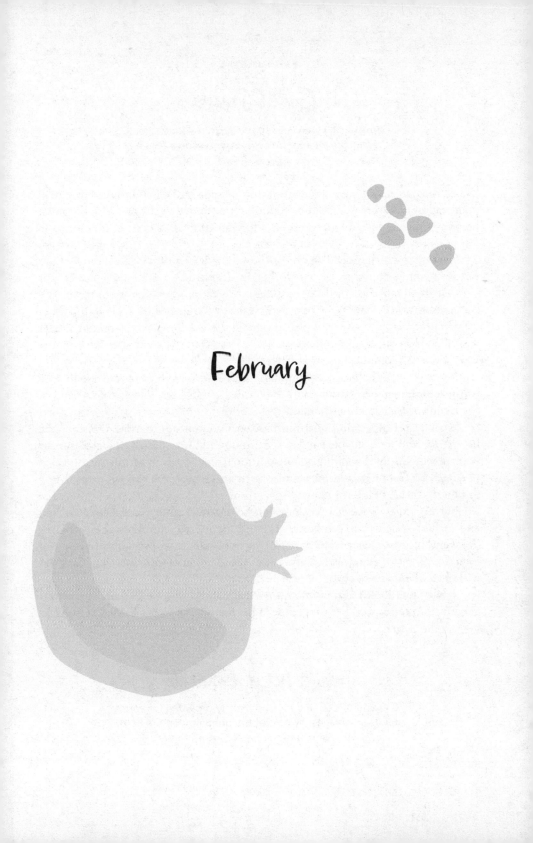

February

God Knew

Those who know your name trust in you, for you,
O LORD, do not abandon those who search for you.

PSALM 9:10

"The Vrbo owner sent me a message offering a discounted rate if I wanted to extend your stay until Saturday," I said to Aaron as we chatted at the end of a long day, he on a work trip to San Diego and I holding down the fort in subzero Minnesota temps.

"I wonder why he'd send an out-of-the-blue offer?" I continued. "Too bad I'm not with you; we could make your work trip a *fun* trip!"

Our small talk soon drifted in a different direction, but after we hung up, my thoughts returned to the Vrbo offer as I washed up dinner dishes. Of all the times we've rented places for work or play, no one has ever offered to extend our stay. It was far enough out of our normal experience to snag my thoughts a couple of times as I moved through the evening's chores.

It wasn't until the next morning's call with Aaron—when he told me that he was sick and unable to return home as planned—that I recognized God's hand in the timing of that seemingly random Vrbo offer.

Work travel in various iterations has been part of our married life since the beginning, and we've adapted and flexed and found ways to make it work, but the years in which I lived with the quiet, additional fear of Aaron getting quarantined in a hotel far from home without someone to watch over him and without healthy food were a time of intense worry.

But God knew what was coming. And he provided a safe place, with a kitchen and enough groceries to see Aaron through, before we even knew he'd need it. We were able to navigate all of the other inconveniences and scrambled plans and frustrations with a grateful heart and the peace that comes from knowing God was with us in the midst of chaos.

While God doesn't always smooth the path ahead of time in quite so obvious a manner, in retrospect, I've so often seen his handiwork in the hardest seasons.

Julie

Today's Act of Gratitude

Can you think of a time God clearly provided for your
needs in advance? Watch for his provision on the hard
days, asking him to reveal himself to you.

Speaking Truth in Love

*We will speak the truth in love, growing in every way more and
more like Christ, who is the head of his body, the church.*

EPHESIANS 4:15

A friend told me recently that her daughter had come to her one day, feeling bad about a situation at school. A young man had expressed interest in her beyond friendship, and although flattered, she politely let him know that she wasn't attracted to him romantically.

A few days later, he showed up at school with a gift for her. The girl again politely declined his advances, to the dismay of several of her classmates. Other girls told her that she should have been nice and just accepted the gift. She explained to my friend, "I felt bad, Mom. I had already told him that I wasn't interested. I didn't want to accept his gift. I don't think that would have been right."

My friend agreed with her daughter. "You did the right thing, honey. You set a boundary in a kind but clear way, and he didn't listen. You weren't wrong to politely decline his gift."

They went on to talk about how she could still be kind and friendly to him, even after this incident. She told her mom that some of the other kids said he was embarrassed, but she went on to treat him just as she always had, and they were able to move past the situation.

We hear a lot in Christian circles about speaking the truth in love. But what does that actually look like? It looks like always leading with love while also being honest. It doesn't look like snide remarks, anger, or put-downs. It esteems the person while also truthfully addressing a situation. And when done well, the person should leave still feeling valued and loved.

It's not an easy balance to achieve consistently, and sometimes we may not do it perfectly, but I'm grateful that Jesus set an example for us to follow.

Kendra

Today's Act of Gratitude

Who is someone that has spoken the truth in love to you? Let them
know you appreciate their honesty and authenticity in your life.

Compassionate Friendship

Make allowance for each other's faults. . . . Above all, clothe yourselves with love, which binds us all together in perfect harmony.

COLOSSIANS 3:13–14

"Would you mind reading that poster aloud?" the leader asked me from the front of the room. Immediately uncomfortable, I watched as every face in the room turned expectantly toward my own. I opened my mouth, gulped, and then—froze.

As for many people, public speaking has always been a source of terror for me. I remember exactly how it started: I attended a small Christian school that required every K–12 student to memorize a poem or other writing and recite it in front of the student body. Though I'm sure the teachers had good intentions, the task went awry for me. As I got up to recite my short poem, I froze. It was too much for my six-year-old heart to take. Embarrassed, I left the stage in tears.

Since then, I've struggled not to freeze up or become overwhelmed when asked to speak in public. Sometimes, I'm successful. Other times, I'm not. The poster-reading night was one of the unsuccessful occasions.

Mercifully, my friend Erin noticed my discomfort and stepped in.

"Do you want me to read it?" she asked me kindly.

"I was a teacher," she explained to the other ladies when I said yes, gratefully, and collapsed back into my chair as the attention turned her way.

At that moment, I felt profoundly grateful for my friend, whose kind offer rescued me from an embarrassing situation. I was so thankful for her compassion. As Christians, we're reminded to lead with love and make allowance for the faults of others. While the fears we face aren't necessarily faults, they can certainly feel like weaknesses. And though sometimes we need to face our fears, other times we simply need someone to walk alongside us in our distress.

My friend's quick response reminded me that in the same way, our gracious God sees our weaknesses and is moved to compassion, not disdain. He does not hold our weaknesses against us; instead, he wants us to lean on him. When we face challenges and choose to turn toward others or God himself, we can be thankful for the reminder that we're never alone.

Kristin

Today's Act of Gratitude

When confronted with a weakness—whether it's your own or someone else's—choose to be compassionate. If you feel weak, thank those who encourage you to be strong.

Blessings from Hard Seasons

*Share each other's burdens, and
in this way obey the law of Christ.*

GALATIANS 6:2

"Working with the toddlers is great. I love it!" A hush fell over our group chatting in the church lobby as the attention suddenly swung to me and my cheery declaration. Noticing several incredulous looks, I continued, "My kids are long past the toddler stage. It's fun to be around kids that age again, especially when I get to give them back to Mom and Dad after service."

After I doubled down on my enthusiastic, nonsarcastic response, our conversation drifted on to more interesting topics, despite a glance or two letting me know that my feelings weren't necessarily the majority opinion.

The truth is, I'd intentionally asked the children's pastor to put me in the hardest-to-fill slot, knowing it was probably with the infants and toddlers. I remember what it was like to be a young mom of very young children and how *amazing* Sunday mornings were when I could spend time worshiping God, soaking up the sermon, and chatting for a few moments after service. I was so grateful to know that my kids were safe and cared for.

I also remember that the volunteers for nursery duty during those intense parenting years were primarily fellow parents of toddlers and infants—me included. We were all in the same exhausted boat, taking turns watching one another's children. It was all those years ago that I promised God that I'd staff the nursery even as my kids grew up, knowing what an immense blessing it was for parents of young children to be in the sanctuary.

Serving God by loving others sometimes simply means noticing a challenging season in someone's life and making it slightly easier. And it has often been in difficult times that my eyes are opened to ways I can quietly love others in similar circumstances. I've gratefully discovered the silver lining of using those experiences to bless others. Personal experience often brings insight into hidden hardships that are otherwise easily overlooked, and it suggests opportunities for being an immense blessing in ways others don't notice.

Julie

Today's Act of Gratitude

Think back to a tough season in your life. Based on what you walked through, list three ways you could make life a bit easier for someone facing a similar situation. Watch for an opportunity to use your ideas.

Rest Is a Gift

*Look at the lilies and how they grow. They don't work or make their
clothing, yet Solomon in all his glory was not dressed as beautifully as
they are. And if God cares so wonderfully for flowers that are here today
and thrown into the fire tomorrow, he will certainly care for you.*

LUKE 12:27-28

The house was still. Blissfully, notably silent. Taking stock of the quiet room, I debated what to do. My husband and children had just left for ice-skating lessons at a local arena, and I had ninety minutes to myself.

I was tempted to rest and read a book but couldn't help noticing the cluttered countertops and dusty floor. *I should clean*, I told myself with a sigh. Immediately, I started putting things to rights. But then I was caught by the thought—*Is this the most important thing to do right now?*

Why did choosing to rest and enjoy my rare time alone feel wasteful?

Sure, I could spend my solitude checking tasks off my to-do list. It's essential to care for our belongings, and a clean environment is healthy for all. But order in the physical world shouldn't come at the expense of our mental, spiritual, or emotional health. And sometimes, rest is the better choice.

Mind made up, I set down the duster and put up my feet. I added some new songs to a playlist. I requested a few more books for my queue at the library. In the time I had left before my kids spilled through the door, I enjoyed activities that weren't technically "important," yet they were investments in future joy, future times of rest.

Instead of feeling lazy, I reminded myself that rest is a gift. Looking anew at my peaceful house, I felt profoundly grateful for the chance to catch my breath. We don't need to work from sunup to sundown to earn God's love. Our achievements don't determine our worth. As my time of solitude neared its end, I spent a few moments in prayer, thanking God for the gift of a quiet home and time to rest from my work.

Kristin

Today's Act of Gratitude

Find a pocket of time when you can rest. Choose an activity that
renews your mind or spirit or otherwise adds to future joy.

Community over Competition

Don't look out only for your own interests,
but take an interest in others, too.

PHILIPPIANS 2:4

"And please, let us know when your book is coming out; we'd love to support you in any way we can!" I recently responded to another author who is in the throes of writing her first book.

We were finishing up a phone call, in which Kristin, Julie, and I had been sharing our tips and knowledge of how to run a book launch team as she prepared for the release of her new devotional in the next year.

"Thanks. Not everyone is so quick to share," she replied.

I knew it was true. I've heard stories of others who've intentionally given false information or withheld knowledge, not wanting to give another writer a leg up. And although it's rare—I'm grateful that most authors I know are very generous with advice—some see everything as a competition to be won.

Whether at work, in church, or in other interest groups we've been a part of, most of us have experienced rivalry with others. There will always be some who act as if they are in (unhealthy) competition with those around them—being stingy with their resources or information and unwilling to help others for fear it will detract from their own success or income. Some people would prefer to go through life independently, seeing others as only a means to their advantage or gain.

Among Christians, this just shouldn't be. Scripture is clear: we are to look out not only for our own interests but also for the interests of others. When we share our knowledge or encourage someone else in their dreams or career, we're taking an interest in them. When we give our time or resources to others, we're taking an interest in them. When we have empathy for others and their situation and step in to pray, we're taking an interest in them. We show God's love to the world when we value people and community over unhealthy competition.

Kendra

Today's Act of Gratitude

Express your gratitude to God for those who have helped
and encouraged you along the way. Share knowledge
that you have with someone else who needs it.

An Encouraging Note

*Let us think of ways to motivate one another
to acts of love and good works.*

HEBREWS 10:24

Mary's request about our mutual friend arrived via a social media message: "Would you write her a note of encouragement? I'm hosting a retreat for several women at my cabin, and I'm asking a few people to write letters for each of them."

My response was an immediate "Yes!" I was honored to be asked, and I admired Mary's thoughtful gift to her guests. I spent the next several days prayerfully asking God what my friend needed to hear, what words she might find most encouraging at this moment. As I slipped my note into the mailbox and raised the little red flag, I thanked God for the opportunity to be a blessing to someone. I pondered who else might need a note of encouragement, a little extra love. Who in my circles was I overlooking? Who in my family was I missing? Even as I racewalked my way back up the snow-covered driveway, a list of faces and names came to mind. I could easily write one letter a week for weeks and still have letters to write.

In a world bombarded with texts, social media messages, and emails, there is something especially lovely about handwritten notes, whether it be flowery words on pretty stationery or a sarcasm-laden-but-genuinely-loving missive in a funny greeting card. We underestimate the value of our handwritten thoughts, no matter how terrible our chicken scratch and how tongue-tied our words when we tell our friends that we love them, that we are proud of them, that they are worthy of God's love, and that they aren't alone as they walk through a hard season.

Our words are powerful, and when we pause and take a breath, noticing and responding to events in the lives of those around us, we are used by God as his hands and feet, his boots-on-the-ground-girls who sow seeds of encouragement and invite others into a deeper relationship with our Savior. Partnering with God is no small thing, and the words of love and hope you send through the mail or secretly tuck into pockets make a difference in ways you likely will never know.

Julie

Today's Act of Gratitude

Prayerfully ask God who needs an encouraging word, then
write them a note, thanking God for the privilege.

The Miracle of Lasts

Whether you eat or drink, or whatever you do,
do it all for the glory of God.

1 CORINTHIANS 10:31

The last time I spoke with my sister was on a Thursday night. She looked tired but laughed at her husband's jokes. I related a funny commercial I'd seen on TV, and we made plans to scrapbook together when she was home from the hospital.

After five years of battling breast cancer, a hospital stay wasn't extraordinary, and neither was our conversation. It was my birthday the next day, and I was in a rush to get home. I told her I loved her and said goodbye.

But by Saturday, her condition had worsened. Keeping her comfortable was all the doctors could do. By the time I arrived, she was no longer able to speak.

I've got mixed feelings about that Thursday night. I wish I hadn't been in a hurry, but I'm glad I visited. And I know she loved me, just as she knew I loved her.

Yet, that lesson of "lasts" remains. Now, as often as I think of it, I try to ask myself: *What if this were the last time? What if this were my final cup of coffee—wouldn't I savor it more? What if this were my last shower—wouldn't I notice the warmth of the water and the scent of my cherry almond shampoo? What if this were the last time my daughter squeezed me around the waist or I saw our home in my rearview mirror?*

The idea makes me pause. Would I reach for patience instead of peevishness when I have a conflict with a loved one? Would I demonstrate grace rather than grumpiness when I encounter an issue at work?

The truth is that all of our experiences will eventually lead to Thursday night conversations. We will always have to reconcile our lasts until we get to heaven. But rather than mourning what we've lost, let's reconsider it as an opportunity for joy. Let's take the time to notice the moments—big or small—that add up to the sum of our days. Let's recognize each moment as a gift and an opportunity to bring glory to God and gratitude to our hearts.

Kristin

Today's Act of Gratitude

Focus on how grateful you'd be for each part of your life if
you knew this would be the last time you experienced it.

Comfort in What Stands Forever

*The grass withers and the flowers fade, but
the word of our God stands forever.*

ISAIAH 40:8

There are times I'll lie in bed at night and imagine what it was like to live in my house years ago. Built in 1907, our home has seen several generations of people come and go. I've heard stories of former residents from all different backgrounds and life experiences: bricklayers and police officers, cement makers and shop owners.

I've heard tales of the renovations done decades ago—the partial basement dug out by hand and the woodwork restored after shag carpet was removed—and the people who've walked these halls. I've been told of card games played around kitchen tables, neighborhood kids who came to play in the large yard, and the twin boys who would often climb out on tree limbs from the second-story windows. I smile when I think about all the holidays, the birthday parties, the wedding and anniversary celebrations. And I reflect on more solemn days, the deaths and losses I'm sure were experienced as well.

These walls that have been repainted countless times, the floors that now squeak, and the doors that take finesse to close—all bear witness to the life that was lived. I find myself being grateful to be a part of this story, knowing there will be other families long after I'm gone to walk these same floors and make memories of their own.

There's consolation in seeing your place in a larger story—acknowledging those before you and those who'll come after you. Just as my house has stood to give shelter and stability to many generations (and hopefully many more to come), the Word of God is steadfast. Even when the grass and flowers fade, structures come to ruin, and people pass away, God will never change. He always stays as our sure and steady anchor. From generation to generation, we can see his consistency in our lives and the lives of the people around us. His Word stands forever. And that is the greatest comfort of all.

Kendra

Today's Act of Gratitude

If you take a step back from your current situation, what can you see that has been consistent in your life and that you can thank God for?

Joy-Filled Service

There are different kinds of service,
but we serve the same Lord.

1 CORINTHIANS 12:5

Snuggled into my favorite chair, I lingered over each page in my newly arrived seed catalog. Of the six or seven catalogs I receive each winter, this is my favorite because tucked between unusual and hard-to-source seed varieties are short anecdotes about the seeds—the history of a tomato variety almost lost to time except for an Appalachian family who'd saved the seeds year after year for six generations, or the effort it took to source a new-to-me melon from the northern China countryside.

One of my great joys in the depths of winter is starting seedlings. For months, I hover over flats of tiny seedlings tucked under artificial lights, eyeballing germination rates and seedling health. It never fails that my eyes are too big for my proverbial stomach—meaning that I end up with far more plants than I could reasonably hope to put into my urban garden.

Several years ago, my overexuberance resulted in a beautiful partnership with a community garden catering specifically to refugee families. I now intentionally grow far more than I can use and donate the surplus to families who don't have the tools or skills necessary to nurse seedlings for twelve or more weeks under grow lights. I am grateful that a hobby that brings me joy is now also a tool for serving others.

You don't have to be a gardener or live in an area of the country with a sizeable refugee population to have a similar impact. We serve the same God—and the people he pursues—with our unique qualifications and skill sets.

I know women who quilt blankets for children entering the foster care system so they have something comforting and bright in the midst of upheaval. One of my friends cooks and freezes meals to gift to new moms. I know men who use their ability to build or tinker to bless someone who cannot. Often there is a way to use the hobbies and skills we love to serve God and others.

Julie

Today's Act of Gratitude

Consider how you might use a skill or hobby you enjoy
in service to God and those around you. Prayerfully ask
God to connect your interests to an existing need.

A Teacher's Influence

In his grace, God has given us different gifts for doing certain things well. So if God has given you the ability to prophesy, speak out with as much faith as God has given you. If your gift is serving others, serve them well. If you are a teacher, teach well.

ROMANS 12:6–7

As a child, I wanted to be a teacher. I was shy and bookish, and teachers were superheroes who could conquer the worst math problems with ease. My fourth-grade teacher, Mrs. Deadrick, helped me overcome some of my shyness by encouraging us to read our poems and stories aloud to the class. My sixth-grade English teacher, Mrs. Decker, made unique spelling lists for me each week because I'd already completed the ones that were part of the curriculum. My high school history teacher, Mr. Mathews, steered me toward books that have influenced me throughout life. Each of my teachers made me feel seen and cared for throughout my school years.

As a parent, I appreciate teachers in a whole new way. I've seen them gently support my child in her weaknesses and encourage her in her strengths. I've witnessed their ability to see my child for who she is and call out the best in her.

Observing their genuine care makes me want nothing more than to respond in kind. Of course, we send Christmas, Valentine's Day, and end-of-year gifts, but I try to check in more frequently. I send my kids on reconnaissance missions to find out their teacher's favorite coffee drink that we can pick up and bring in on a cold day. And at various times in the school year, I make a point of finding out if their classroom needs any school supply refills. These small measures demonstrate just a fraction of the gratitude I feel.

Not everyone has regular contact with elementary school teachers. Still, when we begin to consider other "teachers" in our lives, the list grows long: mentors, pastors, leaders of nonprofits, Sunday school teachers, or team managers. God gave each of us gifts, but when we encourage someone in their gifting—like a teacher—our gratitude can be one more inspiration for them to keep going.

Kristin

Today's Act of Gratitude

Thank a teacher or mentor who has influenced
you, a family member, or a loved one.

Trusting God's Voice

*Whether you turn to the right or to the left, your ears will hear
a voice behind you, saying, "This is the way; walk in it."*

ISAIAH 30:21, NIV

We were watching our kids play together when our small talk turned serious.

"I think we might put Lena on medication for her anxiety," my friend confided to me. "We've tried many other things, and although they've helped, it's not been as much as we'd like. Her doctor is in support of it at this time too."

I paused before responding. "I think you are doing a good thing for her right now. When we finally decided to put our child on medication for his anxiety, we saw a night and day difference. It may not be for everyone, but we found it helpful," I replied, trying to catch her eye.

She nodded as she slowly met my gaze. "Thanks. It's nice to know we're not alone."

I smiled back. "You're doing a good job," I whispered as tears filled our eyes. "You're a good mom just trying to help your child in any way you can—and you'll never regret that."

She nodded as we both wiped our tears, and a shared understanding of wanting what's best for our kids passed between us.

Making decisions for ourselves or our loved ones is not always easy. We wonder if we are doing the right thing. Often, we have to weigh choices and pray for the right answers to life's questionable situations.

But over time, if we continue to bring our needs to God, asking for his help, we will begin to learn and know his voice speaking to us through Scripture, prayer, life circumstances, and even other people. And as we do, we can trust that he'll give us the direction we need, showing us the path we should take, whispering to us, "This is the way; walk in it."

Kendra

Today's Act of Gratitude

Thank God for the ways he has guided your life in the
past, and spend a little time asking him for direction
in an area you are currently unsure about.

The Power of Friendship

Ruth replied, "Don't ask me to leave you and turn back.
Wherever you go, I will go; wherever you live, I will live. Your
people will be my people, and your God will be my God.

RUTH 1:16

As a young woman, I encountered the lie that female friendship was untrustworthy, and I adopted it as truth. I was warily friendly, willing to be cheerful acquaintances but refusing anything further that might require emotional vulnerability.

Oh, how I wish I could pull my younger self aside and unpack with her God's powerful example of female friendship woven throughout the story of Ruth and Naomi, exposing and uprooting that falsehood.

Ruth was Naomi's daughter-in-law, and when both women experienced widowhood and famine, Ruth followed Naomi back to Israel. It is a story of redemption for both women, culminating with Ruth being grafted into the direct lineage of Jesus Christ through marriage to Boaz. But it is also a story of the power found in female friendship, of what can happen when we live in community with other women who love and follow God.

When Naomi despaired, Ruth encouraged her, keeping her moving forward in faith. And when Ruth was uncertain, Naomi advised her, giving her sound guidance on approaching Boaz, their kinsman-redeemer. I've often pondered the push and pull of their friendship—one was strong when the other faltered, and they took turns holding each other up.

Healthy female friendships are one of life's greatest treasures. It's been my girl friends who have given me the final shove out of my comfort zone on any number of occasions, so that I would take the risk of saying yes to God. Girl friends have stormed the gates of heaven for me in prayer, have made me laugh so hard my stomach muscles ached for days, have gently told me I was wrong. Girl friends have been an essential part of my faith journey; I would not be the woman I am today without their influence and love. My heart swells with gratitude for the women God has placed in my life—some for only a season, some for the long haul. And I keep my eyes and ears open for new friends God might send my way in the future.

Julie

Today's Act of Gratitude

This Galentine's Day, tell your girl friends that you love
them and why you are grateful for their friendship.
Ask God to send new friends across your path.

Our Steady Father

*God is not a man, so he does not lie. He is not human, so he
does not change his mind. Has he ever spoken and failed to
act? Has he ever promised and not carried it through?*

NUMBERS 23:19

It was almost the end of the school day, and as the intercom crackled to life, I knew what was coming: Valentine's Day gifts. As the long list of names from each grade was read, students shifted uneasily in their chairs or waited breathlessly to see if they would be one of the lucky ones. When the bell rang, everyone rushed to the lobby, where tables were filled with bouquets organized by last name.

I always had my name called. It wasn't because I was popular or always had a boyfriend. No, it was all thanks to my dad. I can't remember if I initially asked him to send me something or if he came up with the idea on his own—likely with my mom's help—but either way, it sparked a new tradition. Every year, he sent a bouquet to the school. As the names were called, I never worried about being left out. I knew my dad would send me something, just as he'd promised.

I'm grateful for those gifts of flowers, but looking back, I'm more thankful for the steadiness my dad's actions displayed. Like the sun rising and setting each day or the tides advancing and receding, his faithful efforts were a reminder that he could be trusted. His word was true. He would do as he said, and I didn't need to worry.

Unfortunately, I know that's not always the case with earthly fathers. But I'm grateful for the faithfulness of another Father, one whose Word is always true. He, too, delights in giving us good gifts. He is the same yesterday, today, and forever. He is just, good, and trustworthy. When we consider our fast-paced, ever-changing world, that steadiness is a gift we can rely on. With God as our Father, we never need worry about being left out or forgotten. And at the end of the day, we'll hear our name called too.

Kristin

Today's Act of Gratitude

Thank God for his unchanging nature and unconditional love.

Hope for the Future

Anyone who belongs to Christ has become a new person.
The old life is gone; a new life has begun!

2 CORINTHIANS 5:17

"I don't think I can change," he whispered, looking at the floor, disappointment and discouragement almost a visible cloak over his slumped shoulders.

I silently prayed to God before speaking. "Yes, you can. I know you can. With God's help, things can be different. Change isn't easy, but it's possible. I don't care what you've done in the past; you can always choose something different today."

He nodded, unsure if he believed me. My friend has a hard past. He's made mistakes and created patterns that, although they may be tough to change, aren't impossible to break. Even through all the wrong choices and missteps, my friend loves Jesus, and he continues to try for something better. It's not the first time he's heard the truth from me, and it won't be the last. It's difficult for him to believe just how good God is and that he's able to make all things new, so I'll keep reminding him.

Sometimes we need others to encourage us and remind us of the truth in God's Word when we can't believe it for ourselves. But God doesn't lie. We can trust him because we can trust his character. Loving. Forgiving. Merciful. These are all words to describe the nature of God. And no matter who we are or what we have done, God promises that if we belong to Christ we have become a new person. Our old lives are gone, and we've begun new ones! Everything is reset to what he originally intended.

There is always hope. Your past is not an indicator of your future; it can't dictate what will be. Today is a new day, and we can choose something different going forward.

Kendra

Today's Act of Gratitude

Look back at your life and identify a negative thought or behavior pattern that, with God's help, you've been able to change. Spend some time thanking God for his grace that helped you do so.

Stay on Mission

The world offers only a craving for physical pleasure, a craving for
everything we see, and pride in our achievements and possessions.
These are not from the Father, but are from this world. And this
world is fading away, along with everything that people crave.
But anyone who does what pleases God will live forever.

1 JOHN 2:16-17

"Um, what are you doing? That's my left-handed, crepe-flipping spatula. You can have any other spatula in the drawer, but you can't have that one." I'd walked into the kitchen just as a family member was about to scurry away with my prized possession. I bestowed a kiss on my child's forehead as I liberated my beloved spatula from their grasp and provided an ordinary one for their use.

Being left-handed in a right-handed world (only 10 percent of the population is left-handed) means I'm subtly inconvenienced much of the time. I don't even recognize the inconvenience until I stumble upon a tool designed for a lefty. Upon discovering how much easier a left-handed version of a device makes a task, I'm always a bit flabbergasted at how different my daily experience is from that of my right-handed friends.

Instead of being annoyed that spiral notebooks, scissors, watches, guitars, and even the design on my favorite coffee mugs (among a million other things) are backward or awkward to use, I view it as a subtle reminder: this is not my home. This is merely a temporary dwelling place, a way station of sorts, and it should never feel too comfortable. It is so easy to trip headlong into the trap of accumulating possessions, wealth, and accomplishments. These things fade away into nothingness, just as this world will.

Why do we waste our lives chasing temporary pleasures? And what are we to do instead with our precious, blink-of-an-eye time here?

We are to do what pleases God. The two greatest commandments in Scripture (and perhaps the hardest when you unpack all of the ways they apply) can be paraphrased into four words: love God, love others (see Mark 12:28-32; Matthew 22:36-40). May the minor inconveniences in our daily lives remind us to whom we belong and to what we are called.

Julie

Today's Act of Gratitude

Pick a constant, minor inconvenience as a continual
reminder that you are a temporary resident of Earth called
to live differently from the rest of the world. Give thanks
to God for the better world that will be ours one day.

In All Circumstances

*Be thankful in all circumstances, for this is God's
will for you who belong to Christ Jesus.*

1 THESSALONIANS 5:18

At a women's small group, my friend was recently asked to list reasons she was grateful. Enthusiastically, she compiled a list and scrawled it in her notebook. When the leader suggested praying to thank God for those items, she didn't hesitate to bow her head.

After a few minutes, she looked up as the leader began to speak again.

"Great job," the woman said. "Now, think of all the things that have been hard lately—situations that haven't gone the way you thought they would, relationships that are difficult, or work or family issues that have been challenging."

Mentally—and somewhat less enthusiastically—my friend composed a list and waited for further direction.

"Okay," the leader said. "Now, thank God for those things too."

My friend was dumbfounded. *Really? Thank God for the work project that had blown up in her face? The stressful situation with her extended family? The weird, worrisome noise in her car?*

Less willingly, my friend bowed her head. At first, she felt uncomfortable and inauthentic. But as one minute turned to two and then three, she began to breathe more easily. Thanking God for the hard things helped her not only to recognize their influence on her stress level but also to clarify what was true: she trusted God, and she trusted that he would work in and through the challenges. That was a reason to be grateful, after all.

In the same way, we cannot always see how the good and the difficult puzzle pieces of our lives fit together; yet if we choose to trust God, we know that our temporary trials are ultimately for our good and his glory. If we pray about everything and give thanks in all circumstances, we will always find reasons to be grateful.

Kristin

Today's Act of Gratitude

List a few challenging situations you're currently facing,
then spend time praying and thanking God for them.

The Lie of Aloneness

Two people are better off than one,
for they can help each other succeed.

ECCLESIASTES 4:9

"You've got to figure it out yourself."

"No one else will help."

"You're on your own."

These thoughts came to me and festered one morning as I ran around my house, mulling over everything that needed to be done. The weight of it had me feeling and believing that it was all up to me.

By the time my husband returned several hours later, I was disgruntled. Sensing my unhappiness, he tried to step in and help with some tasks on my list. I rebuffed his efforts, already firmly engulfed in my self-pity and anger. He backed off, giving me space.

Later, as we drove together to a gathering of friends, I burst into tears. "I feel very alone."

My husband looked at me and nodded, affirming my feelings; he knows this is a faulty belief I've struggled with my entire adult life.

"But you're not," he whispered. "You're not alone. I'm with you."

I sighed, allowing his words to make their way past my mind and right to my heart. "I'm sorry I was upset."

"I know," he said as he took my hand and squeezed it. His presence reminded me that I really am not alone.

God made us to be in relationship with others. There's nothing the enemy would love more than to make us feel like we are all alone. Alone in our struggles. Alone in our relationships. Alone in life. But this is simply not true. God is there. Always. And he's placed people around us to provide love and support, even if it doesn't always seem like it. (Sometimes we may need to be the ones to let others know we need help.) Scripture reminds us that togetherness is a gift from God because two can help each other succeed. We get so much further together than we ever do alone. Don't believe the lie that no one else is there. God is. People are. You just need to look and see.

Kendra

Today's Act of Gratitude

Reach out to someone, remind them they are not alone, and ask if there is a way you can support them, through your prayers or otherwise.

Welcome Home

*Just as our bodies have many parts and each part has a
special function, so it is with Christ's body. We are many
parts of one body, and we all belong to each other.*

ROMANS 12:4-5

Taking a deep breath to settle the butterflies in my stomach, I opened the car door. "Let's go. Service starts soon."

And with that, we stepped back inside a church we'd left ten years ago—trepidatious and hopeful, scared and excited, knowing there were so many people there whom we still loved and who still loved us, and wondering about all the rest.

Aaron and I had been on a journey during those in-between years—all of it God-ordained, all of it growth and good—and we don't regret that time. But we'd been feeling the tug to return and had been running the other direction for a long while. Finally, we'd had an honest conversation over dinner with the pastor and his wife, asking if we might return, confessing our fear of rejection.

"Welcome home," said Russ, a long-time board member who greeted us at the door to the church. His whispered words amid a bear hug broke the dam of tears I'd been holding back.

Inside, smiles, hugs, and words of welcome from so many others had me openly weeping during the songs. And when the pastor asked later about how the first time back had gone, my slightly choked up response was "It felt like coming home."

Our home, short of heaven, is in community with others who love Jesus. There, we find unity in our love of God and others even as we celebrate our uniqueness. This doesn't mean there is never conflict and misunderstanding. We are complicated, messy creatures, and being in community also means we'll need to both forgive and apologize from time to time.

Creating community means that sometimes we are the ones providing a warm welcome—intentionally creating space for others to come into—and sometimes we are the ones who desperately need to be welcomed home with a hug and words that ease our anxiousness.

Julie

Today's Act of Gratitude

Who around you needs a warm welcome into a community,
whether as formal as a church body or as informal as a
Saturday morning Bible study? Reach out to invite them in
or remind them of how glad you are that they are there.

Taking the Time

Encourage each other and build each other up,
just as you are already doing.

1 THESSALONIANS 5:11

We hadn't seen him in over a year, and as we made our way to his senior apartment complex, I felt excited and a little nervous. I squeezed my daughter Jasmine's hand as we pressed his buzzer before noticing he was sitting in the lobby, waiting for us to arrive. He stood as we walked in, pushing a walker that hadn't been there before, looking frailer than we remembered. We hugged and followed him to his apartment, talking about the weather and how his health had been.

We met Al years ago when we lived in the same neighborhood. He lived alone, right across the street from us. As a mom with little kids, I was often overwhelmed. Jasmine developed a friendship with Al and frequently spent time at his house, especially when he would sit outside his garage in the evenings while my kids circled him on their bikes.

For several years, we shared meals and celebrations on that street until Al decided it was time for him to move to the senior apartment complex one summer. We were sad to see him leave but glad he was still in town. Since then, we've changed neighborhoods as well, but our relationship with Al has remained strong. His friendship has been a gift to my kids over the years, one I could have missed out on if my kids hadn't taken the time to get to know him.

Life can get busy for all of us, and often it's hard to step outside of our regular routines to make a new friend or even get together with the friends we already have. But when we make a point of connecting with others, we walk away feeling better than before. And it's no wonder: God made us for community. He wants us to build up and encourage one another. We just have to take the time to do it.

Kendra

Today's Act of Gratitude

Thank a friend who has been a blessing to you, and
let them know how much they mean to you.

Our Daily Bread

Give us this day our daily bread.

MATTHEW 6:11, ESV

"You don't look like you're having much fun," my husband said.

Blowing a stray hair out of my face to avoid touching it with my flour-covered hands, I sighed. "Nope."

What was supposed to be an exciting experience was turning into—well, a dud. My thoughtful husband had given me a few cooking classes for my birthday. They were live Zoom classes facilitated by a former *Top Chef* contestant I adored, both for her positive energy and the masterful way she incorporated her Vietnamese culture, New Orleans residency, and pastry chef training into mouthwatering dishes.

At first, I was excited. The classes should have been a home run, and most of them were terrific. Bo Kho? Amazing. Turkey gumbo? Mouthwatering. Banh mi sandwiches? Yes, please. Pho? I will eat that all day, every day.

But then the croissant class arrived. And as it went on, my enthusiasm plummeted.

Making croissants is a painstaking process. Butter is placed in the dough in a certain way, and then the dough is rolled out, then folded in. Rolled out, folded in—again and again. By the time we were finished, my arms ached from the effort. It was hard, uncomfortable work.

While the process wasn't my idea of fun, the finished product was delicious. Even more, I left the experience with a renewed respect and gratitude for those who master the skills for creating such a seemingly simple item. All too often, I take everyday things like bread for granted. Yet not only is food necessary for our survival but it's also a source of delight. After all, we live in a world full of delicious fare and have access to cuisines from all around the world. When Jesus taught people to pray in Matthew 6, he specifically mentioned a food we eat each day. We regularly express our gratitude to God for providing our daily bread, but we can also thank the individuals who prepare it for us. Breads and meals of any kind—and the work that goes into them—are worthy of admiration. And they are surely worthy of our gratitude.

Kristin

Today's Act of Gratitude

Thank someone who made an item of food that you consume, whether it's someone in your home, a restaurant chef, a baker, or a company whose products you enjoy.

Timeless Treasures

*The Kingdom of Heaven is like a treasure that a man discovered
hidden in a field. In his excitement, he hid it again and sold
everything he owned to get enough money to buy the field.*

MATTHEW 13:44

One morning my dad sent me a video of my daughter riding a rocking horse when she was three years old. Her little voice and laughter came through the speaker as she talked with my dad about reading books and riding fast, her unruly blonde curls bouncing in her eyes the whole time. I chuckled as I remembered her as such a spunky toddler. The recording was just two minutes long, but it's priceless to me now that she's so much older and has already changed in so many ways. I quickly thanked him for the video, asking him to send any others that he found on his phone.

As I watched the short clip several more times, I teared up hearing the sweet little singsong voice I'd almost forgotten. Realizing how easy it was to take for granted at the time, now I couldn't get enough of it. I saved it to my computer to preserve this treasure I didn't even know I had been missing.

How much of life do we take for granted? Whether people, experiences, or things, we've all missed real treasures from times gone by, and if given a choice to go back, we would value them much more the second time around.

The Kingdom of God is no different. It's easy, especially if we've been following Jesus for a long time, to take our relationship with him and all that he has done for us for granted. But Scripture reminds us that the Kingdom of Heaven is like a treasure that someone finds. When they realize what they have, they sell everything else they own to buy it.

When was the last time I treasured what Jesus has done for me so much that I would give up everything to keep it? Too long ago, I'm afraid. But when I realize that all my comfort, peace, and joy come from him, I remember what matters, and for that, I would leave everything. Give me Jesus above all else.

Kendra

Today's Act of Gratitude

What have you taken for granted in the past?
Stop to thank God and treasure it now.

Flourishing from Afar

*A friend is always loyal, and
a brother is born to help in time of need.*

PROVERBS 17:17

"Hey, friend! How did that meeting go? I've been meaning to tell you about . . ." Smiling to myself as I washed up the dinner dishes, I watched the video message my friend had recorded the night before. She told me about her day, asked follow-up questions about the recording I'd sent her earlier, and commented on a pair of shoes I had asked her opinion on. As I listened, I made several mental notes for the response I would send after the kitchen was tidied and the house was quiet.

My first foray into video messaging apps was as a means of staying in touch with friends when the world shut down. As life slowly returned to some strange semblance of normal, I largely abandoned this form of communication, preferring to be in the same room as my friends. But I've returned to it in the past few months, for two friends I otherwise simply wouldn't see as much as I would like because of current life circumstances.

Relationships are best when face-to-face, and that will always be my first preference. However, video messaging—especially since recordings can be watched at a later time—has allowed these specific friendships to deepen and flourish when an in-person get-together or even a FaceTime call is not a viable option. Having a new video or two to watch as I go about ordinary tasks adds an element of joy to the day and a spring to my step.

I've thanked God for the gift of technology so many times over those several years when it allowed work and school and relationships to continue, even if in a deeply imperfect manner. However, my biggest personal technology blessing has been this video messaging app and my two flourishing together-while-apart friendships. Seeing my friends' faces and hearing their voices on an almost daily basis has added richness to my life as they've given godly advice, prayed over my family, and cracked me up with all sorts of random, silly nonsense. And I've done the same for them.

For as many difficulties and negatives as technology can pose, I'm always looking for creative, healthy ways it can be used to encourage and strengthen us and those we love.

Julie

Today's Act of Gratitude

Consider how you might use technology to be a blessing to others (and yourself). Choose your favorite idea and implement it this week.

The Power of Disruption

*I am certain that God, who began the good work within you, will continue
his work until it is finally finished on the day when Christ Jesus returns.*

PHILIPPIANS 1:6

My credit card information was stolen online. At first, I was annoyed. But as the
days passed, I felt less frustrated and more thoughtful about the fallout.

I make many purchases online. That's convenient, but it also means there are
recurring items I don't always consider in the grand scheme of our finances: a
subscription here, a monthly product there. Updating to a new card meant I was
newly aware of how many of those were no longer serving me. As I reviewed the
sites, I canceled accounts rather than updating information.

Bemused, I realized the disruption I'd been annoyed by had turned out to be
helpful.

That's not always true of disruptions. There have been plenty of times I've
cried out to God, wondering at the injustice or insensibility of something that's
happened.

But just as often, disruptions have been opportunities for growth or changed
my life for the better: A move to a new area brought deep, abiding friendships. A
hard conversation enabled healing in a relationship. A career change I agonized over
opened new opportunities and allowed for peace in my home. A gentle confronta-
tion established much-needed boundaries.

None of those situations were desirable at the time, but in retrospect, those
painful points taught me the most, helped me lean in deeper to Jesus, and ultimately brought hope and healing.

Unlike my limited window into the scope of this life, God's view is a panorama
from start to finish, beginning to end. Paul's letter to the church at Philippi reminds
us that we need to trust in what God is doing—that he will see to completion the
good work he began in us. Yes, we will encounter hard things, but there is always
a glimmer of hope in the distance. God is always and already doing something
new—in or through us —if we have the eyes to see it and the willingness to view
disruptions as reminders of the bigger picture.

Kristin

Today's Act of Gratitude

Reconsider a disruption in your own life that God ultimately used
for good, thanking him for helping you to view it differently.

A Warm Welcome

Encourage each other and build each other up,
just as you are already doing.

1 THESSALONIANS 5:11

I'd arrived for the meeting early, the new girl in a collaboration of amazing women of God. The leader's gentle rap on my driver's-side window revealed the secret I was hoping to keep: me, hunched over the steering wheel, furiously scrawling last-minute notes in purple ink as I rechecked my typed pages and the Bible app on my phone.

I wanted so desperately to do a good job that I was using every last moment to cram for the meeting, not trusting the hours of work I'd already put into the project, not trusting what God had laid on my heart.

Her gentle smile and kind greeting as I sheepishly rolled down the window told me that she knew exactly what I was doing and why. And the welcome extended by everyone else as I entered the conference room had me silently saying a prayer of gratitude for women who received nervous newbies with warmth and encouragement.

After we exchanged introductions and started our meeting, a stray comment by another participant revealed that she, too, was slightly intimidated by those gathered at the table. So later in a quiet moment, I leaned toward her, whispering a thank-you for an exceptionally wise insight she'd shared.

If you've ever been made to feel like you weren't enough or didn't belong, I'm so sorry. It is incredibly difficult to be the new person in a classroom, organization, or team. The people who warmly welcome and reassure us are an answered prayer and a gift from God. And once we understand how precious that gift is, we can become that gift to others, extending the truth to anxious newcomers around us, letting them know that they are enough and they are welcome.

Julie

Today's Act of Gratitude

Think of a time someone intentionally encouraged
you, reminding you that you are enough. Look for an
opportunity to pay that forward to someone else.

Held in His Hand

In his hand is the life of every creature
and the breath of all mankind.

JOB 12:10, NIV

My Grandma Jo died in her mid-eighties after living a full life. She spent the last few years in a nursing home in our town to be close to family. My dad would visit her weekly, making sure she lacked for nothing.

As she neared the end of her life, she would tell us how she longed to go home to heaven. She was so ready. She'd said her goodbyes and blessed her children and had no fear of leaving this earthly home.

My sister Katrina passed away not long before Grandma Jo did, and I noticed that my grandmother didn't shed a tear at that time, so confident she'd see Katrina again soon enough. There was a peace about her, almost a knowing of what would come next. Death wasn't scary or uncertain. She trusted in who Jesus is, fully believing that she would be with him and those loved ones already gone.

When she passed, it was a sad time but also very much a celebration. We knew this homegoing was what she'd wanted. We knew that she was healthy and whole once again, reunited with those she loved, and for that, we were grateful.

Not all deaths are expected or as comforting as my grandma's. Sometimes there's trauma involved, leaving deep pain for those who remain. Sometimes we lose loved ones far too soon.

How do we deal with loss and grief, whether expected or not? We remember who God is. We remember that the life of every creature and the breath of all people is in his hand. Nothing is beyond his control.

Even when life-and-death circumstances come unexpectedly, they are not a surprise to God. He is still in control. Still loving us. Still holding us in his hand. No death occurs without his knowledge. No breath is lost without his notice. And no tear is shed that he doesn't come to comfort.

Kendra

Today's Act of Gratitude

Thank God for the ways that he's comforted you in your grief.

Go Where the Road Takes You

I recommend having fun, because there is nothing better for people in this world than to eat, drink, and enjoy life. That way they will experience some happiness along with all the hard work God gives them under the sun.

ECCLESIASTES 8:15

We'd been cooped up in the house together for too many days, and my family was restless. We needed a change of scenery, so I told my children to put on their shoes. They perked up immediately.

As we piled into our vehicle, I told them that we would go on a little adventure to explore new roads.

"Which way should we go?" I asked when we reached a stop sign. The kids shouted out "left" or "right," and my husband followed their directions. We spent the next hour or so driving backcountry roads, our children indicating which way to turn. Though they were dubious about the idea at first, they quickly settled in and took turns choosing our path. Eventually, we angled back toward town to pick up takeout on the way home.

Going wherever the road takes you—driving simply for the joy of it—is one of life's little pleasures; yet all too often, I tell myself I'm too busy for it. Adventure, fun, and hobbies can all get pushed to the bottom of the to-do list or overlooked in the busyness of life. Yet as we cruised around that evening, listening to music and watching the sun do a slow slide toward the golden hour, life felt good and peaceful, simple and sweet.

God didn't intend for us to forget about fun. If a cheerful heart truly is good medicine, then fun tips the balance from the monotony of the everyday toward a well-rounded life. When we pause to look up from our endless routine to enjoy ourselves, we are better able to appreciate the beauty of creation, the joy of time spent with family and friends, and the things that remind us of God's great plan and purpose for life.

Kristin

Today's Act of Gratitude

Drive or walk an unexpected route on purpose, taking the time to notice your surroundings or the journey itself, thanking God for all you see.

You Don't Have to Be Perfect

*Let everything you say be good and helpful, so that your words
will be an encouragement to those who hear them.*

EPHESIANS 4:29

"I think I'm failing to parent my daughter well," she said with a laugh to veil the honest admission. I was sitting outside one of my kids' activities, watching from the window, when this mom I knew only nominally came and sat next to me. We engaged in small talk while our other kids played around us, but as they went to find a drink of water, the conversation took a turn toward more complicated subjects.

"I think we all feel that way at times," I stated, encouraging her to continue.

"It's probably because she's my oldest," she went on, "but we don't always get along, and I wonder if I'm doing everything right. Maybe I'm messing them all up."

I shook my head as I leaned toward her.

"You're not," I said. "Do you love your kids? Make sure all their needs are being met? Encourage them in the things they enjoy?" I waved my hand at our current surroundings. "Then you're not failing. They're going to be okay."

She nodded and offered a smile.

"Thanks," she whispered as our kids came bounding back toward us and the conversation trailed off to other topics.

There are people around us who need encouragement if we'll only take the time to notice. For us as Christians, it should be second nature to say things that would be good and helpful, encouraging others who may need a little comfort or cheer. No one wants to feel alone, and when we take the time to listen to another's story and offer support through our words, we're following the ways of Jesus.

Kendra

Today's Act of Gratitude

Think of a time you were grateful for someone else's affirmation
in a hard season. Find someone who could use a little support
and take the time to share an encouraging word.

March

Our Daily Gratitude

Oh, give thanks to the LORD, for He is good!
For His mercy endures forever.

PSALM 107:1, NKJV

We're grateful for our washing machine and the many years it has worked faithfully—until it breaks down and we need to replace it.

We're happy that our loved one wants to spend time with us—until they snipe at us over a schedule conflict.

We're thankful that the power company has restored our electricity after a middle-of-the-night outage—until we realize all our clocks are blinking and the coffee pot didn't start automatically.

It's in those moments—when we're forced to find room in the budget for a new appliance or wait a few extra minutes for the coffee to brew (the horror!)—that we're tested the most. Because it's one thing to be thankful for the blessings that come to mind so easily—food, clothing, shelter, family, friends, church, community, a job—and another thing to be grateful in all circumstances. Disruptions can derail our gratitude.

Yet the Bible reminds us that gratitude isn't just a mental exercise we do every once in a while; it's a habit—one that Jesus demonstrated. Consider the Lord's Prayer in Matthew 6:9-13:

> Pray like this: Our Father in heaven, may your name be kept holy. May your Kingdom come soon. May your will be done on earth, as it is in heaven. Give us today the food we need, and forgive us our sins, as we have forgiven those who sin against us. And don't let us yield to temptation, but rescue us from the evil one.

I love how Jesus sets up the prayer. It starts with thanksgiving—*may your name be kept holy*—and an outward reflection—*your Kingdom come . . . your will be done*—before it turns inward. This thanksgiving, this attitude of praise, sets the tone for the prayer. And isn't it true for us, too, that our attitude of gratitude (or not) can often set the tone for how we choose to respond to a situation?

When we start with thanksgiving and look outward, we naturally shift from focusing solely on ourselves to living as Jesus did: loving God, loving others. Let's reframe the challenges of life through the lens of gratitude.

Kristin

Today's Act of Gratitude

The next time you pray, praise and thank God for his blessings
before talking to him about your needs and desires.

Our Faithful God

The LORD is the everlasting God, the Creator of all the earth. He never grows weak or weary. No one can measure the depths of his understanding.

ISAIAH 40:28

I made supper for a friend who lost her father suddenly. She's from a war-torn country and had fled to America with her immediate family, leaving her dad behind. She hadn't seen him in several years, and she grieved the loss, knowing she'd never again have the chance to see him in this life.

She greeted me at the door and I placed the meal on the table, then we sat down on the couch to catch up.

"How are you doing?" I asked, squeezing her hand.

"Okay," she said, shrugging. "I cry a lot."

"That's okay," I said. "Tell me about your dad."

"You know," she responded, "a memory came to me I hadn't thought about in years."

I waited while she wiped her eyes and went on to explain.

She said she was in her late teens, and some troops came through their city, pillaging and taking anything from the homes that they wanted. She was upset because they had taken many of her family's belongings, including her gold jewelry.

She was so troubled over the loss that she cried. Her dad came to her and said, "Why do you cry? These are just things. We can't hang on to the things of this world so tightly that we can't let them go. Even our family members: we can love them, but not to the point of not letting go. Only God we hang on to—he is all we have in life. Everything else could be gone at any moment."

Now, as an adult with a family of her own, she knows his words were true. I agreed—such a wise man.

As I left her home, I thought about her father and the insight he gave her all those years ago. So much in this life can be uncertain. We can believe we have control, but in reality, many things can change without our consent. When times are unsure, what do we have to cling to?

The answer is clear: hold only onto God. He is everlasting. He isn't weak and doesn't grow weary. Everything else in this life can change—it all may come and go—but he remains.

Kendra

Today's Act of Gratitude

Thank God for the ways he's been constant in your life.

Spiritual Sisterhood

*The heartfelt counsel of a friend is
as sweet as perfume and incense.*

PROVERBS 27:9

"Do you realize we've been long-distance friends longer than we've ever been close-distance friends?"

My question was met with several beats of silence as Ceena and I digested that reality individually and collectively. We'd met as coworkers and spent a scant eighteen months in the same community before an incredible opportunity beckoned Ceena to the East Coast. The strength of our friendship after years apart and through busy life seasons speaks to the tenacity of our commitment to one another.

We've worked hard to stay connected, grabbing moments after everyone else is in bed for chats via FaceTime or video messaging apps. We send each other early morning text prayers before important meetings on hard days. And I can always count on my friend for random silliness sent through our social media accounts to make me snort-laugh at some inopportune moment.

We've cried with and for each other, we've stormed the gates of heaven in desperate prayer, and we've reminded each other of the goodness of God, painstakingly pointing out all the ways he has shown up in the past and repeating his promises to show up in the future. We speak life over each other, and just like today's verse reminds us, our friendship brings a sweetness akin to a beautiful perfume to our everyday lives that makes even the most challenging seasons a bit easier.

Spiritual sisterhood is one of my favorite parts of belonging to the family of God, and Ceena is a beautiful example of what it means to be a sister and trusted adviser. She and my other spiritual sisters are a precious gift—one that comes with the intentional investment of time, energy, and prayer support. I am the woman I am today because of women who have built into my life, and I strive to do the same for them and others. These special relationships are some of the most important ones we can have, and we cannot take them for granted.

Julie

Today's Act of Gratitude

Spend time investing in your spiritual sisters, letting them know
how precious they are to you. Prayerfully consider who else might
need a spiritual sister, and start investing time and prayer in her.

Three Good Things

This is the day the LORD has made.
We will rejoice and be glad in it.

PSALM 118:24

"For MOPS, we're supposed to do a '3 Good Things' challenge for the next fourteen days," I messaged my friend Andrea one Wednesday. "As part of it, you're supposed to pick a friend and text them each evening with the list of things you're grateful for. Is it okay if you're my person?" Our moms' meeting the night before had focused on cultivating gratitude, and I was eager to get started.

"Yes! Can you be *my* person?" she responded immediately.

I quickly agreed, excited to try out the challenge and have an accountability partner to keep me on track. Studies have shown that a challenge like this can boost your happiness level for up to six months following the exercise.

As we messaged back and forth each day, I was struck by how small or specific the reasons to be grateful often were: hot coffee, a rosy sunrise, a quiet house, the kids getting along with each other, soaking in the hot tub while it snowed, a chat with a friend, renewed health after a temporary illness, a new book, a visit from grandparents, or an ice-cream sundae.

The good things we listed weren't huge in and of themselves, but they added up to a good life over time—one in which challenges still existed, but so did grace and gratitude. As Christians, we're asked to rejoice in this day. Our gracious God not only made it but he also gave us the opportunity to be alive to experience it. When we wholeheartedly embrace our day, we become aware of how many good things are present in our lives. Naming reasons to be grateful adds joy to our hearts and brings renewed purpose to our efforts.

Kristin

Today's Act of Gratitude

Find an accountability partner and commit to a "3 Good Things" challenge. Over the next fourteen days, send each other three things you're grateful for each day.

An Unexpected Gift

*I am the good shepherd; I know my own sheep, and they know me, just as my
Father knows me and I know the Father. So I sacrifice my life for the sheep.*

JOHN 10:14-15

"I'm willing to consider getting another dog, but I have some preconditions." My stern tone fooled no one as I warily eyed my family around the breakfast table. We'd lost our beloved Peanut a month ago, and it had become clear that we are a two-dog family. Our goldendoodle, Sully, was struggling, and we were sad.

Aaron leaned toward Lizzie and began his familiar chant: "Saint Bernard! Saint Bernar—"

"What? No! No Saint Bernards."

"Husky! Husky!" Lizzie picked up where Aaron left off, throwing a mischievous look toward her father.

"You can have as many huskies as you want in your own home. Be serious, you two!" Smiling, I turned toward Jon. "Our next dog needs to be small, no more than twenty pounds."

And that's how I found myself standing in a park, being introduced to a sixty-five-pound behemoth named Thea. Physically, she is the opposite of what I wanted, but her personality is what trainers look for in therapy dogs. After lots of discussion, that is what ultimately sold us on getting her.

Adopting an adult dog often comes with its own set of challenges. Still, as Thea settled into our family and we settled into her, I realized that she is my personal, unexpected blessing even as she is beloved by all of us.

If I am in the house, Thea is next to me. She shadows me from room to room, content to simply be near as I move through my day. She has declared herself my dog, and her unwavering doggy loyalty is a gift I didn't know I needed during this stage of life.

Jesus knows what we need, usually before we do. And his gifts—big and small, temporary or semipermanent—often come disguised in situations, sizes, and shapes we'd typically overlook. He provides for us physically, emotionally, and spiritually during our life on Earth, including the ultimate gift: salvation through his sacrificial death on the cross so that our sins would be wiped clean.

Julie

Today's Act of Gratitude

Reflect on John 10:14-15, above. List several ways Jesus has been
your Good Shepherd, and pause to thank him for his provision.

Picture Perfect

Confess your sins to each other and
pray for each other so that you may be healed.

JAMES 5:16

While scrolling through our most recent family photos, I paused on the ones of my husband Kyle and me. In them, we're laughing and smiling, even cuddled up in an embrace. As I thought about which one to post, I was immediately struck by how happy we were in the photos, yes, but also by how that could present a deceiving image of our relationship to others on the outside looking in.

Just a short eighteen months earlier, Kyle and I had walked through the most challenging stage of our marriage to date. It was the first time the thought of living apart from each other ever seriously crossed my mind. It was a season of sitting with pain, getting honest, bearing hard truths, and offering apologies and promises of something different, something new.

We shed tears and endured sleepless nights. We were exposing deep wounds. There were therapy sessions, honest ongoing conversations without taking offense, and thankfully, the prayers of friends when we didn't have the words or the strength to believe the good for ourselves.

This is the lie that sometimes permeates social media—the lie that someone else's life and marriage are perfect. Ideal. When that's simply not the case. Kyle and I love each other as imperfect people who both brought baggage to our relationship that needed to be exposed and addressed. With God's help, we're still working on these issues and still moving forward together.

None of us were meant to walk through tough times alone. God is near. And he often uses others to help us find healing. Wholeness. Deeper relationships with loved ones. But we've got to be willing to be honest and confess our heartache and even our sins to others who are trustworthy and will pray for us and with us. When we do, we'll find healing. We'll know we're not alone. God gave us the gift of his Spirit and the family of believers to get us through the good days and the difficult days.

Kendra

Today's Act of Gratitude

Think about a challenging phase you've experienced and spend some time thanking God for bringing you through it. How can you apply all you've learned to a current struggle?

What Have I Received?

He makes the whole body fit together perfectly. As each part
does its own special work, it helps the other parts grow, so
that the whole body is healthy and growing and full of love.

EPHESIANS 4:16

I recently listened to a podcast, and the day's guest posed an interesting exercise. Instead of suggesting a gratitude list, he asked listeners to consider the question "In the last twenty-four hours, what have I received from _____?"

Our answers help us recognize how often we fail to notice what people do for us regularly. We might be grateful for a person's presence in our life, while overlooking the tangible ways they demonstrate care. For example, if I consider what I've received from my husband in the last twenty-four hours, I could list many actions: He hugged me good morning. He picked up donuts for our daughter's birthday and dropped off the kids at school. He filled the gas tank and washed the car. He went to work to support our family. He sent me funny memes and stayed connected via text. He picked up the grocery store order on the way home. He asked about my day and provided support and feedback. The list goes on and on.

All too often, we downplay or overlook the ways people smooth the rough edges of our day. Instead, we focus on what they aren't doing right.

This charge to consider what we've received from others doesn't apply only to loved ones. A coworker who did their part on a team project, a neighbor who always says hello, or a business that provided excellent service can all be added to the tally of what we've received.

In God's economy, we are each meant to work together as various parts of one body. What sounds like an exercise in selfishness—What have I received?—is an exercise in humility. We are a lot more interdependent than we'd like to think. When we honestly consider the balance of what we've received versus what we've given, we recognize that we can never fully repay the small acts of assistance others provide. And when we take time to notice how well someone else is fulfilling their role, we honor each part of the body of Christ.

Kristin

Today's Act of Gratitude

Consider some of the close relationships in your life, both
work and personal. Respond to the question "In the last
twenty-four hours, what have I received from _____?"

Snuggle Chair

Since I, your Lord and Teacher, have washed your feet, you ought to wash each other's feet. I have given you an example to follow. Do as I have done to you.

JOHN 13:14-15

As I stood in the furniture store, eyeballing the oversize chair-and-a-half, I was slightly dismayed by its too-light fabric and less-than-trendy style. The only thing going for it was the larger-than-normal cushion: plenty of room for me and a kid or two to fit with a blanket, books, and sometimes a dog. After years of little butts squeezing next to mine in my favorite, rather petite accent chair, I'd determined to find a bigger one to accommodate fast-growing children rather than give up snuggles.

Smiling at the salesperson, I said, "I'll take it."

When it was delivered and moved into the space previously occupied by my favorite chair, I officially introduced my family to our only piece of furniture with a formal name: Snuggle Chair.

Even in my quest for a slightly more oversize piece, I didn't anticipate that Snuggle Chair would become an important tool for our family. With plenty of room for even Aaron and I to sit comfortably, it is more intimate than the couch, providing a cozy place for, well, snuggles and conversations—silly and hard, tearful and joy-filled. It's given our family the perfect spot for physical proximity as we've wrestled through difficult family moments, as well as offering a lovely place to simply sit side by side while reading separately, together.

God equips us spiritually to love one another, but he also provides physical means and tools. I can't help but think of how the Son of God used something as mundane as the washing of filthy feet to model servant leadership and sacrificial love. And while Snuggle Chair is nowhere near as profound, I'm grateful for its slightly unfashionable presence in my home.

The realization of its usefulness leads me to ponder what other tools I use to love others well, tools that I've perhaps overlooked because of their ordinary presence in my life. For example, lengthy car rides with my teenage children create a nonthreatening space for deeply personal conversations.

When we stop to contemplate which tools help us love others well, we can use those items with increased intentionality, adopt new habits, or make small changes to increase the effectiveness of our tools.

Julie

Today's Act of Gratitude

What tools do you use to love others well? Consider how you might use them more effectively.

The Kingdom Is Already Near

May your Kingdom come soon.
May your will be done on earth, as it is in heaven.

MATTHEW 6:10

The morning after another upsetting event in our country in which innocent people died, I attended a funeral. My mind was still reeling from the flood of information the night before; I felt fearful of people and of an unknown future. I was so unsettled that I almost didn't go to the service.

As I sat in a pew and looked around the church, filled mostly with people I did not know, I let out a quiet sigh. Soft music began to play, and we stood together, showing our respect to the grieving family as they entered the sanctuary. We sang "Amazing Grace," took Communion, and prayed the Lord's Prayer.

And as the scent of incense came to me in the glow of the soft candlelight, I suddenly felt comforted. We were a community, coming together to honor and grieve and love as one. As whispers of *amen* followed each Scripture of hope, every prayer of peace, my spirit was calmed.

I was reminded once again that Jesus brings peace. He is my hope. And he is near. All other allegiances and securities are but vapors that will cease to matter at the mention of his name. Even with all the evil we see around us and in our world, there is still good work to be done right here on earth, just as it is being done in heaven.

We're not waiting only for some future glory. God has already come, and I am so grateful for his presence that surrounds us even amid chaos and fear. And because of this truth, we, as a people who bear his name, are called to bring hope and love into this place. We are the ones who accomplish God's will on this earth in the way that we seek peace, offer love and hope, and remind others that the Kingdom is already near.

Kendra

Today's Act of Gratitude

How have you recently seen and been grateful for God's Kingdom being brought to earth? In what ways could you encourage someone else around you who may be anxious? Look for opportunities to share God's peace with them.

It's Okay to Cry

Jesus wept.

JOHN 11:35

One leg crossed over the other, I traced alphabet letters in the air with the tip of my toe, word after word. The nervous habit was a bid to distract myself from the emotional moment playing out on the video screen above me. But even though my eyes were averted, I couldn't unhear the narrator's words. As the grief in the speaker's voice rose in volume, I felt an answering grief rise in me. Tears gathered in my eyes as I tried to surreptitiously wipe them away, rifling through my purse for a tissue while hoping no one would notice.

The truth is, I've always been a person who cries a lot. I jokingly tell my friends that as long as I'm in the room, they'll never cry alone because their tears will trigger mine. I'm a sympathy crier.

Sometimes I feel embarrassed that I'm moved to tears while others can remain stoic, but I try to remind myself that tears are essential. In fact, our bodies need them to function. Did you know that the human body creates three different kinds of tears? Our bodies produce *reflex* tears to get irritants out of our eyes and *continuous* tears to keep our eyes lubricated, but *emotional* tears have additional health benefits. According to biochemist Dr. William Frey, while reflex tears are 98 percent water, emotional tears collect stress hormones and other toxins that the body then releases during crying. Studies indicate that crying also stimulates endorphins, the hormones that help us feel better.[*] Our tears serve a purpose.

I appreciate how Jesus—when faced with his friends' grief over Lazarus's death—cried alongside them. Even though he held the power of life and death in his hands and knew he could raise Lazarus from the dead, he still wept. His action reminds us that though he was God, he was also fully man, capable of entering into the fullness of our vulnerable humanity. While I'm comforted by the idea that he was moved to tears just as I sometimes am, I'm even more thankful for the unfailing compassion he willingly displayed.

Kristin

Today's Act of Gratitude

The next time you cry, thank God for the gift of tears.

---

[*] Judith Orloff, "The Health Benefits of Tears" *Psychology Today*, July 27, 2010, https://www.psychologytoday.com/us/blog/emotional-freedom/201007/the-health-benefits-tears.

Filling One Another's Gaps

As iron sharpens iron,
so a friend sharpens a friend.

PROVERBS 27:17

"What did you think of the verdict?" I asked one of my dearest friends during our rambling lunchtime phone conversation on a random Tuesday afternoon.

"Oh, yes. Let's talk about that verdict."

And we did. She is my sister in Christ, a fellow attorney, and a woman of color. I knew the outcome of the trial, with its complicated undertones of racism, would lead to a thoughtful, nuanced conversation about complex issues.

I listened as she shared her perspective on a case that had been making headlines for over a year before the hotly debated, nationally publicized trial. I was seeking a deeper understanding of some of the *whys* behind her viewpoint that hadn't necessarily been a part of my own analysis.

As we talked, we analyzed the situation as lawyers but also as women who love Jesus. We carefully teased out areas where our legal system continues to be inequitable in important ways, and we methodically dissected flawed arguments, looking for biblical truth without the taint of propaganda—on either side.

One aspect of our friendship I am most grateful for is our ability to talk about the big and small, simple and complex. In the same conversation, we chortle over something silly, then discuss a situation that brings tears to our eyes. I love her and want to hear her perspective and experiences precisely because they are different from mine, and she'd say the same about me. Because we come from different subcultures and backgrounds, we fill in each other's knowledge gaps, trusting each other enough to be emotionally vulnerable, knowing we won't simply dismiss the other's viewpoint. I am a wiser, more compassionate woman because of our mutual willingness to wrestle with the thorniest of topics, looking for Jesus in the midst of it all.

Julie

Today's Act of Gratitude

Who fills your knowledge gaps, giving you insight or a fresh perspective precisely because of the differences in your background and life? Send that person a thank-you, even as you prayerfully ask God to send you more knowledge-gap-filling friends.

Knowing When to Rest

*It is useless for you to work so hard from early morning until late at night,
anxiously working for food to eat; for God gives rest to his loved ones.*

PSALM 127:2

I love to-do lists. They are one of my favorite things. I thoroughly enjoy crossing off tasks throughout the course of a day, and in fact, sometimes I'll write down an item I've already done just so that I can cross it off.

Most days, this is helpful for me. I feel accomplished and purposeful when I'm checking jobs off the list. It helps me manage my stress level and reminds me of upcoming items that need to be completed or scheduled.

But then there are days when I'm weary. I feel tired or just down, and my to-do list overwhelms me. When I was young, I used to push myself to keep working anyway, but as I've gotten older, I've realized that sometimes my mind, body, and spirit are ready for a break. I must listen to my own needs as well as everybody else's.

It happened again just the other day. As I set to work, I found myself just pushing through. As I finished what I needed to get done and looked at several less urgent items that I could have turned my attention to next, I heard a whisper: *You've done enough for today.*

I sat back in my chair, recognizing the familiar voice of the Lord.

"Okay," I said as I closed my computer, grateful for the wisdom that comes from listening to God and heeding what he tells me to do, even when it's to rest.

We live in a society that values productivity and achievement. Although that's not always bad, it can become unhealthy when taken to extremes. We are not machines. God made our bodies to need rest, and in fact, Scripture says that he *gives* rest to those he loves. That means me. And that means you too.

I'm so grateful that God values work and rest. And so should we.

Kendra

Today's Act of Gratitude

Take some time to rest, thanking God for this much-needed provision.

See the Good

Let all that I am praise the LORD; may I never forget the good things he does for me. He forgives all my sins and heals all my diseases. He redeems me from death and crowns me with love and tender mercies. He fills my life with good things. My youth is renewed like the eagle's!

PSALM 103:2-5

A car accident at age seventeen broke two vertebrae in my back. A week's stay in the hospital for surgery meant I missed the final days of my junior year.

I was released from the hospital into a life that looked a little different. For months, I couldn't drive or lift anything heavy. I wore a back brace everywhere unless I was lying down or swimming. Most activities I'd once been a part of—like marching band and cheerleading—were no longer options.

Nighttime was another challenge, as my movement was limited. I would lie on my side at bedtime while my mom stuffed numerous pillows behind my back to support it. I'd wake a couple of hours later and pull out the pillows so I could rest on my back. Halfway through the night, I'd call Mom, and she'd rush in to help me onto my side again, replacing the pillows behind me.

There were many times I was grumpy about my limitations, but I was grateful too: I could wiggle my toes and know my spinal cord was intact. Faithful friends brought me books and drove me to the lake to swim. And my mom faithfully helped with the pillows, night after night, even though it interrupted her sleep.

Slowly, I improved. By the time school began again, I didn't even need my brace. But for someone who hadn't faced many challenges, the experience was instructive. The accident taught me that we are not invincible and that life is precious. And the aftermath taught me that rarely is an experience all good or all bad—we have a choice about what to focus on. God fills our lives with good things, but we have to have the eyes to see it. Let our prayer be: *May we never forget the good things he does for us.* With this mindset, we'll find renewed gratitude for the good that softens our challenges.

Kristin

Today's Act of Gratitude

Spend time thanking God for the good things that emerged from a challenging circumstance in your life.

New Life

I am about to do something new. See, I have already begun!
Do you not see it? I will make a pathway through the
wilderness. I will create rivers in the dry wasteland.

ISAIAH 43:19

Every year, I wait expectantly for the first signs of spring. Buds on trees, thunderstorms that turn the brown ground green again, flowers pushing up through the dirt. As the temperature in Minnesota slowly begins to rise, each day bringing longer hours of light and warmer sun, my gratitude for seeing new life swells. Spring, to me, comes as a promise and a reminder that no matter how hard winter has been, new life is always on the way.

God's promises do not change. Just as the seasons come and go, so the truth of God and his Word remain. As I think back on the hard seasons I've faced—the death of a sibling after a long battle with cancer, infertility, and a marriage stretched to its breaking point—I see the fingerprints of God on all of them. He was near. And I can see the glimpses of new life that began to come out of those spiritual winters.

This gives me hope for the challenging season I am currently in. As I remember how God showed up with his love and grace, mercy and peace in the past, I can have faith that he will do the same, even now.

There is comfort in knowing and believing Scripture that tells us God will create pathways in our wildernesses and cause rivers to run in places we see as desolate. We just need to have faith that he will do this and eyes to perceive the slightest evidence of the new thing he's doing. Sometimes it takes longer than we'd like, but we can be sure that no matter what we're seeing (or not seeing), he is still at work. Our God is a God who brings new life, always.

Kendra

Today's Act of Gratitude

Spend a little time thanking God for what you know
he can do, even if you aren't seeing it just yet.

Strength in Community

*For where two or three gather together
as my followers, I am there among them.*

MATTHEW 18:20

"Will you pray for me?"

I hit the send button on my text, then paused before adding a few details to my request, trusting friends to hold what I'd shared in confidence but also to petition God on my behalf. As my second text zoomed off, I felt a weight lift. Now that others knew what was going on, the lie that I was alone dissipated, and it felt like I could breathe again.

As two beautiful, simple prayers appeared in the text thread, my eyes welled with tears. I thanked God for friends who immediately drop what they are doing to pray over me, reminded yet again of the power when two or more in the family of God gather in prayer.

While our American culture idolizes fierce independence, that's not the standard outlined in the New Testament for followers of Jesus. The first-century church supported one another financially, emotionally, and spiritually. God never intended for us to walk our faith journeys alone. While sometimes it's necessary because of circumstances beyond our control, we are stronger physically, emotionally, and spiritually when we belong to a committed community of people genuinely trying to love God and love others. We need people who pray for us, encourage us, and remind us of who we are in Christ when we momentarily forget.

If you have suffered at the hands of church people, I am so sorry. Please do not allow that experience to keep you from godly community. A Bible study, a moms' group, a different church—God's family is not a monolith, and there is absolutely a place for you to develop your faith and use the gifts God has given you. If you are already in a faith community but are feeling disgruntled, ask God for clarity on what needs to change, first in you and then in your community. Belonging to a body of fellow believers is a gift from God that is worth the effort.

Julie

Today's Act of Gratitude

Make a list of characteristics you love about your faith community. Prayerfully consider how you can lend your gifts to make that community stronger. If you don't have a faith community, ask God for guidance on finding or creating one.

You've Always Been Known

You saw me before I was born. Every day of my life was recorded in your book. Every moment was laid out before a single day had passed.

PSALM 139:16

"On the surface, you may not think of yourself as lonely, but part of the definition of loneliness is feeling like no one really knows you well. And that can happen even when people surround you." I shared these thoughts with a group of women one chilly spring morning in Minnesota.

As I looked around the room, I saw women slowly nodding, acknowledging this common experience. These were moms of littles, and with kids always underfoot, they often don't think of themselves as lonely. But the longing for connection can be intense. When we unpack loneliness and realize that it's deeper than just feeling alone, we can usually think of a time when we felt misunderstood or like no one could relate to us.

Usually, after we've spoken honestly about this issue, women will approach us, sharing a time when they felt lonely. Often it is a current feeling. With permission to be honest, these women transparently tell us how lonely mothering can sometimes be for them. We nod our understanding, offering encouragement and a reminder that they aren't alone.

We've all experienced loneliness at different points. Whether we were the new kid at school, the new family to a community, or a new member of a church—we know what it's like to come into a space where people don't know us well, at least not yet.

But even when we go through these times of loneliness, we can rest assured that we are always known to God. Scripture tells us that God knew us and saw us before we were born. He has recorded every day of our life—that's how intimately he knows us. And his love and care for us are always near, even when people may not be. Don't be afraid to reach out to him in a season of loneliness; he will always be there.

Kendra

Today's Act of Gratitude

Thank God for the ways he has been close to you,
even if you are in a season of loneliness.

A Dash of Irish

Understand, therefore, that the Lord your God is indeed God. He is the faithful God who keeps his covenant for a thousand generations and lavishes his unfailing love on those who love him and obey his commands.

DEUTERONOMY 7:9

"Scooch closer together!" I called, trying to include as much of the historic town square as possible while omitting random passersby in the picture of Aaron and our two kids. "Great! Okay, now smile!"

My heart fluttered as I snapped the photo of my loved ones standing smack-dab in Birr's town center in County Offaly, Ireland. A multi-great-grandfather of my husband walked these cobblestones, and I—for a tiny moment—wished desperately for my own kinship connection to this beautiful land even as I was thrilled we'd made the trek for Aaron and the kids.

Lord, is it possible I have even one tiny drop of blood tying me to this place? If I do, could you reveal it to me? That was my unspoken prayer as I trotted my way back to my family, ready to spend the afternoon exploring the surrounding area.

As we stood on a hill overlooking Birr, reading the historic caption about the ruins of a monastery, I felt the Holy Spirit gently stirring in my heart. People who loved Jesus had prayed and worshiped and walked upon this same land hundreds of years before Aaron's direct ancestors. That means I have "family" from this gorgeous place, and you do too.

While our human lineage can sometimes be complicated—filled with hard stories, less-than-virtuous forerunners, or DNA tests leaving us with a longing to be from a physical place we've grown to love—we're also adopted into a spiritual lineage and a spiritual family. And that spiritual family is filled with imperfect people who were courageous and brave, who loved God and others, and who set the example for us to follow.

Isn't it encouraging to remember that others have walked in the same faith that we walk, have encountered God intimately through hard and joy-filled moments, have failed before repenting and trying again successfully? We are not alone on this journey, and our faith ancestors are encouraging and cheering us on.

Julie

Today's Act of Gratitude

Read the list in Hebrews 11 of faith heroes who have gone before us, thanking God for our incredible spiritual lineage. Keep these heroes in mind the next time you feel alone in your faith.

Experiencing God

May you experience the love of Christ, though it is too great to understand fully. Then you will be made complete with all the fullness of life and power that comes from God.

EPHESIANS 3:19

We bought a hot tub. After a vacation we'd been planning for a long time fell through, using the money for a fun purpose seemed like a reasonable trade-off. But I was skeptical at first: maintaining it sounded like work, and I wasn't sure how much use it would get.

But after mulling it over, we decided to purchase it. My worries were unwarranted; to tell the truth, it's the best "vacation" I've ever experienced. I'm grateful for the peace I feel when I climb in with a cup of coffee to watch the sunrise. I'm thankful for it on nights when I look at the stars and try to identify constellations. Chilly winter days when snowflakes fall softly, coating my hair and melting on the surface of the water, have become my favorite hot tub experience. It's magical.

But what I love most are the connections that tub has fostered. We live in a distracted world, but the time with my family in that space is a moment of connection. No screen, book, toy, or work commitment is present to interfere with the quiet conversations, the eye contact, the simple pleasure of not feeling hurried.

Although we initially purchased an *item*, I think the reason our joy and gratitude have lingered is that it's now become an *experience*—one that keeps on giving. Research consistently demonstrates that experiences foster happiness much more than material goods do, in part because we are not tempted to compare our own experiences with someone else's the way we do with possessions. We simply enjoy them.

So, how can we bring the joy of experience into our relationship with Jesus? Relationships grow through shared activities. When we intentionally seek time with him—by adding a reminder or time slot to our calendar, singing songs of praise at church, or studying or discussing his Word with a small group—we will appreciate his love and presence to a greater degree. And when we foster connection via experience, we will find ourselves more grateful for the time we've had with him.

Kristin

Today's Act of Gratitude

Choose one concrete activity you can do to bring the joy of experience to your relationship with Jesus.

Steadfast Hope

Let us hold unswervingly to the hope we profess,
for he who promised is faithful.

HEBREWS 10:23, NIV

The first day of spring is a turning point for me, a firm reminder that regardless of the snowy yard, bare tree branches, and chilly nighttime temps outside my front door, change is coming.

Spring—for me—is hope made tangible. It is the fulfilled promise of a fresh start and new beginnings as it ends winter's dormant days. Growing up on a farm, I knew that this season brought the birthing of lambs and hatching of ducklings, and that we would soon be tilling fields with our 1950s Massey Ferguson tractor and hunting for pussy willows along the edges of a secret meadow, accessible only by a footpath through marsh and forest.

While the first day of spring has me taking a deep breath and pausing to thank God for the official arrival of my favorite time of year, I know better than to think there won't be a snowstorm or two before summer comes. This date simply acknowledges our seasonal progress: snow melts faster, the sun's rays are warmer, and I hear the chorus of newly returned songbirds on days it's warm enough to open my windows.

As much as I love spring and the hope it brings after wintry weather has outstayed its welcome, it is nothing compared to the hope I find in Christ. His death on the cross provided a way for our eternal redemption, and his life on the earth gave us a blueprint for spending our time here wisely. For those of us who love and follow Jesus, there is no uncertainty about the meaning of life, how we are called to live, what is important and what is not, or what happens when we die. We know that no matter what is happening in the world, God wins.

And he gifted us with a book containing all the answers we need for living in a way that spreads the same hope to everyone around us. Just as the first day of spring reminds us of what is coming seasonally, the Bible is the inspired Word of God, reminding us that Jesus is our ultimate hope in a broken world and that he who gave promises to us will be faithful to fulfill them.

Julie

Today's Act of Gratitude

Sing God a hymn or worship song about hope. "It Is Well" and
"Raise a Hallelujah" by Bethel Music are two of my favorites.

Learning to Be Content

*If we have enough food and clothing,
let us be content.*

1 TIMOTHY 6:8

He woke in the night, crying out in pain. My husband Kyle and I jumped out of bed and ran to his room as soon as his cries reached our ears.

"My stomach really hurts," our eleven-year-old son said, clutching his midsection.

He'd been sick all the previous day, alternately vomiting and sleeping. We thought he just had a bug but now worried it could be something more.

"Maybe you should take him in," I whispered to my husband. He nodded in agreement.

I helped our son put on some clothes and shoes while Kyle started the car to heat up against the cold winter night. As we waited for it to warm, we whispered a quick prayer for him. After they left, I checked on our girls before crawling back in bed, turning on the sound on my phone. I knew I wouldn't sleep, but I laid my head against the pillow to rest.

Twenty minutes later, my phone dinged.

"He's seeing the doctor now. They're ordering tests, but they think it's his appendix."

Relief washed over me. They had a plan to help our child. A few hours later, Kyle called to let me know he was in surgery and everything was going well.

By the time our girls woke up the next morning and I let them know what had happened, the operation was over, and our son was resting in a hospital room.

Several days later, I was struck by an overwhelming sense of gratitude for the doctors, nurses, and hospital staff who quickly acted to care for our son. At the same time, I pondered the reality that medical care is not so easily accessible worldwide.

There are millions of people living without access to some of the things that I can easily take for granted—medical care, schooling, shelter. How often do I go through my days feeling disgruntled when my basic needs are already met? Too often, I'm afraid my family won't have what they need. The Bible says that if we have clothing and food, we should be content. That may not seem like much, but when I focus on just today, it's enough.

Kendra

Today's Act of Gratitude

Think of all the simple things that you often take for granted. How can you focus on contentment in light of what you already have?

Walking through the Middle

When you go through deep waters, I will be with you. When you go through rivers of difficulty, you will not drown. When you walk through the fire of oppression, you will not be burned up; the flames will not consume you.

ISAIAH 43:2

Aaron's phone and mine both buzzed with a loved one's text: "I woke up with symptoms that need to be checked by my doctor. I've got an appointment for 10:00 a.m."

Our friend has been on a journey with his health, and his brief text contained layers of unspoken thoughts and emotions. We knew the possibility of certain complications, and our friend had confessed his fear even as he stood firmly on his faith. As we rallied in prayer for peace, wisdom, and discernment, and ordinary and extraordinary miracles, I asked Jesus to be a tangible presence, a steady assurance to our friend that he is seen and loved even in these scary, uncertain moments.

The middle is my least favorite part of any journey. Even fun journeys tend to have an un-fun middle, a space we quietly gloss over when sharing the highlight reels with others. Middles are often filled with hard work, uncertainty, and chaos as we journey through them, sometimes toward an unknown end. The middle requires trust, patience, and reliance upon God, pulling us out of our comfort zone and shattering our illusions of control.

There is one unconditional guarantee about the middle: God accompanies us. We are not left alone in those dark places. My wisest, most deeply faith-rooted friends would tell you that their unshakable faith foundations were forged in the middles. And I would say the same. It is there that we learn to rely upon God in new ways, entrusting him with our loved ones and ourselves when there is nothing else left to do. I hate the middles, but I acknowledge that my faith has a sturdy and strong footing because of them.

Can we pray for rescue while simultaneously thanking God for drawing near and revealing more of himself to us? I believe so. There is space for prayerful pleas even as we praise and thank him in every circumstance, including the hardest ones.

Julie

Today's Act of Gratitude

Instead of resorting to clichés that are meant to soothe but often feel flippant, specifically pray for God to be tangibly present as loved ones walk through difficult circumstances. Isaiah 43:2, above, is a wonderful place to start.

We Want You

See how very much our Father loves us,
for he calls us his children, and that is what we are!

1 JOHN 3:1

My friend is a supervisor for a large organization in our town. During the past year the business went through several transitions, and as often happens, the employees weren't happy with the changes. My friend was required to meet with each employee under her supervision to discuss their concerns.

One evening as we prayed for her work situation, she said her boss told her to approach each of these meetings with one goal in mind—to say to the person across from her, "We want you here." And to truly mean it.

She'd already had several meetings, and she said it disarmed people when they knew they were wanted and valued—not only as an employee but as a person. From that point on, the interactions went well—even when there were differences of opinion—because the employees knew they were a valuable part of the team.

I left our time together thinking about what she said and wondering about conversations I have with family, friends, and strangers throughout my day. Do these people walk away feeling wanted? Sometimes, I'm sure, but not always. I'm determined to do better.

Don't we all want to know that we are included, loved, and wanted? I know I do. My friend's work situation is an important reminder for all of us—that no matter who we interact with or the differences we may have—letting people know that they are wanted and cared for is always our greatest goal.

And isn't this what God does for each of us? He calls us his children, dearly loved. So regardless of what we've done or who we are, we know that if we come to him, we will be loved. This is what I desire for myself and for those around me.

Kendra

Today's Act of Gratitude

Thank God for the ways he has let you know that you are loved and wanted. Think of someone who needs to know that they are wanted and reach out to let them know it.

Unexpected Beauty

*When you have eaten and are satisfied, you shall bless the LORD
your God for the good land which He has given you.*

DEUTERONOMY 8:10, NASB

We went house hunting in the late fall. The home we owned at the time was lovely, but I could see right through the window to my neighbor's kitchen sink. It was also on a corner lot, with the yard situated in the front. There was zero privacy and no backyard to speak of.

In our search for a new place, we were determined to make sure it included a backyard. I grew up on an acre of land in northern Minnesota, with a big backyard that butted up to trees. Wild beauty was all around us; the Mississippi River was just a couple of blocks from our house. Even now, trees and water remind me of my childhood and the comfort of home.

But as we began to walk through potential homes with our realtor, I had to revise my hopes. Many homes had yards, but most were small squares with little privacy. I felt a little disappointed but figured that a smaller space was better than none at all.

By the time we toured the home that was to become ours, checking the yard felt like an afterthought. We peered outside, saw patchy brown grass and scraggly branches, and moved on. Backyard—check.

Imagine our surprise when spring arrived. The once-barren branches filled in with glorious foliage, and the pond in the wetlands behind us came alive with the sound of countless frogs. At night, I would open the window just to hear them sing. The best part is the trees, which lie thickly across the back and side of the property. They remind me of my childhood. They feel like home.

Over time, we added to the bare slabs of concrete behind the house: an area for fires, a patio, a playset for the kids. The backyard we'd given only a cursory glance had become a haven.

It's good land, and I'm grateful that I get to see it out my window each day. But I'm even more thankful that God knew the desire of my heart and answered it in a way that makes me smile just to think about it. What a gift—the gift of home.

Kristin

Today's Act of Gratitude

Thank God for something in his creation that holds special
meaning for you, whether it's a piece of land or something else.

My Earring Collection

*This will be a symbol among you. In the future your children may ask,
"What do these stones mean to you?" Then you will tell them that the
water of the Jordan was cut off before the LORD's covenant chest. . . .
These stones will be an enduring memorial for the Israelites.*

JOSHUA 4:6-7, CEB

Standing before my simple, homemade earring display case that hangs near my vanity mirror, I contemplated my options. I'm a jewelry minimalist, except for earrings. Most frequently, I reach for a big, dangling pair that can be easily spotted from across a room, although I have several favorite sets of petite, hard-to-notice studs that make my day when I slip them on. If I'm going to walk out the door, I put on earrings—even on the days I skip makeup and tuck my hair into a hat.

Why earrings? This habit started quite accidentally but has become a beloved part of my morning routine. Years ago, I purchased a beautiful pair while on vacation. Every time I slipped them on, I recalled the fun we had on that trip and even the warmth of the experience. Realizing that those accessories triggered a cascade of lovely memories every time I saw them, I started buying an inexpensive pair on each subsequent trip as a memento. A few years later, I began adding sets to mark significant milestones in my walk with Jesus. And now, here I stand in front of my own version of the Gilgal stones mentioned in today's verse.

What are Gilgal stones? God commanded Joshua to pull twelve stones from the middle of the temporarily dry Jordan River to memorialize the miracle of parting the flood-stage Jordan so that the Israelites could cross on dry ground. Those stones were then stacked in a pile as an enduring memorial for subsequent generations to what God did for his people that day.

My earrings will never be a memorial for future generations like the actual Gilgal stones. Still, they are a daily reminder to me of God's goodness, his enduring faithfulness, and some of the beautiful places I've been blessed to explore during my travels. They are tiny remembrances of my blessings, and I rarely leave the house without a pair.

Julie

Today's Act of Gratitude

How do you remember God's provision and blessing
in your life? Consider whether you could establish
your own version of the Gilgal stones.

Pride and Joy

*Well done, my good and faithful servant. You have been
faithful in handling this small amount, so now I will give you
many more responsibilities. Let's celebrate together!*

MATTHEW 25:21

Our faith community met on an early Sunday morning. One of the couples had a young baby, and they were feeling overwhelmed. As others in our group talked of volunteering in our city and of neighbors they were building relationships with, I looked over at my friend. Her face fell as tears filled her eyes.

"What's wrong?" I whispered.

Everyone stopped talking as she looked toward her husband, a knowing glance passing between them.

Kim let out a sigh.

"Everyone is doing something for God, and it's really exciting," she started. "I guess we're just frustrated. We thought we could be doing more, but Ellie has been a challenging baby, and with Tim's work schedule and being out of town during the week, we just haven't been able to connect with other people like we were hoping we'd be able to. We feel like we're not doing anything."

We all stared at them for a moment before another woman spoke up. "You *are* doing something. You've started your family."

"I feel like we're just a disappointment," Kim said with a shrug.

"God's not disappointed in you," I responded. "He knew what this season would bring for you and your family. Yes, there are things you want to do, and there will be time for that, but just know, he is not disappointed with your current season of life."

Kim nodded. "Thanks. I needed to hear that."

Sometimes our lives don't look like we'd hoped. But what God values is not always what we see as valuable. I am grateful that he is not always looking for us to do big, elaborate things for him. He's just looking for us to be faithful—in big and small things. And sometimes, being faithful in the little is even more important than the big. No matter what, God is not disappointed because his love is not dependent on our actions; he is pleased when we are simply faithful to follow through in what he asks of us for today.

Kendra

Today's Act of Gratitude

How are you being faithful to what God is asking of you in this season, whether in big or small ways? Thank him that he will never demand more of you than you can handle in your stage of life.

Take It to Jesus First

*God showed his great love for us by sending Christ
to die for us while we were still sinners.*

ROMANS 5:8

I know better than to handle disagreements via text. Still, here I was, reading and rereading her message, frustrated at her perceived lack of compassion over my situation and wanting desperately to reply with a passive-aggressive "That's fine. I'll handle it."

Knowing I should pick up the phone and continue a potentially tension-filled conversation verbally instead of by text doesn't always mean that's what I'll do. And that's where I found myself this particular day: grumpy, in the proverbial ditch emotionally, and about to respond to my friend in a way not recommended by conflict management professionals.

One of the things I am most grateful for about Jesus is that he can handle the rawest, ugliest parts of me. There is no pretense or polite dithering; Jesus gets the straight-to-the-point, emotionally-in-the-ditch Julie more than I care to admit. And he can handle it. I can tell him all the ways someone is irritating me without fear that he will suddenly realize I'm a sinner with an unhealthy passive-aggressive streak and disown me. He already knows this about me and isn't one bit surprised when I tell him all about whatever has me tied in knots as I drive down the road. The beautiful thing about Jesus is that he always meets me in that ugly place but never allows me to stay camped there.

When I take my complaints to him first, I often find perspective and clarity as I process the situation. As I confess my ugliest uglies, the Holy Spirit has the space to comfort while gently convicting me, reminding me of biblical truth, and setting my feet back onto firm ground spiritually and emotionally.

Jesus *intentionally* died for me—and you—becoming the blood sacrifice necessary to put us back into right standing before God. He knew us at our worst and chose us despite ourselves. I don't know about you, but when I meditate on that realization, I'm able to reconsider even the hardest situation from an eternal perspective, and it never fails to both challenge my intended response and change my heart.

Julie

Today's Act of Gratitude

Thank God for loving you even when you are at your worst. Entrust Jesus
with your ugly initial responses, allowing the Holy Spirit an opportunity
to change your heart and mind before you text or pick up the phone.

The Sun Still Rises

Long ago you laid the foundation of the earth and made the heavens with your hands. They will perish, but you remain forever. . . . You will change them like a garment and discard them. But you are always the same; you will live forever.

PSALM 102:25-27

I read the news on a Wednesday evening. A friend who had been battling cancer for the past year and been in remission for a mere two months had been diagnosed with stage IV pancreatic cancer. Though the doctors had suggested chemotherapy to slow its progress, there was no cure.

Tears rolled down my face as I grasped the full magnitude of a thirty-something woman receiving such a life-changing diagnosis. I scrolled up from her post to see a photo of her with her husband and three beautiful children. Grief consumed me as my friend's current reality reminded me of the complex emotions I had felt two decades earlier as I watched my sister walk through a five-year cancer battle that ultimately took her life.

We can feel battered by life and its constant shifting. In a moment, the world as we know it can become a vastly different landscape, one filled with worry, stress, or fear. A diagnosis, a divorce, a job loss, a natural disaster, or a single poor decision can have life-altering consequences and ripple effects that spill over and trickle down.

I went to bed that night full of lament and fervent prayers for my friend. But the following day, as I found a quiet moment to eat breakfast, I looked outside and was struck by how everything had changed—and yet nothing had changed. The sun still rose. Birds still fluttered past. Neighbors still drove by on their way to work or school.

I don't have all the answers on why evil exists or why we experience such suffering. But I take heart and feel comfort knowing that our God is unchanging. He is not surprised by the tragedy that befalls us. He remains our comforter, our peace, our provider. And he is the same yesterday, today, and forever.

Lord, thank you for your unchanging nature. In a world that is often confusing, we are grateful that your constant love is always available to comfort us. Amen.

Kristin

Today's Act of Gratitude

Thank God for his unchanging nature, even amid life's constant shifting.

Caring for Others

This is what the LORD of Heaven's Armies says: Judge fairly, and show
mercy and kindness to one another. Do not oppress widows, orphans,
foreigners, and the poor. And do not scheme against each other.

ZECHARIAH 7:9-10

We'd been watching the news and following along for several days. War was causing people to flee their homes and country for safety. We kept in close contact with a friend who works for a Christian organization that helps resettle immigrants and refugees around our state.

We talked together as a family about what it means to be a refugee, having to flee everything familiar to you and travel a great distance just to be safe. We wondered together what it would be like to walk in their shoes and then prayed together for their safety and peace.

Afterward, we messaged our friend. "How can we help with this current crisis?" we asked. "We have an extra room if people are coming and need a place to stay."

"I'll let you know," she responded. "I'm not sure how many are coming yet or where they'll want them to be resettled."

"Thanks," I responded. "We'd really like to help; please let us know if there is anything else that we can do."

A few days later, she let us know of a way we could help, and we, along with our kids, were able to offer support and encouragement to an immigrant family in need.

As Christians, we are called to show mercy and kindness to others. It is a way to show our gratitude to God for his provision to us, and it's a reminder that all we have comes from him. And God is clear: our mercy should not include only people we know or like but should extend to "widows, orphans, foreigners, and the poor." We don't get to leave anyone out; everyone is to be cared for. At times this may feel overwhelming because of all the needs around us. That is when we need the Holy Spirit to guide us as we ask, *What needs can I help with currently? Where would you like me to use my resources to help others?* And when we ask, we can be sure he'll answer.

Kendra

Today's Act of Gratitude

Find an organization in your community or state serving immigrants or refugees and offer to help in some capacity, whether buying supplies, volunteering time, or donating monetarily. Thank God for his provision to you that enables you to help others.

Encouraging the Competition

Give, and you will receive. Your gift will return to you in full—pressed down, shaken together to make room for more, running over, and poured into your lap. The amount you give will determine the amount you get back.

LUKE 6:38

"Are you here for the fiction brainstorming session? Here, come sit next to me."

She'd caught me lingering in the doorway, quietly reconsidering whether to join this breakout session as I recognized the faces of several women well known in Christian fiction circles. But when a famous author tells you to sit next to her, you do it. And so I did.

If you have ever wondered whether fiction authors are as amazing as you think they might be, I'm here to tell you that they are—at least this particular group of them. The group brainstormed about plot holes and about characters that needed to be developed, and I got to listen in as the behind-the-scenes magic unfolded. It was marvelous . . . until it was my turn.

"So Julie, what would you like to discuss?" As eyes turned to me, I stammered my way through the secret idea for a cozy mystery I'd been carrying around for years. "And so I'm trying to think of a way to murder a few people." I finished a bit lamely, wondering why I was asking for help with killing off characters instead of a million other questions I could ask about my novel.

The ensuing conversation in that beautiful Victorian drawing room at our retreat center was delightfully hilarious as my deadly question was pondered with creative seriousness. Everyone chimed in with clever ways for my villain to (temporarily) get away with murder.

Whether or not that villain ever has the opportunity to commit a crime on the written page, I often think of these women and their warm invitation and thank God for them. They fanned the flames of my tentative dream, even though I was a potential future competitor.

I want to be the woman who sees the new girl hovering in the doorway and invites her in. I want to be someone who sincerely encourages another's gift, knowing there is zero scarcity in the Kingdom of God and that she is no threat to me. God's math is not our math, and our generosity returns to us pressed down and overflowing into our lap.

Julie

Today's Act of Gratitude

Thank God for someone who has encouraged your tentative dreams. Trust him as you, in turn, are generous with potential competitors.

The Comfort of Being Known

O LORD, you have examined my heart and know everything about me. You know when I sit down or stand up. You know my thoughts even when I'm far away. You see me when I travel and when I rest at home. You know everything I do. You know what I am going to say even before I say it, LORD. You go before me and follow me. You place your hand of blessing on my head.

PSALM 139:1-5

My kids love selling items door to door. As a shy child who once hated participating in fundraisers, I don't completely understand it, but I've come to accept it. Whether it's chocolate bars, nuts, or Girl Scout cookies, all three of my children are thrilled to go from one house to the next, asking if the person would like to support their school or troop.

It takes courage to knock on someone's door, but I think what tips the balance for my kids is knowing that they're welcome. Our house is located on a quiet cul-de-sac, and we've lived here since 2010. Most of our neighbors have known my daughters since they toddled around as babies and have spent the last decade watching them doodle chalk creations on the driveway, race their bikes on the street, or trudge each morning to the bus stop. They've seen them sled down the hill created by the snowplow, argue with each other, or run through sprinklers on hot summer days. They've let my daughters pet their animals, fed them ice cream and snacks, and listened to them talk incessantly while they weeded their gardens. Over time, those shared memories add up. And as a result, when my children knock on doors to ask about Girl Scout cookies, they are warmly welcomed.

What a comfort there is in being known.

In the same way, you and I can experience that level of comfort in our relationship with Jesus. We need not approach him with hat in hand, unsure of our welcome. The Bible details how God knows everything about us—not so he can trip us up or shame us, but because of his great love for us. He goes before and behind us, and his hand of blessing is upon us. What a loving Father we have. I'm thankful that he knows us completely and always welcomes us into a relationship with him.

Kristin

Today's Act of Gratitude

Thank God that he knows and loves you, and
that you are always welcome.

Loving Those You'll Never Meet

It's not important who does the planting, or who does the watering.
What's important is that God makes the seed grow.

1 CORINTHIANS 3:7

"Mom, I need something sweet. Do we have anything?"

My daughter's pajama-clad, whirlwind entrance into the kitchen had me pausing from unloading the dishwasher as she frantically pawed through our snack drawer.

"Um. It's 7:15 a.m. on a school morning; what's going on?" My voice revealed my skepticism over what could require sugar this early in the day.

"Mom, today is Chloe's birthday, and she's having a terrible week! I need something sweet to bring her as a present."

My initial annoyance faded as I absorbed the weight of her words, and soon we were both digging through the snack drawer. Tucked in the back corner, we simultaneously spied an unopened package of Reese's Peanut Butter Cups originally intended for milkshakes. After checking the expiration date, I offered them to Lizzie. "Do you think she'd like these?"

"Oh, perfect! Thanks, Mom. She'll love this!" A quick hug and my daughter was off, back up the stairs, clutching her present as she raced to get ready for school.

I've never met Lizzie's classmate, and while I know her a bit through stories shared over the years, I'd walk past her on a sidewalk without recognition. I thought about this young woman off and on as I went about my own day, praying over some of the details Lizzie had shared as we drove to school, grateful that I got to be a small part of Lizzie's plan to brighten Chloe's day.

That's the beautiful thing about being in community with others who know and love Jesus—we get to touch the lives of people we'll never meet by partnering with those who know them. Lizzie's presence in her school, in her classrooms, and in her after-school activities puts her in community with people I'll likely never meet. And yet, through Lizzie, I can provide support in several ways—whether it be something physical like providing the birthday treat or something less tangible like listening to Lizzie and helping her discern what she might say or do to help someone else.

Julie

Today's Act of Gratitude

How can you be the silent partner in loving someone you'll never meet? Watch for opportunities as you go through your day.

April

God Can Handle Your Worst

I am convinced that nothing can ever separate us from God's love. Neither death nor life, neither angels nor demons, neither our fears for today nor our worries about tomorrow—not even the powers of hell can separate us from God's love.

ROMANS 8:38

Grunting, I manually lugged our beast of an ancient snowblower into position, pausing to swipe at my partially frozen bangs before starting back down a neighbor's driveway.

I was grumpy. Aaron was traveling, so a task that falls firmly into his realm of duties was unexpectedly placed solely on me. The larger-than-normal pile of compacted snow left by the early morning snowplow seemed to sneer at me from the end of the driveway, daring me to attempt to move it. And the fact that I was plowing out two driveways with a massive, cumbersome machine I barely knew how to use meant that an ongoing small act of kindness—for a neighbor in the midst of their own crisis—was currently being performed with a grinchy heart. I told God exactly what I thought about all of the above as I worked.

The freedom to be brutally honest is one of the things I am most grateful for in talking to God. If God already knows that I'm a bit of a hot mess, what can be gained by pretending I'm not? Nothing. There is not one thing to lose and yet so much to gain.

God's knowledge of my secret worst self means I get to be honest in a way I'm mostly not with my fellow humans. I get to be blunt and completely vulnerable as I pour out my thoughts and feelings with a refreshing rawness, knowing that he is safe and that I am loved.

That doesn't mean I get to stay in ugly emotional spots or wallow in ongoing sin; it simply means I am safe to process all of it—the good, the bad, and the ugly—so that I can move past it, reframe the situation before me, and course correct if I've started to stray. Of all the good gifts our heavenly Father bestows upon us, this might be one of the least appreciated and most precious.

Julie

Today's Act of Gratitude

Express your gratitude to God that you can trust him with your ugliest of uglies. But don't stay there: allow him to guide you, show you a different perspective, and redeem the unredeemable.

Sharing Your Passion

*Whether you eat or drink, or whatever you do,
do it all for the glory of God.*

1 CORINTHIANS 10:31

My husband loves to cook. It wasn't something he did or enjoyed when we were first married, but it's become a passion of his over the years. He loves to grow food, has several gardens on our property, and makes meals from what he produces.

He enjoys trying new foods and new combinations of flavors and is constantly experimenting with different varieties of plants. Each winter, he scours seed catalogs looking for interesting fruits and vegetables, and every year he adds something that he's never grown before. I've come to appreciate the time and effort he puts into his gardens, knowing how much he loves the work.

But Kyle's greatest joy from gardening, cooking, and creating new cuisine is sharing it with others and seeing them enjoy what he makes. It's really not even about the food. It's about his love for serving people and seeing their reaction to his latest creation. Whether it's grilling or smoking lamb or tenderloin or assembling a veggie dish from his imagination, his passion is people and loving them well, and one way he shows it is by feeding them. I'm thankful for the people and dishes it's brought to our table that probably wouldn't be there otherwise, as he invites others in, along with their ethnic dishes, and shows us the vast array of God's unique creations.

We all have distinct passions; God made each of us with the desire to pursue different things. But no matter what they are, we can use them to love God and others and bring glory to him. Scripture says that whether we are eating or drinking, or whatever else we are doing throughout our days, we should do it all for God's glory. No activity or interest that we pursue is too great or too small to matter to God. It can all be used to honor him.

Kendra

Today's Act of Gratitude

What is something that you have a passion for and enjoy doing? Make plans to share it with someone else.

Looking for Beauty

I have seen the burden God has placed on us all.
Yet God has made everything beautiful for its own time.
He has planted eternity in the human heart.

ECCLESIASTES 3:10-11

Waves rippled over our feet as we walked along the shoreline. The dark, wet sand dragged at my heels as I followed my Aunt Debbie, who urged us on with a smile.

That morning, she'd asked my sister and me if we wanted to go searching for sea glass, and we'd agreed. As we strolled along one of her favorite beaches, the people thinned out until it felt like we were nearly alone, the cliffs at our backs, blue water ahead, and a vast sky above us.

This trip—my first to Washington—was unexpected. I'd gotten a call from my sister, her voice solemn.

"Uncle Michael isn't doing well," she'd said. "The cancer is worse. Mom, Dad, and Aunt Delpha are visiting in a couple of weeks. We should go too."

In the flurry of preparation, I hadn't given much time to thinking about the reason for our visit—not until I saw my uncle's diminished stature, his exhaustion, and the muted pain in his kind eyes. But his voice was just as warm as always, and for the next few days, we basked in our time together. As we sat around the table and reminisced, we captured my uncle's words, along with family memories from the rest of us, on an audio recorder. That trip was the last time I'd hear his voice in person.

But on the day we were searching for sea glass, I couldn't help but feel grateful. With my eyes downcast, each glimmer of blue, white, or green reminded me of how beauty could be found in unexpected places. The Bible reminds us that everything is beautiful in its time. But the flip side to this fleeting beauty is that it points us to an eternal God. Though the beauty we experience is temporary, God is not.

And in every moment of that trip—when we stopped at a farmer's market, drove up the mountainside, visited coastal boutiques, sipped cider at an orchard—beauty was evident. Though the threat of loss hung like a heavy pall, the hope of an eternity with God was on the horizon. And every fleeting moment of beauty served as a reminder of the unchanging nature of our eternal God.

Kristin

Today's Act of Gratitude

Thank God for small reminders of the beauty of his creation.

The Giver of Good Gifts

Whatever is good and perfect is a gift coming down to us from God our Father, who created all the lights in the heavens. He never changes or casts a shifting shadow.

JAMES 1:17

"I'm sorry, Kendra. By the time I got there, she'd sold out of her gnomes." I was parked at the art fair, staring at the last tiny clay gnome I'd snagged from a favorite local potter, as I told my little white lie. This so-ugly-it's-cute little guy was Kendra's birthday gift, and I'd rearranged my entire morning so I could be one of the first people at Danielle's booth, ready to snatch him up. I knew she only had a couple left and wasn't intending to make more.

I felt a tiny bit guilty hearing the disappointment in Kendra's voice but managed not to confess. The anticipation of surprising her with something I knew she'd love barely kept me from spilling the beans.

Gift giving does not come naturally to me, and having a perfect gift to give someone I care about isn't something I take for granted. The thought of making her day made my day, and as I drove to my first of several meetings, I silently thanked God for the opportunity to give my friend a gift I knew she'd appreciate.

As I drove, my thoughts turned to all of the gifts God showers on us, big and small, obvious and inconspicuous. How often do I pass by them, oblivious to the tokens of his unconditional love for me? Recognizing my ingratitude made me wince. Far too frequently, I listen to the lies that I am not enough, allowing my inner critic to speak louder than the still, small voice of the Holy Spirit. And far too often, I neglect to thank God for the good gifts, taking his blessings for granted when it is smooth sailing and turning to him mostly when life's waters are rough.

God is with us in the good and the bad, and becoming sensitive to noticing his provision builds our trust so that when we are in crisis, we have a firm foundation of faith upon which to stand.

Julie

Today's Act of Gratitude

Ask God to nudge you into noticing his good gifts. Practice looking for them and thanking him when you find them.

Empty and Filled

This hope will not lead to disappointment. For we know how dearly God loves us, because he has given us the Holy Spirit to fill our hearts with his love.

ROMANS 5:5

"Oops." I winced, closing the app on my phone. It was the second day of the Lenten season, and I had given up social media for the duration. Out of habit, I'd clicked into one of the apps.

Quickly realizing my error, I exited and repositioned my social media apps several screens to the right. I hoped the extra distance would give me enough pause to remember my goal.

As a child, my only experience with Lent was secondhand knowledge from friends who gave up Coke or candy. As an adult, I appreciate the tradition in a new way. Because now, every time I forgo social media or sweet treats for those forty days, I experience the paradox of becoming both empty and filled.

What does this mean? Practically, it means creating space in our hearts and schedules for more of Jesus. Our modern world bombards us with messages, tasks, and busyness. We are packed to the brim with worries, to-do lists, work woes, and current events. Lent, on the other hand, can help us refocus. One of my pastors described Lent as a pause, a sacred space in which we recall the past with gratitude—remembering what was accomplished by the life, death, and resurrection of Jesus—while also being joyfully expectant of the future and Jesus' glorious return.

When we take the time to get rid of the things that have entangled us, refocusing our attention on Jesus, we can experience his peace. When we give him our burdens, we make room for him. In his economy, hearts can be healed. Worries can become avenues toward peace. And the mess in our lives can be transformed into a message of hope. We can live in confident expectation because of his work on the cross and the subsequent joy of our salvation. No striving. No hurry. No worry. Just Jesus. In that Lenten pause, the hope of more sustains us.

Kristin

Today's Act of Gratitude

Choose to fast from something for a predetermined length of time.
Plan an alternative activity to help fill you with Jesus' love.

Hope Is Alive

There is hope for a tree, when it is cut down,
that it will sprout again, and its shoots will not fail.

JOB 14:7, NASB

"I just don't know if I can start over," our friend Jim said early one Saturday morning. He sat in our living room, coffee in hand, slowly sobering up from drinking the night before.

I sat across from him on the couch next to my husband, Kyle, praying for wisdom and the words to speak love and truth to him.

"Don't look at the whole of your life," I began. "Just start with today. What healthy step can you take today?"

He shook his head and sighed as we discussed some things he could start with: stop drinking, get rid of the alcohol in his house, and eat a good meal. We continued to encourage him not to get overwhelmed by thinking about the future, but to focus only on what he could do differently on this day. Jim spent the day with us, and as the hours went on, his mood lifted. We played games, made dinner, and laughed together. And as we hugged and he went home for the night, I saw it. Just a glimmer, but hope had returned to his eyes. The day had been a clear reminder that something different is always possible.

Maybe you don't struggle with alcohol like our friend Jim. Perhaps it's something else you've grappled with or sought to overcome. Sometimes we get so set in unhealthy patterns that we feel helpless to change them. But Scripture constantly reminds us, in all kinds of ways, of the hope we can find through God. As when a tree is cut down, a shoot will surely sprout and grow again. That's the very definition of hope. For a tree. For us.

Thankfully, even when we fail or feel that all is lost, hope comes along to remind us that today is a new day, that different choices are always available to us, and that God is there offering us his love and grace through it all. Hope is always alive.

Kendra

Today's Act of Gratitude

What have you been discouraged about lately? Bring your
situation to God, asking him for wisdom and the next right
step to take, while also clinging to hope for the future.
Thank him that he is with you each step of the way.

Celebrating Your Age

LORD, remind me how brief my time on earth will be. Remind me that my days are numbered—how fleeting my life is. . . . And so, Lord, where do I put my hope? My only hope is in you.

PSALM 39:4, 7

"Um, I think I saw a picture of your husband the other day?" another parent mentioned at preschool drop-off.

"Oh!" I said, recognizing her hesitant tone. "Did it happen to be at the entrance to the neighborhood?"

"Yes!" she said, relieved that I knew what she meant. We shared a laugh as I explained that my husband's friends had created the enormous banner for his fortieth birthday. It included a photoshopped picture of him wearing a weird, hairy bikini. They'd placed it in front of his gym first, then moved it over to our neighborhood, where everyone who drove past could see it easily.

I couldn't help but roll my eyes at the practical jokers we call friends, but the truth is, that milestone is one I appreciate. I can't say I'm glad, exactly, to be getting older. But I am grateful for the wisdom of experience and for what we've learned over the years. I'm a lot more sure about who I am now than I was at eighteen or even at twenty-eight, and most of that is because my life experiences have made me more and more sure of who Jesus is and why he can be trusted.

When we consider our age in the context of the brevity of life, we are more likely to recognize our need for God and his wisdom. It's easier to trust God when we've walked through fiery trials, his hand in ours, and come out the other side intact. We can trust him because he has walked with us through unsettling diagnoses for our loved ones, the ups and downs of marriage and parenting, and the stresses of conflict at work or in the community. Our experience demonstrates that God is who he says he is and will do what he promises.

Kristin

Today's Act of Gratitude

Consider your age, thanking God for the life experience
and wisdom you've gained over time.

Cheer Each Other On

Dear friends, let us continue to love one another,
for love comes from God.

1 JOHN 4:7

My daughter Jasmine loves to dance and has made some wonderful friendships with other girls at the studio. These girls have spent several years together, and although they aren't all on the same team anymore, they continue to cheer each other on.

One spring day, we were on our way to a competition in the next town. It was going to be a long day of dancing, and Jasmine's team was second to last on the schedule, with her friend Brooklyn's solo as the last performance of the day.

By the time my daughter's team took the floor, many attendees had already left, and just a handful of us sat toward the front of the auditorium. After their performance, Brooklyn stepped onstage. As her music began, we heard a voice yell from the back of the room, "Go, Brooklyn!"

One of the moms leaned over and whispered, "That's your girl."

I nodded as I smiled to myself.

Later, I asked Jasmine about what she had done and why. She explained that she knew Brooklyn would be the last dance of the day and that most people would have already left.

"I wanted her to know she still had a friend cheering her on, so as soon as we were done, I ran back through the hallway and into the room to watch Brooklyn dance."

My eyes filled with tears as I hugged her. "I'm proud of you, honey," I said.

If there's ever been a time for us to cheerlead for one another, it's now. With the world the way it is and the negativity barraging us through social media and news outlets and even sometimes in our own heads, we need to support each other. Scripture is clear: we are to continue loving one another because love is from God. One way we can show our gratitude for God's love is to be a cheerleader to others. It sounds simple but can have a significant impact on those around us.

Kendra

Today's Act of Gratitude

Find a way to be a cheerleader for someone,
whether at work, school, or home.

Our Living Hope

According to his great mercy, he has caused us to be born again to a living hope through the resurrection of Jesus Christ from the dead. . . . In this you rejoice, though now for a little while, if necessary, you have been grieved by various trials, so that the tested genuineness of your faith—more precious than gold that perishes though it is tested by fire—may be found to result in praise and glory and honor at the revelation of Jesus Christ.

1 PETER 1:3,6-7, ESV

Standing in line, my six-year-old shifted her feet.

"How much longer, Mom?" she asked.

I sighed, checking my watch. My husband and older daughters had headed straight for the Tower of Terror at Disney's Hollywood Studios, but we had opted for the Rock 'n' Roller Coaster. Finally tall enough for the ride, she was thrilled about speeding through the darkness and looping the loop upside down.

At first, the line moved quickly, and our spirits were high. But as it slowed to a crawl, my daughter's little shoulders began to droop. An announcement over the loudspeaker about a technical problem was met with a collective groan. Still, we persisted, and the joy on my daughter's face as we exited the ride an hour later made the wait worthwhile.

Waiting is never easy. An abnormal test result, job dissatisfaction, or relationship turmoil can leave us floundering, wondering what to do or how long to wait before making a change. The messy middle of in-between can often feel painful.

Unfortunately, while we're here on earth, we are stuck between the "now" and the "not yet." Although Jesus' death and resurrection have occurred, he has not yet come again, so we are still subject to the sickness and suffering of our broken world. Yet because we know Jesus will return, we have hope. This "living hope" is something to which we can cling. In the three days following Jesus' crucifixion, his disciples must have felt dismayed by the messy middle they found themselves in. Thankfully, the Resurrection was still to come.

Even while we are waiting, God is still at work. Even if our external circumstances aren't changing, he is working in our hearts. Let's thank him for the confident hope we can place in him as we wait.

Kristin

Today's Act of Gratitude

In what area of your life are you waiting? Turn it over to God, asking him to help you endure. Thank him that he is with you as you wait.

The Sound of Change

Be strong and courageous! Do not be afraid and do not panic before them. For the LORD your God will personally go ahead of you. He will neither fail you nor abandon you.

DEUTERONOMY 31:6

Drip. Drip. Drip. Drip. Drip. A lull in the conversation during our early evening walk had Aaron and me tuning in to the soundtrack playing around us. The pitter-patter of ten thousand drips interspersed with an occasional plop as snow slid off a roof or branch was music to my winter-weary soul, a subtle symphony assuring me that the recent snowfall would soon be gone.

As I splashed through sidewalk puddles, I glimpsed muddy flower beds alongside house foundations and around mailboxes and pondered the musicality and the mess accompanying the transition from winter to spring.

If I'm honest, I rarely like the process of change, even if the outcome is one for which I've longed. Chaos, disarray (emotional and physical), and occasional discomfort are my least favorite things, even when I know they are leading to a better place. And if I don't know what the outcome will be, the added layers of uncertainty bring me to my proverbial knees.

For me, facing change from a posture of prayer has become an essential tool for navigating the good, the bad, and all things in between. The promise that God goes before us, neither failing nor abandoning us, is one I've whispered under my breath as I stood at courtroom and conference room thresholds on the cusp of life-altering decisions. I made today's verse my mantra as I sat with pencil and paper alongside thousands of fellow law school graduates, waiting for the bar exam questions to be slowly passed out, one by one. I've clung to it with desperation next to hospital beds while waiting on the results of important tests.

God is trustworthy in the midst of change—even change we didn't ask for and don't want. He stands with us in turmoil, bringing his peace and solace amid earthly discomfort. On more than one occasion, knowing that I am not alone—even for one moment—has left me in tears of gratitude.

Julie

Today's Act of Gratitude

Memorize Deuteronomy 31:6 so you can face change with gratitude, knowing that you are not alone.

It's All about Perspective

*Be thankful in all circumstances, for this is God's
will for you who belong to Christ Jesus.*

1 THESSALONIANS 5:18

It was a blistering cold spring day. I pulled my jacket tight around me as I quickly ran to the car to avoid the swirling wind. "Brrrr!" I said to myself as I turned up the heat and waited for the vehicle to warm.

As I made my way to a local antique store to buy a birthday present for my daughter's friend, small flakes of snow began to fall.

"Great. Really, Minnesota? It's April already," I grumbled under my breath as I pulled into the parking lot.

I spent the next twenty minutes perusing all of the lovely antiques, sending my daughter pictures of things her friend might like before settling on an old bottle filled with beautiful dried flowers.

When I meandered up to the checkout, an older gentleman greeted me there. As we made small talk and I paid my bill, he teasingly said, "Enjoy the beautiful weather!"

"Right?" I said. "This is just crazy. I'm tired of snow."

"You know," he said, handing me my bag, "that's true, but if this were January, we'd be celebrating that the temperature was above thirty degrees."

I paused. "You're right. It's all about perspective," I said, as I smiled and left the store. All the way home I thought about our interaction and how perspective changes everything. What had me grumbling in April would have left me overjoyed in January, when anything above zero degrees feels like a reprieve in Minnesota.

And isn't that true of so much in life? Our perspective on our circumstances, relationships, and life in general matters. If we go about our days complaining, thinking about everything that is negative or wrong, that will sour our mood. But the opposite is true as well: if we can find a way to be thankful for even something small in any circumstance, we'll go through our days grateful for what we do have.

Kendra

Today's Act of Gratitude

Is there an area of your life you've been complaining about recently? How could a change in perspective help you find even the smallest thing to be grateful for in this season?

The Gift of Help

*God . . . will not forget how hard you have worked for him and
how you have shown your love to him by caring for other believers.*

HEBREWS 6:10

Entering the small anteroom, I began the in-depth process of washing my hands. As I finished the familiar procedure, I exited into a larger room that was humming with activity. Long curtains separated infants in Isolettes from one another, and beeping medical machines were accompanied by the soft murmurs of families mere feet apart.

Smiling at the nurses I passed, I headed directly to the area where my newborn slept.

Our daughter had arrived six weeks early. At just over five pounds, she was enormous compared to many of the other premature babies in the NICU, but she still had challenges that would result in a twenty-day stay.

Even as I yearned for the day we could take her home with us and struggled to leave her there each night, I was profoundly grateful for the care she experienced. One nurse, in particular, was my favorite. Roland was a tall man with graying hair, and though his hands seemed too big to hold such tiny infants, he cared for them with ease. His calm, kind nature was reassuring.

As a new parent, I felt myself floundering, wondering how to care for such a tiny person. But with patience, nurses like Roland assisted us in bathing our child for the first time and gave us tips on how best to attend to her needs. A class offered by the March of Dimes taught us how to do infant CPR and help a choking child. Recognizing their expertise, I soaked up the knowledge. By the time we were able to leave the NICU and bring our daughter home, I felt equipped and encouraged.

We all benefit when people use their skills and knowledge to help others—whether it's a customer service representative fixing a computer, a baker providing bread, a math teacher explaining a difficult concept, or an accountant navigating the tax code. Another person's expertise is valuable and worthy of praise, and you and I can participate by thanking others who provide it.

Kristin

Today's Act of Gratitude

Whose expertise have you benefited from
lately? Take time to thank them.

I Surrender

*Jesus said, "Come to me, all of you who are weary
and carry heavy burdens, and I will give you rest.*

MATTHEW 11:28

As I turned the key in the ignition, I sighed deeply. Weary. I was weary. The week felt dogpiled with burdens beyond my immediate control and with overwhelming concern for people I loved.

Lord, this is too heavy. I can't carry this.

With my silent confession aimed heavenward, I put the car into reverse. I slowly began backing down the driveway, my thoughts swirling, trying—once again—to find a solution to a situation without solutions.

*All to you, I surrender
Everything, every part of me*

My bewilderment over how and why music was suddenly and unexpectedly filling the air turned to gratitude as I recognized the song by Kim Walker-Smith. My phone's Bluetooth had connected with the car stereo. While it usually connected with whatever recent podcast I'd been listening to, this time, it connected with my worship playlist and this particular song. I don't know whether it was mere coincidence or divine intervention, but it was the gentle reminder I needed in a moment of hopelessness.

I felt the tension release as the biblical truth of the lyrics washed over me: I wasn't alone. And as I drove, I realized that some of the cares I'd been shouldering were not mine to bear. I'd been running around taking up worries when I should have been on my knees in surrender, giving loved ones and challenging circumstances to God.

With the awareness that I'd been trying to deal with these issues on my own, I again repented: *Lord, thank you that I'm not alone. Thank you that I don't have to carry this too-heavy burden. I'm sorry I sometimes forget to run to you; forgive me for my arrogance.*

I won't pretend that I didn't fret about my loved ones or wrestle with how to solve the impossible after that precious moment in the car. But now, I took my fretting and wrestling to God, lifting the situation to him in prayer rather than handling it on my own, trying to be a superhero, unsurrendered.

Julie

Today's Act of Gratitude

Think of one burden you've been trying to carry on your own. Surrender it to God, thanking him that you aren't the superhero in the story. He is. Always.

Our Lives Are a Sweet Perfume

Our lives are a Christ-like fragrance rising up to God.
But this fragrance is perceived differently by those
who are being saved and by those who are perishing.

2 CORINTHIANS 2:15

"What's that sweet smell?" my mom asked as we drove down the highway. I exchanged an incredulous look with my sisters in the back seat as we sniffed the pungent air.

"Mom—that's a skunk!" we said, eyes wide.

"Oh, I didn't know!" she said, laughing a little.

For as long as I can remember, my mom's sense of smell has been either absent or a little wonky. How else can you explain the mistaken interpretation of a stinky smell as a pleasant one? While she will occasionally catch a hint of a scent, most of the time she has to rely on someone else to tell her if a candle or perfume smells pleasant.

Though our sense of smell can be protective, such as when smoke signals a fire or a rotten-egg scent warns us of a gas leak, it's a mix of practical and poignant for many of us. I can't smell lilacs without remembering the bushes that separated my childhood backyard from that of my best friend, and the smell of hay always reminds me of younger days spent jumping from one bale to the next on my aunt and uncle's farm. Freshly baked brownies, lavender on a pillow, pho that's been simmering overnight on the stove—all are smells that instantaneously evoke good memories.

In the same way, as Christians, our faith is a defining characteristic of who we are. Just as the smell of fresh-cut grass reminds us of lazy summer days, our faithfulness emits a fragrance that—like incense—rises to God. What a welcome image, that our lives should produce something that brings such joy to the Lord. In the same way that we are filled with delight or expectation when we open the door to our home and smell bread or a chocolate cake baking, may we continue to serve and honor Jesus in such a way that we remain a delight to him.

Kristin

Today's Act of Gratitude

List five items you enjoy smelling. Thank God for them.

Render to Caesar What Is His

*"Give to Caesar what belongs to Caesar, and
give to God what belongs to God."*

MATTHEW 22:21

Today is a day of reckoning for those living in the United States. We're either bemoaning the additional tax payments we owe to our state and federal government, or we're doing a little jig over the refund checks that will soon be coming our way for overpayment. Conversations about how tax funds are spent versus how they should be spent cause heated debates in the media and in our homes and workplaces, reaching a crescendo today before tapering off until the next year's tax season.

Today reminds me that we are citizens of two kingdoms—our temporary earthly one and Jesus' eternal one. Jesus recognized that we would be living under imperfect earthly governments and that we would be required to obey laws and pay taxes. Generally speaking, our acquiescence to these earthly requirements does not make us disloyal to his Kingdom.

As I was pondering this duality, the following question came to mind: *If our taxes belong to earthly governments, what is it that belongs to God?* The answer is in the greatest commandment, found in Luke 10:27. We are called to love God with every ounce of our heart, soul, strength, and mind. It is in these places that God asks to reign, above all earthly authorities. And when we love God like this, our resources (finances included) naturally follow.

The Creator of the known and unknown universe doesn't *need* our money; he asks us to entrust him with a portion of our earthly treasure as part of our relationship with him. As we do so through our tithing and generosity in caring for those around us, we find our spiritual, emotional, and physical needs met in ways that are immeasurably greater than whatever we surrendered in offering. This Kingdom generosity creates a cycle in which we hold our earthly treasures loosely, trusting God's provision and goodness in whatever forms they might take. There is something about seeing God supply what we need just in time that creates humble gratitude like nothing else.

Julie

Today's Act of Gratitude

Ask a fellow believer to share a story of when God provided
for them spiritually or physically, and share your own
story of God's provision. Spend a few moments in prayer
together, thanking God for supplying your needs.

My Favorite Gift

*Whenever we have the opportunity, we should do good
to everyone—especially to those in the family of faith.*

GALATIANS 6:10

I walked into the church sanctuary, excitement running through me. I looked down at my white gown with some disbelief that this day was finally here. My gaze traveled around the room to the lovely decor that my sister Katrina and friends had put up so beautifully, and then my eyes stopped on a man setting up a video recorder behind the last row of chairs. He smiled and waved as I nodded.

I didn't think much about it that day; it was a whirlwind of events—ceremony, pictures, greeting guests, dinner, and reception. To this day, I have more of a sense of joy about the experience than actual vivid memories.

But one thing that stands out is seeing Larry, a friend's father, quietly setting up that video camera in the back of the sanctuary. We didn't ask him to do it; the thought hadn't even crossed my mind. But he knew how important this day was to us and was wise enough to know that we'd want a record of it. To this day, it is the greatest gift we received and the one I didn't even know I'd want or need.

When I talked with Larry's son Andrew later about what his dad had done, he told me he wasn't surprised. His dad was always doing little (and big) things for others. He had a heart for people and loved them well. Larry has since passed away, but his legacy and the kindness he offered others are not forgotten.

The Bible encourages us that whenever we can do good to others, we should—especially those who are fellow believers. But to do that, we must think about what might be beneficial or helpful to them. Establishing a habit of doing good starts with small things; holding the door for someone whose arms are full, smiling at the checkout person and thanking them, or allowing a mom with young kids to go ahead of you in line are simple ways to start. Over time we'll find that our lives, like Larry's, are defined by the loving acts, both big and small, that others will remember about us for years to come.

Kendra

Today's Act of Gratitude

Do something good for someone else.

The God of Details

What is the price of five sparrows—two copper coins? Yet God does not forget a single one of them. And the very hairs on your head are all numbered. So don't be afraid; you are more valuable to God than a whole flock of sparrows.

LUKE 12:6-7

Growing up, we had big windows that ran nearly from floor to ceiling in our living room. On sunny days, they cast large rectangles of light across the length of the room.

As a child, one of my greatest delights was lying in the warmth of the sun as it streamed in. Sometimes I'd grab a blanket or pillow, other times a book, but I loved to lie there and doze. The temperature outdoors could be below zero or unbearably hot, and it wouldn't matter, so cozy was my spot on the floor.

Sometimes, as an adult, it's easy to forget about those small pleasures that bring us joy: a fan that blows toward our face on a hot day, the way grass feels under our bare feet, the bracing chill of waves racing across sand to wash over our toes. While we might notice the larger details—the mountains that rise before us, the ocean's rolling waves—we overlook those tiny pleasures, those little reminders that help ground us in the moment.

I love the passage in Luke in which Jesus talks about how God is the God of details. He says that even the hairs on our heads are numbered. Sometimes it's easy to get so caught up in our worries over the big parts of life that we forget to enjoy the small things. But just like the hairs on our heads, little things matter. They are important to God, just as we are important to God. Because of this truth, we can rest assured that the God of details cares about every part of our lives—both the big and the small things. We can trust him with all of it and thank him for every small pleasure this life offers.

Kristin

Today's Act of Gratitude

Take time to notice tiny pleasures—the weight of a cozy blanket, the coolness of a glass of ice water in your hands, or the warmth of the sun on your skin.

Hope Personified

*No power in the sky above or in the earth below—indeed,
nothing in all creation will ever be able to separate us from
the love of God that is revealed in Christ Jesus our Lord.*

ROMANS 8:39

Eyeballing the forecast, I knew my favorite, fleeting moment of spring would likely be arriving in the next seven days. While the exact timing changes from year to year, the conditions heralding its entrance are so consistent that I can reasonably predict it about a week ahead of time.

What is this mysterious moment? When the weather finally flips from overcast, clammy cold to a mix of sunny, warmer temps and rain, there is this brief interval in which all the world is covered in the softest, haziest veil of green—every shade represented—as trees and shrubs just barely begin to leaf out. For a day or three each spring, a fog of the lightest greens blankets everything, a gentle promise of the lush, verdant greenery to come. These few days are possibly my favorite of the entire year, and I wait all winter long for their arrival. For me, they are hope personified.

Summer in Minnesota means you cannot step outside without being enveloped in green—whether it be carefully cultivated or unruly and weedy. No matter the aesthetic, the coming of summer never fails to remind me of Jesus' triumph over death through his resurrection.

Just as I anticipate these few, precious days every spring, I do the same with the promises of God when walking through a hard season. I look for evidence of his fingerprints in the situation, the assurance that he is in the midst of the chaos, tangible confirmation that I am not alone and that—no matter what happens—at the end of the story, God wins.

Sometimes, it's a close friend who points out the quietly consistent signs of God's presence, knowing my emotions are clouding my ability to see with spiritual eyes. And sometimes it is the whisper of the Holy Spirit in my thoughts, assuring me that this earthly adventure is temporal and temporary and that, no matter how hard it is, I am never alone. The promise in today's verse is one I've clung to with gratitude time and again.

Julie

Today's Act of Gratitude

What tangible signs remind you of the promise in Romans 8:39?

The Hope of Resurrection

Blessed be the God and Father of our Lord Jesus Christ! According to his great mercy, he has caused us to be born again to a living hope through the resurrection of Jesus Christ from the dead.

1 PETER 1:3, ESV

I am a gardening wannabe. Herbs, cherry tomatoes, and a few flowers are as good as it gets at my house, although I keep trying. My friend Molly, who is much better at keeping things alive than I am, recently told me about a calla lily that she had thought was dead. Even though she had trimmed it down and didn't see any new growth, she still watered it every once in a while along with her other plants—just in case.

Amazingly, over time, it began to grow again.

Like that calla lily, there are often things in our lives that we assume to be dead. And though we will indeed experience pain and loss in this life—in our relationships and communities—Jesus' resurrection reminds us there is always hope. In Jesus, we know that death is never the end of the story. In God's economy, he is making all things new. He is the God of resurrection, restoration, and renewal.

Baptism by immersion is a beautiful embodiment of this spiritual truth. As a public affirmation of a personal decision to follow Jesus and live for him, it illustrates the change in our lives when we decide to become a Christian. When we are submerged in the water, we demonstrate laying our old ways of living to rest. But when we emerge, we rise to new life. We are no longer the same person we once were.

Because you and I have the hope of resurrection, we know that God can restore that which was lost. Though Jesus entered into our suffering and brokenness with his death, he also brought the hope of more when he rose from the dead. Jesus is alive; he is our living hope. And he is making all things new.

Kristin

Today's Act of Gratitude

Thank God for the living hope we have in him
through the power of his resurrection.

Risk-Takers

This is my command—be strong and courageous! Do not be afraid or discouraged. For the LORD your God is with you wherever you go.

JOSHUA 1:9

We'd invited our friends over for dinner. While we enjoyed pizza and chicken shawarma, we updated each other on our lives—jobs and work, dreams and school. As our kids cavorted around us, our friends explained a new business venture they planned to launch in the coming months.

I watched as the husband's face lit up, excitement brewing for all that was ahead. I sat in awe as his wife nodded and smiled, seemingly unworried about this exciting but unknown future.

I thought of all the questions that would have swirled in my mind but were not bothering them in the least. *Do we have enough money to start this? How much time will it take? Will we make enough money to live?*

They had a plan that was well thought out and organized. But even so, all I could see were the risks involved. After we hugged goodbye a little while later with promises to help in any way that we could, I looked at my husband. "They have a lot of courage," I said after closing the door behind them.

As we continued to discuss their new venture, we realized our friends had been through a lot in their young lives. They had moved to the United States from a war-torn country within the last five years, leaving everything and everyone familiar to them, to come to a safe place here. They've lost far more than I have ever known, and because of it, they're willing to step out and try new things. What seems risky to me does not appear that way to my friends. Their example is one I'd love to follow.

Scripture tells us over and over again to be strong and courageous. That God is with us and will go before us. And because of it, we don't need to fear. We can step out in faith into all the places he calls us to go. It can be too easy for many of us to live a life of comfort and safety, but I'm so grateful that God would invite us to be risk-takers and pursue all the dreams he's given to us.

Kendra

Today's Act of Gratitude

Is there something you've been dreaming of pursuing but haven't yet? Step out of your comfort zone and take the first step toward it. Express your thanks to God for being with you as you take the risk.

You Aren't Alone

*Take my yoke upon you. Let me teach you, because I am humble
and gentle at heart, and you will find rest for your souls. For my
yoke is easy to bear, and the burden I give you is light."*

MATTHEW 11:29-30

As a gardener, stories of planting and harvesting used in the Bible often resonate with my own experiences, providing me with a deeper understanding of the point being made. Still, teaming up oxen to plow the ground is completely beyond my frame of reference, and the thought of taking on Jesus' yoke has always left me feeling slightly bewildered. The invitation sounds—on the surface—vaguely lovely, but it evoked confusion rather than adding clarity and understanding to the verses found in Matthew 11.

It wasn't until Pastor Dave added cultural and contextual background one Sunday morning that I had tears welling up as I reconsidered this invitation. To my understanding, yoking involves tying two oxen (or other beasts of burden) together so that their strength is used jointly, making the hard work of plowing soil significantly easier.

I didn't initially understand that wise farmers yoke one strong animal with one weaker animal, with the bigger end of the yoke going on the more powerful beast. The weaker ox's strength is used, but it's leveraged: the weak animal can do more, go further because it's tied to a stronger one.

In other words, Jesus is asking us to go on mission with him, but he is the stronger of our two-person team, and he is going to take the heavier end of the burden. We are never in ministry alone (note: if you strive to love God and love others as commanded in Mark 12:28-34, you are in ministry), and the seemingly private struggles we encounter are never born single-handedly.

My tears that Sunday morning were of gratitude as I reconsidered Jesus' promise. When we agree to go on mission with him, he promises to carry the bulk of the load, never leaving us to plow hard, rocky ground on our own.

Julie

Today's Act of Gratitude

With this deeper understanding of being yoked with Jesus, what is one burden you'll bring to him, asking to be yoked together with him as you carry it?

The Power of Our Words

The soothing tongue is a tree of life,
but a perverse tongue crushes the spirit.

PROVERBS 15:4, NIV

"The first time I met Sara, I thought to myself, 'She will be my friend,'" I said to a packed auditorium of women at a conference I was emceeing. I glanced over at Sara, whose session I was cohosting, and caught the stricken look on her face. Confused, I wondered if I'd said something wrong. She quickly recovered, and the rest of the session went off without a hitch.

"Why did you say that?" she asked after we'd finished and were once again backstage.

"What?" I asked.

"Why did you say you knew you wanted to be my friend?"

Confused, I tried to explain. "Because it was true. That's really what I thought the first time I met you. Why?"

Tears filled her eyes. "You don't understand," she whispered, voice strained. "I was bullied for years as a kid. Nobody wanted to be my friend."

We both wiped our eyes as I took a moment to respond. "First, I am so sorry that happened to you, and second, you just need to know, you're the kind of person that when women meet you, they think, 'I want to be her friend.'"

She smiled as I hugged her, affirming the gift she was to those around her.

I had no idea of the past pain my friend had experienced or how my words would hit that place in her heart that was still so tender to the harsh treatment she'd endured. But God knew, and I'm thankful that he used my words to soothe that hurt.

Our words matter. There is power in the things that we say. We don't know how we might impact someone else. When we use our words wisely, they will soothe and give life to all around us, but the opposite is also true. A harsh tongue can crush the spirit. Let's use what we say to soothe rather than to destroy.

Kendra

Today's Act of Gratitude

Use your words to soothe someone, and if
you've spoken harshly, apologize.

Finding God in the Midst of Hard Times

When you go through deep waters, I will be with you. When you go through rivers of difficulty, you will not drown. When you walk through the fire of oppression, you will not be burned up; the flames will not consume you.

ISAIAH 43:2

"I've been praying for you. How did today go?"

Her text made me pause, uncertain about how best to answer. The last several weeks had been rough. And while I smiled prettily in response to most inquiries and had a ready list of all the ways I was grateful in the midst of the bumpy ride, my friend was looking for the unvarnished truth.

I knew God was in the mess with me because I could see his provision. And I was beyond grateful for both his presence and his interceding. But I was so, so sad. I was a weird, simultaneous mix—deeply grateful, while also heartsick.

My text confession was met with one of her own, and we both acknowledged the truth: a grateful, thankful heart can also be a heart in lament, deep frustration, and even anger. We are complex creatures living in an often ugly, unfair, and grueling world. While it's tempting to think gratitude automatically wipes away and replaces physical or emotional pain, that's not always true. And we are not disloyal to God when we embrace thankfulness even while hurting.

Searching for gratefulness amid hard circumstances doesn't remove the circumstance; it acknowledges and makes room for God in the *midst* of it. And that's where we need him most—smack-dab in the middle of the most difficult parts of our story.

God promises to be with us in our worst moments, days, weeks, and seasons. We are not alone, not for one moment. And when we embrace gratitude, intentionally watching for silver linings, practicing thankfulness for the smallest bits of good among the hard, we find God present with us.

Julie

Today's Act of Gratitude

Actively search for silver linings, thanking God for the big and small during challenging moments.

Unchanging God

If we are unfaithful, he remains faithful,
for he cannot deny who he is.

2 TIMOTHY 2:13

I was upset. Someone close to me had broken a promise, and it wasn't the first time. I was discouraged and angry, but mostly just hurt that it had happened again.

As this person and I talked through the events that led to their poor choice, it was logical to my brain, but my heart still hurt. I knew that their history of trauma added to their unhealthy decisions. I also knew they wanted better for themselves and for our relationship.

Over the next few days, I brought all my emotions to God—all my anger, hurt, and even fear over an uncertain future. All of my "what ifs" I laid out in prayer. *What if things don't change? What if it happens again? What if this is the best our relationship will ever be?*

As I prayed, the Scripture that came to my mind again and again was that even when we are unfaithful, God remains faithful because "he cannot deny who he is." I thought about my loved ones and how God's grace still extends to them. I thought about my own imperfect life and how often I sense God's peace and forgiveness when I mess up. How I never worry that God will abandon me or tell me he's had enough. He stays faithful. Even when I am not. Even when those around me aren't. I was reminded that my full reliance is to be on Christ—he is my constant. Even when others disappoint me, God will never change.

As we reconciled and put new boundaries into place, I was encouraged to love those around me fully while remembering that God will stand by me even if they disappoint me again.

God is many things, but one quality I am most grateful for is his faithfulness. Sometimes people we love will let us down. Sometimes we will be the ones to let others down. Sometimes we will need to establish boundaries to be healthy, but God will remain steadfast no matter what happens in our earthly relationships. Of this, we can be sure. Don't be afraid to put your complete trust in Christ; he will always be near.

Kendra

Today's Act of Gratitude

Spend some time thanking God for the ways he's been
faithful to you even when others disappoint.

A Forced Rest

It is useless for you to work so hard from early morning until late at night,
anxiously working for food to eat; for God gives rest to his loved ones.

PSALM 127:2

I'd been looking forward to our spring break trip for months. We were headed to Red Lodge, Montana, so Aaron and the kids could ski a mountain after having practiced on the small hills of Minnesota. And while they enjoyed the snow for a few days, I had big plans for prepping classroom materials, writing, and working on other tasks requiring uninterrupted hours of deep thought. We'd reunite around 4:00 p.m. for dinner and games, and everything would be perfect.

My first inkling that something wasn't quite as it should be with me was the evening we arrived in town. By morning the inevitable was impossible to ignore: a head cold of epic proportions. I spent the better part of the next three days in bed, feeling miserably congested and fatigued, and having completely given up my grand designs for accomplishing anything except healing.

My body is remarkable in the sense that it can push through busy seasons and looming deadlines like a champ while seemingly having a sixth sense for the precise moment in which it can simply let go. After too long a stretch of pushing, pushing, pushing, it collapses in on itself—regardless of my good intentions and best-laid plans. And instead of feeling frustrated over spoiled expectations—although there was some of that as well—I was grateful for my earthly body and all it does for me, even imperfectly.

I'm learning—once again—to watch for smaller signals that I'm pushing too hard. I'm trying to treat myself a bit more gently and accepting that sometimes what my mind, body, and soul need most are sleep and rest. There is no shame in taking a break; today's verse tells us that God gives rest to those he loves. Isn't that a marvelous reminder in a culture that demands a frenzied pace?

Julie

Today's Act of Gratitude

In what area(s) do you need to practice rest? Set aside time for
your favorite pampering activity, thanking God for your body
and for all the things it enables you to do, even imperfectly.

He Understands Us

This High Priest of ours understands our weaknesses, for he faced all of the same testings we do, yet he did not sin. So let us come boldly to the throne of our gracious God. There we will receive his mercy, and we will find grace to help us when we need it most.

HEBREWS 4:15-16

I was settling into my seat at a women's conference when I heard an unexpected noise from the level below.

At the front of the room, the speaker, Lisa Harper, had barely started her message when a woman in the audience began to wail.

Instead of being rattled by the interruption, Lisa seemed unperturbed. After quietly asking the woman's friends to help her into the hallway where they could pray for her in private, she addressed the crowd with words that resonated in my heart.

"Jesus never told anyone to stop crying," she said.

Huh, I thought. *Though I've cried plenty of times, I've never considered Jesus' reaction to tears or other emotions.*

Yet over the next few days, as I continued to mull over her words, they reminded me of the story told in John 11. Jesus receives word from Mary and Martha that Lazarus—their brother and Jesus' friend—is sick. By the time Jesus returns to their home in Bethany, Lazarus has died.

What's interesting is that Jesus already knows that Lazarus is dead—he tells his disciples before they even arrive. He also knows that he has the power to raise Lazarus from the dead. But in that moment, when he is faced with his friends' grief over their brother, he doesn't say any of that. Instead, he weeps.

What I love about Jesus is that even though he sees the big picture, he meets us in the moment. Jesus doesn't wave away Mary and Martha's grief or reassure them that he will raise Lazarus from the dead, as he later does. Instead, he demonstrates compassion. The same is true of the way Jesus cares for you and me. Hebrews tells us that he understands us—our weaknesses, our humanity—and loves us anyway. We can be grateful that we don't serve a distant God who cares nothing for us. No matter our circumstances or situation, his mercy and grace are always available to us.

Kristin

Today's Act of Gratitude

Thank God for his compassion.

Whispering Truth

"Go out and stand before me on the mountain," the LORD told him. And as Elijah stood there, the LORD passed by, and a mighty windstorm hit the mountain. It was such a terrible blast that the rocks were torn loose, but the LORD was not in the wind. After the wind there was an earthquake, but the LORD was not in the earthquake. And after the earthquake there was a fire, but the LORD was not in the fire. And after the fire there was the sound of a gentle whisper.

1 KINGS 19:11–12

You don't need to perform for me. I heard a gentle whisper as I prayed quietly before everyone else in the house was up. It'd been a particularly tough couple of weeks, nothing terrible, just busy. A lot to do and not enough time to do it. *I love you just as you are. Beyond behavior or titles or to-do lists. I am near. Ready to help. Always. Call to me.*

I wiped tears as the words became a balm to my weary heart. As I took a little extra time that morning to sit with my Bible and journal open, pen in hand, I was struck by the fact that God's words are true. And always available to me. Sometimes I just have to slow down, turn off outside noise, and listen. God is waiting to give us all we need for the day when we pause for a few moments, quietly listening for that still, small voice.

In the Old Testament, there's a story of a prophet named Elijah who was waiting to hear from God. As he waited, a mighty storm passed by, followed by an earthquake and then a fire. But God wasn't in any of those things. After all of that had passed, Elijah heard a "gentle whisper." The voice of the Lord had come. Probably not in the way that Elijah had expected, but it had come just the same.

We aren't so different from Elijah. We may not face storms or earthquakes every day, but we all have things swirling around us that can distract us from hearing God. Sometimes we have to shut everything else off and just be with him. It's not always easy to do, but it's so worth it.

Kendra

Today's Act of Gratitude

Whether you sit quietly, go for a walk, or go for a drive, intentionally listen for that small voice of God.

Tempted by Anger

A hot-tempered person starts fights;
a cool-tempered person stops them.

PROVERBS 15:18

Is this even the same lawsuit? Their versions of what happened are so radically different . . . did the clerk misfile the briefs? I turned back to the legal caption on the top of both parties' motion arguments, comparing the names and the file numbers. Same captions, same case number. Nothing was misfiled. A bit bewildered, I gathered the documents and my legal pad, and I headed for Judge Hoolihan's chambers —my boss and the judge who would be hearing this motion at the end of the week.

As a brand-new attorney, I firmly believed there were good and bad guys, liars and truth-tellers, and a legal system to sift fact from fiction and dispense justice. I didn't know what to do when confronted with two stories around the same set of events that were different but not opposite. Both individuals' interpretations of the facts could be the truth as they saw it, with neither being a liar. It was possible that neither side was the "bad guy" and that what we had before us was an unfortunate misunderstanding fueled by anger that had spiraled so out of control that lawyers and a judge were now involved.

I've often thanked God for the lesson I learned in that memorable-to-me case. It was my first experience with two "good" people who, through a series of escalating, angry miscommunications, found themselves pitted against one another in an emotionally exhausting and expensive lawsuit. Unfortunately, during my years in the legal profession, I saw dozens of such situations involving angry litigants but no true evildoers. Many times, people had assumed the worst about one another, and their angry, hurt responses served to inflame the conflict, eventually to the point of litigation.

While anger is a legitimate emotion that even Jesus felt, it is powerfully destructive when we allow it to dictate our actions. Scripture exhorts us not to cede control and respond in rage. We cannot see clearly at these times, and we make decisions harmful to ourselves and others. I counseled incensed clients to wait at least twenty-four hours before communicating with the other party or taking action, allowing time for their anger to dissipate and for rationality to return. It's been so successful that I'm committed to the same rule for myself.

Julie

Today's Act of Gratitude

Do you currently find yourself feeling upset with someone?
Adopt the twenty-four-hour waiting rule when anger has
you in its grip. Intentionally spend time thanking God for
wisdom, discernment, and clarity as you wait, prayerfully
asking the Holy Spirit how best to respond.

A New Heart

I will give you a new heart, and I will put a new spirit in you. I will take out your stony, stubborn heart and give you a tender, responsive heart.

EZEKIEL 36:26

I spent two years working in the outpatient mental health and chemical dependency program at our local veterans hospital. Most veterans would stay for the intensive treatment anywhere from thirty to forty-five days.

The visits often started the same. The person would come to my office the first morning looking tired and upset. They were disoriented and angry. Exhausted by life. We'd develop a plan for their stay and discuss which classes they thought would most benefit them, what they hoped to get out of the program, and how long we recommended for them to stay. They would leave my office that first day still deflated but determined to stick to the plan.

Then, slowly, I'd see the change. Day after day. Week after week. Eyes would become brighter. Shoulders no longer slumped. They'd engage in group sessions and start having deeper insights into their thoughts and behaviors. They'd have honest conversations with family and friends and begin the process of restoring relationships. They'd laugh again. The transformation took place before my eyes—a stony heart being turned back to tender—and it was awesome to behold. Witnessing it never got old.

God still restores lives, replacing stubborn, hardened hearts with softened, responsive ones. Sometimes it is a pronounced change, and other times it occurs gradually. But there is always the promise and the hope given to each of us that God will give us a new heart, a new spirit—one that mirrors his own heart for us and all his people. One that can give and receive love, showing compassion and mercy to those around us.

Kendra

Today's Act of Gratitude

What stony parts of your heart has God replaced with tenderness?
Spend some time thanking him for the transformation.

God Knows What We Need

*If you sinful people know how to give good gifts to your children,
how much more will your heavenly Father give good gifts to those who ask him.*

MATTHEW 7:11

"Um, honey? I just texted you a picture of a toy poodle. I think we need to adopt him." My phone call was met with several beats of silence as Aaron digested my out-of-the-blue pronouncement. He was on a work trip and was a passenger in the car his coworker was driving.

"Where are you guys?" His slightly suspicious tone had me grinning. My husband knows me well and likely knew exactly where I was—and that the kids were with me. We'd agreed that we'd be getting a dog, but this was perhaps a bit sooner than either of us had anticipated.

"Well . . . we're at the animal shelter, but don't worry, the kids think we're at the dog hotel. They don't know the animals are available for adoption. They think we're just here to visit and pet the animals. We thought it would be fun." I rushed to get the words out, trying to head off any protest. "Plus, I've been watching online, and there was a poodle named Peanut that I wanted to meet. I think he would be perfect for us."

"All I can see in the picture is a little ball of super-thick brown fuzz. Is that even a dog?"

I laughed at his teasing question because Aaron was right. Peanut hadn't been properly groomed in at least six months and looked like a bouncy brown cotton ball.

"I know he doesn't look like much, but trust me. He's exactly what we need."

And I was right. Peanut turned out to be a source of immense comfort during some hard elementary years for my daughter, and toward the end of his life, he taught us patience and gentleness as he lost his sight and hearing.

Eight years later, as I drove home from the vet with Peanut's ashes, I smiled through grief. Peanut *had* been just what our young family needed, at just the right time. I've offered up prayers of thankfulness for him on many occasions, but that drive home was a special time with God as I realized the fullness of the gift of Peanut.

Julie

Today's Act of Gratitude

What good gift has God given you that has taken years to fully understand the depth and breadth of its magnitude?

May

The Gift of Creativity

Now, O LORD, you are our Father; we are the clay, and
you are our potter; we are all the work of your hand.

ISAIAH 64:8, ESV

"Wow," I breathed, staring around the room in disbelief. Two of Botticelli's enormous paintings covered the length and breadth of the walls, the dreamy depictions characteristic of the Renaissance period. Finding a spot on a bench in the center of the room, I soaked in the view.

In the few precious weeks I'd spent backpacking around Europe after my spring semester ended, I marveled at the art and history on display. I love my small Minnesota hometown, but growing up, I never had many opportunities to visit museums. Now, suddenly, treasures seemed to be everywhere—from the Ashmolean Museum in Oxford to the opera and symphony in Vienna, from the Trevi Fountain and the Colosseum in Rome to the buildings in Prague and London built long before the United States was even a country. These works of beauty aren't just a minor representation from long ago; they are part of the cities and people I visited, a witness to humanity's creativity.

On rocking overnight trains and in the quiet of early mornings, I read a dogeared biography of Michelangelo. Then, during the day, his story seemed to come to life as I viewed his sculptures, from the quiet sorrow of the Pietà to the powerful David.

I love art because it reflects and reveals life. It bridges cultural divides and brokers understanding; it can last generations. Even more impressive is that the creative impulse and sheer talent people are endowed with is all thanks to our creative God. He is the ultimate Creator, a master artist who paints the skies in brilliant shades of lavender and cerulean blue, coral and ocher. Like a potter, he has molded us with purpose; like a sculptor, he refines our edges and reveals who we truly are inside. When we appreciate the works people have created, our gratitude reminds us of the God who created us and the masterpieces he's made in us and this world.

Kristin

Today's Act of Gratitude

Thank God for the gift of creativity. Consider a piece
of art—a sculpture, painting, song, or landmark—and
how its creation reflects the ultimate Creator.

When Gratitude Surprises You

Your Father knows exactly what you
need even before you ask him!

MATTHEW 6:8

We arrived early, ready to set up our booth for the day and acclimate ourselves to where we'd be spending the next several hours as a part of a women's retreat, the first one we'd been to in a while. We were greeted by Elizabeth, the event organizer, who hugged us and showed us where we could set up. She then explained the grounds as we walked around the old farmstead, now turned into an event space mainly hosting weddings and small gatherings.

As we set up our book table and women started to arrive, they filtered through the old barn doors and found open seats around the handcrafted wooden tables decorated with flowers. As their chatter began to swell, I whispered to Julie, "I've missed this." She smiled back as she nodded in agreement. We spent the afternoon visiting with women, being encouraged and offering encouragement in return. The participants shared stories, laughed, shed a few tears, and nodded in understanding as truth lay bare. The day went more quickly than I wanted.

As we began the drive home, my heart was full. I hadn't even realized how much I had missed gathering with others. Sometimes things seep so slowly from your life that it's not until you experience them again that you realize how much you had missed their presence. Community. I didn't realize how much I longed for it until I found it again.

God knows what we need, even before we ask him. Even when we do not know or have forgotten. He is so good. We never have to worry whether God has our best in mind (he does!), and since he already knows what we need, we can trust that he will gently remind us of what is most beneficial and what we're missing in our lives.

Kendra

Today's Act of Gratitude

Can you think of something you've slowly let go of lately
that God would remind you is good for you? Thank God for
it, and make a plan to incorporate it back into your life.

Basking in the Son

"I am the light of the world. If you follow me, you won't have to walk in darkness, because you will have the light that leads to life."

JOHN 8:12

"Whatcha doing?" Aaron's question caused me to peer over my shoulder from my crouched position, a tray of seedlings half pulled from beneath the artificial lights.

"I'm checking my baby plants. These florescent bulbs can only do so much. Where is the warmer weather? Where is the sunshine?!" I sighed heavily as I shoved the tray back where it belonged and stood. "Things are going to start dying if I can't get them outside and in the sun, even for a few hours a day."

The wordsmith in me appreciates the phonic irony of calling that life-sustaining orb of light and warmth the "sun" even as we refer to Jesus as the "Son." But the gardener in me sees the practical reality in the sun/Son analogy every year we have an unseasonably cold spring.

Living in The Tundra (aka Minnesota) means I need to start many of my seedlings indoors, long before the soil and daytime temps are warm enough to sustain tender, green life. My grow lights are usually enough to get the seeds sprouted and life started, but left too long with only artificial light, my plants limp along, small and weakly, barely surviving, and certainly not thriving.

It's always amazing to me that spending afternoons outside on temperate days, even when the sky is overcast, is a far better option for my seedlings than grow lights hovering less than an inch above them. It's a beautiful reminder of how necessary the presence of Jesus is to my own day-to-day emotional and physical well-being.

I can read all the self-help books and follow all the self-care routines in the world, but those are—at best—temporary fixes for surface symptoms. They are not a permanent fix for the real issue: my need for ongoing spiritual rootedness in an often dark, confusing, chaotic world. As today's verse reminds us, following Jesus means we have the light leading to life and that we will no longer walk in darkness. His presence brings spiritual life to me, similarly to the way the sun brings physical life to my seedlings. I don't know about you, but that is a promise to which my grateful, winter-weary soul clings.

Julie

Today's Act of Gratitude

How can you add a little extra Jesus to your day-to-day spiritual health?

A Heart for Hospitality

*Cheerfully share your home with those
who need a meal or a place to stay.*

1 PETER 4:9

"Are you guys big Derby fans?" the man asked quizzically.

"Um, actually—no. Not really," I admitted with a laugh, shrugging. "We don't know much about it."

A few months earlier, we had decided to host a Kentucky Derby party and—despite not being horse racing fans or knowing the traditions and customs—threw ourselves into it with gusto. I spent the morning setting up games I had printed off online, decorated the house with red roses, and ensured we'd have what we needed to host forty people.

Less than an hour after I'd told the man that I didn't know much about the Derby, our house and the outdoor patio were full of friends, music was playing, and the dining room table and kitchen island were groaning under all the delicious food. Our guests had risen to the occasion, with most women wearing hats or fascinators and brightly colored dresses while the men wore suspenders and bow ties.

Looking around at the groups of people chatting and laughing together, I couldn't help but feel grateful. After the isolating winter months, the return of spring and a group of friends to our home is the reminder I need of how much I appreciate the gift of community.

We endeavor to host friends in our home at least once a week. It's not because I have an immaculate house or am a social butterfly, but because I believe that life is simply better when we experience it alongside others: the joys and sorrows, challenges and celebrations. The Bible reminds us to open our homes with cheerfulness, and the early church abounded with examples of the community of faith meeting together, eating together, and serving with one another. Jesus is less interested in making sure we adequately clean our baseboards or prepare a gourmet meal; he's much more interested in ensuring that our hearts are ready to receive others into our home. With Jesus' help, a heart for hospitality is a gift we can give others—no derby knowledge required.

Kristin

Today's Act of Gratitude

Write down a list of friends you're grateful for. Make plans to invite one of them over to your home in the next few weeks.

From Generation to Generation

Your faithfulness extends to every generation,
as enduring as the earth you created.

PSALM 119:90

My husband and I were foster parents in our county for six years. During that time, we took in twenty kids. Some came for a month or two, others stayed a year or more, and three we adopted into our family permanently.

When the children first arrived, we generally knew very little about them and their families, but over time, we would often meet parents, grandparents, aunts, and uncles. We would hear stories of past trauma, and of hurt parents caught in unhealthy patterns, in turn wounding their children. Many times it was a cycle of dysfunction passed down from one generation to the next.

And then you'd see it: one child or parent who was determined to do something different than what they'd been taught or known. Someone who wanted a healthier way of life than they'd had. Someone who wanted to break the cycle of abuse or dysfunction.

We'd watch in awe as they made different choices, healthier ones, even when it didn't feel comfortable at first. They'd leave behind family patterns of drug use and instability, trusting God to lead them to wholeness and health. It wasn't always a perfect transformation—there were stumbles and missteps along the way—but there was transformation just the same, and it was awesome to behold.

I'm so grateful that God's faithfulness extends to every generation. It never ends. Our family history—for better or worse—can't undo it. Even if we come from dysfunction or from long decades of unhealthiness, with God's help, we can choose something different going forward. We are not bound to the past. Each day, we can make better choices than yesterday. With God's strength and his promise to be with us, we can believe that better days are coming both for us and for those who'll come after us.

Kendra

Today's Act of Gratitude

What unhealthy patterns have you been able to change with God's help? Thank God for his faithfulness to you and your family.

A Little Dose of Adventure

The earth is the LORD's, and everything in it.
The world and all its people belong to him.

PSALM 24:1

"Okay, everything else in the box has been *so* good, but that was weird," my daughter commented.

"What is that taste?!" her younger sister moaned, while the littlest one unceremoniously spat her mouthful in the garbage.

Despite my own displeasure over a taste reminiscent of pine trees, I finished chewing the mastic-flavored toffee. "It's definitely the most unique."

It was Friday night, and my family and I had gathered for our monthly tradition: opening a subscription box full of treats from another country. Over the last couple of years, we've had boxes that featured countries like Poland, Taiwan, Greece, and Colombia. My husband reads the descriptions of each item while I divvy them up, and each child takes a turn recording our reactions, whether positive or negative. The included score sheet provides an area for us to record our favorite, least favorite, and weirdest items.

While most of the snacks are varying degrees of deliciousness, occasionally we encounter one that doesn't agree with our taste buds. But we keep trying them because it's fun to explore new places, even from the comfort of our homes.

We tend to think that we need to travel far and wide to appreciate the world and its treasures. But even something as simple as a subscription box reminds us that we can enjoy new adventures without going anywhere. Each time we try a cocoa-dusted chocolate truffle bar from France, yogurt candy from Poland, or bubble tea popcorn from Taiwan, we're reminded that God has created a wide array of flavors, experiences—and people too. We are each as unique as our fingerprints. Yet each of us is made in his image. Let's delight in the variety present in the world, thanking God for how he has endowed us with fascinating, unique, and beautiful cultures. Let's celebrate and appreciate the beauty of the world and its people.

Kristin

Today's Act of Gratitude

Try cooking a recipe or eating an item from another country. Thank God for the variety of flavors and people in his world.

Comfort in Creation

God, the LORD, created the heavens and stretched them out.
He created the earth and everything in it. He gives breath
to everyone, life to everyone who walks the earth.

ISAIAH 42:5

I'd had a tough day. My head swelled with information and with trying to check everything off my never-ending to-do list. I felt frazzled and at the end of my emotional rope. Then I glanced out the window to see the sun shining.

I decided to take just a ten-minute break and go outside, so I stepped out my back door, intentionally barefoot, down the back steps, past the patio, and onto the green grass. I spent the next several minutes just walking around the yard. As I did, I thought about the young men I'd once counseled at the VA hospital who had severe anxiety. I remembered a common counseling tool we'd teach them to use when they felt overwhelmed: finding a way to ground themselves. We encouraged them to think about where their feet stood and to touch the things around them to remind their bodies of where they were in time and space. It had a way of calming them.

I turned my face toward the sky, taking a deep breath, feeling a light breeze twist through my hair. I wiggled my toes, feeling the blades of grass tickle the bottoms of my feet. My heart rate slowed, my thoughts calmed, and I felt a sliver of peace permeate my brain. I knew I would still have to go back inside and face the rest of my tasks for the day, but taking a few moments outside was just what I needed to make it through.

God created the world and everything that is in it. It's no wonder that we would be comforted by his creation, by all the things he's given life to on the earth. We can often more easily experience God's peace while sitting by a river. Or perhaps he calms us with the sounds of wildlife as we walk through our town or along a path. Sometimes, spending time with God and reflecting on all he has made is just what our souls need.

Kendra

Today's Act of Gratitude

Spend some time outside, being intentional about
noticing your surroundings—all the life right outside
your door—and then thank God for his creation.

A Little Wonky

When they call on me, I will answer;
I will be with them in trouble. I will rescue and honor them.

PSALM 91:15

". . . And I responded, we're all a little wonky. Your painting beautifully reflects the wonkiness in all of our lives."

My friend was recounting a conversation she'd had at the community art night she'd helped host, and my attention snagged on her "We're all a little wonky" phrase. One woman's painting was—in her own words—"wonky." She thought it was not quite as perfect as canvases other women were creating and therefore, in her eyes, it was less lovely.

I don't know about you, but I often feel slightly out of sync as I navigate the various roles I play and the relationships in my life. Just as one role and set of relationships moves toward firmer, solid terrain, another area or set of relationships starts to feel slippery and uncertain. Something in my life is usually a bit wonky, no matter how hard I try to keep everything and everyone steady and stable.

It's easy to forget that most of us have at least a little wonkiness in our lives at any given time when we're accustomed to seeing pageantry and pretense on social media and in our cursory interactions with those around us. To be a little out of whack is part of the human condition, I'm starting to realize—there is always something or someone I'm entrusting to God because it's beyond my ability to control.

The wonky parts of our lives often draw us nearest to God as we recognize how desperately we need him. I must acknowledge the blessings I've found in the harder parts of my story: the closeness I've found with God, as well as his provision when my efforts have fallen short. It's often in the wonky that my faith is refined, growing broader and deeper as I surrender, allowing God to accomplish his will in his way and timing.

It's not particularly fun to be grateful for the hard things; we fear that our acknowledgment will somehow invite additional heartache, but that's not how it works. Recounting and being grateful for God's ongoing goodness and provision—no matter the circumstances—serves to sustain and strengthen our faith, creating a resiliency that sees us over the next bump in the road.

Julie

Today's Act of Gratitude

With gratitude, surrender your current wonkiness to
God, asking for his will to be accomplished.

Sweet Sleep

When you lie down, your sleep will be sweet.
. . . for the LORD will be at your side.

PROVERBS 3:24, 26, NIV

"Shhhhh!" I quieted my daughter as she came careening around the corner of the kitchen. I nodded toward my husband in the next room, gently snoring on the living room floor. "Dad's sleeping."

Her look of surprise turned to understanding, lips tilting down at the corners. "Poor Daddy," she said, eyes bright with sympathy. "He's so tired."

The truth was, he was always tired back then—and for a good reason. For several months, a pinched nerve in his neck meant that he was constantly in pain. He rarely slept soundly, and it was for small snatches of time when he did. Each morning I would awaken to see his side of the bed rumpled from his tossing and turning, abandoned when he was unable to find rest.

He'd tried several solutions without success. But after sustaining nerve damage, he realized he needed surgery. Afterward, he felt immediate relief. And with the pain gone, he was finally able to sleep again.

Sleep is restorative for both the body and the mind, and it's an essential part of our overall health. It's a chance for us to slow down, rest, recover. It gives our brain time to consolidate our memories, releases hormones that regulate everything from metabolism to stress, and helps us maintain alertness and executive functions during the day. Yet, it's not always a priority for us. Lured by the entertainment of one more show in our Netflix queue or the fast-changing pace of social media, or even just wired up by the day's worries that weigh on our minds, we sometimes struggle to gain true rest. When we do find rest, we are reminded of what a gift it truly is to us.

And even though God does not promise us a trouble-free life, he is there during the darkest hours of the night when we feel most alone. He is always by our side. As we close our eyes and drift off to sleep, we can feel secure knowing that he provides rest to those he loves (see Psalm 127:2).

Kristin

Today's Act of Gratitude

As you get ready for bed, spend time thanking God for the gift of sleep.

Comfort Food

*People should eat and drink and enjoy the fruits
of their labor, for these are gifts from God.*

ECCLESIASTES 3:13

It happened quite by chance. We were planning to get together for dinner with friends and were deciding what food to make. Someone suggested pasta from scratch—something we'd never made before—and everyone agreed it'd be fun to do together. The day we gathered, Julie and Aaron dusted off the pasta maker they'd received years earlier as a wedding gift, and we set about measuring the ingredients. As we poured flour and broke open eggs onto Christa's countertop, one of her boys came to help. We kneaded dough and laughed, wondering if we were doing it correctly.

While the guys grilled steaks and Kyle fried polenta, the smell of the food mixed with our chatter and laughter. We worked together to push the pasta dough through the maker several times until it was ready. As the water boiled, we assembled salads, then we sat together around the table, prepared to partake of the things we'd just made.

The pasta was the best I'd ever had. Melt-in-your-mouth good. As I looked around the table at a group of people I've known for years and hold dear, my heart swelled with love.

There's comfort in food. And there's comfort in the relationships of those who know you well. These friends have prayed for us, cried with us, celebrated with us, and loved us deeply.

That night we left determined to do it again soon, making plans for the other dishes we'd like to make together. Beef Wellington, ravioli, and banh mi sandwiches. Comfort food. Comfort friends. All gifts from God.

There are so many good things in life that God has given us to enjoy. And when we share them with others, grateful for the goodness of God in them, we sense the joy he meant for us to experience. Enjoying the fruits from our daily work, the food and drink, and the friendships we've made—this is good and right, and truly, a gift from God.

Kendra

Today's Act of Gratitude

Invite a friend (or multiple friends!) over for dinner, and
if you're so inclined, make the meal together.

The Gift of Mothering

Love each other with genuine affection, and
take delight in honoring each other.

ROMANS 12:10

My mom is steady, loving, and wise. She loves me despite knowing my worst and tells me the truth in love, even when I'm not sure I want to hear it. She mothers me (and others) well. The older I grow, the more I appreciate her—both as a woman who walks alongside me and as my mother.

The beautiful thing is that my mom, as much as I love her, is not the only woman who mothers me. As I've found myself in community with other women of all ages and backgrounds, their compassion, encouragement, and—at times—gentle correction have helped form who I am physically, emotionally, and spiritually. My connection with fellow faith-filled women keeps me grounded and moving forward.

I feel it in the surprise delivery of a fancy coffee to my office during a horrible, terrible, no-good week. I see it in our music teacher, who knows everyone by name and quietly meets needs no one else notices. I feel it in Christa's bear hugs, a squeeze so tight you can't help but understand that you are loved. It is the middle school language arts and math teachers who create a loving, safe space for my children to be their goofy, authentic selves. It is my mother-in-law, a woman who pours love over my children in ways that bring tears to my eyes.

I am surrounded by women whose words and actions reveal their faith. They mother others, in the best possible definition of that word, regardless of whether or not they have birthed a child of their own. My family has been blessed beyond measure by women such as these during challenging moments and chaotic seasons. These women are the very definition of church—the people, not the building—a living embodiment of today's verse.

I owe so much of who I am to women who have taken the time and energy to mother me and those I love. It's a debt of gratitude that gets paid forward and forward and forward through encouragement, cheerleading, intercessory prayer, wise advice, laughter, and an occasional hug as we do our best to love God and love others together.

Julie

Today's Act of Gratitude

Who has mothered you well? Send her a note of thanks.

God's Endless Supply

*From his abundance we have all received
one gracious blessing after another.*

JOHN 1:16

Looking at the credit card bill from the previous month, I felt a little surge of guilt as I considered the charges one by one. With the benefit of hindsight, there were a few items that I wished I hadn't bought at all.

I love finding a good deal at the grocery store or cute items at the thrift store. That's not necessarily bad, but it sometimes means that I purchase more than I need. Even though we've heard that contentment is key to living a peaceful life, the world lures us in with the promise of more. Stocking our pantry or filling our homes offers a false sense of security. Trendy clothes or gorgeous decorating upgrades—all ours for the asking with the click of a button or two—can seem to promise us health, safety, comfort, or prestige.

When we see the world around us through the lens of scarcity, we never will have enough—whether resources, time, or possessions. Unfortunately, "more" is never enough, and the safety and comfort we seek can never be fulfilled by our belongings.

Thankfully, the Kingdom of God is one of abundance rather than scarcity. I love the reminder in John that we already have received "one gracious blessing after another"! Our gracious God lavishes us with his love, power, and peace. He gave us a world overflowing with light and color, twinkling stars, and a brilliant sun. He provided us with community, imbued us with purpose, and gave us the ability to breathe deeply and savor every moment.

When we shift our mindset from scarcity to abundance, we recognize that we don't need to strive for more. Because of Jesus, you and I already have all that we need. His generosity never runs out, never goes dry, and never fails. Our abundant God has more than enough for you and me.

Kristin

Today's Act of Gratitude

Take a minute to survey your life, making a mental
list of all God has provided. Thank him for the people
and the possessions he has blessed you with.

New Experiences

Keep putting into practice all you learned and received from me—everything you heard from me and saw me doing. Then the God of peace will be with you.

PHILIPPIANS 4:9

"They won't listen to me. They can't even have a conversation. Anything that would make them question or consider another way to think or believe they dismiss without discussing it," my husband, Kyle, lamented to me about a family member he loves dearly.

My husband has done a fair amount of reading over the past several years and has grown in his faith and how he views God and others. It means a lot to him to be able to share his heart with people, but there are those in our closest circles who would prefer not to hear.

As I thought more about his comments and the person he was referencing, I said, "You know, I don't think it's just topics of faith they don't want to discuss. That person has done the same actions for many years and isn't open to new things, whether it's food, trips, or even simple changes to their daily schedule. If we want to learn and grow, we have to be willing to try new things, and I don't see that person being open to new experiences."

He nodded in agreement as we prayed together again for them, asking God for wisdom and compassion to love them well while continuing to speak the truth.

It's easy to get into a rut in life. And although there's nothing wrong with routine, sometimes we get so stuck that we are unwilling to try unfamiliar things or be open to alternative ideas. But Scripture is clear: we must keep putting all we're learning into practice. We never fully arrive here on earth as followers of Jesus; there is always room to grow. And I am grateful for the assurance that when fear tries to stop us, the God of peace is with us.

Kendra

Today's Act of Gratitude

Try something new—a food, a place you've never visited before, or an activity you've been interested in but haven't taken the first step to try yet. Express your thanks to God for continued opportunities to grow and learn.

Our Spiritual Heritage

Your testimonies are my heritage forever,
for they are the joy of my heart.

PSALM 119:111, ESV

Hundreds of years ago, an ancestor of mine was a mercenary soldier. He crossed the sea to work for the British Army, but once he landed here in the colonies, he defected and fought on behalf of the American forces. After the War of Independence ended, he lived on a well-known general's land until settling down in his own home. Rumor is that the woman he married was a spy for the French during the war.

I love hearing stories about the past, but knowing that a particular story is interwoven into who I am today makes it even more special.

Family genealogy fascinates me, but the rich spiritual heritage I possess is even more valuable. My parents became Christians in their twenties, and I grew up knowing about Jesus and the radical life change he had wrought in their lives. Even now, if you walk into my parents' home in the early morning hours, you're likely to see them sitting quietly in the living room with coffee in hand, a Bible open beside them.

I'm grateful for my family's spiritual background, even though I know that's not everyone's story. Thankfully, our heritage can encompass far more than our family. The testimonies we hear from others and the way we see God's work in the lives of those around us contribute to it. My spiritual upbringing includes the leaders who poured into my childhood, the mentor I met for coffee in college, the pastors who have made biblical concepts relevant to everyday life, and the friends who continue to challenge and renew my faith with gentle questions and a loving community.

Those who shape our spiritual heritage encourage us with a clear call to live a life of faithfulness, and that shapes who we are and what we know to be true about Jesus. The stories we, in turn, choose to tell of God's faithfulness are not only a reminder of the past; they are part of the legacy we are passing on to those around us.

Kristin

Today's Act of Gratitude

Consider who has contributed to your spiritual heritage. If possible, reach out to them to express your thanks.

A Fresh Perspective

Two people are better off than one,
for they can help each other succeed.

ECCLESIASTES 4:9

"Whoa, you need to vacuum your office." She paused just inside my door, taking in the almost-dead Boston fern and the carpet around it littered with shriveled leaves. "I'm sorry, that was rude. I didn't mean to say that your office is messy."

"No, you're right, and that's not rude. I've been trying to save that fern for months, and I probably need to acknowledge defeat and toss it." I peeked over my desk at the mess resulting from my ongoing reluctance to throw out any plant until it is deader than dead and completely beyond rehabilitation.

Her accidental honesty was refreshing, and it reframed my perspective concerning that Boston fern. By that afternoon, it was in the dumpster, my entire office had been swept clean, and I felt lighter and happier having a tidy space once again.

I've periodically wondered how long I'd have lingered in limbo with my messy office and mostly dead fern without her comment. And I've wondered where else I've perhaps grown too complacent, allowing spiritual, emotional, or even physical clutter to gather, preventing me from seeing the situation clearly until someone walks in with a fresh perspective and the bravery—or foolhardiness—to say something.

Allowing a trusted someone a peek into our thought processes, physical spaces, or any other area where we can grow stagnant and blind to the status quo can be a gift, especially when we are willing to accept feedback without offense. Listening to suggestions doesn't always mean we'll make a change. Still, considering another's viewpoint can reawaken us to ideas or things that have crept into our normal and ordinary when they should not have, or it can remind us of truths we've let slip away.

I am grateful that God created us so that community, intimate friendship, and familial relationships are there to gently course correct us when our perspectives start to get a bit skewed. Rather than shut down conversations when views differ from our own, let's practice listening with discernment, asking God to help us sift well-meaning feedback, showing us when it requires change and when, though lovingly said, it can be gently ignored.

Julie

Today's Act of Gratitude

What areas of your life could use loving feedback? Invite someone you trust out for coffee and a chat, asking God to refresh your perspective.

Fully Accepted

How precious are your thoughts about me, O God. They cannot be numbered! I can't even count them; they outnumber the grains of sand!

PSALM 139:17-18

"Mom, Kari told me she's going to straighten her hair every day because that's what the popular girls do," Jasmine said late one evening after returning home from an activity.

"What?" I responded. "But she has such pretty, curly hair. I love it."

"Me too," my daughter said as she sat on the edge of my bed where I had been reading. "I told her she doesn't need to do that, but she said she doesn't have any friends at school, and she thinks it will help her."

"Oh honey," I said, realizing the ache behind her young friend's actions. I fully understood where she was coming from, and it grieved my heart. "She doesn't need to do that. She's beautiful just the way she is. It's a shame the other kids at her school don't see it."

"I know," Jasmine whispered with a sigh.

"Why don't you invite her over this weekend? See if she wants to sleep over?" I asked as I hugged Jasmine. She nodded as I kissed her cheek. "And remind her how much we love her, just as she is."

"I will," Jasmine said, and before I sent her off to bed, she texted her friend to make plans.

How often have you and I tried to change things about ourselves so that others would like us? It's a familiar feeling, and although wanting to be included is good, changing who we are so others will befriend us is not the best approach. We need to remember that we are already fully accepted by God. His thoughts about us are precious and too plentiful to be counted, outnumbering the grains of sand. He loves us so much.

This truth can uphold us even when others shun us or leave us out. We are fully known, entirely accepted, truly loved. We are valuable, just as we are.

Kendra

Today's Act of Gratitude

Thank God for his acceptance of you, and then remind someone else of his love

The Power of Prayer

Devote yourselves to prayer with
an alert mind and a thankful heart.

COLOSSIANS 4:2

I bought a prayer journal this year.

Prayer has always been an area where I've struggled to remain consistent. Compared to "prayer warriors" I know, my own prayer life has felt—well, a little lackluster.

So when a friend mentioned that she'd started using a journal with monthly prompts, an area to record Scripture and prayers, and a section to jot down reasons to be grateful, I ordered one for myself. Ever a list maker, I love the mix of practicality and purposefulness.

Now, each morning, I spend my coffee time in prayer. The gap between when I wake my oldest daughter and when she finally makes her way downstairs for school provides just enough space for me to have my first cup and reach toward my journal. Those early morning minutes with Jesus are exactly what I need to help center my thoughts. By the time my cup is empty, I feel better prepared for whatever the day will hold.

Even with my newfound habit, I've been challenged to widen the lens of prayer, think bigger, and pray for more. Speaking at church a couple of weeks ago, my friend Eli asked: What would happen if everything you prayed for last week had come true? Would big, audacious prayers have been answered? Or would they have been pretty unremarkable things—an enjoyable dinner, a good night's sleep for a loved one, or a road cleared of traffic so you could make it to work on time?

It can be easy to get caught up in questioning whether prayer changes anything. We see loved ones struggle and wonder if our intercession for them matters. Yet, in the months since I've started my journal, I've come to believe that there is value in the practice of prayer. Even if the answer doesn't look the way I hoped it would. Even if the answer is "not yet." Prayer can change our external circumstances, but it can bring the most significant changes in our hearts. I'm grateful that even on days when hope and healing feel hard won, peace is always ours for the asking. When we come to God in prayer, he provides the peace we need to face each day.

Kristin

Today's Act of Gratitude

Spend time in prayer, thanking God for the peace he provides.

Tasting God

Taste and see that the LORD is good.
Oh, the joys of those who take refuge in him!

PSALM 34:8

As I pull away from the drive-through window, I take a tiny sip of my favorite coffee drink before putting it into my cupholder to be savored later. Releasing a deep sigh, I feel my shoulders drop and tension leak from my body. I flip on the blinker and take a left turn, headed toward my classroom and a day full of obligations.

It might sound silly, but I've come to associate that occasional cup of fancy coffee with God's love for me. That is to say, as those particular flavors explode across my taste buds, I automatically think of God, marveling at the creation of our senses and the emotions and memories that can be provoked by them. This drink tastes of serenity, of the knowledge that God goes before me into my classroom as I do a final mental review of the day's materials and silently pray over my students and myself.

Certain foods remind me of loved ones long since gone to heaven. I think of them whenever I whip up the recipe for my own family or come across a brand of cookie they always stocked in their pantry. And I know I'm not the only one who associates emotions, memories, and people with taste. I've laughed with many women about weird pregnancy cravings for childhood comfort food that we hadn't thought about in fifteen years, let alone yearned for before pregnancy.

If we experience God through the melody of a favorite hymn, the beauty of a spectacular sunrise, or the hug of a beloved one, why wouldn't we experience God through food or drink? He is the creator of our taste buds, which help us savor salty and sweet and sour and bitter. He created the original ingredients from which all else is derived. As we thank God for beautiful vistas, for melodies that move us closer in intimacy with him, for blessings and material provision, let's also thank him for the gift of taste. My family is learning to pause over something that tastes amazing and proclaim, "This is a little taste of heaven!"

Julie

Today's Act of Gratitude

What favorite meal or beverage is a little taste of heaven for you?
Practice lingering momentarily in gratitude as you take a bite or sip.

Well-Timed Words

The tongue can bring death or life;
those who love to talk will reap the consequences.

PROVERBS 18:21

"What are you going to do with an English major?" was a common question from friends and family during my college years. Most people assumed I planned to be a teacher or work in academia. Although I think that the world can always use more people who are good communicators, I understood my loved ones' concern about the practicality of my chosen path.

As a result, I decided to earn a mass communications minor to increase my marketability. I hoped the public relations and marketing classes would provide the business-minded foundation I needed.

One of the classes I took was an introduction to newspapers. A few of the assignments dealt specifically with editing, and after one of them, my professor pulled me aside.

"You've been really good at the editing we've done in class," he said. "Have you ever thought about joining the copydesk at the student newspaper?"

I was simultaneously flattered and caught off guard. *Work for the newspaper? What would that even entail?* I had never considered it.

I wasn't sure, but—bolstered by his encouragement—I headed down to the lower level of the building where the newspaper was located. The student editor was in his office, and I stumbled nervously over my words as I explained that I'd like to work on the copydesk. To my surprise, he agreed to take me on.

I'm grateful for my professor's timely words. They gave me the push I needed to try something new and led to a career in journalism that I continued to pursue for the next decade.

Our words matter in profound ways. Depending on how we wield them, they can "bring death or life"—they can spur doubt or destroy our identity, or they can foster a skill or birth new dreams. My professor's generous advice led me to consider a skill I didn't realize I possessed, sending me down a new path. His words had an impact long after the semester was over.

Kristin

Today's Act of Gratitude

Think of a person who said something positive to you
that changed the direction of your life in some way.
Reach out to thank them for the gift of kind words.

What Do You Want to Be Known For?

*You died to this life, and your real life
is hidden with Christ in God.*

COLOSSIANS 3:3

Recently, a friend of mine who is a Christian shared a social media post on a topic they were passionate about, only to find out it was false information. A mutual friend told me they had stopped following this person because they thought differently about the issue and didn't care to see false information come across their feed.

My daughter heard our exchange, and after the friend left, she asked, "Mom, what was that about?"

I shook my head as I tried to explain how differing opinions can sometimes cause rifts, especially online. When issues are not discussed face-to-face, it's hard to see the other person as a whole being with thoughts, feelings, and emotions.

We talked about being careful in sharing things on the internet, and then I told her, "You know, before I post anything, I always ask myself, 'What do I want to be known for?'"

"How do you decide?" she asked.

"Well, that's a good question," I responded. "My dad used to say, 'I want to know Jesus and make him known.' That was his goal. And I think that's mine as well. Is what I'm sharing going to make Christ known? Will people come to a deeper understanding of who he is, his love and grace? If not, it might not be worth sharing. I am grateful for Jesus' love, and there's nothing I want more than to draw others to him. Anything that would turn them away from him isn't worth it to me."

Jasmine nodded. "That makes sense."

There are so many things that pull our attention in this world and many issues we can become passionate about. Often, these are good and worthwhile. But nothing should matter more to us than Christ and sharing his love with those around us. As Scripture reminds us, we've "died to this life," and our real life—the only life that matters—is "hidden with Christ in God." Our highest goal as Christians is to gratefully share his love, mercy, and grace with a world that could desperately use some good news.

Kendra

Today's Act of Gratitude

Take time to assess how you use social media and whether what you post is worth sharing for the sake of the gospel.

The Gift of Inclusion

The whole law can be summed up in this one command: "Love your neighbor as yourself."

GALATIANS 5:14

"I just left Whole Foods. What a fun—but expensive—store!" My friend's prerecorded video message kept me company as I loaded the dishwasher. I worked as she chatted, smiling as she told me to try a particular sauce brand to see if I liked it as much as she did. Then she turned the one-sided conversation to why she'd stopped at Whole Foods in the first place.

She was on the hunt for vegan cupcakes—cupcakes that looked and tasted enough like regular ones that a preschool classmate would be included in her son's birthday treat later that week.

"Julie, it breaks my heart," she continued. "The teacher sends pictures of the class smiling while holding cupcakes for these little celebrations, except for this one child who always has a package of fruit snacks. I figured it had to be a food allergy, so I asked whether there were any in the class, and it was eggs. It's a bit challenging, but I'm determined that this child will have a cupcake for my son's birthday."

I love my friend's fierce determination to see and include those sitting on the sidelines in life, even if that means driving to the most expensive grocery store in town to hunt down vegan treats in the same flavor as the regular ones her son would be bringing to school. Her family knows firsthand the unintentional but very real exclusion that occurs because of an allergy to a common food ingredient. She was willing to be inconvenienced—in several ways—if it allowed another person's child to be wholly included.

Her story was gently convicting, even though I'm sure she'd tell me that was not her intention. And as I finished wiping down my countertops, I asked God to show me where I've put convenience over inclusion and where I've been too preoccupied to see someone on the sidelines. I thanked him for the more difficult seasons and moments in my own life that have made me sensitive to others walking a similar road. I resolved to slow down and look more carefully for opportunities to be inclusive, even when it's inconvenient.

Julie

Today's Act of Gratitude

Thank God for a time someone went out of their way to make sure you were included. Ask him to help you notice those who could be included with just a little extra effort from you.

Famous to One

The master said, "Well done, my good and faithful servant. You have been faithful in handling this small amount, so now I will give you many more responsibilities. Let's celebrate together!"

MATTHEW 25:23

"What does your tattoo mean?" she asked as we were hiking a trail along one of Minnesota's many rivers one warm May morning.

"Which one?" I said with a laugh. She pointed to my back, and I paused to explain. "Well, it's the first tattoo I ever got. It says, 'Famous to One.' I got it after hearing a message about making ourselves famous to Jesus." She nodded as I continued.

"The speaker did a great job explaining how so many people are concerned about impressing people here on earth, when our greatest desire should be that Jesus knows who we are and is proud of us. That when we get to heaven, he would hug us and say, 'I know you.'" I turned to look at her as I finished. "Being famous to Jesus is my ultimate goal in life."

She nodded understanding as I explained that the pastor's words affected me, a self-proclaimed people pleaser, because what I wanted more than anything was to please Jesus in the way that I love him, love others, and share his kindness with the world. I had the phrase tattooed on my body so I would never forget what, or who, I am living for.

It's so easy to get caught up in worrying about what others think of us, and although there's nothing wrong with striving for a good reputation, there comes a point where we can cross over into simply trying to please people. When we remember that as believers, we want nothing more than to hear God say, "Well done," we'll be faithful to do what he asks of us rather than worrying about what others may say or think. And when we're faithful to handle the small things that come our way, he'll give us even more responsibility —increasing our witness and influence with those around us.

Kendra

Today's Act of Gratitude

Do something that Jesus would be proud of you for— offer forgiveness, love someone who doesn't deserve it, or share with someone in need. Ask God for just the right opportunity, and then take the initiative to follow through.

Shoes of Peace

*Put on every piece of God's armor so you will be able to resist
the enemy in the time of evil. Then after the battle you will still
be standing firm. . . . For shoes, put on the peace that comes
from the Good News so that you will be fully prepared.*

EPHESIANS 6:13, 15

"Hey, Lizzie. Can I pull these off?" I called out as my daughter rounded the corner and started toward where I was hunched over in the shoe aisle.

I straightened as she approached, and we peered down at my feet in the moderately heeled, shiny, classic black patent leather pumps with a sassy, barely-there, iridescent shimmer reminding me of oil on asphalt.

"If I buy them, I think they deserve a name. Maybe Oil Slicks?" I'd never given a name to a pair of shoes before, but these delightful heels cried out for one.

"Mom, those are awesome. They should be your 'I don't listen to mean people' shoes."

Startled for half a moment as I processed her words, I pulled her in for a tight, quick hug. "You are right, thank you," I whispered into her ear before releasing her.

Lizzie's simple statement realigned my perspective with God's Word. There is a difference between accountability and honest conversations about where we've fallen short, and the nasty spew that steals our peace for any number of reasons, almost always having more to do with the other person than with us. And I'd recently allowed my peace to be stolen by nasty spew.

I'm grateful that my inherent worth has nothing to do with my ability to coherently string words together, my inability to add numbers accurately, or any other good and bad comments about my skill sets and talents. My peace comes from God, unshakable and unavailable to be stolen by my fellow flawed humans.

And while the armor of God is spiritual in nature, my Oil Slicks represent being shod in the peace that comes from knowing the Good News. And just as knights donned armor before battle, I wear my Oil Slicks to remember that the peace of God cannot be stolen by circumstance or by other people. I know that my shoes have zero actual power, but I am grateful for their tactile reminder.

Julie

Today's Act of Gratitude

What part of the armor of God in Ephesians 6 might you
need in tactile form as you stand firm in battle?

Grateful for the Help

God has given each of you a gift from his great variety of
spiritual gifts. Use them well to serve one another.

1 PETER 4:10

When I arrived, she was sitting by the practice room, sewing kit out. Relieved, I sat down next to her.

"You have no idea what this means to me," I said as I started to pull my daughter Jasmine's dance costumes out of a bag.

"It's no problem at all," Staci said with a laugh as she set to work on the first of several outfits. I'd texted her earlier in the day, asking for her help. Staci has many giftings, one of which is being a seamstress, and since I can barely sew a button on a shirt, I knew I'd need her assistance before the competition season started.

We sat and chatted while she worked. Jasmine tried on each costume, and Staci made adjustments as needed. It took a few hours, and as we said our goodbyes, I left relieved to have it all done in just one sitting. What Staci saw as no big deal was massive to me, as one who couldn't have done the alterations on my own. I'm grateful for a friend who has strengths that I do not.

Peter reminds us that God has uniquely gifted each of us and that we should use our gifts to serve others. I think this applies to our natural abilities as well as our spiritual gifting. What unique talents do you have? Are you someone who loves to invite others into your home or circle of friends? Are you an encourager? An excellent planner or gift giver? Maybe like Staci, you have a talent that could be shared with others. No matter what our gifts and talents are (and we all have something!), we can use them to love and help those around us. We aren't to hoard our gifts, only using them for ourselves, but to generously serve others with them. They are meant to be given and received. Let's thankfully acknowledge the abilities God's given to us while also recognizing the gifts of those around us.

Kendra

Today's Act of Gratitude

Use a gifting you have to serve someone else, and the next time
a friend offers, allow them to serve you with their abilities.

Freedom in Truth

Dear children, let's not merely say that we love each other;
let us show the truth by our actions.

1 JOHN 3:18

"Can we talk for a minute?" a voice called out. I paused, fingers still hovering over the light switch I'd been about to shut off. For a moment, I thought longingly of the warm bed and cozy book I'd been headed toward, but as I turned around and noticed the tension on her face, I dredged up a smile instead.

"Sure," I said, moving toward the dishes on the counter. As she settled into a chair and I began to fill the sink with hot water, I listened as hurt poured out of my loved one. She felt overlooked, ignored, unwanted. She questioned motives—including mine—and revealed the pain she'd been holding on to.

I felt a mix of sadness and concern, but as she wound down and I was able to respond, I was also glad for the opportunity to set the record straight. That worst-case scenario she'd been envisioning? It wasn't true. She *was* cared for, loved, wanted. Though we differed in opinion on a few issues, I always valued her viewpoint and genuinely looked forward to our time together. So why had she believed the worst and suffered needless harm? My spirit grieved with her over the trust that had been damaged, and I apologized for the unintentional hurt I'd caused.

The conversation was painful. But by the time we said good night a couple of hours later, we both felt better. And I was grateful for the opportunity I'd had to set things right.

Scripture has many references to the truth, reminding us that it sets us free, that hidden things will always come to light, and that Jesus himself is truth. Truth is a hallmark of our faith, yet our actions are often the bellwethers that reveal what we believe to be true. My nighttime conversation had revealed how someone I loved was writing a narrative in her mind that wasn't true, and our honest conversation offered a way to rewrite that narrative. Our pain-filled discussion was the first step toward composing a new story filled with forgiveness and hope for a better tomorrow.

Kristin

Today's Act of Gratitude

Are you harboring anger or pain toward someone else? Consider
whether a truthful conversation would be beneficial.

Just Breathe

*The Spirit of God has made me, and
the breath of the Almighty gives me life.*

JOB 33:4

My daughter Jasmine has been dancing competitively for several years, but this was the first year she'd compete with a solo. As I watched her take the stage, I was nervous but excited for her.

She danced beautifully, but I observed she seemed a little off partway through the performance. No one else seemed to notice, but being her mom, I knew something wasn't quite right.

As we watched the judge's comments and critiques a few days later, I looked at Jazz. "Honey, it seems like most of what they're commenting on comes down to your breath. Because I've seen you do this dance so many times in the studio, it looks like you forgot to breathe here."

"Yeah," Jasmine agreed. "I was just so nervous."

"It's understandable," I reassured her. "It was your first time; I just think many of their critiques would go away if you simply remembered to breathe."

She nodded in agreement. "I know. Next time, I'll breathe more deeply."

Later on, I thought about how often I can go through life tense, nervous, holding my breath. And how, just like in Jasmine's performance, that can restrict the actions and even the risks I'm willing to take. Because if I'm walking through this life tense and anxious, I'll miss all that God has for me. I won't give myself over to fully trusting and moving into the things he has planned.

I'm thankful that it is the breath of the Almighty that gives us life. If we remember this, we are free—free to breathe deeply, have peace, and step into all that lies ahead. We needn't fear; God is there.

Kendra

Today's Act of Gratitude

Be aware of your breath today and when you may be holding it instead of breathing deeply. When you realize you are tense, imagine God breathing into your being and take a few deep breaths. Thank God that he has made you and given you life.

Interruptible

*Let us think of ways to motivate one another
to acts of love and good works.*

HEBREWS 10:24

"How did Luke seem to you today?" Jon and I were driving home from an activity, and I asked the question about his friend during a lull in our conversation.

"Luke? Oh, he was fine, same as always." Jon's response was preoccupied as he dug through the passenger seat glove box, searching for a stray piece of gum.

"Hm. What if I told you that he has been struggling a bit lately?"

"What? Nah. He's fine." Jon paused from his search to look at me. "How can you tell? Do you know something?"

I did know something, and while I didn't share the particulars, we talked about what it means to struggle silently while publicly acting like everything is fine. Jon was contemplative as we pulled into the garage, and after we walked into the house, dinner, homework, and the evening's tasks sidetracked me from any further conversation about Luke.

But Jon took my words to heart. Several days later, he mentioned Luke, having struck up a conversation with him about something mutually interesting. And several days after that, Jon brought up Luke again, and how they'd shared chocolates Jon had been given. This pattern continued, with Luke popping up in casual conversation as Jon quietly and without fanfare simply began seeking him out, including him, intentionally demonstrating friendship.

I got a bit teary-eyed as I thanked God for Jon's tender heart and his quiet stepping up once he realized Luke was having a tough time. But more than being grateful, I asked God—once again—to make me interruptible, giving me his eyes to see who around me might be struggling. I prayed that he would allow me an inside tip with a Holy Spirit nudge so I could be a bit gentler in my expectations of them, and a bit bolder in my reaching out. I've prayed this before, but as life gets busy and the day-to-day gets distracting, I have to recommit, ceding space to the Holy Spirit and remembering to discern between tasks with eternal value and tasks that feel momentarily important but will fade away into nothingness.

Julie

Today's Act of Gratitude

Who has encouraged you in a difficult season? Make a list of what they did well, and ask God whom you might encourage similarly.

Making the Most of It

*People should eat and drink and enjoy the fruits
of their labor, for these are gifts from God.*

ECCLESIASTES 3:13

"Okay, guys, it's that time of year again," I said, passing out sheets of paper with the words "Summer Bucket List" printed at the top. "Come up with your best ideas, and then we'll decide on our final list as a family."

"Ooh, I know what's going on my list," one of the kids crowed, hiding her paper from her sister so she couldn't sneak a peek.

For the next several minutes, all that could be heard was the faint scratching of pens. Turning to my own list, I wrote down some of our favorite traditions from years past: a rainy day pajama party, made-from-scratch raspberry shakes from a local drive-in diner, visiting the state's biggest candy store, the summer library reading program, a trip to the science museum, cones at a new ice cream parlor, painting pottery, and more.

Each year, we come up with a summer bucket list of ideas. Although some of the items cost money or require extra planning, many are free and can be done at home. Eating breakfast in bed, Backward Day (where everything is backward, including meals—in the morning, dessert is first, then dinner!), or creating a life-size game of Chutes and Ladders with chalk on the driveway cost us nothing but time, yet are richly rewarding experiences. We never get to all of them, but creating our list and posting it on the refrigerator reminds us to prioritize adventures and togetherness during the all-too-brief summer months.

Though working hard is essential, the Bible reminds us that we should also eat, drink, and delight in the fruits of our labor. Life is not meant to be drudgery but something to enjoy! Let's celebrate by recognizing and making time for the "good stuff." Each moment and memory is a gift from God that we can be grateful for. In the same way that we write down appointments and obligations, let's take the time to write down—and schedule in—the fun activities.

Kristin

Today's Act of Gratitude

Come up with your own bucket list, whether it's three
items or thirty. Ideas: travel destinations, friends to have
over for dinner, meals to make, or books to read.

A Friend of Your Own

*There are "friends" who destroy each other,
but a real friend sticks closer than a brother.*

PROVERBS 18:24

My daughter Eleanor had always been a bit shy and quiet in public. Being the youngest of five, she tended to follow along where everyone else was going, content to just be a part of the family's bluster of activities.

But two years ago, something changed. She wanted a friend—not just her siblings' friends who were kind enough to let her tag along, but a buddy she could call her own. That's when we met Alayna and her family.

The interesting thing is that Alayna is very different from Eleanor in many ways. She's spunky and loud, outgoing and curious. They seem like an odd pairing on the surface, but they complement each other perfectly, and they clicked immediately.

I've noticed that Alayna brings out all the best things in my daughter. Eleanor is more courageous and outgoing, welcoming new friends into their circle, because that's how Alayna is. And as her mom, I couldn't be more grateful. They dance together, are in the same class at school, and have even shared birthday parties. In Alayna, my daughter has a friend who is an absolute gift to her and an answer to her young prayers.

Introverted or extroverted. Loud or quiet. Serious or silly. We all need friends. People who understand us, who listen to us and love us. But they don't have to be just like us to fit. In fact, sometimes being our opposite is even better because they can fill in what we lack, just as we do for them.

Scripture reminds us that a true friend is someone who doesn't destroy others around them but instead sticks closer than a sibling. Someone who loves unconditionally and always looks out for the good of their friends. Someone who lifts others and encourages them to be the best version of themselves. That's the God-given gift of friendship offered to each of us, and I'm so grateful for it.

Kendra

Today's Act of Gratitude

Text, call, or message a friend who has been a blessing to you,
and let them know how grateful you are for their friendship.

Manifested Joy

I pray that God, the source of hope, will fill you completely with joy and peace because you trust in him. Then you will overflow with confident hope through the power of the Holy Spirit.

ROMANS 15:13

It happens at the same time each weekday afternoon. As I pull on my coat and reach for my keys, our goldendoodles Sully and Thea begin a doggie tap dance. They twirl in circles, toenails clicking across the vinyl floor, tails wagging so hard that their entire rear ends swing left to right, right to left. They know it's time to pick up the kids from school, and they are desperate to tag along for the ride. And on the days that we aren't running errands or going anywhere else after the pickup, I swing the door wide open and call out, "Hey, doggos, let's go get the kids!"

At my invitation, it's every creature for him or herself as a pell-mell dash of furry bodies streaks out the door and to the car, followed by an eager waiting as I catch up. They pile into the back seat and settle into their specific spots, delighted and content to be along for the relatively short ride.

I cannot help but grin as I shut the rear driver's-side door and climb into my seat; their exuberant joy over an ordinary and routine task is contagious. We're off to gather up our family after a school day apart, and that—in and of itself—is reason for rejoicing.

Can one be convicted by the joy of their pet? I'd never before considered it, but the answer is yes, at least for me. Can I trust God enough—even in the hard times—to be filled with his peace and joy? Can I search for joyful moments to cherish and abiding peace in even the chaotic stretches of life? If we can, and when we do, we're promised the overflow of confident hope through the Holy Spirit. This promise is a rare and priceless gift in a world often teetering on the edge of hopelessness. It has challenged me to be a hunter of joy and peace, intentionally searching it out and basking in even the smallest glimpses.

Julie

Today's Act of Gratitude

Be a hunter of joy and peace, seizing small moments while recognizing God's handiwork.

Road Trip Memories

"You are worthy, O Lord our God, to receive glory and honor and power. For you created all things, and they exist because you created what you pleased."
REVELATION 4:11

My family and I love to travel, especially by car. We make a game of seeing how many license plates from different states we can find, and we play a lot of the alphabet game. We listen to music and sing along, and we look for interesting stops to make along the way. Although there are moments of boredom, the drive has become a favorite part of any trip for me.

On one trip, we drove from Minnesota to Texas, and as we traveled, I was struck by the vastness around us. The barren land that seemingly went on for miles. The change in terrain from forests to fields to grazing land. As I stared out at the enormousness of the earth and the very different landscapes we passed, I couldn't help but feel enamored once again with the greatness of our God, who creates all things with care and creativity. The more I travel, the more I wish to see all he has made. The earth indeed is incredible, and I am grateful for a God whose cleverness and imagination know no bounds.

No matter where we live, it's easy to get accustomed to the scenery around us—to no longer be enthralled with what God has created because it is too familiar. Sometimes going to a new place, even just a few hours away, can change our perspective. Doing so reminds us of just how great our God is.

Scripture tells us that God created all things, and they exist because of him. As a result, he is worthy to receive glory and honor and power. When we are intentional about stepping into a new place or even looking outside with fresh eyes, we can't help but be in awe of the greatness of God and grateful for all he has made.

Kendra

Today's Act of Gratitude

As you go about your day, notice what God has made and thank him for his creation.

June

The Firmest Identity

My old self has been crucified with Christ.
It is no longer I who live, but Christ lives in me.

GALATIANS 2:20

"Tell me about yourself."

For the longest time, whenever I heard that comment, it would tie me in knots. *Do they mean professionally? Do they mean personally? Which labels are the right labels for this occasion?* I'd find myself carefully evaluating the social situation and responding accordingly, identifying myself through the labels I thought most relevant in the particular setting: attorney, board chair, adjunct professor, or wife to Aaron, mom of two, dog owner, proud lefty. I'd gauge what my questioner was looking for and respond with the pieces of me that best fit their desired narrative.

And while chunking myself up into various pieces is a function of navigating the world, I've learned that those pieces of me are not my full identity. They are merely describers of roles and attributes, and adopting any one of those as my identity is a formula for heartache and confusion—a trap the world often trips into.

If I've mistaken roles and attributes for my identity, when one of them changes—whether by my choice or not—I risk being cast into an identity crisis. And what of the *negative* roles or attributes placed on me, things I would not choose if it were up to me? Those are also not my identity. And they are not your identity either.

When we decide to love Jesus and abide by his Word, our identity becomes rooted in him. I am thankful that with an unshakable foundation in Jesus, our labels and attributes can shift and change without tossing us into a crisis over who we are and what we are called to do. Our mission is clear: we are to love God with our whole hearts, strength, minds, and souls, and we are to love others as ourselves (see Matthew 22:34-40). When we adopt Jesus as our foundation and the greatest commandment as our primary mission, every label and every attribute is viewed through and informed by the lens of loving God and loving others because we belong to Jesus.

This realization has been breathtakingly life-giving to me, even as the journey of periodically re-rooting my identity remains ongoing. Jesus is our Savior and our firm foundation, and my soul rejoices in that truth.

Julie

Today's Act of Gratitude

Prayerfully evaluate where you have conflated your identity
with roles and attributes. If necessary, make changes,
thanking God for your firm position in Christ.

The Gift of Knowledge

Don't forget to do good and to share with those in need.
These are the sacrifices that please God.

HEBREWS 13:16

"Mom, how do I make tea?" The call had come in while I was helping at an event, and I left the noisy hubbub of volunteers to find a quiet room. Sinking into a chair, I clutched the phone as my daughter repeated her question. "I wasn't sure if I just turn the kettle on or if I have to do something else."

Smiling, I gave her a few basic instructions and hung up, returning to my work.

It seems like a simple thing, but it makes a difference when someone is willing to share their knowledge. Whether it's a tip about a new restaurant to check out, a stain remover that works, or a show we enjoyed watching, passing along what we have learned reveals a generosity of spirit that is always a reason to be grateful, regardless of whether we are the recipient or the one who provides the information.

The first time I made chicken noodle soup from scratch, I was overwhelmed at the thought of working with a whole chicken. It looked huge. I didn't know if I needed to clean the inside or if I had to cut it up before cooking it. I was so nervous that I called my mom at least five times to ask her advice. Each time, she patiently answered my questions and reassured me that I could do it. I was so thankful that she had taken the time to bolster my flagging spirits and send me back to the recipe. By the time it was ready, soup had never tasted so good.

While sharing with others can often involve our time or treasure, sometimes it simply requires our knowledge. Let's not waste the wealth of life experience we carry; instead, let's pass it on. Being willing to come alongside someone else and offer our expertise allows us to provide hope or reassurance to a person who may be struggling. It also reminds us that we matter and are uniquely positioned to help those around us. During his ministry on earth, Jesus often shared his knowledge in parables that made it easy for his followers to recognize what he meant and apply the concepts to their daily life. When we follow his lead by sharing our knowledge, everyone benefits.

Kristin

Today's Act of Gratitude

Share a tip or piece of knowledge with
someone or ask for their best advice.

Standing Firm

The LORD's plans stand firm forever;
his intentions can never be shaken.

PSALM 33:11

I was up late, worried. One of our kids was making some poor choices, and I was wondering (in vain) how I could stop this cycle. Though they were old enough to make their own decisions, it didn't keep me as a mom from willing them to do something different.

Instead of even trying to sleep, I took my concerns to God. I imagined handing my child over to the Lord, placing them in his hands. I reminded myself of God's love for my child and for me. I prayed for the plans that I knew the Lord had for them and their future. And as I did, slowly, peace began to settle over me. Enough that I could lie down and rest.

It's been a while since that night, and my child hasn't magically started making perfect choices. Sometimes our prayers take time, but I believe and stand firm on the promise that God is holding my child close and that someday they will respond to God and follow his plan.

Life doesn't always turn out as we hope. Circumstances happen beyond our control, people make choices that hurt themselves or loved ones, and sometimes we're the ones who make poor decisions. Yet even when chaos seems to reign, even when prayers aren't being answered in the ways we'd hoped, I'm thankful that God's promises are still there for us to cling to.

In these harder moments, we can remind ourselves that the Lord's plans will always stand firm and that his intentions will never be shaken. He reigns. He is sovereign. And he will make everything right in his time. All we have to do is trust him, stand firm on these truths, and rest in his love that holds us all.

Kendra

Today's Act of Gratitude

What has been burdening your heart lately? Spend a little time bringing it before God. Imagine him taking it from you, and then remind yourself that his plans always stand firm.

The Yellow Mixing Bowl

Remember the days of long ago; think about the generations past. Ask your father, and he will inform you. Inquire of your elders, and they will tell you.

DEUTERONOMY 32:7

Bewildered, I stared at my family gathered around our kitchen island. I had just casually announced that after almost twenty years, I was replacing our unsightly green and yellow plastic mixing bowls, and their howls of protest caught me off guard.

"Um, you want to keep the ugly plastic bowls?" I turned from reaching into the cupboard where they were stored to look at my family, certain they were teasing.

"Mom, the yellow one is Dad's Pancake Making Bowl. We can't get rid of it. We need it." Lizzie spoke, but Jon's head was nodding furiously in agreement.

"But we can make pancakes in this new one—look, it has a handle and a spout, plus it's stainless steel . . ." Pleading eyes and shaking heads melted away my argument as I realized that those bowls had become an essential component in my husband's Saturday morning homemade buttermilk pancake tradition.

There are a thousand memories tied to those bowls, and they have become precious, their weekly use layering memory upon memory filled with banter and laughter, and all of it underpinned with their daddy's love.

The mixing bowl fiasco soon had me rethinking other family heirlooms. I began looking for ways to put sentimental pieces into regular use so that new memories are embedded among the old until they, too, become as precious as those plastic bowls.

But even more important than building new memories around Great-Grandma's Depression-era glass is passing forward the stories of God's faithfulness, how he has provided for Aaron and me as individuals and collectively for our family. Today's verse reminds us to share those stories, making sure Lizzie and Jon know our unending gratitude for God's ongoing generational faithfulness as far back as I've been able to trace.

Just as those plastic mixing bowls remind my children of their earthly father's love, it is the ongoing recounting of God's stories during ordinary moments that helps launch their own relationship with their heavenly Father. It gives them a foundation for building memories of their own interactions with God's faithful love.

Julie

Today's Act of Gratitude

Recount God's faithfulness to you and your ancestors.
Share those stories with a new generation.

A Friendly Neighborhood

Yes indeed, it is good when you obey the royal law as found in the Scriptures: "Love your neighbor as yourself."

JAMES 2:8

"I think you're fine," our neighbor Jim said, taking one final sniff of the garage. I had run inside a little while earlier to tell Tim that the garage smelled strongly of gasoline, even though neither of us had refueled our car in days. Tim was unsure whether it was a problem, so we'd asked Jim for a second opinion.

Minutes later, he'd arrived and sniffed the air experimentally, looking around our garage as he did so. His reassurance that nothing was wrong was the confirmation we needed to go on with the day as planned.

My husband and I often joke that we are inept homeowners. Thankfully, we have lovely people nearby who are always willing to lend a hand—or, in Jim's case, a nose.

Our neighbors have brought in our mail and rolled the garbage to the curb when we're out of town, loaned us a wheelbarrow for an outdoor project, and helped us chop wood. They've attended birthday parties and bought cookies from our kids, hosted brunch, and watched a movie together in the cul-de-sac. And though each family has their own life and friends, they still stop to chat when they step outside to get their mail or work in the garden.

We are meant to live with one another in a healthy community, but sometimes, it can be easy to overlook those closest to us. And while we may find our most genuine sense of community in a church or small group, we're also called to love those who reside beside us. The very nature of God—as the Trinity, three in one—is communal. There is value in loving our neighbors. When we know we can count on one another in times of crisis, we are more likely to overlook minor offenses and appreciate the neighborhood in which we live.

Kristin

Today's Act of Gratitude

Drop off a note of thanks or a small gift to a neighbor. Or consider someone in your circle of friends who lends a helping hand when you need one, and take the time to say thank you.

Embracing Discipline

I correct and discipline everyone I love.
So be diligent and turn from your indifference.

REVELATION 3:19

Hands on hips, I surveyed my raised garden beds. It was late spring, and while my seedlings were growing, they certainly weren't thriving. I'd checked for insects and disease, and now I was considering whether there might be something lacking in my soil.

I can water, prune, mulch, and otherwise care for my plants diligently and in accordance with the latest scientific studies. Still, if I neglect the soil in which my seedlings are rooted, they will never reach their full potential—whether that be a bountiful crop or a glorious bouquet of blooms. A healthy garden requires that I amend the soil by replenishing nutrients from season to season.

As I stood pondering my sad plants and next steps, the Holy Spirit's still, small voice asked whether I had been an amender of the proverbial soil in the lives of those around me. Was I building others up, or was I being critical and frustrated with them?

Ouch. The question stung and still stings. But it's the right question, and I find myself reexamining it regularly. Are the words I speak over others life-giving and encouraging? Do I treat others as beloved children of God worthy of the same mercy and grace I know I need?

The answer, if I'm being truthful, is not always. Sometimes my emotions are like a dumpster fire, and my tongue gets sharp. Just as I intentionally care for my garden soil, I must practice intentionally speaking words of life over my relationships and treating those around me with tenderness, grace, and mercy as a default response to difficult moments, regardless of my feelings at that particular time.

And when I feel that nudge of conviction, I remind myself that God loves me enough to tell me I'm missing the mark. It's not my favorite way to spend time with God, but his discipline is meant to refine me. There is gratitude to be found in those hard conversations with him as we pause to reconsider the path we've been on, repent, and realign ourselves with him. He loves us so much that he invests the time and energy in correcting us.

Julie

Today's Act of Gratitude

As you feel the nudge of conviction when you fall short of
the mark, pause to thank God for his loving correction.

Change Is Possible

Since you have heard about Jesus and have learned the truth that comes from him, throw off your old sinful nature and your former way of life, which is corrupted by lust and deception. Instead, let the Spirit renew your thoughts and attitudes. Put on your new nature, created to be like God—truly righteous and holy.

EPHESIANS 4:21-25

A few years ago, my husband, Kyle, decided he should see a therapist. He'd had silent struggles for years that he'd dealt with alone, and after he shared them with me, we determined it might be helpful if he went to counseling.

Because it was his decision, he took it seriously. Over several months, he worked to change old patterns of thinking and behavior that he knew had never been healthy but simply familiar. As I watched Kyle learn and grow, I was appreciative, knowing he wanted to be the best possible version of himself.

But I was surprised when I'd hear him in conversation with other people about things he was learning in therapy. He wasn't embarrassed or ashamed. He didn't keep it a secret from anyone around us. He told me that he wanted to normalize getting help and set an example for others that it's okay to seek out support when you need it. I was impressed by his vulnerability and willingness to allow others to see that he wasn't perfect.

Not long ago, I told him how proud I am of him and the changes he's been able to make. Is he perfect? No. But with God's help and the wisdom of a counselor, he's become healthier, healed in ways he wasn't before.

No one is perfect. We may live out of unhealthy habits for years and wonder if we could ever be different. But God promises that change is possible. I'm thankful that when we throw off our old nature and former way of life that no longer serve us, the Holy Spirit will renew our thoughts and attitudes, allowing us to put on a new, healthier nature. God-breathed. Righteous and holy. What hope we have! We are not stuck in old patterns of thinking or living. With God's help, change is possible.

Kendra

Today's Act of Gratitude

Is there something you feel helpless to change in your life? Reread the Scripture above, and then ask God to help you take one first step toward a positive change.

Candy Dinner

Teach us to realize the brevity of life,
so that we may grow in wisdom.

PSALM 90:12

"Okay, who's ready to dig in?" I could not help but grin as I took in the eager faces of the crew gathered around the kitchen island. Based on a long-running inside joke, I call them my Wild Poodles: Kendra's youngest three and my two kiddos. They have known one another since birth and are as much family as friends.

Kendra and I had challenged our kids to participate in NaNoWriMo (National Novel Writing Month). We had promised a dinner made solely of sugar if they met age-appropriate writing goals.

They had, and now several months later, we were making good on our promise. I'd even picked up a box of Twinkies after realizing the Wild Poodles had never tried the legendary treat with a shelf life of—apparently—forever. We (parents included) raised a candy toast to their hard work and dedication, cheering for the surprisingly complex and creative works resulting from their month of work. It was a delightful evening filled with laughter, silly photos, and great memories.

I haven't always paused to celebrate accomplishments, being so often too consumed with striving and too future-focused to remember the fleeting nature and importance of being present today. I was long into adulthood (and parenthood) before I began to truly comprehend the brevity of our days, years, and entire life, and the importance of living intentionally in the present rather than always living with a future focus. There is a place for both, to be sure, but I tend to swing too much toward the future and too little toward moment-by-moment living.

Candy Dinner was a lovely reminder to pause in joyful celebration over life's milestones. Small victories are worthy of an intentional pause and grateful reflection over our progress before setting new goals and marching onward. There is something so encouraging in recognizing our forward movement along the journey instead of always waiting until we've reached a far-off finish line. Life is too short not to celebrate every chance we get, being grateful for smaller accomplishments along the way, even as we've set our sights on audacious goals.

Julie

Today's Act of Gratitude

What small victory can you celebrate this week even as you pursue a bigger goal? Pause to prayerfully acknowledge your forward movement, even as you make plans for the next steps in your goal.

Real Talk

You will know the truth, and
the truth will set you free.

JOHN 8:32

It was a busy Monday morning, and our earlier communication had been curt. My friend and I were upset with one another, and it was showing. I decided to call her instead of continuing to communicate through text, which only seemed to be adding to our misunderstanding and hurt feelings.

"I just feel abandoned," she said as she burst into tears over the phone. My initial annoyance dissipated as my own throat clenched with emotion in response to her honest confession.

"It's okay," I responded as we discussed an issue that we'd both miscommunicated to one another. Before we hung up, I quickly added, "You are not alone. I'm here. I'm with you. I love you."

"Love you too," she whispered as we both cried for a moment together before ending the call.

It was only a few minutes of conversation, but it was just enough to cover over any hard feelings and remind each other of the truth. We love each other. We are there for each other. We always want good things for each other. We are friends. I texted her again a little while later, reminding her of what she means to me.

Sometimes we need those around us to tell us what is true. Life circumstances can throw us curveballs that we weren't expecting, leaving us reeling, unable to fully remember what is true. But when we know the truth, it will set us free.

And what is the truth we can gratefully cling to today? We are loved. We are chosen. We have good work to do. We can walk in peace and love. We are called by name. No one can remove us from our Father's hand.

So many good things that God promises to each of us. They are all true. And that knowledge does set us free.

Kendra

Today's Act of Gratitude

What lies have you believed lately about God, yourself, or your circumstances? What truth would Scripture remind you of? Take time to write out that truth and read it throughout the day.

A Lazy Summer Afternoon

You make known to me the path of life; in your presence there is fullness of joy; at your right hand are pleasures forevermore.

PSALM 16:11, ESV

Drowsily, I heard my littlest daughter approach, sandals scuffing on the concrete pavers. I opened my eyes to see her surveying me with a twinkle in her blue eyes.

"Found you," she said.

Thirty minutes earlier, I'd quietly slipped on flip-flops and grabbed pillows as I made my way outside. Finding a spot to curl up and close my eyes, I enjoyed the stillness even as I wondered how long it would take my children to discover my hiding place.

As I waited, I took in the world around me: The breeze whispered through the trees, insects buzzed, and a lawn mower motored in the distance. Frogs chorused in the pond behind me while squirrels bounded from branch to branch in the tree above. I couldn't help but wonder, *Is there anything more marvelous than the joy of an unexpectedly lazy summer afternoon?* Despite little noises all around me, the world felt quiet, and as time passed, I felt my spirit calm too.

My daughter wandered off to find some chalk; when she returned, I helped her create a pattern on the ground. Finally, she looked up at me.

"You can go back to resting now, Mom," she said. I fell asleep to the sound of her chalk scraping the concrete.

Each little noise and small pleasure reminded me that when we appreciate the beauty of creation, we thank our Creator. When we enjoy the solitude of a sunny afternoon, we find the peaceful rest God promises to his loved ones. When we take time to quit worrying about yesterday's woes and tomorrow's concerns, we demonstrate our trust in him. As his children, we can believe what he says. His presence is a soothing balm, always and already available. In him, we can find joy and pleasure—we simply need to take the time to do so.

Kristin

Today's Act of Gratitude

Find an hour in the afternoon—preferably sometime in the next week or two—in which you can simply rest. (If you need to schedule it, that's okay.)

Trusting the Master Gardener

I am the true grapevine, and my Father is the gardener. He cuts off every branch of mine that doesn't produce fruit, and he prunes the branches that do bear fruit so they will produce even more.

JOHN 15:1-2

"Dad, wait! What are you doing?" My tween-aged self had wandered into our garden and stumbled across the carnage of pruned tomato branches my dad was leaving in his wake as he moved swiftly down the row of plants.

"I'm pruning the suckers off the tomatoes." His response floated up from his hunched-over form as he kept right on moving and pinching off branches, despite my fluttering about with horrified gasps. "We need to remove these suckering branches. Otherwise our tomatoes will suffer and won't produce as much fruit."

Of course, Dad was right, despite what initially looked to me like a plant murder spree. The suckering branches of tomato plants—if left to grow—steal nutrients and shade the growing fruits, leading to higher instances of disease and fewer tomatoes. What looked like the removal of important greenery and intentionally inflicted damage was an act of loving-kindness by the wise gardener, caring for and multiplying his crop.

As a farm girl who grew up around various garden and agricultural crops, I have found that the parables Jesus told about sowing, growing, pruning, and harvesting strike particularly close to home. I've planted, grown, pruned, and harvested plants myself. The temporary hardship inflicted to create a future crop that is both healthier and bigger is one with which I'm intimately familiar.

While that understanding doesn't necessarily make my own pruning at God's hands more enjoyable in the moment, it does create trust. Having been the pruner and having seen the results in the plants I cared for, I trust the process, knowing that God is the master gardener and is far more skilled than I am in knowing what or who needs to be removed from my life and when. I understand that the temporary reductions create resiliency and a better outcome based upon what God deems eternally important. Sometimes, our gratitude is forward looking, knowing that present circumstances, though temporarily uncomfortable, are an investment in God's molding of a better version of you and me.

Julie

Today's Act of Gratitude

How has God's past and present pruning created a better version of you? Write him a thank-you and tuck it into your Bible for future discovery.

Who Are You Friends With?

Don't you realize that friendship with the world makes you an enemy of God? I say it again: If you want to be a friend of the world, you make yourself an enemy of God.

JAMES 4:4

During family devotionals with our kids, we often find ourselves in James because his words are so practical and straightforward. After reading the fourth chapter, we asked our kids, "What does it mean to be friends with the world?"

"It means putting yourself first, keeping all your things to yourself, and not caring who you hurt to get ahead," my daughter Jasmine said. I nodded.

"And what does it mean to be a friend of God?" I followed up.

"It means that we don't love the things the world loves," she responded.

"And we care about other people. We don't just think about ourselves but what could benefit others. We love people," my son Abram added.

"Does being a friend of God mean we should avoid certain people?" I asked.

"No," Jasmine said. "We're supposed to love people. It's how we treat people that matters to God."

I smiled as I looked at my kids. They're getting it. There are many parts of following Jesus that can seem complicated or complex, but the basic premise isn't difficult to grasp. Love God. Love others. And a question we often ask in our house is: *How does everything else in my life honor these two commands?*

Do we respond in kindness, even when faced with unkindness? Do we show love to people others wouldn't deem worthy? Do we put our own needs aside from time to time to meet someone else's needs? Do we look not only to our interests but to those of others around us?

If we are going to be God's friend, these are the questions we need to ask ourselves, a check of our hearts to make sure we're following his ways. Because it's too easy to fall into the trap of being a friend of the world, it's often harder to assess how we're doing and make changes when necessary. But I'm so thankful God's friendship continues to extend to each one of us, even if we have to make adjustments.

Kendra

Today's Act of Gratitude

Have your actions lately shown you to be a friend of God or a friend of this world? Take some time to assess yourself and adjust where needed.

The Domino Effect

As iron sharpens iron,
so one person sharpens another.

PROVERBS 27:17, NIV

I smiled as I saw the message drop into my inbox. "Dear friends and customers," it began. "I am pretty sure it has been too hot at your house lately also, so I will not even bring that topic up. We certainly could use rain, but we survived last summer and that was even drier and hotter. On these hot days, we take care to see that the herds have shade in their pastures. All the hogs have mud puddles to cool in. Otherwise things are going just peachy. (Granddaughter Ella says that sometimes.)"

Over the past several years, we've bought beef, pork, chicken, and even bison from this local farmer named Tom.

Though I appreciate the ability to purchase products locally, I also appreciate Tom. Whenever we meet up to exchange items, his calm demeanor and his age remind me of my dad, but his personality shines best in his newsletter updates. In every newsy email to his customers, he describes the weather and the rhythms of the season, as well as what's happening day to day.

Tom's letters offer a bird's-eye view of the everyday life of the farm, but what I enjoy most is his evident appreciation for his life. In every line, it's clear that he cherishes his ability to continue to work the farm and provide something of value for others. This, in turn, spurs my own sense of gratitude. As I read his letter, I'm constantly reminded of how thankful I am for the respect he shows the animals in his care.

Someone else's gratitude often serves as the fuel that sparks appreciation within our hearts. What we choose to say matters, and the things we focus on will influence what those around us focus on. If we make it a habit to thank God for his many blessings—the day, the food, the sun, a friend, the coffee we hold in our hands—in the presence of others, our focus on gratitude will spill over into them. They, likewise, will be encouraged to thank God.

Scripture reminds us that we sharpen one another, and when we focus on Jesus and encourage others to do the same, it spurs them on in their faith. Let's continue to find ways to encourage those around us. Let's carefully consider the words we choose to speak, always seeking to inspire others to live a life of thankfulness.

Kristin

Today's Act of Gratitude

Ask someone else to tell you what they're grateful for.
Take time to consider how it increases your thanksgiving
for something or someone in your life.

What's Your Superpower?

*Love never gives up, never loses faith, is always hopeful,
and endures through every circumstance.*

1 CORINTHIANS 13:7

It wasn't until I'd backed down the driveway and put the car into gear that I noticed my fuel gauge's little red marker. I knew it had been hovering around a quarter tank the afternoon before, but now it was filled to the tippy-top. Aaron had—once again—filled my car with gas when he picked Jon up from soccer the night before and had not mentioned it upon his arrival home.

If he isn't filling my gas tank, he's charging my phone, which if left to my tender loving care, also consistently hovers around a quarter charge. And it's not just me: Aaron frequently plugs in school-issued devices when the kids forget before they head upstairs for bed, ensuring a full charge for the next school day. His tendency to quietly stroll behind us, refreshing all the things we use, has become a bit of a running joke in our marriage and our family, earning him the affectionate superhero nickname Super Charge-Up Man.

His love language is acts of service. The simple ongoing gift of charging our batteries and gassing up my car without complaint—other than periodic teasing about me and our teens walking through life uncharged—is a tangible manifestation of his love for us. In turn, I make it a point to express my gratitude with sincere thanks, a kiss, and sometimes a cheeky grin as I dash off, fully charged, to wherever I'm headed next.

Ongoing kindness in the face of a loved one's foibles is indeed a superpower. My family's relatively constant state of low batteries and my consistently empty gas tank could easily be an irritation (and admittedly is some days), especially at twenty years into our marriage. And yet Aaron generally turns my annoying quirk into an opportunity to love me (and us) well.

His ongoing act of love has me reconsidering the eccentricities in others, Aaron included. Instead of being slightly annoyed or irritated, I'm pondering how I can reframe idiosyncrasies into an ongoing opportunity to serve and love someone well. It's my prayer to quietly show the type of ongoing, enduring love laid out in today's verse, a love that goes beyond words.

Julie

Today's Act of Gratitude

Consider whose actions reveal their ongoing love (platonic, familial, romantic) for you. Let them know. And consider how you might reveal your enduring love for someone else through an ongoing act of service.

Music and Memory

I will sing of your love and justice, LORD.
I will praise you with songs.

PSALM 101:1

We sang a new version of an old song at a recent church service. The leader mentioned that Hillsong had released an album of revamped songs, including the one we were about to sing. I loved the new version, so I added the album to my queue when I arrived home.

One of the updated songs was "Eagle's Wings," which was first popular almost twenty years ago. It was a song my sister Katrina and her husband, Jim, both members of their worship team, often sang together.

When the music began to play through the speaker, tears fell as the song instantly reminded me of the last time I'd heard it.

On that day, Katrina could no longer sing it with us. We knew it was her final day on earth. With my family gathered around her hospital bedside, Jim began to sing. As I held my sister's soft hand and joined in, my voice wobbled. The song is about surrendering to God and asking him to live and breathe in us. The reality that my sister was taking her final breaths and would soon meet Jesus face-to-face made the lyrics resonate anew.

Years later, as I listened to the new version, I found myself smiling through tears. Because the opportunity to relive that moment when love surrounded us and eternity was on the horizon? That was a priceless moment I don't ever want to forget. I'm so grateful for the song that reminded me of that truth.

God designed music as a beautiful way for us to connect with one another and with him. It has the uncanny ability to circumvent our thinking brain and engage our emotions. It's why we can't remember what we ate for dinner last night but can sing a song from junior high word for word.

Songs can instantaneously remind us of a crush, a road trip, a job, a season, or a friendship. And when we use the gift of song to tell of God's love and justice and mercy—when we choose to praise him in every circumstance—we connect with others in a powerful way. We create memories that linger long after the notes have ended.

Kristin

Today's Act of Gratitude

Listen to a song that reminds you of something or someone
memorable. Thank God for the gift of music.

Endings and Beginnings

*I focus on this one thing: Forgetting the past and looking forward to
what lies ahead, I press on to reach the end of the race and receive
the heavenly prize for which God, through Christ Jesus, is calling us.*

PHILIPPIANS 3:13–14

It was a sunshine-soaked afternoon as the doors to Madison Elementary School burst open and families of the graduating sixth-grade class emerged. Temporarily blinded by the bright sunlight, we blinked our way down the sidewalk toward the small park for a postgraduation picnic. As I passed by the line of teachers and staff stretched along the walkway to wish their students well, a thousand memories floated through my mind.

My own furious blinking had more to do with my futile attempts to keep tears at bay as I said a silent goodbye to the community that had played a vital role in our family's life. Beloved teachers and staff members had poured love into our children daily for six years, and I had so many delightful memories of music concerts, plays, and activity nights.

I knew I would feel a weird mix of grief and joy as I prepared for this day. Yet, the gut-punch of emotion as my youngest child chatted excitedly with his friends, all of them eager to move on to middle school and the increased independence it represents, still caught me a bit off guard. As I walked, I prayed, thanking God for all the life my family had lived in that building.

Standing on the cusp of a new adventure often requires goodbyes to something or someone you are leaving behind. Even the most exciting change, the most desperately anticipated new adventure, often has a thin thread of lament and grief woven inextricably into its fabric. And that's okay. You often cannot have firsts without lasts, and pausing in that in-between place for a moment to acknowledge the complicated emotions associated with new beginnings and final endings is a way to honor the journey we are all on. But don't linger. Move into that new undertaking, knowing that God is calling you forward on your faith journey, with new people to influence and new tasks to complete.

Julie

Today's Act of Gratitude

Pause for a moment to prayerfully honor what God has done through
the lasts you have experienced before casting your vision forward.

Called to Be You

*We keep on praying for you, asking our God to enable you
to live a life worthy of his call. May he give you the power to
accomplish all the good things your faith prompts you to do.*

2 THESSALONIANS 1:11

Surveying the screen, my heart sank as I read through the list of potential topics for an article I'd been asked to write: *camping activities for kids, baking with toddlers, tagging games.*

On one hand, I love checking items off a summer bucket list with my kids, playing board games with them, and spending as much time together as possible. And if you look at my social media profile, it's easy to see that those are things I highlight. The fun things.

But when somebody tells me that I seem like "a fun mom," I have to laugh a little. I'm not a big camper, baking with kids can be a challenge, and I wouldn't say I like playing tag. Based on that list, maybe I'm not a fun mom at all?

Thankfully, God doesn't expect me to be someone I'm not. God gave me my children, knowing my personality. He knew that the adventures we placed on our summer bucket list would sometimes be out of my comfort zone. He knew I'd rather read quietly or play board games with my kids than hike or go fishing. And that's okay.

The same is true for you. You are called to be you—no one else. And when you and I see people who seem like they've mastered some aspect of their lives—their career, parenting, or friendships—the truth is that we probably caught them on their best day. We don't see how they struggle with anxiety, the hours of work that went into winning the award they're proudly holding, or the way their kids hollered at each other moments after the picture-perfect photo was taken.

God gave you the gifts and talents you were meant to have. He endowed you with your sense of optimism or good humor, your love of nature, or your ability to observe others or listen well. Instead of trying to measure up to others, let's live a life worthy of his call. His grace is sufficient for us, no matter what. Let's celebrate who we are, take a deep breath, and move forward in love.

Kristin

Today's Act of Gratitude

List five things you like about yourself, thanking God for them.

The Gratitude Race

You made all the delicate, inner parts of my body and knit me together in my mother's womb. Thank you for making me so wonderfully complex!

PSALM 139:13-14

"Ready, set, go!" I flipped the game board hourglass over, and my husband and kids immediately began scribbling on the sheets of paper I'd placed before them. Picking up my pen, I joined our informal competition to write down as many things as I could that I was grateful for before our time was up. We had thirty seconds to make our lists and then were going to compare notes to see how many different items we could come up with as a family.

My ultimate goal was to create a list that I could type up, print out, and hang on our bathroom mirrors and on the pantry door concealing our frequently used microwave to serve as a reminder to each of us of the many blessings we enjoy.

The results were along the lines of what I expected. Our lists began with similar entries related to family, food, shelter, friends, and the like. As we each got further into our lists, we started including items unique to our interests, our circles of influence, our experiences. We started general and became increasingly specific as the timer slowly ran out. We tallied the items that were on all of our lists before sharing the rarer, individual items and the *why* behind including them. It was a fun experiment and one we'll repeat on occasion.

This game was a lovely reminder that even though we are members of a close-knit family living under the same roof, God loves us as individuals, with personalized blessings inviting us into our own deeper relationship with him. We truly are fearfully and wonderfully made, known to him even as we were knit together in the womb. It was an unexpected but profound takeaway as a lighthearted exercise in gratitude suddenly veered into deeper spiritual territory than I'd originally anticipated.

Julie

Today's Act of Gratitude

Conduct a gratitude race with loved ones. Compare
your lists, acknowledging similar items but also hunting
for those things unique to how God loves you.

Love over All

All of you should be of one mind. Sympathize with each other. Love each other as brothers and sisters. Be tenderhearted, and keep a humble attitude.

1 PETER 3:8

My first job out of graduate school was at our local Veterans Affairs Medical Center. I worked in the residential treatment program and was hired alongside several new grads. One of those was Katrina, who had an office next to mine, and who, on the surface, appeared to be my opposite. She was raised in the South by her grandmother, so we'd certainly grown up in different environments.

And yet, Katrina and I had a lot in common. We both were raised in strict Christian homes, attended college and graduate school, and were passionate about becoming therapists. Over the two years I worked with Katrina, she taught me much about her history and upbringing—things I hadn't ever learned or been taught about in school, like Juneteenth and Black Wall Street. She explained things that had happened to her, the discrimination she had known. And because I knew her, it broke my heart. I couldn't imagine anyone treating her as anything less than the valuable person I saw and knew her to be. She was kind and caring, generous and funny. I found myself grateful for her friendship and her willingness to be open with me, teaching me things I hadn't previously known.

The first Christians faced many of the same challenges that we do today with regard to differing backgrounds and traditions. They were a diverse group of people gathering together in ways they hadn't before Jesus came. They were Jews, Gentiles, Samaritans, and more—all trying to navigate a new way to live and follow God together. Paul, Peter, and other New Testament writers were constantly encouraging them to be of one mind, to sympathize, and to listen to one another. Love one another. Be tenderhearted.

Today, the church is just as diverse, and we would do well to follow this same encouragement. Listen. Love. Sympathize. Treat one another as brothers and sisters. Because that's who we are in Christ Jesus.

Kendra

Today's Act of Gratitude

Find someone who has had a different upbringing than you and listen to their story. See what you can learn from their life.

An Unexpected Gift

Work willingly at whatever you do,
as though you were working for the Lord rather than for people.

COLOSSIANS 3:23

Watering my lawn felt like a colossal waste of time. We'd recently replaced a boulder wall and overgrown bushes with a tidy stone wall and lights that lined the driveway, which required us to add new sod. The landscaper had told us that we needed to keep the sod moist or risk it dying—which is how I found myself, if it didn't rain, faithfully watering the new grass every day.

At first, I was annoyed at the task. It took me about thirty minutes to ensure the sod received a good soaking, and during that time, my mind would race with all the other things I could be doing instead: work, my to-do list, chores.

But after a while, I found myself enjoying those half-hour interludes. I began to look forward to the break in my day: the warmth of the stones under my bare feet, the peaceful quiet of the moment, the tiny rainbow that shimmered in the water from my hose, or a neighbor who stopped to chat with me as they walked their dog or grabbed their mail.

The time I spent outdoors, unwanted as it may have been, was a gift in disguise.

How often is that true in other areas of our lives? Maybe we used to dread exercising but now appreciate the boost of energy it provides. Perhaps we once loathed cooking but now enjoy sharing our favorite recipes with others. Maybe we used to dislike our commute to work but now appreciate the opportunity to listen to podcasts or enjoy a little silence in our day.

The work or task doesn't change in these circumstances, but our attitude can. When we choose to see all that we do—including seemingly thankless jobs—as working for the Lord, even mundane tasks feel exceptional. Worthwhile. Essential. With the grass I continued to water, growth was not possible without the work. So it is with us—we can't grow without resetting our hearts and minds to appreciate the big and small tasks we've been given each day.

Kristin

Today's Act of Gratitude

Think of a task you don't enjoy doing. Brainstorm ideas to help you shift your attitude about the job and appreciate the work it requires.

Fan the Flames

I know that same faith continues strong in you. This is why I remind you to fan into flames the spiritual gift God gave you when I laid my hands on you.

2 TIMOTHY 1:5-6

She was fifteen when God called her to ministry. There was zero fanfare or public pronouncement; her calling came quietly one afternoon when she was alone, spending time with Jesus in her bedroom. And it was a secret she kept because women simply did not enter formal ministry positions, at least not in her corner of American church culture.

Instead, her ministry was lived out through an ordinary life as a wife and mother in a small community—fanning the flames of faith in neighborhood women and children who gathered in her home and church. And then, when her children were mostly grown, God opened the door to a formal leadership role in ministry where she fanned the flames of faith in thousands, encouraging them to follow God's unique calling—big and small—in their lives.

Now, newly retired from her ministry position, she stands on the cusp of becoming a credentialed minister in her seventh decade. It's a beautiful example of the fulfillment of God's calling over the entire course of our lives, of humanity's inability to thwart those plans—intentionally or not—and of God's perfect timing that often looks nothing like our own. Just as she fanned all of our tiny flames of faith, encouraging our spiritual giftings, we have the privilege of standing alongside her, fanning the flames of *her* faith, and cheering her on as she takes the next steps in a lifetime of faithfully serving God, informally and formally.

Being a person who actively fans the flames of faith—in ourselves and others—is a blessing passed down from generation to generation, reaching back thousands of years to Paul's encouragement of his young disciple in 2 Timothy 1:5-6. Encouraging another in their spiritual calling is among the greatest gifts we can give. Its ripple effects will extend far beyond anything we'll see this side of heaven. I am forever grateful for how my friend has encouraged my faith over the years, and I show her my thanks by doing the same for others.

Julie

Today's Act of Gratitude

Prayerfully ask God whose spiritual flames you can fan.

Safe in His Hand

From eternity to eternity I am God. No one can snatch anyone out of my hand. No one can undo what I have done.

ISAIAH 43:13

One evening we were talking with our kids about life after death. Someone had just passed away in our community, and our children had questions. My husband and I answered them as well as we could and attempted to alleviate any fears.

As we talked, our eight-year-old daughter, Eleanor, began to cry.

"What's wrong?" we asked, as my husband took her and held her on his lap.

"I don't want to die!" she exclaimed, placing her head in her hands. "It sounds scary."

My husband and I agreed. There is a part of the unknown that is troubling. But then I reminded her of the Scripture in Isaiah. "Honey, God promises that no one can be snatched out of his hand. That person is with Jesus, and that is always good."

She nodded understanding as she wiped her eyes, and we hugged her close.

A week or so later, we discussed a family friend whose cousin had suddenly and tragically passed away. Without hesitation, Eleanor said, "But it's okay, Mommy, they're in God's hand, right?"

"Right," I responded, grateful that she remembered what we'd been talking about the week before.

Often if we do not know the character of God, we can question why bad things have to happen in life and what will become of us when we die. But when we know that God is good and kind and loving, we needn't worry or fear. We can trust that even if we do not have all the answers, God will take care of us, and he is in control. He is God. For all of eternity. And no one can snatch us out of his hand. No one will be able to undo what he has done in life or death. And because of this truth, we do not need to fear what is to come.

Kendra

Today's Act of Gratitude

What has made you feel afraid or anxious lately? Tell God, and then imagine yourself in his hand, with his protection all around you.

Instilled with Purpose

Not that we are sufficient in ourselves to claim anything as coming from us, but our sufficiency is from God.

2 CORINTHIANS 3:5, ESV

Rummaging through documents in my office, I ran across a file folder. Inside was a collection of emails, note cards, and other memorabilia from my years at a local newspaper.

As I rifled through the items, I smiled at the tangible reminders of working alongside supportive coworkers. Reading through an email congratulating me on successfully laying out the front page for the first time reminded me of a conversation I once had with my boss.

At the time, I was struggling to feel qualified in the design work I'd been tasked to accomplish each day. Repeatedly, I'd ask my boss what he thought of my designs.

Although he always provided helpful feedback, finally, he gently told me, "You're doing fine. You need to trust yourself more."

His confidence in me boosted my own belief in what I was capable of accomplishing. Though I still sought his opinion from time to time, it happened less and less. I had the knowledge and experience, but I lacked self-assurance. My boss's wise words gave me the boost I needed to move forward.

In the same way, we are equipped to fulfill God's purpose for our lives. It's not that we have to do it all ourselves—he is not asking us to be superheroes—but rather that we can lean on him when we need to. God gave us the gifts and talents we possess. Instead of being paralyzed by self-doubt, let's recognize that our abundant God can provide what we need to accomplish our purpose. His wisdom is ours for the asking. Let's not belittle ourselves or envy someone else's abilities. Let's rejoice in the recognition that God will help us continue the good work, equipping us with resources and confident hope to accomplish the purpose he has instilled within us.

Kristin

Today's Act of Gratitude

What is one area of purpose in which you have felt self-doubt or fear creep in? Ask God for the wisdom you need, thanking him that it's yours for the asking.

Don't Judge a Book by Its Cover

The LORD said to Samuel, "Don't judge by his appearance or height, for I have rejected him. The LORD doesn't see things the way you see them. People judge by outward appearance, but the LORD looks at the heart."

1 SAMUEL 16:7

I walked into the women's event by myself.

As I entered the venue, I was greeted by the planner, who quickly went over with me all that the morning would entail. Since there were about twenty minutes of downtime before I would have to speak, I stood quietly off to the side while women began to show up.

As they arrived, the women were smiling, engaged in conversation. And slowly, my insecurities began to come to mind. These women were very put together—with beautifully coiffed hair, and with makeup and outfits that would rival any magazine. I looked down at my scuffed boots, fighting the thought that what I was about to say wasn't going to be good enough. I quickly said a prayer as they called me up to speak.

As I began to share, the first story I told was one of a friend being bullied when she was younger. As my throat clenched with emotion, I looked out at the crowd and was surprised by what I saw. Some of the most beautifully accessorized women had tears in their eyes, nodding as I spoke. I could tell there was a shared understanding of the hurt I was talking about.

I shouldn't have been surprised; it's often the most put-together people who are the first to shed a tear. It's as if they use the external to hide their pain or insecurities. But when given the opportunity, they are the first to be open and tender.

We all face the temptation to hide who we are or the hard things we've gone through. As followers of Jesus, we can lead the way in sharing honestly, inviting others to do the same. It's so easy to judge people based on their outward appearance, but I am grateful that's not how God judges us. He sees our hearts. He knows our pain. And because of this truth, there is no need to be something we're not or to hide from him or others.

Kendra

Today's Act of Gratitude

Determine to look beyond outward appearances
to the heart of those around you.

Overcoming the Darkness

*The light shines in the darkness, and
the darkness can never extinguish it.*

JOHN 1:5

Thunder boomed and lightning flashed as the storm raged outside. Rain pelted the ground as once-small rivulets turned to big puddles, pooling on the ground and rapidly filling the storm sewers. Though it was morning, the storm had darkened the skies to an eerie green color. Suddenly, the lights flickered once or twice, then went out. I heard our generator grind to life a few seconds later, lights and appliances around the house beeping as they revived.

As I peered out the front windows, I noticed that our house was the only one on the block that was still lit. In the gloom, it stood out like a beacon. I glanced at the coffee mug I held in my hands, and it occurred to me that others might not have been lucky enough to get their morning cup in before the storm hit and knocked out the power.

I shot out a quick message, starting with our nearest neighbors.

"We've got lights. If you need coffee, you're welcome to drop by," I said. Luckily, most were already sipping on their own cupfuls. They thanked me for the invite, then waited for the electricity to return, which it did after a couple of hours.

Though electricity powers the lights that brighten our homes and businesses, the spiritual light we emit in the world is equally important. As children of God, we are called to shine for him in our community, our lives demonstrating who he is and serving as a beacon to all those around us. Light is powerful enough to overcome darkness, but darkness can never overpower light—it is only when light is extinguished that the darkness can take over. In the same way, the love and truth and mercy we display shine brightly in the world, an invitation to neighbors and all those around us that if they need help, it's available.

Kristin

Today's Act of Gratitude

Send a short message of thanks to a friend or mentor whose
faith has been a light to you on your spiritual journey.

Look for the Good

Finally, brothers and sisters, whatever is true, whatever is noble, whatever is right, whatever is pure, whatever is lovely, whatever is admirable— if anything is excellent or praiseworthy—think about such things.

PHILIPPIANS 4:8, NIV

One evening, we were eating dinner on our patio when we heard a commotion. Suddenly a young man on a bike raced across the street, making his way down our alley, a police car with blaring sirens close behind.

Before we had time to absorb what was happening, several more police cars pulled up on our street as neighbors made their way out of their houses to see the commotion.

The young man on the bike was now lying in the middle of our street, being arrested for a fight and stolen property a few blocks away, as we found out later. Our neighbors gathered, talking with one another and the police as we watched the young man walk with an officer to a police car. Soon, everyone slowly began to leave the scene.

As I turned toward our house, I looked at my kids, who were wide-eyed and scared. My husband and I hugged them as we walked back to our abandoned dinner.

"That was scary, wasn't it?" I affirmed before any of them spoke. They nodded.

"Yes," I responded. "But did you notice all of our neighbors who came outside? If you ever had an emergency, any one of them would be there to help you. Ernie. Claire. Doug and Heather. They'd all come to assist you. Look for the good, kids; it's always there." Their expressions showed the shift in their thoughts as they pondered what I'd said.

It is so easy to focus on the negative things in life, but Scripture encourages us to look for what is true, noble, right, pure, and lovely. And when we do, we will find it. Does this mean we don't face the more complicated things in life? Not at all. It simply means that we see things for what they are while also looking for the good that is available to us. Don't get overwhelmed by the harder things; there is always good to be found too.

Kendra

Today's Act of Gratitude

In what ways can you focus on what is true, right, or lovely, even if you are currently facing something hard?

Breath in Our Lungs

Thus says the Lord GOD to these bones:
Behold, I will cause breath to enter you, and you shall live.

EZEKIEL 37:5, ESV

As someone who lives in a state with more than ten thousand lakes, I should be well-versed in all things water. Unfortunately, I'm not the strongest swimmer. I still have to plug my nose when I jump into a lake.

Though I enjoy plunging into cool water on a scorching hot day, it's in those moments of silent stillness when I'm submerged that I truly appreciate air or—more precisely—the lack of it. Because the longer I try to hold my breath under water, the more uncomfortable my body becomes. At that moment, something I usually take for granted becomes the most essential thing in the world, and I'm desperate to recover it. Breaking the water's surface and gulping in oxygen is a sweet relief.

We don't usually need to prompt our bodies to inhale oxygen and exhale carbon dioxide; our lungs function without a conscious reminder. We even describe circumstances as being "as natural as breathing" when they are effortless. Yet most of us can't go very long without a breath unless we've had special training. It's only the absence of air that reminds us how essential it is—not just for our well-being but for our very survival. It's not an understatement to say that we can't live without it.

Yet the air we inhale is also a good reminder of the God we serve. With a word, he breathed life into us. And even though it has become automatic, our bodies have never forgotten it. Many people look for miracles or wonders to remind them that God exists, yet refuse to notice the everyday miracle of our breath. You and I are miracles—walking around, living, and breathing—a symphony our body executes effortlessly.

Let's use our breath to praise God. Let's thank him for every inhale and exhale, every time our lungs fill. He alone gave us life and breath, and they are a remarkable reminder of our Creator.

Kristin

Today's Act of Gratitude

Take five deep breaths, thanking God on every exhale.

Unshackled

You say, "I am allowed to do anything"—but not everything is good for you. And even though "I am allowed to do anything," I must not become a slave to anything.

1 CORINTHIANS 6:12

"Hey Lovie, how was your day?"

From a hotel balcony in Albania, I quietly chatted with my daughter back home about ordinary moments in her school day before she turned the phone over to her brother so I could start the process all over again, asking about soccer practice and an English project. Hanging up the phone ten minutes later, I returned downstairs to circulate with my traveling companions and our Albanian hosts, my homesickness eased and my heart reassured that all was well.

Our phones can be a wonderful tool. The ability to stay connected with loved ones far beyond our physical reach is an incredible blessing previous generations could not have fathomed. And social media—so often a frustrating, difficult beast to tame—has reconnected me with cousins I'm lucky to see once a decade, allowing me to keep alive relationships that would otherwise lapse entirely.

But sometimes, too much of a wonderful thing can turn into something insidiously damaging. While today's verse isn't specifically about electronics and our culture's tendency to be distracted to the point of spiritual and physical harm, it's certainly applicable when terms like "addiction" are often used to describe people's relationship with their phones.

If we're honest, this principle applies to far more than technology. Jesus doesn't want you shackled to anything: phones, food, addictive substances, appearance, shopping, gambling, to name a few. He died that we might be free from bondage of any and all kinds. And the enemy of our souls desires to steal that freedom, crippling us physically and emotionally so that we become ineffective in fulfilling God's plans.

I don't know about you, but I periodically need to reexamine my life, looking for shackles—big and small—and bringing them before God, thanking Jesus as he shakes me free once again. He will, and he does, and that gift of freedom is one we need to protect carefully.

Julie

Today's Act of Gratitude

What is trying to steal your freedom in Christ? Use 1 Corinthians 6:12 as a starting point as you bring those shackles to him, seeking an intentional plan toward liberty.

Photo Memories

The thief's purpose is to steal and kill and destroy.
My purpose is to give them a rich and satisfying life.

JOHN 10:10

When my husband and I were first dating, his mom pulled out their family photo album. Starting when she and my father-in-law wed almost fifty years ago and continuing through the next several decades, there are pictures of their family each year—a documentation and testimony to a rich family heritage. As we chuckled over feathered hairstyles and old-fashioned outfits, themed shirts and outdated perms, I smiled as I glimpsed my husband's upbringing long before I knew him.

As we started our own family, I realized that I wanted to create the same tradition for our kids. So, every fall we take family photos and put them in an album. My kids aren't yet full-grown, but we still enjoy pulling out the book and looking at each year. We smile at baby pictures and laugh at outfit choices.

As a parent, I browse through these portraits and am reminded of all the good and hard years. The fall I almost didn't book a photographer because we were walking through a very challenging season with one of our kids. The year my husband and I struggled to keep our relationship going. Not every memory is a good one. But when I look through the album as a whole, I see how God continues to weave the difficult times with the happier ones. And there is so much good to be found when I look for it.

Jesus reminded us that the thief wants to steal, kill, and destroy. Nowhere else do we see this more prevalently than in our closest relationships. But Jesus also promises that his own purpose is to give us a "rich and satisfying life." Not a perfect life. Or an easy life. But a satisfying life. And if we'll take the time to notice, we'll see all the ways he's done that—even through the hard seasons (outdated hairstyles and all).

Kendra

Today's Act of Gratitude

Think of several ways Jesus has made your life rich and satisfying.
Express your thanks to him for the evidence of his purpose in your life.

Prayer Is a Choice

Don't worry about anything; instead, pray about everything. Tell God what you need, and thank him for all he has done. Then you will experience God's peace, which exceeds anything we can understand. His peace will guard your hearts and minds as you live in Christ Jesus.

PHILIPPIANS 4:6-7

Worriedly, I flipped on the television. The news channel showed army tanks rolling across the landscape while a journalist narrated the scene, videos of explosions in the distance flickering on the bottom quarter of the screen. Half a world away, a brewing conflict had erupted overnight. I wept as I listened to the stories of those impacted by the violence, felt an answering ache in my heart as I watched fleeing parents try to remain calm and brave for their children.

What can I possibly do to assist those who are hurting? I wondered. I felt overwhelmed by helplessness. The chaos had uprooted charities from the region, and I had no expertise or influence of my own to provide relief in this situation.

As I sat down for a moment to better absorb what I was watching, my attention was caught by my prayer journal, lying open on the table in front of me. Muting the television, I read again the verses I'd handwritten that morning from Philippians. In them, Paul calls on the church at Philippi not to worry but to pray and thank God for his provision. He reminds them that their choice to trust God by praying specifically and telling him what they need leads to peace. It's this peace, ultimately, that guards us against fear, helping us to live unafraid.

Bowing my head, I prayed for the worries that weighed on my heart. I asked God to move in this ongoing situation to bring peace and healing. As I raised my head again, I thanked God for the gift of his peace. Though the problem wasn't resolved immediately, the burden of concern felt lighter. Even when the world is warring, we can experience an internal calm. He is the source of peace, come what may. Thank you, Jesus, for the peace you offer to us.

Kristin

Today's Act of Gratitude

Spend a few minutes writing down the heaviest burdens on your heart. Spend time in prayer, asking God for his peace.

July

Finding Purpose in Grief

In his kindness God called you to share in his eternal glory by means of Christ Jesus. So after you have suffered a little while, he will restore, support, and strengthen you, and he will place you on a firm foundation.

1 PETER 5:10

It was a cool summer day. We'd been invited to the lake by our friends whose family members, Sue and Rick, owned a small cabin close to town. As soon as we arrived, we were greeted by our friends and the owners.

As our kids put their suits on and ran out to the lake, Rick was waiting, ready to take them out tubing. We spent the next few hours watching the kids laugh and play in the water. Afterward, as we got dinner ready and the kids played yard games, Sue told us how much she enjoyed having us over.

She went on to share about her daughter Ellie who had died in a car accident at just thirteen years of age. My friends and I sat quietly as she talked about the kind of person Ellie was—a joyful girl who loved to dance, and who was kind and compassionate. Her life's motto had been "Be a friend to everyone."

We smiled, holding back tears as Sue went on to explain about their daughter's legacy, an organization called Ellie's Army that each year supports kids in school by creating a buddy system of friendship between older and younger students.

As we left their cabin that day, I was grateful they had shared their inspiring story. Ellie's legacy lives on through her parents and all who knew her, and it was evident from their hospitality and kindness toward us where she got her open-hearted spirit from.

We all experience hard things in life. Spend any amount of time on this earth and we'll know suffering. But Scripture says that afterward, God will restore and strengthen us and put us back on a firm foundation. He won't leave us alone in our trials. With God's help, we can find a purpose, just as Sue and Rick did, in our grief and our pain. And hopefully, our story can be an encouragement to others about the goodness of God, even in the hard times of life.

Kendra

Today's Act of Gratitude

Look for someone in your local community who has experienced tragedy and now works to inspire change in the world. Find a way to partner together.

World of Wonder

O LORD, what a variety of things you have made!
In wisdom you have made them all. The earth is full of your creatures.

PSALM 104:24

"Does anyone want to see a sloth?" the tour guide called from the front of the bus.

"Yes!" The bus full of adults chorused agreement, excited chatter following in its wake.

We had just finished a trip to the Mistico Arenal Hanging Bridges Park in Costa Rica. During the hours we explored the rain forest, we'd seen a small yellow viper curled up on a branch, watched monkeys swing through the trees with babies on their backs, and admired the industrious leafcutter ants as they carried vegetation. We'd walked across bridges that swayed with every movement—feeling like intrepid explorers with each step—spied a hummingbird nest, and even watched a tiny, poisonous frog disappear into the mass of leaves and trees.

But the one thing we hadn't seen was a sloth.

The excitement was palpable as the bus pulled up alongside a couple of vans and a gaggle of people. As a group, we sounded like unruly kids, not middle-aged tourists. One by one, we exited the bus and gathered to watch a sloth painstakingly make its way up a tree.

Looking around, I saw wonder reflected on the faces of those near me and felt joy rise from within.

God's creation is full of wonder, but sometimes it takes a moment that feels extraordinary to jolt us from the mundane nature of our everyday lives. We spy deer along the side of the road, the flash of a cardinal snags our gaze, or the scent of lilacs reaches our nose, and we are reminded of how enchanting and miraculous our world is. Our imaginative God—Creator of all, seen and unseen—gave humans a beautiful gift when he designed the world. Experts say that we have yet to discover all of the creatures on our planet. Yet every plant and animal demonstrates and reflects the creativity of our God; each one is a reason to marvel. He designed them perfectly and purposely.

Let's choose to seek wonder. Let's use it as a reason to rejoice in the miracle of God's creation.

Kristin

Today's Act of Gratitude

Look for something out of the ordinary—or take a closer
look at the birds, flowers, or trees you usually see—
to remind you what it's like to feel wonder.

Cleansed

*If we confess our sins to him, he is faithful and
just to forgive us our sins and to cleanse us from all wickedness.*

1 JOHN 1:9

"We should pull the car into the garage. The weather radar is showing red." Aaron was peering out our southwest-facing sunroom windows at the thunderheads brewing on the horizon as I came down the stairs.

Joining him to peer outside, I realized just how dark the sky had suddenly grown. "I'll do that now. Can you help me move the bikes? Is there anything else we need to get inside?" Grabbing my keys, we headed out the front door to batten down the proverbial hatches in a race against the storm system rolling in on the leading edge of a much-needed cool front.

I love thunderstorms (although not severe ones), especially when they bring relief from baking temperatures and humidity so thick you feel like you are swimming through the air. As the thunder rumbles fade and the rain slowly pitter-patters to an end, I'll step out on the porch to survey the world left fresh and clean in its wake.

The refreshment my senses encounter after a summer storm is tangible: the light breeze with cooler temps raising gooseflesh on my arms, the wafting scent of ozone, the sound of water dripping off tree branches, even the slight twinkle to the earth as the sun reappears, its light refracting off raindrops. Those first moments after a storm are some of my favorites because they subtly remind me of being forgiven and cleansed.

Of all the promises in Scripture, the gift of forgiveness and the assurance of a fresh start when we confess our sins before God is among the most powerful and life changing. We are not stuck with the poor choices we've made. We are not forever defined by our mistakes and miscalculations. There is always a way out and a way back to God. And his willingness to redeem and restore us is far better than any post-storm refreshment we'll ever encounter.

Julie

Today's Act of Gratitude

Before you thank God for his blessings, spend time
confessing your sins. Make it a habit to confess and thank,
including both actions as prayer companions.

Freedom to Serve

You have been called to live in freedom, my brothers and sisters. But don't use your freedom to satisfy your sinful nature. Instead, use your freedom to serve one another in love.

GALATIANS 5:13

"Mom, I can't reach," my youngest daughter said. Looking down, I had a hard time repressing a smile at the sight of her—pint-size, wearing a hairnet and gloves, and looking up at me with a grin.

"No problem," I said, finding a stool for her to step on. I slid it over to the tables and gestured toward it. "Hop up."

Clambering onto the stool, she gave me a thumbs-up to let me know she was ready.

Our family had signed up to work a shift at Feed My Starving Children, an organization that provides food for those in need.

As I scooped grains and sealed bags over the next couple of hours, I couldn't help but be thankful for the day's work. Though I enjoy volunteering and helping others, the truth is that I benefit just as much as the person receiving the assistance. Nothing gets me out of a funk quicker than serving someone else. Whether it's cooking a meal at a local homeless shelter, scooping grains that will be packaged and distributed to those facing hunger, or picking out school supplies for local kids who can't afford them, serving others is the best way to overcome our selfish tendencies.

Of course, we don't serve God or others in order to earn our salvation—that is a gift, freely given. No, our desire to serve should arise from our response to our salvation. Gratitude—not guilt—is our motivation. Even Paul recognized this idea, writing to the church at Thessalonica, "We think of your faithful work, your loving deeds, and the enduring hope you have because of our Lord Jesus Christ" (1 Thessalonians 1:3). We have freedom in Christ—to laugh, to sing, to praise him—and to serve. And when we do, our service glorifies God and celebrates the freedom we have in him.

Kristin

Today's Act of Gratitude

Find a way to serve someone.

Extravagant Complimenting

Don't use foul or abusive language. Let everything you say be good and helpful, so that your words will be an encouragement to those who hear them.

EPHESIANS 4:29

A few years ago, Julie and I were traveling together to speak at a women's conference. As we made our way through the airport, she suddenly stopped.

"That dress looks so lovely on you," she said to a woman who was sitting on a bench, waiting for her flight.

The woman blinked as she made eye contact with Julie.

"Thanks," she responded. "I just got it. I wasn't sure that I'd like it."

"Well, it looks really nice," Julie said. The woman smiled, and we continued on our way.

As we reached our gate and sat down to wait, Julie again leaned over to a woman sitting across from us.

"Those shoes are so cute," she whispered.

The woman smiled as she told Julie the brand and how she'd gotten them on sale.

Afterward, I gave Julie a confused look.

"What is going on?" I asked.

She sighed. "The world is hard enough the way it is, and I've just decided that when I see something that looks nice or that I like about a woman, I'm going to tell her. Even if she's a stranger," she responded.

Since then, Julie's habit of what she calls "extravagant complimenting" has rubbed off onto me. I now find myself giving compliments to complete strangers as I go through my days. And I am most often met with smiles and thank-yous from those who receive them.

Being critical, cutting, or cynical is a common practice in our day, but Scripture tells us that as Christians, we aren't to "use foul or abusive language." Everything we speak should be beneficial, encouraging all who hear our words. Sincerely complimenting others is one way that we can uplift those we know and even strangers we may never see again. We'll never know the blessing we may be to someone who really needs it if we start practicing extravagant complimenting.

Kendra

Today's Act of Gratitude

Look for people you can genuinely compliment.

Wisdom and Discernment

If you need wisdom, ask our generous God, and he will give it to you. He will not rebuke you for asking. But when you ask him, be sure that your faith is in God alone. Do not waver.

JAMES 1:5-6

"Um, I'm going to grab a portable ultrasound machine. I'll be right back."

With that departing statement, Amy, my nurse, bustled out of my hospital room. In the midst of labor with my first baby, and with drugs already pumping through my system, I didn't fully comprehend the seriousness of her statement until she'd come back, scanned my pregnant belly, and immediately disappeared again.

Her concern was due to the fact that my baby was breech, and within a few minutes I was headed into an emergency cesarean section. I've often thanked God for Amy. She caught what several others had missed, and her intuition and quick action protected both Lizzie and me.

Amy isn't alone in her quiet heroism. As I've walked alongside loved ones through a variety of medical challenges, I've often thanked God for women and men who have noticed and reacted in ways that protect, heal, and support people important to me. And while I don't know whether Amy or others started their shifts with a prayer for God's wisdom and discernment, I pray for it over the nurses, doctors, and everyone involved whenever loved ones find themselves navigating a medical journey.

But I don't stop there. I pray for divine wisdom over my husband in his workplace and over my children and the friendships they are navigating. And I pray that I have the Holy Spirit's discerning wisdom as I step into my college classroom—that I would strike the perfect balance between mercy and accountability as I encounter student situations.

Since God offers wisdom freely and without rebuke, I want it! If I can walk through my days with the Holy Spirit's wisdom as a filter overlaying every interaction and decision, then I'm leaving a powerful spiritual tool unused when I live on my own terms and on my own inadequate knowledge. God sees the whole picture, including situations where emotion colors my perception, and I am determined to trust his lead, asking him to guide me and others, that we might avoid pitfalls and missteps and wrong turns.

Julie

Today's Act of Gratitude

Start praying for God's wisdom as you brush your teeth each morning. Make this prayer a tooth-brushing double habit.

Living Water

The LORD will send rain at the proper time from his
rich treasury in the heavens and will bless all the work you do.

DEUTERONOMY 28:12

Looking up, I blinked my eyes as raindrops landed on my face. It was summer break, and my twelve-year-old best friend and I had decided to play in the rain. Even though I usually avoided getting caught in the weather, I enjoyed dancing and jumping around with abandon. The warm shower felt cleansing. Afterward, we came inside, soaked and muddy-footed, breathless with laughter and the sheer exuberance of being alive.

Since that long-ago afternoon, I've visited places where rain is bountiful—like the months I lived in England, where an umbrella was my constant companion—and I've visited dry places—like South Point on Kona, the southernmost point of the United States, where the land is cracked, the vegetation parched. Though we may sometimes overlook the importance of precipitation, it is essential for survival. Water is a necessary part of life; rain is integral to that. It fills aquifers, which in turn keep rivers and lakes filled. When it pours over the land that surrounds us, it not only contributes to what we need for household use but brings life to farmers' crops and helps sustain the plants and animals in our environment.

Just as rain is needed to bring about new life and sustain every living thing that depends on fresh water, the living water Jesus provided is necessary for us to experience a rich and satisfying life. In his wisdom, God gave us physical water by sending rain from the heavens. But the spiritual water we receive is equally essential. Just as the ground needs rain, we need the living water of Jesus to bring vitality to our parched souls and provide purpose each day.

Kristin

Today's Act of Gratitude

The next time it rains, spend a minute listening to its patter and thanking God for its presence. Then, pray and thank God for the living water available to us through Jesus.

Welcome the Stranger

You shall treat the stranger who sojourns with you as the native among you, and you shall love him as yourself, for you were strangers in the land of Egypt: I am the LORD your God.

LEVITICUS 19:34, ESV

The first summer we moved to our new house across town, my husband decided he wanted to take down the large privacy fence. One morning as he worked outside, I noticed he had stopped to talk to some of our neighbors who lived across the alleyway from us.

Later that day, he came inside to tell me about his conversation and let me know that he had invited the young men for dinner that week.

"What?" I asked nervously. "They looked young. Are you sure they'd want to hang out with us?"

My husband nodded. "Yes, they're college students from Saudi Arabia. They said they'd love to come over."

"Okay," I answered, still unsure, thinking about our spunky kids and how dinnertime can sometimes be a mess.

A few days later, they showed up, dessert in hand. As we sat around our table, passing dishes of grilled chicken, rice, and salad, they told us about their families back home, explained how they had come to school in the United States, and laughed at the silly antics of our kids. As we said goodbye, we promised to get together again soon.

I couldn't have known at the time what a gift the next few years would be with these young men—we hosted several game nights, bonfires, dinners, and fish fries. They got to know our friends and their families, watching soccer matches and visiting local restaurants together.

I didn't understand how much these young men missed their families back home or how being with us reminded them of their own parents and siblings. They became so dear to us and, even now, we remain close.

Sometimes it's hard to know how to invite people who are different from us, but the Bible tells us that we are to welcome the strangers who sojourn with us, loving them as we do ourselves and our own family. I'm thankful for the richness found in including others who have different backgrounds from ours. We can learn from the experience and grow as people. Don't miss the goodness of God we can glean from inviting others into our lives and homes.

Kendra

Today's Act of Gratitude

Invite someone who comes from a different
background to coffee or dinner.

Missing Ladder Rungs

*Since God chose you to be the holy people he loves,
you must clothe yourselves with tenderhearted mercy,
kindness, humility, gentleness, and patience.*

COLOSSIANS 3:12

"What do you mean the swim ladder is gone?" I paused from scooping a spoonful of pasta salad onto my plate to look at my husband.

"The swim ladder attached to the back of Boaty McBoatface has rungs that fold down so people can climb into the boat from the water. Those rungs are missing." Contemplating this new information, we both looked toward where Boaty (our circa 1993 Larson ski boat) was bobbing cheerily at the end of the dock.

"When a few people told me how hard it was to get into the boat after tubing, I teased them that they just weren't doing it right . . ." Aaron trailed off thoughtfully as he reached for a plate and began to follow me down the line of potluck goodness.

We were at a small private lake with friends and friends of friends—many of whom hailed from parts of the world where they didn't grow up with tubing and water skiing. We'd spent the day pulling them around the lake on whatever they wanted to try. It had been great fun, even with the missing ladder, Aaron's explanation and apology, and our laughter over people having to be bodily pulled into the boat.

During the long drive home, the missing ladder rungs circled in my thoughts. How often have I insisted (even if only to myself) that something was easy when, in actuality, it was near impossible for someone else? How often have I been unaware of crucial information? How often have I assumed there was a "ladder" when there wasn't, using that wrong assumption to springboard into judgments about inability, laziness, or ineptness?

Today's verse is countercultural in its call toward mercy, kindness, humility, gentleness, and patience. Those traits require intentionality and effort as we set aside our default tendencies and reconsider what might be tripping up someone else instead of assuming they, themselves, are the problem.

Gentle conviction in this area is a blessing as I strive to see others as God sees them. And those missing ladder rungs have become a poignant visual reminder not to make assumptions.

Julie

Today's Act of Gratitude

How might you be making unfair assumptions? Prayerfully ask
God to see people and situations through his eyes, thanking him
for revealing where you've fallen a bit short of Colossians 3:12.

You Get to Do This

Let the message about Christ, in all its richness, fill your lives. Teach and counsel each other with all the wisdom he gives. Sing psalms and hymns and spiritual songs to God with thankful hearts. And whatever you do or say, do it as a representative of the Lord Jesus, giving thanks through him to God the Father.

COLOSSIANS 3:16-17

I get to do this.

Scrolling through social media, I paused when I saw my friend Samara's post. The words were written in chalk, with "get" underlined for emphasis.

"This will be my summer mantra," she wrote in the caption, explaining that summer necessitates a constant juggling between her career and her kids' activities. "It's easy to spiral into overwhelm, but I also feel so lucky that I GET to do this. I don't HAVE to do this; I GET to."

I appreciated her words. Because all too often, it's easy to lament our busy schedule and daily tasks. We see them as obligations rather than opportunities. But when we reconsider through the lens of *getting* to do them rather than *having* to do them, our perspective shifts.

I don't *have* to work just to provide for life's needs; I *get* to work at a challenging and fulfilling job.

I don't *have* to cook dinner for my family; I *get* to be thankful I have loved ones with whom I can share a meal.

I don't *have* to doodle on the sidewalk with chalk next to my seven-year-old; I *get* to enjoy this all-too-brief age.

I don't *have* to spend time in God's Word; I *get* to learn from him and soak up the peace only he can offer.

The Bible reminds us that we need to let the message of Christ permeate every part of our lives, remembering that we should always seek to reflect his love. As followers of Jesus—wholly and deeply loved—his example is our starting point. During Jesus' earthly ministry, he didn't grouse about walking dusty roads with his disciples, teaching his many followers day after day, or healing those in need. Instead, he was ever conscious of the good news of God's love.

We, too, can be ambassadors who demonstrate God's love. And our to-do lists are simply opportunities to praise him.

Kristin

Today's Act of Gratitude

Write a list of five tasks you have to accomplish. Read the list aloud, telling yourself that you *get* to do them.

Better Together

Two people are better off than one,
for they can help each other succeed.

ECCLESIASTES 4:9

For years my husband worked mostly alone, building his business. A couple of years back, he came to me, upset. It had become too much for him to do on his own. That summer, I started helping in the office as much as I could, and he began to share more and more of his daily activities with me.

Then this past year, I took over ownership from his partner, and together Kyle and I decided to bring several other people in to work with us. Every Monday morning, we have a meeting where everyone shares what they're doing that week, tasks they need help with, wins they've had, or questions that need to be answered. It creates excitement and momentum as we go into our week. It has renewed my husband's spirit and love for what he is doing.

"I didn't realize how lonely this was for you all those years," I said not long ago after one of our meetings.

"I didn't either," Kyle responded. "I'm so glad to be working with others."

As we listened to the conversations and laughter of our staff, all working toward the same goal, we smiled at each other, feeling grateful and encouraged just to know there were others all reaching for the same goals.

We're often praised in our culture for our individual accomplishments. Meeting goals and completing tasks independently of others is often seen as a strength. But God has a different idea in mind when it comes to humanity—and that is to see us work together. To build community. To create and support and lean on each other when we need it. Two are better than one because not only can we help each other succeed but we can shoulder together the work to be done. No one should go through life alone, not the whole of it, anyway. We are definitely better together.

Kendra

Today's Act of Gratitude

Is there an area of your life you've been trying to handle all by yourself? Choose someone you could reach out to and ask for help.

Encountering Vibrancy

*He made heaven and earth, the sea, and everything
in them. He keeps every promise forever.*

PSALM 146:6

"Mom, there is a bird whose song goes like this: co-OOO-oo co-OOO-oo." Jon stomped his feet on the front door rug, then bent to take off his shoes. "It's my favorite birdsong. I wish I knew what kind of bird it is."

"That's a mourning dove, buddy," I responded from where I sat folding clothes. "And I agree, they have one of the prettiest songs."

One of my favorite parts of summer is the birdsong soundtrack to my outdoor life. My dad taught me to identify several bird species by sight as well as solely by their songs, which means the recognizable trills and tweets of robins, cardinals, nuthatches, chickadees, and—of course—mourning doves accompany me on walks, in my garden, and even as I dash from house to car, late for a meeting or errand. And my ability to identify a variety of local rocks and plants means that a walk with me results in frequent starts and stops as I pause to examine flora and fauna. While my walking companion may (or may not) enjoy my meandering, having a rudimentary knowledge of the rocks, plants, and birds around me brings me immense joy.

One of the ways I feel close to God is through encountering his creation. And there is something—for me at least—that brings a vibrancy and a richness to that experience when I can identify small, beautiful details that otherwise tend to fade into the background unnoticed—like birdsong. This desire to find vibrancy fed my interest in identifying planets visible to the naked eye and constellations in the Northern Hemisphere, and it fuels my search for agates, rocks I've been hunting and collecting into an ever-growing stash since childhood.

The vibrancy of God's creation reminds me of his authority over the heavens, the earth, and every tiny detail in between. If he holds the stars in the palm of his hand and yet also cares for the lilies of the field, I can entrust myself and my beloved ones to his all-encompassing sovereignty. That ongoing, constant reminder swells my heart with thanksgiving.

Julie

Today's Act of Gratitude

Consider the details you love to notice as an ongoing
recognition of God's authority over the heavens and earth.

Unexpected Paths

Show me the right path, O LORD;
point out the road for me to follow.

PSALM 25:4

"I don't think we're going the right way," my husband said from the driver's seat as he carefully negotiated the narrow mountain roads.

Checking the navigation app on my phone, I sighed. "I'm sorry, I have terrible service here. I don't know either."

Though we had planned on a picturesque drive through the Colorado mountainside, we'd taken a wrong turn. Worried about getting lost, we decided to go back the way we came.

As we brainstormed alternative destinations, my mother-in-law threw out an idea. "How about the Ski Tip Lodge? It's one of my favorite places."

We quickly agreed and arrived in Keystone a short time later. As we strolled down the path toward the lodge's rounded front door, we were immediately charmed by the lush flowers and a glistening pond that reflected the mountains. It looked like something out of a storybook. My mother-in-law poked her head inside and asked if they would mind us looking around. Luckily, the front desk employee agreed to give us a tour since it was a quiet morning. As we walked through narrow hallways and admired well-appointed rooms, we learned that although it's now a B and B with an excellent restaurant, it was once an 1800s stagecoach stop and later a private residence. Unexpectedly, the lodge had a reservation available the following evening, which we gladly signed up for.

The next night, as we enjoyed dinner together and marveled at the majestic mountains and cool evening breeze, I couldn't help but be grateful for the wrong turn that had led us there. That evening was the highlight of our trip.

The Bible talks a lot about following the Lord's path. And though our little detour didn't have long-term consequences, the truth is, sometimes life mirrors the confusion of that day. Sometimes we question whether we're going the right way or should turn around.

We aren't sure where to go next. Yet it's not the *path* we should trust—or our navigational skills—but instead, the God whose lead we are following. Even when we lose our way, we can turn to him. He is worthy of our trust.

Sometimes, those wrong turns and detours may even lead to unexpected beauty. Let's trust in the Lord to help us navigate the way forward.

Kristin

Today's Act of Gratitude

Reflect on a time when you felt like you had lost your way.
How did God's faithful presence help you move forward?

Praise through Poetry

Let everything that breathes sing praises to the LORD!
Praise the LORD!

PSALM 150:6

As the sun rises
Thankful a new day is here
Birds burst into song.

Setting down my pen, I sat back and rubbed my eyes. Rereading my haiku (a poem consisting of only three lines, the first with five syllables, the next with seven, and the third with five), I contemplated my morning's attempt at praising God via poetry. While I won't be winning any awards, the exercise of following the precise rhythm required by this format, and of letting my creative juices flow for a few moments before a busy day intruded upon silence, was just what I needed.

Heavenly Father, thank you for warmer days, this beautiful sunrise, and the bird-song filling my sunroom this morning. Please accept my bad poetry written with an adoring heart as worship pleasing to your ears.

And with that whispered prayer, I set aside my prayer journal and pen and stood up, ready to refill my coffee and wake my slumbering family.

When I take time to remember God as the creator of the universe with every living creature called to worship him, I regain perspective over the inconveniences and challenges. I am reminded to whom I belong and to what I am called, shaking off the temptation to be distracted by things that ultimately don't matter. Being creative as an act of praise to the Master Creator can be a form of worship, drawing us into intimacy with God as we busy our hands and focus our minds. It provides another avenue for those of us who are not particularly musical to spend time in God's presence, without worrying about how we sound or who can hear us.

The beautiful thing is that no one besides Jesus needs to read our bad poetry. If we choose, it can be silent worship, vulnerable and raw, as we sit alone before God. He does not care if we haven't written poetry since seventh-grade English class. And he doesn't care how beautifully we string together our words. He cares about our heart's condition, the sincerity of our effort, and the time spent sitting in his presence, focused on his majesty and goodness.

Julie

Today's Act of Gratitude

Write God a haiku of praise and thankfulness.

Put on the Shorts

Kind words are like honey—
sweet to the soul and healthy for the body.

PROVERBS 16:24

"What do you think?" I asked as I sent a picture of myself to my sister. I waited in the dressing room for her response.

"Cute!" she replied.

"Thank you! I never buy shorts, but I'm trying to get over it," I said.

"Why not? You have cute legs!" she said. "You should totally wear shorts. I don't even like my legs, and I refuse to wear capris anymore. I'm wearing what's comfortable."

I reflected on her statement as I stared in the mirror. *Why haven't I ever worn shorts?* I wondered as I changed back into my clothes. *I'm starting today,* I told myself as I took the pair of shorts up to the cash register.

Driving home, I continued pondering why I never wear shorts and where the idea came from that I couldn't or shouldn't. I realized that I had started telling myself as an insecure teenager that they didn't look good on me, and I had never challenged that belief. Now, as a forty-something-year-old, I realize how faulty (and damaging) those thoughts were to me then and still are even now.

When I got home, I put the shorts on, looked in the mirror, and—because I'm determined to change how I think and feel about my body—I told myself, *You have nice legs. They look good in shorts.*

We can all have negative perceptions or beliefs we hold for years without even realizing it. It takes intention to notice and then replace ideas that may not have been true or healthy in the first place. But to do this, we must become aware of how we talk to ourselves.

Do we build ourselves up or tear ourselves down with critical self-talk? If the latter we must take a different approach. I'm grateful for my sister's wise words, as well as for the reminder in Scripture that "kind words are like honey—sweet to the soul and healthy for the body." If we want to care for ourselves—mind, body, and soul—we must consider what we say.

Kendra

Today's Act of Gratitude

Pay attention to how you talk to yourself. What faulty thoughts or beliefs need to change? Once you realize what they are, decide how you will speak to yourself more kindly. Thank God for the amazing work he did in creating you.

Letting Her Go

*We know that our old sinful selves were crucified with Christ so that
sin might lose its power in our lives. We are no longer slaves to sin.
For when we died with Christ we were set free from the power of sin.*

ROMANS 6:6-7

"I'd like to take a moment to introduce my new law clerk, Julie Brotzler." Judge Hoolihan made the announcement from the bench to a courtroom of attorneys, deputies, a court reporter, and other court staff. It was my first official day of my first official legal job, and we were momentarily in between court hearings, waiting on parties to finish a last-minute negotiation.

"Um. Judge? She's now Julie Fisk. She got married last weekend." The court reporter's friendly, matter-of-fact correction had me melting into my chair with embarrassed relief, grateful she'd spoken up. But I was also feeling the extra weight of a roomful of eyeballs considering Judge Hoolihan's newest law clerk and her new name.

It wasn't until that slightly mortifying moment that I realized my wedding and subsequent name change meant that Julie Brotzler had done all the work of becoming an attorney—including taking the bar exam—but it was Julie Fisk who would be the licensed attorney. And while I have never regretted changing my name, there was a small part of me that weirdly mourned the timing of my name change, sad that Julie Brotzler had put in all that effort but would never practice.

Years later I realized that my reluctance to let my former identity go in that one particular context sometimes plays out spiritually as well. When we profess our faith in Christ, committing to follow him, we are set free from the sin that ensnared our pre-Jesus life. And yet we sometimes trip back into our old patterns, tricked into thinking sin still has us tangled up, believing the lie that we can't get out.

That's not what God intended when his beloved Son died on the cross. Our new identity is an undeserved gift, freely given, and we must gratefully abide in the truth that sin no longer holds us hostage rather than wallow in old ways.

Julie

Today's Act of Gratitude

If you haven't yet accepted Jesus' gift, it's never too late.
And if you find yourself wallowing in that past self, let her
go, thanking God for the precious gift of a new identity.

You're Not Alone

*The light shines in the darkness, and
the darkness can never extinguish it.*

JOHN 1:5

"You should come," Abbi said as we talked about an upcoming event where she would be sharing about her battle with an eating disorder.

"I would love to," I responded. "I know someone else who struggles with an eating disorder and has been trying to get into treatment. Would you mind if I brought her too?"

"Of course not!" Abbi responded.

Two weeks later, I found myself, along with my daughter and the young woman I'd invited, at the small venue where Abbi would be sharing her story publicly for the first time.

As we sat down to listen, I suddenly felt nervous. I wanted so much for my guest to connect with what Abbi had to say. I knew their struggles were similar, and my prayer was that her words would be an encouragement. My concern dissipated as soon as Abbi began to speak.

She was honest and kind, vulnerable and loving. She shared from her heart everything that she had gone through, and as I listened, my throat tightened with emotion. She commented that all of us could find bits of ourselves in her story, and she was right—we've all experienced some unhealthiness in the way that we view our bodies, food, or just caring for ourselves.

I smiled as she finished by offering encouragement to anyone in the room battling an eating disorder as she did, inviting them to connect with her.

"You don't have to go through it alone," she finished.

As we hugged her goodbye, thanking her for the wonderful evening, I couldn't help but think about how often the enemy tries to separate us from the love and support of others. Alone in our thoughts, we can grapple with issues that no one else knows. But thankfully, when we bring them to light, the darkness will not overcome us. Sharing honestly about our struggles and allowing others to walk alongside us is one way that we find strength and bring light to any battle we are facing. It's a lie to believe that you have to go through difficulty by yourself in the dark. You're not meant to be alone.

Kendra

Today's Act of Gratitude

Bring light to something you've been trying to manage on your own by sharing your struggle with a trusted family member or friend. Thank God for providing this person for you to talk to.

Living in Vacation Mode

O people, the LORD has told you what is good, and this is what he requires of you: to do what is right, to love mercy, and to walk humbly with your God.

MICAH 6:8

"People on vacation are different. I've had more pleasant interactions with random strangers than I've had in a long time." I sighed while snuggled beneath the covers in my hotel room, holding my phone sideways as I chatted with Aaron for a few moments before bed.

"It's because they are in vacation mode."

I paused for a long moment, considering Aaron's observation.

"Well then, we should live more often as though we are on vacation." And with that thought lingering, we signed off for the night.

I was in Lake Country on business—an area filled with resorts and touristy towns nestled between the woods and lakes of northern Minnesota. It wasn't until the third time a stranger held the door for me with a cheery smile and a friendly comment that I first noticed the vacation mode atmosphere.

While most of us cannot literally live on vacation 24-7, why can't we practice the attitude of vacation mode as we go about our ordinary days? It takes no money and almost no time to smile warmly for strangers as we hold the door or to bestow the gift of patient grace for parents with young children (or slightly surly teenagers) as they navigate parenting in public. And extending mercy to those who inadvertently annoy us is often a matter of our internal heart condition, but it is made clear in our facial expressions and verbal responses.

For as easy as these small acts are, when done consistently, they completely change the atmosphere and the experience for all around, and they become contagious—encouraging others to adopt the same grace, mercy, and warmheartedness in their own interactions.

Awakening the next morning, I thanked God for the gentle reminder that walking through day-to-day life with an intentional attitude of humility, mercy, and seeking to do right by one another is incredibly powerful. We impact the atmosphere of the places we go—for good or bad—by how we engage with others.

Julie

Today's Act of Gratitude

How will you wield the power of your words and attitude?

Why Friendships Matter

*They devoted themselves to the apostles' teaching and
the fellowship, to the breaking of bread and the prayers.*

ACTS 2:42, ESV

Though our family usually makes a summer bucket list and fills it with experiences and adventures, in the wake of months of isolation, we were hungry for deepened relationships.

So we decided to do something new. We prioritized inviting others into our home and dubbed it the "Summer of Friends." We included old friends and new acquaintances, families and couples. We hosted neighbors for bonfires and friends for dinner. We went to fewer places but saw more people, and it was glorious.

As we gathered around tables and campfires, living rooms and porches, I realized how much I'd missed those moments of connection. How much they mattered.

There's a fascinating study in which participants were asked to climb a hill. The ones who climbed it alone judged it to be steeper than those who were accompanied by a friend. Interestingly, the longer a pair had been friends, the less severe the incline appeared.[*] In the same way, when we have friends who support us and walk through the highs and lows of life alongside us, the obstacles we face feel more manageable.

We're not meant to walk through this life alone. In the book of Acts, the author details how the early church prioritized gathering together. As a result of their generosity toward one another and the way they met together consistently, the church grew. Although our twenty-first-century society doesn't quite resemble our first-century counterparts, the value of community is unchanging. When we gather together, we're more likely to focus on others than ourselves. Our problems will seem smaller, and our ability to handle challenges will seem easier to manage. Rather than stewing in worry, we'll grow in grace and contentment.

Let's celebrate the joy of being in community with one another. When we do, we'll see friendship with others as a precious gift to cultivate—an essential part of life—rather than one more item to check off our to-do list.

Kristin

Today's Act of Gratitude

Make time for a friend in your schedule.

---

[*] Simone Schnall et al., "Social Support and the Perception of Geographical Slant," *Journal of Experimental Social Psychology* 44, no. 5 (2008): 1246-1255, doi:10.1016/j.jesp.2008.04.011.

Following His Lead

My sheep listen to my voice;
I know them, and they follow me.

JOHN 10:27

It was a hot afternoon. I was driving home to pick up one of my kids for an appointment. As I made my way down the busy street and stopped at a red light, I noticed a man standing on the corner.

I felt a small nudge to stop and offer him something from my car. But I was two lanes over, and traffic was heavy. I argued with myself all the way home about turning around but finally called my husband and asked him to look for the man on his way home from work.

A few hours later, he told me the man was already gone by the time he passed the corner. Disappointed, I asked God to give me another opportunity.

Later that week, I bought water bottles, determined not to pass up another nudging from the Holy Spirit to offer assistance to someone. I explained to my kids, who were watching my actions, that I had missed being obedient to God's voice earlier but didn't want to miss it again.

I read them Galatians 6:3, which says, "If you think you are too important to help someone, you are only fooling yourself. You are not that important." Ouch. That stung a little bit. But as we put the water bottles and snacks in our vehicle and began driving around town as part of our everyday routine, my kids joined me in noticing people asking for assistance on the side of the road. And each time, we would stop and offer a warm greeting and a cold drink.

I may have missed God's nudging the first time, but I was determined not to do it again.

All of us will fail from time to time at hearing and being obedient to the prompting of the Holy Spirit. But thankfully, God's grace is limitless, and his mercy knows no bounds, so we don't have to feel shame when we realize our error; we can ask forgiveness and move on, course correcting and taking the appropriate action steps.

Jesus said that his followers listen to his voice and follow him—and this includes not just what we say or believe but the actions we take in obedience to his prompting.

Kendra

Today's Act of Gratitude

Be obedient to a nudge from God. Thank him
that he prompts you in this way.

His Unfailing Love

*Your unfailing love is better than life itself;
how I praise you!*

PSALM 63:3

I was angry at God. I'd fallen for the tantalizing lie Christians sometimes believe—that bad things won't happen to us if we serve God well. Or, if something bad happens, we will eventually be healed or triumph over the challenge.

But when my sister Katrina died after a five-year battle with breast cancer, I felt confused and ashamed. I asked myself, *Didn't we pray enough? Was our faith not enough?* I had trusted in God's mercy, his justice. What could seem more unjust than a sister dying at twenty-eight? How could the loss of a wife, mother, sister, daughter, and friend possibly "work together for the good of those who love God" (Romans 8:28)? Though I've heard countless times that we'll have trouble in this world, it still feels counterintuitive. Shouldn't our goodness be rewarded?

The truth is that earthly healing doesn't always happen. And instead of the grand testimony we envision ourselves telling about a miraculous outcome, we are often left with a quieter story of God's faithfulness in helping us pick up the pieces afterward.

Looking back, I'm grateful for Jesus' gentle comfort and love in the wake of Katrina's death. Even in my darkest moments, I was never abandoned. Instead, I felt cushioned by his comfort and buoyed by his love through the shock and grief of loss. As my family clung to one another, God's love felt near, tangible, and present—more so than at any other time in my life.

David, the psalmist, writes about praising God for his unfailing love. What's remarkable is that David was someone who understood pain, sorrow, and the danger of this world—after all, he was hunted by King Saul and lived in the wilderness—and yet he remained willing to give up his life for God's favor. How valuable God's love is to us! Though it's worth more than any treasure we could possess, it's free and constantly available.

In our darkest times, his love is unfailing. And sometimes, that's the best testimony we can offer to others—the hope and the knowledge that he will not forget us; we are not alone; we are loved.

Kristin

Today's Act of Gratitude

Think of a difficult time in your life. Consider that God was near to you, even then, and thank him for his presence.

Friendship Bucket Lists

*The heartfelt counsel of a friend is
as sweet as perfume and incense.*

PROVERBS 27:9

What on earth did you agree to? My inner voice quivered a bit as the chestnut mare shifted impatiently under my weight for the fourth time. *You don't know how to ride a horse, so why are you sitting on one?!* I quelled inner Julie as my horse—Casey—and I eyeballed one last rider swinging into a saddle. Then our guide cheerily called, "Everyone ready? Great! Let's head out."

Casey lurched into the slowly rolling gait of a horse accustomed to taking strangers on hour-long trail rides and fell into position somewhere toward the head of the line. I clung with nervous tension to the reins and the saddle horn, and it took several minutes of gentle motion before I relaxed and began taking in our surroundings: the gently sloping hills, the verdant patches of forest, and the glint of a small lake reflecting the afternoon sun.

Glancing backward, I grinned at Maha and Kendra on their own horses as they, too, lurched and swayed along the dirt path. We were here because horseback riding was on Maha's bucket list, and after facing down my initial reticence, I was beginning to enjoy the adventure. As we tumbled into my car after returning to the stable, we were dusty but happy, and our conversation on the ride home was lighthearted, introspective, and everything in between.

Checking items off my friends' bucket lists wasn't something I'd considered prior to our horsey adventure, but it's become a favorite way to show my love, support, and appreciation for those someones dear to me. The laughter over newly created shared memories, the opportunity to know friends in a new way or under new circumstances, and the heartfelt conversations along the journey add depth and breadth to our relationships. It's a marvelous way to express how much we appreciate their presence in our life.

Julie

Today's Act of Gratitude

Ask a friend or friends to exchange their adventure
bucket list with you. Look for opportunities to cross
items off one or both of your lists together.

Never Too Late

Always be humble and gentle. Be patient with each other, making allowance for each other's faults because of your love. Make every effort to keep yourselves united in the Spirit, binding yourselves together with peace.

EPHESIANS 4:2-3

"I wish you had told me sooner," I said as tears filled my eyes. "I would have done something."

My friend sighed. "I didn't want to complain."

"No one would think of you as a complainer," I said as she went on with explaining her child's sudden exit from an activity our kids had done together for years. We cried as she told me of the bullying and challenges they'd faced all year. Unbeknownst to me. I listened and offered as much support as I could, letting her know that I loved her and that, after hearing about the situation, I knew she was doing the right thing.

As I hung up the phone, my heart ached. I looked at my husband and began to cry once more. "Why didn't she tell me what was going on?" I asked.

My husband just shook his head. "Sometimes people keep things to themselves; they don't want to risk being vulnerable, or they worry how other people will respond," he offered.

"Yeah," I replied. "It just hurts."

As the day went on, I continued to think about my friend and our conversation. I felt so sad and, if I'm honest, guilty for not being the kind of friend she felt she could trust.

But as I continued to pray for her, I gratefully realized that our dialogue, although painful, was also honest and loving. We came together, cried with each other, and finished, still friends, with both of us feeling seen and heard.

The goal of friendship is not simply to always get along but to be able to share honestly, even when it's difficult. But to do this we must remain humble and gentle. We must be willing to listen and be patient—even making room for people's faults because of our love for one another. We are to do all we can to keep ourselves united, even if it means having difficult conversations, binding it all together with peace and love. It's a lofty goal, but with God's help, one we can attain.

Kendra

Today's Act of Gratitude

Have you been avoiding a difficult conversation with someone? Spend some time praying for God to give you wisdom, and then reach out to the person.

Relaxing into Rest

It is in vain that you rise up early and go late to rest, eating the bread of anxious toil; for he gives to his beloved sleep.

PSALM 127:2, ESV

Although I ride a stationary bike several days a week in my home, I hadn't seen the inside of a gym in more than a decade. Over time, my muscles have weakened. To make up for this, I recently started working with a personal trainer to develop a strength training routine.

One day, after the workout, I asked her how to stretch my chronically tense neck muscles. Together, we spent the next several minutes working through her demonstrated technique. As I focused on the slow stretch of my muscles and the inhale and exhale of my breath, I felt calmer, more at peace.

Although I could initially stretch a muscle to a certain point, it wasn't until I waited long enough for it to fully relax that I could sink into a better stretch. Waiting for that release took time and patience.

Just like those neck muscles, I often find myself wound tight. Though I may appear relaxed—sitting on the couch, taking a break, or reading a book—my body is constantly on the verge of movement. I'm poised to spring into action, should my presence be required somewhere.

The Bible reminds us that rest is a gift from God, but it can be one we struggle to accept. We are often too busy with our tasks—or, as Scripture puts it, "eating the bread of anxious toil"—to slow down and appreciate the joy of proper rest. With to-do lists running through our brains and more activities than hours in the day, it's no wonder that it's hard to remind ourselves to slow down. It's not until we truly pause and focus on the present—the space that our body is in, the breath going in and out of our lungs, the stillness of the space around us—that we can truly relax.

Yet, when we choose to slow down and sink into the moment, there is a sacredness to a true pause. Rather than simply putting up our feet for a minute, let's be mindful to relax and rest in the promises of God.

Kristin

Today's Act of Gratitude

Spend time stretching your muscles. Spend at least thirty seconds—or roughly four breaths in and out—on each stretch, allowing your body to relax.

The Golden Rule

*Do to others whatever you would like them to do to you. This is
the essence of all that is taught in the law and the prophets.*

MATTHEW 7:12

Having arrived in the intimates section of my local department store, I paused at the sheer volume of choices. I lifted a silent prayer for the women I was shopping for and began perusing the racks for practical, pretty undies and bras for people I've never met. Twenty minutes later, I was out the automatic doors, a bag of unmentionables swinging from my arm.

It was years ago that Bridging the Gap first started gathering brand-new bras, panties, and socks for the single moms attending its retreat weekend filled with worship and practical breakout sessions, as well as pampering opportunities. We quickly realized that single moms are often juggling the care for a myriad of others before themselves and that simple necessities like fresh undergarments rarely rise to the top of the priority list. And so began the SUB (socks, undies, bras) Project as part of each year's conference, challenging donors to purchase and donate new undergarments.

It's an honor to come alongside others with loving care, meeting a basic but essential need. There is nothing quite like new socks and lovely new underthings to boost my mood and confidence, and I want the same mood and confidence boost for the women at that retreat.

Supplying new undergarments for another woman is but one tiny, practical example of today's verse—the Golden Rule—in action. We're commanded to love others as we love ourselves in Matthew 22:39, and treating others according to the Golden Rule is the practical reality of embracing that commandment. This requires us to filter our days, our interactions, our experiences through the lens of God's love for everyone we meet, considering their interests in addition to our own.

I've been the recipient of Golden Rule behavior on a number of life-changing occasions, and one way to express my gratitude is by paying it forward. Instead of focusing on how someone can help me reach my goals, I'm asking God for divine wisdom about what allows both of us to thrive. This looks different with every circumstance, and there is no formula other than prayerful consideration for the needs of those around us.

Julie

Today's Act of Gratitude

View others through God's lens, looking for
a way to be a blessing to them.

The Great Outdoors

O Sovereign LORD! You made the heavens and earth by your strong hand and powerful arm. Nothing is too hard for you!

JEREMIAH 32:17

Our oldest son, Donnie, discovered a love for the outdoors at a young age. Whether it was BMX biking and racing, snowboarding with friends, ice fishing, or hunting every fall with his grandpa, Donnie would always choose to be outdoors rather than inside. We encouraged him from a young age to try new things, from football to lacrosse, and he found that he loved them all.

Donnie's life was a bit chaotic as a child before he came to live with us at eight years old, and we could see how his growing interest in outdoor activities brought a calmness and stability to his life like little else did. It's a passion my husband and I have seen and encouraged over the years. What started as simple activities have now become interests that he engages in often as a young adult, inciting a love for the outdoors in others, teaching friends how to snowboard or fish, making plans to visit mountains and try new diversions. As a parent, it's encouraging to see how God's creation brings purpose and peace to his life.

Are you drawn to the outdoors too? Sometimes people will make us feel like God and his Spirit are found only in a church building or during a service, but that isn't true. Scripture reminds us repeatedly that God's strong hand created the heavens and earth. Just stand before a mountain or look out over the vastness of the sea, and you will find yourself in awe of God and his creation. There is nothing he cannot do! There is no place his Spirit cannot go, and if we pay attention, we'll see creation bringing glory to God simply by being. The earth and all that's in it are alive because of God, and I am so grateful for the glory we can find.

Kendra

Today's Act of Gratitude

What outside activity do you enjoy? The next time you are engaged in it, take a few moments to notice and thank God for the beauty and power displayed in his creation.

Repeating His Promises

*Repeat [these commands] again and again to your children. Talk
about them when you are at home and when you are on the road,
when you are going to bed and when you are getting up. Tie them
to your hands and wear them on your forehead as reminders.
Write them on the doorposts of your house and on your gates.*

DEUTERONOMY 6:7-9

". . . forgiving one another, as God in Christ forgave you," one of my older daughters finished reciting Ephesians 4:32 (ESV), voice ringing with triumph.

"Great job!" I cheered. It was Monday, and I'd written a new verse on the black chalkboard inside the pantry. We'd recently started memorizing a new verse each week, with a small prize as an added incentive.

Though the verses were easy for my older daughters to rattle off, their six-year-old sister struggled.

Looking over, I saw her little face droop toward the floor, tears welling.

"I can't do it! It's too hard!" she wailed.

"Aww, it's okay. We can help you," one of her sisters said, patting her arm soothingly.

The littlest one brightened when her nine-year-old sister bounded out of her chair, saying, "Let's make up a dance for it!"

Amused, I watched as the two older girls came up with simple choreography to help their sister remember the words. By the end of the day, she had gained enough confidence to approach me and repeat the words to the verse, face beaming with pride.

When I was a child, my dad recited 2 Timothy 1:7 to me each time I was afraid. Now that I am an adult, its words still come to mind whenever I encounter fear. Over time, that constant repetition of God's truth became *my* truth.

Though we often brush off moments like these as ordinary, the truth is that repetition is a reason to be grateful. Jesus himself used ordinary parables to help his followers connect with the truth in ways that made sense and were easy to remember. When we spend time each day focusing on the Word of God and talking about Jesus, we gain the knowledge we need to approach situations with holy confidence. Just as children mimic their parents, over time our regular consumption of God's Word helps us walk and talk the way Jesus would.

Kristin

Today's Act of Gratitude

Which of God's truths are you absorbing daily?
Write out a verse to memorize.

Out of Practice

Keep putting into practice all you learned and received from me—everything you heard from me and saw me doing. Then the God of peace will be with you.

PHILIPPIANS 4:9

"What? No. Look again; we *have* to have paper plates!" I called back to Aaron. He was combing through our basement pantry even as I frantically searched for our rectangular serving platters, opening and shutting kitchen cupboards, wracking my brain for when we'd last used them and what on earth I'd done with them.

In the end, we hosted our first BBQ after two summers of canceled plans with no platters and a small stack of flimsy paper plates we'd found tucked in a forgotten corner. We'd also had to text one of our guests (a good friend of ours), sheepishly asking them to pick up American cheese for cheeseburgers and ice for the cooler as they passed the nearest grocery store.

"Well. We're clearly out of practice." Sighing, I dropped onto the couch next to Aaron hours later, happily tired but also slightly frustrated. "How did we forget the cheese and ice *and* not think to check on plates?"

"Everyone was happy to be together again, and that's what counts the most. We'll get back into the swing of hosting. It's just one of those things that require consistency."

Aaron was right. When we were entertaining regularly, we had established patterns and practices that had gotten rusty during our long hiatus. Restarting felt a lot like starting from scratch as we bumbled around, and that was initially discouraging. But as I reflect on the experience, I appreciate the lesson found in pressing out of inertia and through the difficulty, back to the worthwhile practice of opening our home.

There is value in rebooting the good habits we've let slip—for whatever reason. Prioritize spiritual practices that create intimacy with God and that encourage you to love those around you. Have you gotten out of the habit of talking to God? Chat with him while you apply your deodorant and brush your teeth. Have you stopped being part of a faith community? Set Sunday mornings aside to visit churches until you find the right one.

It's okay to admit that you are out of practice, but don't stay stuck in that inertia. Life is too short, and your calling is too valuable to remain sidelined.

Julie

Today's Act of Gratitude

Prayerfully consider what spiritual practice
you need to reboot. Start now.

Food Is Fun

*Go ahead. Eat your food with joy, and drink your wine
with a happy heart, for God approves of this!*
ECCLESIASTES 9:7

"I gotta say—that was the best meat I've ever had," my husband, Tim, said slowly.

"Aww, Eli, what do you do with that type of compliment?" my friend Ashley asked.

"Uh, it's a little dusty in here," Eli said with a smile, pretending to wipe a tear as the rest of us laughed.

Our families were on vacation together, and Eli had just spent the last few days using a sous vide method for tri-tip, a triangular beef cut from the bottom of a sirloin. He and my husband have an ongoing, friendly food competition, so Tim's compliment was hard-won. Wanting photo proof, I'd asked Tim to repeat his words for the video I was recording.

Now, each time my husband takes out our sous vide cooker to make something, I'm reminded of that memorable week away with our friends. The truth is that many of our best memories are tied to food. My mom's cheesy potatoes remind me of Thanksgiving holidays; pho and banh mi sandwiches remind me of cooking classes my husband and I took together. Seeing my oldest daughter bake cupcakes reminds me of my second daughter, who only eats the frosting. I've got childhood memories of eating my dad's Norwegian pancakes or drinking Kool-Aid at Aunt Delpha's house.

Many foods remind me of places I've been—arepas in Venezuela, papayas fresh off the tree in my brother-in-law's yard in Hawaii, hot and salty chips and cheese in Oxford on a dreary night. Sometimes food even reminds us of people we've loved and lost, like my sister Katrina's handwritten recipe card for "Fanciful Fruit Pizza" and the fudge my Grandma Jo made every Christmas.

Yes, food is fuel, but that doesn't mean it can't be joyful. When we choose to enjoy the food we have to eat, it's just one more way to thank God for his provision. Today is a gift, and so is the food that graces our table. Even the simplest of fare can taste wonderful if we take the time to notice the flavors or simply be present with those around us.

Kristin

Today's Act of Gratitude

Choose to eat something that's tied to a fond memory.
Or visit a restaurant and make a new memory.

Investing in the Next Generation

*Let each generation tell its children of
your mighty acts; let them proclaim your power.*

PSALM 145:4

We walked in on a Sunday morning and could feel the excitement as we took our seats near the stage. All of the youth, including our daughter Jasmine, were sitting in the front two rows—ready to perform.

Jasmine turned and smiled at us, and we waved hello. Our daughter loves to dance and sing and takes any opportunity she can to share her talents with others. This Sunday all the youth would be performing things they'd written and rehearsed for the upcoming Fine Arts Festival to be held the following weekend.

We sat back and watched as teens gave short sermons, taught lessons about God's love to kids, performed piano pieces they'd composed themselves, and danced and acted out "human videos" set to music that told a story.

As Jasmine took the stage before her dance, we could hear the youth leaders and teens cheering her on. My heart swelled with pride, not just at the sight of our girl doing something she loved, but at seeing the support she had in the group. I was struck by how the leaders loved these students so well.

As the teens all went up at the end for prayer, the pastor asked that the elementary kids—the next generation—also come forward. He had the teens pray for the kids coming up after them because, as he told them, "Just as we support you, you want to look for and support those coming up behind you." As they prayed, I wiped tears, grateful once again for the wise mentors in my daughter's life.

Every generation is to tell its children of God's mighty acts—of his faithfulness, love, and mercy. We are to remind those behind us of his great power. To do this we must have a relationship with other generations. We must love them, teach them, and train them to instill the same understanding in those even younger.

As my daughter has found out, you're never too young to start encouraging and mentoring others. We all need people before us who mentor us and after us who we are pouring our lives into as well.

Kendra

Today's Act of Gratitude

Thank someone who has mentored you, and then
encourage someone you are mentoring.

Measuring Success

Jesus replied, "'You must love the LORD your God with all your heart, all your soul, and all your mind.' This is the first and greatest commandment. A second is equally important: 'Love your neighbor as yourself.' The entire law and all the demands of the prophets are based on these two commandments."

MATTHEW 22:37-40

Some days, I go to bed feeling a little dissatisfied. It's not that something went wrong that day; it's that not enough things went right.

Ensuring that I end the day on a better note requires that I start out right. Though I love crossing items off to-do lists, I've realized that the real question I need to ask myself each morning is this: *What do I need to accomplish today to feel successful?*

Though one might assume that the answer is something significant—achieving a big goal or a lifelong dream—the truth is that it's often something small. Maybe it's finally picking up the phone to make a dreaded call. Perhaps it's organizing a single drawer so I feel less worried about the clutter in my home. Maybe it's spending one-on-one time with a loved one after an overly busy week.

Though I still write down all the items I'd like to accomplish each day, that question helps me gauge what's essential for peace in my mind and heart. It helps me wade through everything that vies for my attention to discern what matters most.

The question reminds me of a story told in Matthew. Some religious leaders were trying to trap Jesus in a false teaching, so they asked him, "Which is the most important commandment in the law of Moses?" Instead of wading through a laundry list of rules—a to-do list for his followers—Jesus cut to the heart of the matter. He told them that loving God and loving others were the most important commands; all other priorities should reflect those essential truths.

Like the religious leaders, we can get so caught up in following rules—in Christianity and life in general—that we forget about the most important things. I'm grateful that Jesus' simple answer reminds us to reconsider our priorities. Refocusing on what's essential for today can provide us with the peace we need, ensuring we never again fall asleep with dissatisfaction hanging over our heads.

Kristin

Today's Act of Gratitude

Ask yourself: *What do I need to accomplish today to feel successful? How can accomplishing that item give me some peace of mind about my to-do list?*

August

Change the Atmosphere

*Your love for one another will prove to
the world that you are my disciples.*

JOHN 13:35

We were nearing the end of summer. One of the families in our small group invited all of us to an event being put on by another local church to reach out to an immigrant community in our city. The plan was to meet at a park each night for a week and have games, crafts, and snacks for kids and families so everyone could get to know one another.

The first night we went, our kids helped serve snacks, played soccer, and chased little ones around the playground. As we pulled out of the parking lot several hours later, they begged us to go back the next night.

Because of their excitement, we decided to return. As my kids settled in to help out with the activities for the night, I struck up a conversation with a young mom, a recent refugee resettled to our area after spending years in a camp, waiting to be moved to a permanent home. We started talking about our mutual friend Samantha, who had helped to welcome her when she first arrived.

The woman shared about a situation that had happened to her children, an activity in which they did not feel welcome to participate. Sam stepped in to bridge the gap between the two cultures and to help bring about a resolution.

"Sam changes the atmosphere," she explained. "She changed the feeling from hostility to peace and love. She is such a good friend to me."

I nodded, feeling sad for all that this woman has had to face in her life and also proud to have a friend who sees the needs of others and takes the initiative to help.

Her words challenged me days later as I wondered, *Do I change the atmosphere of the places I find myself? Do I bring peace to my workplace? To my kids' school and activities? To interactions with my friends who don't yet know Jesus?*

John tells us that the world will know we are Jesus' disciples because of our love for one another. This love is shown through our words and our actions. And it has the power to change the atmosphere in all of the places we find ourselves, if we'll let it.

Kendra

Today's Act of Gratitude

Determine to change the atmosphere wherever you are by
showing the love of Jesus through word and deed.

Unspeakable

The Holy Spirit helps us in our weakness. For example, we don't know what God wants us to pray for. But the Holy Spirit prays for us with groanings that cannot be expressed in words.

ROMANS 8:26

A ten-year-old girl had died. Though I didn't know her personally, the tragic circumstances surrounding her death—and the fact that I had a daughter the same age—made the loss hit a little harder than it might have otherwise.

I found myself tearing up at odd moments over the next couple of days, grieved over the heavy weight of her death, the terrible injustice of the situation, and her family's profound and irrevocable loss. I couldn't help but wonder, *How is it possible to feel grateful in this circumstance?* The situation felt irredeemable.

The truth is that this world is often brutal and cold. Evil exists, and people can make bad decisions with ripple effects that spill over to innocent people. In the face of tragedy, we can feel helpless, not knowing how to respond.

Over the next few days, each time the child's family came to mind, I tried to pray yet felt helpless to find the words. All I could muster was the whispered plea, *Jesus, be near.* As time passed, peace began to steal over me—not because the words I said were magical but because they reminded me that I wasn't alone in my grief.

In fact, the Bible tells us that we are never alone when we pray. When Jesus left this earth to return to the Father, he sent the Holy Spirit—our advocate and comforter—so that we need never be alone. When the reality of life feels unspeakable—when the pain of this world silences us—the Spirit comes alongside us in our distress, speaking in ways that we cannot find the strength or courage to do ourselves. He has not left us. He is still here, even now. We are never alone. That is a reason to be grateful.

Kristin

Today's Act of Gratitude

Ask the Holy Spirit for help in a situation that feels impossible. Thank him for his presence.

Her Last Letter

Do not talk much about tomorrow,
for you do not know what a day will bring.

PROVERBS 27:1, NLV

Dear Pen Pal . . .

My pen wobbled to a stop as I realized I didn't know how to proceed, didn't know what to say next. As unshed tears obscured the pretty stationery I'd bought just for this purpose, I laid down my pen and sat back. *Lord, how many more letters do I get?*

Thirteen years older than my dad, Aunt Claire was struggling with her health, but the terminal diagnosis and the news that she wouldn't be returning to her cozy townhome made this letter matter more than all of the silly, nattering letters we'd been exchanging for years—letters filled with our respective rambling scrawls, sharing tidbits of memories or small, funny moments in our ordinary lives.

The tears started in earnest when I realized I'd likely received the last of Claire's letters, no matter how many more of mine might zip through the mail. In an era of texting and emails, I had learned to savor the envelopes bearing her name, setting her letters aside to be read as I sipped my tea, taking a quiet moment to linger over the pages and her stories. We'd agreed that we were kindred spirits: women who loved Jesus, who loved the same people, and who—despite the age difference—physically resembled each other so closely that we could be mother and daughter instead of aunt and niece.

Thank you, Lord, for the time we've had, for the warmth and laughter we've brought to one another. Thank you for slowing me down, for impressing upon me the importance of writing these letters when I had been sporadic, for giving me this precious friendship. Help me to write the letter Aunt Claire needs at this moment.

Having breathed that prayer, I picked up my pen and began to write.

We aren't promised tomorrow, which makes appreciating yesterday and today all the more important. And yet so much of our lives is consumed with tomorrow—worrying, planning, anticipating—that we neglect to be fully present, now. God knows this and asks us to release tomorrow to him. Today is the day we have. The question is, What will we do with it?

Julie

Today's Act of Gratitude

Seek to be intentionally present, and look for joy—the kind you can bring to others as well as what God is gifting to you.

A Listening Ear

*Share each other's burdens, and
in this way obey the law of Christ.*

GALATIANS 6:2

"I'm so overwhelmed," I said through my tears to Julie as she listened over the phone. I'd just gotten back some medical results on my hormone levels and my thyroid, and although it was good to know areas that needed to be addressed, I was overcome with emotion.

"Why did I wait so long?" I asked. "So many of the symptoms the doctor mentioned I've had for years."

"But you know now," Julie answered. "What did she tell you to do?"

Julie affirmed me as I listed the medications and supplements that I'd need to take to begin the slow process of fixing systems in my body that hadn't been working correctly for quite some time. As she listened and encouraged me, showing her understanding of what I was going through, I started to feel better. We hung up after she prayed for me.

Several hours later, I got a text from Julie. "I left a little package on your doorstep."

Curious, I went to retrieve the pretty gift bag she'd left. When I opened it, I began to cry. Inside were each of the supplements I needed to take. I had no idea that as I shared the list with her, she was taking notes. Then she stopped at the pharmacy to pick up what she could, and left them at my door. Knowing a friend had been listening and had understood what I was feeling made me so grateful for her. The heaviness of what I was facing began to lift because of her thoughtful gift.

If we are going to share another's burden, we will first have to take the time to really listen to them. We've got to slow down long enough to empathize with what they are saying and not just be waiting for our turn to speak again. When we listen well, it is powerful—not only for those we are listening to but also for us, since this is how we obey the law of Christ, the law to love others well.

Kendra

Today's Act of Gratitude

Take time to really listen to someone and offer encouragement.

Hearing His Call

My sheep listen to my voice;
I know them, and they follow me.

JOHN 10:27

My sister Katrina used to tell the story of how, despite growing up in a Christian home, she had walked away from her faith for a time.

During the day, she distracted herself with a full round of activity, noise, and friends. But nights were a different story. Though she tried to tire herself out so she would fall asleep quickly, she didn't always succeed. And in the quiet of the night, she was faced with silence and the weight of her own choices.

One night, just as she was drifting off to sleep, she heard a gentle voice call out, "Katie!"

Turning on her light, she looked around the room but saw nothing. Yet, she felt convicted by the call.

"Katie was the name that those who loved me and knew me best always used," she said. "I felt strongly that it was God."

A little while later, she heard the voice a second time. Again, like Samuel, she felt sure that it was God gently calling her name (see 1 Samuel 3). As a result, she decided to recommit her life to Jesus.

While many of us have never audibly heard the voice of God, he calls to each one of us through his Word. The stories Jesus told his followers—about the shepherd who left the ninety-nine sheep to find the missing one, the doctor who came to heal those who knew they were sick, and the loving father who welcomed his prodigal son home—serve as reminders of just how much Jesus continues to pursue us. Even when we walk away, he is always and already looking for us. He is the God of second chances and seventy-seventh chances. We are his children, and he knows us by name.

Yet, you and I have the opportunity to choose how to respond. May we listen for his call and the nudges of the Holy Spirit, responding with obedience and gratitude.

Kristin

Today's Act of Gratitude

Thank God for his persistent pursuit of your heart.

Thankfulness Lived Out

*Live a life filled with love, following the example of Christ. He loved us
and offered himself as a sacrifice for us, a pleasing aroma to God.*

EPHESIANS 5:2

One morning as I was spending a little bit of quiet time with God, I read through
Ephesians 5, which in my Bible has the header, "Living in the Light." As I thought
about all the ways we are to imitate God, in conjunction with writing a book about
gratitude, I asked myself the question, *What might God be inviting me into as I
consider both gratefulness and imitating him?*

I sat quietly for a few moments, just thinking about what that would look like,
practically, in my life. An answer of sorts came to me. *Being grateful pulls me out of
myself, enabling me to see others' needs while also being thankful for all that I have. It
allows me to love others and take steps to show that love.*

When I focus on others, not only can I be a blessing to *them*, but I *myself* am
blessed. I am encouraged. I feel love. And when I start each day from a place of
thankfulness, I can live out that thankfulness by loving others while simultaneously
feeling gratitude to God for all that I have. It's an invitation to remember what God
has done for me, and because of that truth, my life will spill love and kindness on
those around me.

But the opposite is true as well. If I am ungrateful, I have a hard time noticing
all that God has provided, and I am unable to see the needs of those around me.
I am focused only on what I don't have or how someone has wronged me. This is
not how I should live as a follower of Jesus. We ought to live a life of love, following
Christ's example. The easiest way to do this is to wake up each morning, remembering all that we can be grateful for that day.

Kendra

Today's Act of Gratitude

What might God be inviting you into as you consider
what gratefulness looks like when it is lived out? Think
of one practical way you can show love to others.

A Steady Perspective

*We fix our eyes not on what is seen, but on what is unseen,
since what is seen is temporary, but what is unseen is eternal.*

2 CORINTHIANS 4:18, NIV

"You're going to want to put this on." The tour guide handed me what looked like a water-repellent snowmobile suit, then, more suits in hand, moved toward the next couple.

Raising an eyebrow at Aaron as we donned our respective garments, I said, "How close are we planning to get to the whales? Is this going to be dangerous?"

My somewhat rhetorical question was answered soon enough as our small boat splashed through the trough of yet another larger-than-life ocean swell, leaving me a wet, salty mess. I clung to my bench as we navigated our way to a site where whales like to frolic.

As I clung, I considered two things: (1) ocean waves appear far tamer and milder when one is walking along the shore rather than hitting them head-on in a teeny, tiny boat, and (2) the beachfront cliffs looked minuscule from my vantage point on the ocean, though they towered above me each day (with accompanying signs warning of rockslide and sudden, erosive collapse) when I strolled along the sandy strip of beach where the tide ebbed and flowed.

My perspective on the strength of the ocean's waves and the height of those sandstone cliffs shifted, based upon my proximity. With some distance, each was a beautiful vista, while up close, each felt unpredictable and dangerous under the right conditions.

I'm guilty of perspective shifting in my personal life as well: a task or situation feels harder (or easier) based on my emotions or the busyness of my schedule. Rather than allowing outside influences to determine whether (or how much) I have peace, joy, or contentment from moment to moment and day to day, I'm gratefully fixing my eyes toward the eternal, looking to build stability and consistency into my perspective based on the truth of Scripture and my assurance of God's love.

There is no question that we will face challenging circumstances during our time on Earth; however, we can keep a steady perspective by focusing on unseen, eternal truths rather than allowing ourselves to be tossed to and fro by visible, temporary conditions.

Julie

Today's Act of Gratitude

What unseen, eternal truths hold your perspective steady?
Pick a verse or two to meditate on when events
tempt you into perspective shifting.

Memories of Faithfulness

I recall all you have done, O LORD;
I remember your wonderful deeds of long ago.

PSALM 77:11

Every time I see the painting on the wall between my living and dining rooms, I can't help but smile.

In it, windswept clouds hover, suspended, over the tranquil waters of a lagoon. Trees along the shoreline are mirrored in the water's surface; white and yellow flowers dot the edges of the canvas.

The painting is an exquisite portrayal of the lagoon at Big Bay on Madeline Island. A local artist used my photographs for inspiration, and her work perfectly encapsulates the peaceful beauty of one of my favorite places to visit. It reminds me of the dozens of times I've paused to gaze at this same view before descending weathered wooden steps to the sandy shoreline below.

While I love the painting, it's not the artist's skill or even the subject itself that truly matters—it's what it represents. It's the way it reminds me of a lifetime of memories stored in my heart: lazy days lying in the warmth of the sun, wading into the water, searching for sea glass, and building castles in the sand. It reminds me of roasting marshmallows on the beach and donning sweatshirts as the sun sets. I can't look at it without imagining the shaking of dice or shuffling of cards as my family plays games. I remember noticing the bell-like birdsong on morning walks or holding my hair out of my face as the wind pummels it on the ferry ride to Bayfield and back. Seeing it takes me back to all the times I've spent celebrating my sister's birthday, finding books and old records at the local church bazaar, and strolling down the main street with a dripping ice-cream cone from Grampa Tony's in my hand.

Memories are wonderful. Even the hard ones—of challenges faced or loved ones lost—remind us of things we've learned. In the same way, our remembrances of what God has done in the past can give us the courage to face what lies ahead. Our memories of his faithfulness, mercy, and love can buoy us on hard days, giving us the hope we need to continue. When we consider all he has done, we are more likely to see our current circumstances positively.

Kristin

Today's Act of Gratitude

Jot down memories of God's faithfulness. Post them on
your mirror as a visual reminder of what he has done.

It's Okay to Take a Break

*I will satisfy the weary soul, and
every languishing soul I will replenish.*

JEREMIAH 31:25, ESV

I'd been feeling overwhelmed for several days but ignoring my feelings and just pushing through. Until one morning I woke up very aware that my energy was low and the things I normally loved to do—exercising, running kids to activities, helping Kyle with our business, and tackling my to-do list—seemed more than I could handle. At the same time, even though my body felt tired, my mind began to berate me over all the things I "should" be doing.

I sighed and opened a social media site instead of starting on the list of things awaiting my attention. The first image that popped up was the face of a woman I follow. Immediately I knew her message was for me. She encouraged those who were watching to listen to their bodies, to rest when they feel like they need to. I wiped my eyes as she reminded us that we aren't meant to run ourselves ragged, we aren't machines, and some days it's okay to take a break.

I closed my phone and whispered a prayer, thankful that God had used the words of someone else to speak to me, and the guilt I'd been feeling began to lift.

We can face a lot of pressure each day. Pressure to work hard. To get things done. To feel like we've accomplished something. And although there is nothing wrong with having goals, sometimes we can put too much emphasis on completing tasks, wearing down our bodies, minds, and spirits in the process and ignoring our need to rest.

That's when we need to remember that God promises to satisfy weary souls and replenish languishing ones. My heart fills with gratitude as I read these words. God made us as living beings, not machines. Knowing we'd need rest, he offers it freely. God doesn't expect us to run ourselves ragged, and neither should we. Rest is a gift from God. All we have to do is receive it.

Kendra

Today's Act of Gratitude

Take time to rest, thanking God for the opportunity
to replenish body, mind, and spirit.

Becoming Lake People

*May God give you more and more grace and peace as you
grow in your knowledge of God and Jesus our Lord.*

2 PETER 1:2

"You guys have become lake people."

My brother's comment as Aaron and I bustled about, getting ready to pull Boaty McBoatface from the lake, was a compliment.

He knew how *not* "lake people" Aaron and I were when we had bought our small ski boat several summers earlier. Despite living several states away, he'd heard the stories of that first summer—of having to be towed off the water by kind strangers . . . of frantically troubleshooting electric systems with a thunderstorm prowling toward us in the distance . . . of semi-panic ensuing as we struggled to get Boaty in and out of the water at boat launches while others waited in line.

His offhand observation as he watched us work was an acknowledgment that—in his eyes—we'd moved from the category of "what were you thinking buying a boat" to "lake people." Our actions silently revealed our growing experience, comfort level, and competence around launching and operating a ski boat.

Living a life in which our actions proclaim our faith as loudly as (or more loudly than) the words we speak is not unlike learning to become "lake people." Proclaiming Jesus with our deeds in addition to what we say requires embodying the fruits of the Spirit found in Galatians 5:22-23 (love, joy, peace, patience, kindness, goodness, faithfulness, gentleness, and self-control). Learning to launch a boat properly is not unlike learning to be a person of peace—to choose but one example—as both require ongoing practice, fixing of mistakes, and multiple do-overs until one day an outside observer's comment has you realizing how far you've quietly come in that particular area.

Thankfully, God does not abandon us as we strive toward holy living. Being a person who responds with kindness despite being irritated or chooses gentleness instead of anger is difficult and requires continual, intentional practice. Today's verse is a beautiful encouragement that as we intentionally grow toward God and holy living, not only are grace and peace available to us, but more and more of them.

Julie

Today's Act of Gratitude

Pick one spiritual fruit as an intentional focus for the next
twenty-one days, thanking God as you spot his provision of
grace and peace, even during the challenging moments.

The Gift of Imagination

When I look at your heavens, the work of your fingers, the moon and the stars, which you have set in place, what is man that you are mindful of him, and the son of man that you care for him?

PSALM 8:3-4, ESV

"Flight attendants, prepare the cabin for arrival."

When the announcement sounded through the loudspeaker, I paused to place a bookmark and slide my book closed. Reaching over to the window, I cranked the small shade open, blinking at the sudden brightness of the sun.

As my eyes adjusted, I caught my breath at the sight outside: puffy white clouds piled high like whipped cream, their pale shade a startling contrast to the cerulean sky. We were at the perfect altitude to sail through them.

For just a moment, I couldn't help but be gripped by wonder, and I began to smile over the sheer joy of floating effortlessly through clouds. As a child, I had stared at them in the skies above from my place on the ground, wondering what they were like; our family trips usually involved a minivan and an open road, not an airplane.

But because of the gift of imagination, I'd dreamed about how they might look up close. I'd looked for shapes and animals in them; I'd envisioned jumping from one to the other or lounging on one the way I'd seen characters do in cartoons. I thought about eating them up; they looked like the very best of marshmallows.

Now, the wonder of floating past them felt pure and right, a reminder that our imagination is a reason to be grateful—even as adults.

The gift of imagination inspires us to create story lines in our heads, gives us dreams of visiting far-flung places, and prods us to anticipate people and places that bring us joy. It spurs inventors and artists to new innovations; it sparks the ideas that change the future of a life, a family, or a community. And when we pause to enjoy our imagination, it reminds us of our inventive God. He made the heavens and the earth—so many beautiful, fantastic creations!—yet he still cares for us. He imbued each of us with the ability to think and create and imagine.

Kristin

Today's Act of Gratitude

Spend some time using your imagination.

The Meaningful Mix-Up

If you have two shirts, give one to the poor.
If you have food, share it with those who are hungry.

LUKE 3:11

"I know we don't know her, but I think we should help," I told my husband early one Monday morning just minutes after he'd left for work.

"That's fine with me," he said. Over the weekend an envelope had come to our home, with our address mistakenly written on it. Thinking it was something for us, one of our kids had opened it.

But as I read the note, I realized it wasn't meant for us. It was from someone's tenant, with a check for half the current month's rent and an apology and explanation as to when she'd have the second half. I looked up the name on the envelope and realized it was a rental management company on our street. Kyle and I put the note and check in a new envelope with the correct address, ready to send out the next day. But as I went to put the letter in the mailbox, I felt a little nudge— a reminder of all the times others have helped us.

Thus, my call to Kyle. After I hung up, I wrote a check for the other half of the rent and a simple explanation as to how the letter had ended up in our possession and how we wanted to help. I said a prayer for the woman involved as I dropped it in the box, grateful for the opportunities God gives us—to receive help when we are lacking and to extend it when we have more than we need.

The older I get, the more I see God putting small things in my path for me to notice and act on. Scripture reminds us that if we have two shirts, we should give one away, and if we have food, we should share with those in need—we don't have to wait for a sign to follow God's instructions. And once we start, we'll come to view our actions not as a burden but as a blessing when we see all the small and large ways God is showing up in our lives and the lives of those around us.

Kendra

Today's Act of Gratitude

Look for ways that God might be nudging you
and then be moved to act.

Teamwork Makes the Dream Work

Obey your spiritual leaders, and do what they say. Their work is to watch over your souls, and they are accountable to God. Give them reason to do this with joy and not with sorrow. That would certainly not be for your benefit.

HEBREWS 13:17

"Soooooo, what's next?" My friend ambled her way to my side as I finished putting the last flier into a bag for later distribution.

Grinning, I said, "I'm not in charge, so I'm not sure. Shall we go ask?"

As we worked, we chatted generally about the roles of leadership and followership and what it means to be a good follower. Because we've both worn the mantle of leadership in various areas of our lives, we know the value of a strong team filled with people who can be focused on implementing rather than envisioning.

I hadn't considered the importance of good followership in terms of pastors and other spiritual leaders until I read today's verse, but many of the same concepts apply to being a healthy member of a faith community.

Good followers are thoughtfully committed to the same vision as their leader. This is not a blind following but a conscious choosing to work toward a common goal.

Good followers engage in healthy conflict resolution. If we are frustrated or uncomfortable with a leader, we go to them directly and discreetly before pulling others into the disagreement. We also acknowledge that there are often several perfectly reasonable ways to go about the same task and accept that our leader might go about it differently than our preferred way, and that's okay.

Good followers work toward finding and building unity between the larger team and leadership rather than sowing seeds of discord and division through murmuring and gossip.

There are times and seasons in which I cannot serve as a leader, but I'm grateful to know that I can still be part of God's kingdom-building team in equally important ways by being a committed and servant-hearted follower. God doesn't always call us to leadership. And, truly, even those in leadership roles are—first and foremost—followers of Christ.

We aren't tasked to be world changers and kingdom builders alone; isn't that a relief? The moment I finally realized I can change the world in my followership, a weight lifted that I didn't know I was attempting to carry.

Julie

Today's Act of Gratitude

Where are you called to be a committed, excellent follower? In what ways could you apply some of these concepts of good followership within your team?

A Love for Reading

All Scripture is inspired by God and is useful to teach us what is
true and to make us realize what is wrong in our lives. It corrects us
when we are wrong and teaches us to do what is right. God uses
it to prepare and equip his people to do every good work.

2 TIMOTHY 3:16-17

I'm a bookworm. In fact, when I was a child, my sisters used to tease me about having ghostly pale skin despite it being summer because I spent so much time indoors, reading books.

With no real responsibilities until school began in the fall, I would often walk to the public library a few blocks from my home and return with a giant stack of books. Ignoring the whirlwind of siblings and parents around me, I worked my way through one to two novels each day. In those early days of Christian fiction, there wasn't much to read beyond Janette Oke and Gilbert Morris, but I read everything I could get my hands on. I loved how the authors' stories of God's love and faithfulness—with a bit of romance mixed in—took me to previously unknown worlds.

Over the years, I've expanded the genres that I read, but I still feel the same sense of joy each time I pick up a book. I've also reread a few favorites, and one thing I've realized is that the aspects I focused on as a teenager weren't the same as they are now that I'm an adult. I pay attention to previously overlooked characters and themes I didn't pick up the first time around; I sympathize with the hardships and revel in the pursuit of redemption or joy.

Just like those other books, God's Word is a book that lasts for a lifetime of reading and rereading. It's full of richness and truth. It's got drama, intrigue, romance, poetry, parables, and timeless truths that help us follow Jesus and love others well. It corrects, equips, teaches, encourages, challenges, bolsters, convicts, and confounds us. And even though I love reading fictional books, the Bible is the most influential book I've ever read, one that continues to reveal truths previously unknown. What a privilege it is for us to live in an era in which we have the opportunity to hold the Word of God in our hands.

Kristin

Today's Act of Gratitude

Spend some time reading a book or listening to an
audiobook, thanking God for the truths you find in it.

Trying My Best

*The godly may trip seven times,
but they will get up again.*

PROVERBS 24:16

"Thanks, Mom, for always being there and trying your best."

My daughter's note caught me momentarily off guard before I smiled, grateful that she and I are on the same page. It's not easy being the first-time mother of a teenager, and it's not easy being the oldest child and the first teenager in the house—the one who paves the way, the one who always bears the brunt of her mother's first attempts to parent through a new season or circumstance.

Lizzie—as my oldest child—is my parenting guinea pig. As she grows up, encountering new situations, new decisions, and new opportunities, I'm along for the ride, new in my parenting through each of those same circumstances.

Parenting is not for the faint of heart, and she and I agree that sometimes I get a gold star on the first try and sometimes I fall short and need a second, third, or more attempts before I land on the right balance between giving her increasing freedom and keeping her emotionally, physically, and spiritually safe.

What she does know is this: (1) I'm trying my best, and (2) I love her unconditionally. After a difficult parenting interaction, I whisper these two foundational truths in her ear as I hug her tight, even when I've had to apologize for missing the mark on what she needed in that moment versus what I thought she needed.

Intimate relationships involving close friendships, spouses, parents, and children require hard, committed work. Reminding our loved ones of how much we love them and that we are doing the best we can—even as we navigate our own insecurities and shortcomings—challenges us to do better next time, reminds us to assume the best of one another, and helps keep us connected, even when we disagree.

It's important to understand that the shortcut phrase "trying my best" isn't an excuse to ignore improving in areas where we repeatedly fall short. It's an acknowledgment of being a work in progress and committing both to improvement and to having grace for our loved ones—as they, in turn commit to a reciprocated grace and acknowledge that they, too, are a work in progress.

Julie

Today's Act of Gratitude

What shortcut phrase(s) can you use with a loved one that acknowledges love, commitment to growth, and grace over missteps?

A Lesson in Patience

The LORD is a faithful God.
Blessed are those who wait for his help.

ISAIAH 30:18

"You kids have no idea," I stated as my daughter showed me another sweatshirt she wanted me to buy for her while browsing at a local boutique. "When I was your age, we went shopping at Kmart for clothes twice a year—early spring for the summer and about a month before school. Then my mom would put everything on layaway and we would have to wait several weeks until it was paid off and we could pick up the items."

My kids chuckled as I smiled. They've heard my story many times before, but it bears repeating.

"But Mom, that was so long ago!" my daughter responded. "Times have changed."

"They certainly have," I said. "But some things are still worth waiting for. Why don't you add that to your birthday list if you really want it."

Jasmine sighed and rolled her eyes for dramatic effect. "Fine, I can wait." Now it was my turn to chuckle as I leaned in for a hug before we left the shop.

We've all heard that patience is a virtue, but no one likes to be told to wait. In a fast-paced world, we've gotten used to getting things quickly—the faster the better. But there is still a benefit in learning to wait for something we really desire: a refinement and building of our character.

And when we find ourselves in a season of waiting, we can rest assured that we're in good company. Just scan the Bible and you'll see. Abraham waited for decades before he had a son. Paul spent years in prison. And even Jesus waited until he was thirty to begin his ministry.

It is no different for us. We will sometimes have to wait a long time for things we want. Scripture reminds us that God is faithful, and we are blessed when we wait for him. I am thankful that he remains close to us, even as we wait.

Kendra

Today's Act of Gratitude

What is something you are waiting on? Spend some time asking God to meet you as you wait and thank him in advance for his faithfulness to you.

What's Saving Your Life?

The LORD God is our sun and our shield. He gives us grace and glory.
The LORD will withhold no good thing from those who do what is right.

PSALM 84:11

In her memoir, author Barbara Brown Taylor writes about being asked to speak at a church. The host invited her to answer the simple question: What's saving your life right now?*

She points out that it's easy to list what's killing us. Most of us have a litany of hard things cluttering up our minds and hearts. We can feel as though we are drowning beneath the weight of work, school, errand-running, or other people's expectations, making it a cinch to rattle off what makes life difficult.

But asking ourselves "What's saving your life right now?"—that is, making it more bearable—can lead to endless answers too. Perhaps it's a new recipe for Thai chicken tacos topped with slaw and peanut sauce, a morning cup of coffee, or the worn-in feeling of your favorite sweatshirt. Maybe it's a friend's steady presence or a hug on a hard day. It could be a book you can't wait to finish, the promise of an after-dinner walk, or laughing so hard that your sides hurt. Maybe it's a promise from God that you scribbled on a Post-it Note and placed next to your kitchen sink to look at each time you plunge your hands into hot water.

Whatever it is, taking the time to list the things that are saving our lives can be just what we need to redeem the day. God is our source of light and joy ("our sun"), protection ("our shield"), favor and friendship ("grace and glory"). As a loving Father, he doesn't withhold good things from us. He delights in lavishing on us his love, the beauty of creation, and the peace and comfort of his presence.

When we choose to consider what's saving our lives, we are reminded of the good gifts we have access to every day, little reminders from our generous God. He delights in us! When we take the time to thank him for the things that make life feel a little easier, we recognize both the gift and the Giver.

Kristin

Today's Act of Gratitude

List ten things that are saving your life right now.

---

* Barbara Brown Taylor, *Leaving Church: A Memoir of Faith* (New York: HarperOne, 2013), 225.

Choosing Contentment

I know what it is to be in need, and I know what it is to have plenty.
I have learned the secret of being content in any and every situation,
whether well fed or hungry, whether living in plenty or in want.

PHILIPPIANS 4:12, NIV

"You work in pest control? I bet you have some interesting tales to tell!" Her comment snagged my entire table's attention. Apparently, everyone loves pest control horror stories, and the conversational floodgates on that topic had been thrown wide open.

I was in Southern California, the only Minnesotan among a table of locals, and I grew a bit green around the gills as I listened to stories of venomous and poisonous critters in backyards and basements. Ready for a conversation change, I asked one table companion— a transplant from the Midwest and a fellow gardener—about her SoCal garden and some of the plants I'd been desperately wishing would grow in my Zone 3a yard. But her response cast those flowers in a different light. Those gorgeous bougainvillea vines I'd been sighing over all week? Filled with thorns so prickly and painful that pruning was a carefully undertaken task. And the jasmine hedgerows I'd fallen head over heels in love with at the botanical garden? Water hogs requiring too much moisture in a drought-ridden landscape.

Our conversation wasn't all gloom and doom, but her honesty about the realities of gardening in San Diego's sunny Zone 10 as compared to her colder Midwestern experience was exactly what I needed to hear. There is something to be said for living in a place where it gets so cold that your nostrils freeze together. The trade-off for frigid winter temps is that I don't worry about shaking an occasional scorpion out of my shoe.

In a world filled with photoshopped images and curated social media posts, contentment is elusive. Someone said, "The grass is greener where you water it." I've taken that statement to heart. Longing for the illusion of what someone else has rarely accounts for the realities of what they face. And if you knew the hidden costs and downsides, what they have wouldn't be nearly as alluring.

Cultivating contentment bolsters gratefulness. We do this by understanding that the glossy facade others present, intentionally or not, isn't the whole truth, and by anchoring our hope in Jesus, viewing our circumstances through the lens of faith.

Julie

Today's Act of Gratitude

What illusions have you been believing as truth? How might you
replace longing with contentment in these circumstances?

Asking for Help

*Do to others as you would
like them to do to you.*

LUKE 6:31

I got a text early one morning. "I hate to ask, but I have an appointment. Would you mind watching June for me while I go?"

I sat for a moment, thinking about all I had planned for the day. I would love to tell you that I am instinctively a generous and kind person, but the truth is, I'm not always. I'm not someone who cares to switch plans, especially on short notice.

I sighed as I thought about my friend, someone who is new to the country and has no family here. *What would I hope someone would do for me if I were in her shoes?*

I quickly texted her back. "Of course, I would love to. I do have some errands to run this morning, but she's welcome to come with me."

A little while later, my friend dropped June off with a bag of books and a smile.

"I'm so excited to be at your house today!" June said as she skipped through the front door.

I smiled. "I am so glad too. Keep your shoes on, though. We're going to run some errands."

As we waved goodbye to her mom and got in my vehicle, June began to tell me all about her mornings spent at school and what she liked to do in the afternoons. We had a lovely morning together, and I found myself grateful for her cheery little voice engaging me in conversation as we went from store to store.

A few hours later, when my friend came to pick up June, she once again thanked me.

I hugged her as she prepared to leave.

"Anytime," I said, "that's what friends are for."

Asking for help isn't always easy to do and neither is offering, especially when we have to change our own plans to accommodate someone else. But when we remember that Scripture tells us to do to others as we would like them to do to us, it can help us to be willing—both to help and to be helped. Putting ourselves in another person's shoes and having empathy for them is a skill we want to develop as followers of Jesus.

Kendra

Today's Act of Gratitude

Thank God for the times others have stepped in
to offer help to you, and then look for someone
who may need assistance and offer it to them.

Seeking Justice Obediently

He has told you, O man, what is good; and what does the LORD require of you but to do justice, and to love kindness, and to walk humbly with your God?

MICAH 6:8, ESV

"Good morning, do you have a moment?"

My friend's greeting accompanied her quiet knock on her manager's office door. And at his invitation, she stepped inside, silently praying that Jesus would guide her next words.

Their department had a Jewish employee, and her manager had scheduled an after-work meeting on what was an important holy day on the Jewish calendar. My friend knew it was an unintentional oversight, but she also knew her Jewish coworker was unlikely to say anything but felt—once again—like an outsider. So she, as a follower of Jesus, had the slightly awkward conversation with her manager, explaining the situation and gently encouraging him to note Jewish holidays when scheduling future events, which he immediately agreed to do.

As daughters of the living God, we need to be sensitively outspoken in situations involving inclusion and justice of all kinds. If I want freedom of religion, shouldn't I support it for my coworker of another faith? If I want opportunities based on my experience and knowledge without being disqualified or discounted because I am a woman, shouldn't I want the same for my Black colleague? If I am part of the dominant culture, don't I have an obligation to be protective of those who are treated differently simply because they are not part of that culture?

This has nothing to do with politics from the right or left. We are required to be just, love kindness, and walk humbly with God. When we speak up for the widows, orphans, foreigners, and others, people cannot help but notice Jesus in us, in part because it's countercultural to align with the least powerful. My friend's quiet conversation on behalf of her colleague opened the door for future conversations around faith, building relationship and creating an invitation for her to freely speak about Jesus later.

Do not discount the power of your witness to colleagues, neighbors, and family as you live out today's verse. When confronted with exclusion (intentional or not) or injustice, I want my response to proclaim Jesus' love so loudly that others cannot help but be drawn toward him. And I gratefully entrust the rest to God, knowing that I've done my small part in obedience.

Julie

Today's Act of Gratitude

Prayerfully consider what obedience looks like for you in living out Micah 6:8.

Internal Renewal

*Throw off your old sinful nature and your former way of life,
which is corrupted by lust and deception. Instead, let the Spirit
renew your thoughts and attitudes. Put on your new nature,
created to be like God—truly righteous and holy.*

EPHESIANS 4:22-24

Looking around in amazement, I surveyed our main level as the smell of fresh paint stung my nose. A pale blue had replaced the mustard yellow walls of my kitchen; the neutral light brown of the living room was now a soft gray. The rooms looked brighter, bigger, and airier. I loved it.

"It looks like a completely different house!" I said, turning to my husband. "Why did it take us so long to do this? I can't believe we lived with those walls for ten years!" Eyebrows raised, he nodded in agreement.

"It's incredible," he said.

Though the essential nature of the space had not changed—it still had the same walls and windows, flooring and furniture—one simple alteration had made all the difference. Of course, no one looking at the outside of my house would notice anything. But inside, it was radically different.

This kind of simple change demonstrates a spiritual truth. In Jesus, we are made new—not just once, but again and again. He renews our thoughts so that we can become more like him. This transformation is accomplished from the inside out.

As when I selected the soft blue and gray of my freshly painted walls, we have the privilege of deciding what our internal landscape looks like. Thanks to the guidance of the Holy Spirit, we can actively choose to follow his lead, take our negative thoughts captive (see 2 Corinthians 10:5), and replace them with the truth of his Word. We can refresh and restore our lives, viewing our current circumstances through the long-term lens of God's love, mercy, and grace. He makes all things new—including us. Let's follow the Spirit's lead and choose to be renewed, inside and out.

Kristin

Today's Act of Gratitude

Consider what your internal landscape looks like by checking your
thoughts and attitudes. Pray for the Spirit to renew your mind
and heart to experience peace, gratitude, and joy throughout
your day—no matter what external circumstances you face.

The Most Important Ingredient

*You are the salt of the earth. But what good is salt if it
has lost its flavor? Can you make it salty again? It will
be thrown out and trampled underfoot as worthless.*

MATTHEW 5:13

Bending low, I pulled my second-ever loaf of sourdough bread out of the oven. It looked perfect with its lightly toasted exterior and adorable heart expertly carved (by me!) into the rustic crust.

"Hey Aaron, I'm officially a bread-baking diva!" I aimed my excited shout toward the stairs, hoping my hubby would come running up. I was inordinately excited by my immediate success in this new adventure, especially because I'd been too intimidated to try bread baking for more than a decade, convinced it was too hard.

"Cut it open, let's see how it tastes!" Aaron's voice carried up the stairs as he joined me in the kitchen, grabbing the bread knife even as he admired my masterpiece. After a quick swipe of butter, we took a first, simultaneous bite. As we chewed, our faces morphed from excited into a contemplative puzzlement; something wasn't quite right.

"NOOOOOOOOO!" I wailed. "I forgot to add the salt!" The realization hit hard. And with my devastated proclamation, Aaron's face went from puzzled to a polite frown as the taste mystery was solved. It took me until just before bedtime to toss my beautiful loaf, acknowledging that there was no saving it. I'd done all the big, hard things perfectly right, and yet it was ruined by my failure to add a tiny amount of seasoning.

It was a painful lesson, but one that has reverberated in my spirit. If I live a "good" life but am not salty, what is the point? If I do all the hard work of living lovely but don't point others toward Jesus, careful to give God the glory, am I any better than beautiful, unsalted bread?

That loaf has become a poignant reminder that good works, apart from God, don't have eternal value. God's presence and my acknowledgment of him is the key, salty ingredient in my calling here on earth. Letting others know *why* I strive to live faithfully is my spiritual salt. I've never been so grateful for a cooking disaster (and I've had more than my fair share) as for my saltless bread.

Julie

Today's Act of Gratitude

Prayerfully ask God if there are areas in which you've lost
spiritual saltiness. Thank him for his redemptive work in you.

Come As You Are

*Accept each other just as Christ has accepted
you so that God will be given glory.*

ROMANS 15:7

"When we first went, I didn't have anything to wear other than ripped jeans. I didn't own a dress," my mom recalled about the days she and my dad first started attending church together in the late 1970s.

"We were accepted, just as we were. And we were a little rough," she added with a laugh. "But the people at the church loved us so well. We really grew in our faith during that time."

I smiled as I recalled those formative years of my childhood. I too remembered that little country church and the people who attended—bankers and convicts, former addicts and stay-at-home moms—all sitting together, joining in worship because of the acceptance and love they'd found in Jesus. It wasn't always easy, and sometimes people's lives still got a little messy, but the love that flowed was evident and transformative to all who showed up at their doors.

Not everyone has had a church experience like my family did when I was young. I've been in other church communities that weren't as loving or inviting, and I've heard plenty of stories of people who've been hurt. Although their feelings are valid, that's simply not the way it should be. In Christ, we are to accept one another because Christ has accepted each one of us. And when we do this, people outside (and inside) our church walls notice and are drawn in, and ultimately, God gets the glory.

If you've been hurt by a church or a faith community, don't lose hope. God's design is one of inclusion for each one of us. Keep searching, asking God to lead you, and he will bring you to people and a community who will love you and accept you, just as you are.

Kendra

Today's Act of Gratitude

Who do you know that may be an outsider who needs to be included in a faith community? Reach out and let that person know you care.

The Gift of Noticing

Encourage each other and build each other up,
just as you are already doing.

1 THESSALONIANS 5:11

"Oh, thanks! I got the shirt on the clearance rack. And the pants are a really old pair . . ." She rambled on, subconsciously rejecting my genuine, freely given compliment about an outfit that fit both her body shape and her personality in a particularly lovely way.

Why do we women tend to deflect the lovely things others say about us? It's a question I've rhetorically asked the Holy Spirit hundreds of times over the years. I've witnessed compliments about naturally thick curly hair, a knack for organization, or a job well done as an event emcee be politely refused as the recipient immediately points out that someone else has prettier hair or a better organized fridge, or confesses that she flubbed a certain part of the event announcements.

In fact, I've noticed that women are far more likely to engage in lengthy conversations focused on their flaws, criticizing their God-given bodies and their abilities—often in front of daughters, nieces, and other young women who quietly soak it all up and then emulate the same behaviors.

Rather than deflect compliments, what if we simply said thank you, genuinely accepting and appreciating lovely words spoken over us as the gift they were intended to be? And what if we became compliment gift-givers ourselves, building up those around us through the simple act of looking for loveliness in all its forms and letting another woman know that we see something beautiful in or about her?

The simple act of noticing another's loveliness is often remembered by the recipient decades later because it is so rare and unexpected a gift. I don't know about you, but I have an inner critical voice that *loves* to tell me all the ways I've fallen short, constantly. And I may—at times—have others in my life who speak harsh words over me. Being noticed for something positive—especially by the woman standing in line behind me at the grocery store or by a woman further up the chain of command in the same organization—is a blessing and an encouragement.

Julie

Today's Act of Gratitude

Reflect on a time someone spoke words of lovely,
affirming life over you. Pay it forward by
giving the gift of noticing to a stranger.

He Knows Your Name

The LORD replied to Moses, "I will indeed do what you have asked,
for I look favorably on you, and I know you by name."

EXODUS 33:17

"Mom, did you get rid of Violet?" my daughter asked.

Stalling for time, I paused and asked a question of my own. "Why?"

"I can't find her," she said. "I've looked everywhere. Do you think you donated her?"

"Hmm," I said noncommittally, knowing full well that I'd purged Violet—a purple stuffed animal who talked—long ago. (Noisy toys are the bane of a parent's existence.) I sighed, deciding to be honest. "Yeah, I'm pretty sure I did."

Crestfallen, she left the room. I couldn't help but feel bad; I would never have given the toy away, noisy or not, if I'd known how much it mattered to my daughter.

Why would she remember Violet when she has forgotten the hundreds of other toys, clothes, and books I've donated over the years? I think it's because Violet was customizable. After we programmed her online, she sang a song with my daughter's name, remarking on her love of peanut butter and penguins.

Violet knew my daughter's name, and that was remarkable to her.

What's more remarkable is that *God* knows our name. The story of Moses is a great example. When Moses encountered God in a burning bush, I imagine that he wanted nothing more than to live a quiet, anonymous life. After all, he'd left everything behind—including his wealth and position of privilege—in his flight from Egypt. Though he had rebuilt his life in a new land, I doubt he broadcasted the circumstances of his former world to those around him. Yet, when God appeared in the burning bush, he called Moses by name. He wasn't fooled by the fact that Moses was far from his homeland. He knew Moses was the person he wanted to use in freeing the Hebrews from slavery in Egypt. He called him by name to fulfill a specific purpose.

There is power in names—the names we are given at birth, our nicknames, the good or bad names we internally call ourselves. Though there are billions of people alive today, each is as unique as fingerprints to our Father God. I am grateful that he knows us by name—and more staggering, that he has a purpose for each of us. We are irreplaceable.

Kristin

Today's Act of Gratitude

Reflect on what it means to you that Jesus knows your name.

Insiders and Outsiders

Every knee will bend to me, and
every tongue will declare allegiance to me.

ISAIAH 45:23

As I stood along the back wall of a tiny, one-room church near Fier, Albania, the Albanian words of a faintly familiar worship song swelled to fill the entire space. The English words tickled along the edges of my memory while ultimately remaining elusive.

As the congregation sang (and I hummed), I felt the living God among us, just as I do back home. His presence filled that space just as it's filled the sanctuary of my home church or filled hospital rooms, conference rooms, and courtrooms—all places I've invited God to walk alongside me and loved ones.

God stands apart from humanity, and his unchanging, unconditional love for his people exists outside of differences in language or culture. Those were my thoughts as my early morning flight lifted off Albanian soil, carrying me back across an ocean to worship songs whose words I understand. It was a lot to process.

In the weeks following that Albania trip, I had to repent of a weirdly unrecognized, ridiculous assumption that God speaks English as his primary language. Of course, he doesn't. But, at some point, I'd subconsciously defaulted to a belief that God is like me. The problem in thinking that way—besides being unbelievably arrogant and *wrong*—is that it makes me an "insider" while believers from other cultures and places are "outsiders." When we play the insider/outsider game with God, we are tempted to believe that we "insiders" have just the teeny-tiniest bit more of God's love than everyone else, and that is incredibly dangerous territory upon which to tread.

This insider/outsider game is an insidious tendency of human nature found in preschools, workplaces, and church denominations. We must stomp it out wherever we find it, especially when it comes to how we look at fellow brothers and sisters in Christ. We are all "outsiders" conforming to God's culture as set forth in Scripture. It requires bending our knees, giving our allegiance, and there is no room for arrogant pride or the secret belief that we are one iota more loved than believers anywhere else in the world.

While it's humbling to confess to unconsciously thinking that God is like me, I'm grateful for a fresh start.

Julie

Today's Act of Gratitude

In what ways might you be playing a spiritual insider/outsider game? Who do you consider an "outsider"? Repent.

Let's Ask Jesus

You will call, and the LORD will answer;
you will cry for help, and he will say: Here am I.

ISAIAH 58:9, NIV

Kyle and I signed up for a two-session training on Christlike healing. As the speakers shared how they had ministered to people over the years, bringing their faith into counseling, one of them said something that struck me.

He explained that so often people have an unhealthy view of Jesus because of what has happened to them or ways people have treated them, which we must address first. We must show them how much Jesus has always loved and cared for them.

He gave an example of someone lamenting to him about the traumas that had occurred in their life. When the person asked, "Where was Jesus?" the trainer leaned in and said, "Let's ask him."

He said he often answers people's hard questions with "Let's ask Jesus." And Jesus answers. Sometimes with words, but often with a sense of peace or love that the person hasn't experienced before. They often leave feeling loved and lighter than they had before they arrived. I sat back in my chair as the full weight of his words hit me.

I said to my husband later on, still pondering all we'd heard, "You know, I pray all the time, but I never just all-out think 'Let's ask Jesus.' I know God answers prayers, but I never thought to be so direct. I'm going to start."

How often do we pray, really expecting that God will answer? So many times, we can go through the motions of talking to God without waiting for his response. But Scripture is clear: when we call, the Lord will answer. And not just when things are going well. When we're in a hard place and cry for help, he will say, "Here am I." I'm so grateful that we don't have to wonder if God is listening or if he cares or if he'll respond to us. We can be confident that he will. We just have to ask.

Kendra

Today's Act of Gratitude

Ask Jesus about something that's been troubling you and wait to see how he answers—whether in word, a sense of peace, or some other response you weren't expecting.

Remembering Those We've Lost

The memory of the righteous is a blessing.

PROVERBS 10:7, ESV

Sometimes, I daydream about what my sister would be like if she were still alive today. Whether or not she would still have the interior design business she planned to start. What other creative endeavors she might have pursued over the years. How her love of traveling, hospitality, and serving others would have looked over time. If she would still love drinking mochas or watching *Gilmore Girls*. What she would think of my husband and kids, whom she never got to meet.

Although she died more than fifteen years ago, she's still part of who I am. And one of the greatest gifts I've received over the years has been the instances in which friends have reminded me of her or said something to let me know that she's not forgotten.

Like when a friend and I were shopping together and she asked me what Katrina would think of the items we were considering.

Or when a friend texted me to say that even though she'd never met my sister, she missed her with me.

Or the nurse who told me, years after my sister had passed, that she was still remembered by the other nurses at the hospital.

Sometimes people think that they are being merciful when they don't bring up the loss of our loved one, when the truth is, many of us welcome the opportunity to talk about those we've lost. Our greatest fear is not that we will feel renewed pain at the reminder, but that our loved one will be forgotten.

The Bible tells us that the memories of those who have passed are a blessing. I'm grateful each time someone tells me how much Katrina meant to them or how her story of faith impacted them positively. Those little comments always help me feel less alone in my grief. When we give someone the space and grace to reminisce about their loved one, we remind them that they aren't alone. In Jesus, we have the hope of more (see 1 Thessalonians 4:13). But while we wait, we can choose to celebrate and thereby honor the memory of those we continue to love after loss.

Kristin

Today's Act of Gratitude

Reach out to someone whose loved one has passed.
Tell them how much that person meant to you.

We All Need a Jasmine

If one person falls, the other can reach out and help.
But someone who falls alone is in real trouble.

ECCLESIASTES 4:10

Glancing at Lizzie as she slid into the front seat, I said, "So . . . we have to run to the grocery store before we head home to celebrate your birthday."

"Hmm. Does that mean Jon and Daddy are still decorating? You're stalling, aren't you?"

"Busted!" Grinning mischievously, I told my daughter a half-truth. "We ran into trouble because there is a helium shortage. They're blowing up balloons manually, and it's taking a bit more time than we expected. So let's give them just a little longer."

While Aaron and Jon *were* manually inflating balloons, the full story was that Lizzie's dear friend Jasmine was in our house, putting the final touches on a surprise birthday tea party. And while the balloons were taking longer than expected, my primary concern was giving Jasmine a little extra time to finish her preparations.

When we walked into our house thirty minutes later, the delighted surprise on Lizzie's face as she took in Jasmine's efforts—including a beautifully set tablescape—was worth the slight subterfuge and the last-minute errands.

But what makes Jasmine a truly wonderful friend is the loving, godly advice she gives Lizzie—even in the midst of these teen years. She listens carefully, and then, instead of saying what she thinks Lizzie wants to hear, she tells her the truth, wrapped in love. I'm grateful that she gives Lizzie a safe space to process ideas and feelings out loud while being brave enough to disagree when she senses Lizzie is believing a lie about herself or others.

We all need a Jasmine, a friend brave and bold who loves us enough to gently hold us accountable and speak up when we are venturing away from the best God has for us. And we need to be that kind of friend for others, willing to reach out with help when we see a loved one floundering.

Julie

Today's Act of Gratitude

Send a note of thanks to someone who has been lovingly honest with you at the risk of making you frustrated or angry. Prayerfully consider who might need the same from you.

Joy from Within

You are the light of the world—
like a city on a hilltop that cannot be hidden.

MATTHEW 5:14

"It's kind of amazing when you hear about someone's life," I commented to a friend as we left a women's event. "Someone can look so put together on the outside but then you hear their story and you realize how much they've overcome."

"Yeah," she responded. "It's easy to think someone else has had a perfect life or has never struggled when you see how they're doing today."

At the event, our new friend Autumn had shared her story for the first time to a group of women. I had met her a couple of years earlier because she worked at a boutique I would shop at regularly. We became Instagram friends, and I was drawn to her outgoing and positive personality. She has a way of lifting the atmosphere in a room, allowing others to feel loved and accepted.

But what I found out that night was that Autumn's joyful disposition doesn't come from an easy life. She's had many experiences that caused heartache and pain. More than most. As she spoke, I realized that part of her joy comes from authentically sharing *all* of her life and using even the hard things that have happened as a way to connect with others. She's not fake. She's real. And her ability to encourage others in whatever they're facing through her own story is a gift. She is a light. And she shines brightly.

Oftentimes, people can look so composed on the outside, leading us to assume that their lives are perfect. In turn, this can make us want to hide our own imperfections or past mistakes because we feel like we're the only one with our history.

But just like Autumn has learned that part of the secret of experiencing joy is to be true to who you are and share your story with others, we can do the same. We can be honest and use even the difficult times we've walked through to encourage those around us, letting them know they're not alone. And when we do, we become a light that others are drawn to. We become like a city on a hill that no one could overlook.

Kendra

Today's Act of Gratitude

Who can you encourage by sharing part of your own story?

Our Body Is a Gift

Don't you realize that your body is the temple of the Holy Spirit, who lives in you and was given to you by God? You do not belong to yourself, for God bought you with a high price. So you must honor God with your body.

1 CORINTHIANS 6:19-20

Balancing on my left foot, I maneuvered the sock between two toes of my right foot and slowly angled my leg upward until I could snag the dangling sock with my hand. *Success!*

I first learned this dubious skill more than two decades ago. After breaking vertebrae in my lower back in a car accident, I spent the summer wearing a brace that covered my torso and supported my spine. As a result, I couldn't bend over. So when things fell on the floor—whether they were clothing items or something else—I used my toes to retrieve them. The improvisation allowed me to do more tasks on my own.

Before then, I'd always taken my mobility for granted. Even now, it's not something I notice all that often—I can usually bend, lift, walk, and move without discomfort. It's only when something isn't working as it should—when my back is too sore from lifting, or my foot falls asleep and tingles when I try to step on it—that I think to be grateful for my physical abilities.

The idea that our body is a temple of the Holy Spirit probably isn't new to you. People often mention it when they talk about choosing to eat healthily or avoid certain habits, but I think the concept applies to more. Because when we choose to be thankful for our body's ability to do things—without comparing it to someone else's ability—we honor God. Instead of focusing on what we don't like about ourselves—the aches and pains we might have, or the parts that aren't functioning well—let's consider what works. Thanking God that our lungs utilize oxygen, our heart can beat on its own, and our brain can think or pray are ways to honor him for the gift we've been given.

Kristin

Today's Act of Gratitude

Spend time thanking God for all the things your body can do.

September

Giving with Love

*You must each decide in your heart how much to give.
And don't give reluctantly or in response to pressure.
"For God loves a person who gives cheerfully."*

2 CORINTHIANS 9:7

"Do you want to see what I've been working on lately?" my mom asked one day. We'd been sipping coffee in her sunroom when she posed the question.

Moments later, I stared at a riot of color and patterns in the spare bedroom that doubled as her workspace. Many of her half-finished quilts and projects were pinned on the wall, while others draped over tables or racks.

"Wow," I marveled, approaching one to take a closer look. "These are beautiful."

My mom has been quilting for many years, and as her daughter, I've been lucky enough to be on the receiving end of many of her creations. I appreciate the combination of beauty and practicality, but even more, I appreciate the time that went into making them. Each one takes hours to piece together, sew, and eventually quilt. I'm grateful that she chooses to share something she's spent so much time on with those she loves.

Just as my mom's quilts can provide warmth and comfort, many of us have gifts and talents we can share with others. My friend Sam bakes beautiful bread that she generously gives to neighbors and friends. My friend Sandy volunteers the gift of time to help complete administrative work for a women's ministry. My friend Steph's best friend bakes fabulous cakes for Steph's daughters on their birthdays.

What a joy and privilege it is for us to share with others! Whether it's through something we've made, a helping hand, the gift of time, or a listening ear, we can spread beauty, hope, or love in the world. Rather than feeling pressured to give, let's consider our talents and skills as part of the blessing that our generous God has endowed us with, and let's use them to honor him. Everything we have and do is a resource. When we choose to serve others or give them something we've created, we bless the recipients and demonstrate the same care for them that Jesus has shown to us.

Kristin

Today's Act of Gratitude

Share a skill, talent, or item with someone else, or
thank someone for something they shared with you.

A Well-Lit Path

*Your word is a lamp to guide my feet
and a light for my path.*

PSALM 119:105

"Julie, come see my wisteria! We installed a pergola this spring, and I decided to plant wisteria around the four posts so it'll grow up and over the entire structure. Won't that be gorgeous?"

I followed my acquaintance into her backyard, trying to mentally smooth the furrow I could feel between my eyebrows as I processed her words.

Be tactful. Be gentle. Don't completely smash her pergola hopes and dreams, my inner voice scolded even as my thoughts swirled with frustration at whoever sold her a plant that likely wouldn't survive more than one or two of our Minnesota winters, depending upon snow cover and prolonged subzero temps.

While I love living in Minnesota, purchasing plants from national retailers and big-box stores means we must be hypervigilant in our independent assessment of whether that particular variety can actually thrive here. Just because they stock plant varieties with glossy photo promises of pergolas draped in twisty vines and positively smothered with glorious, fragrant blooms doesn't mean that's what will happen this far north.

And isn't that true with so much of life? We scroll through illusions on social media (or in books and magazines, or on television) promising that if we follow a particular diet or use a certain product, we'll be thin or rich or wrinkle-free and thereby happy. We get sold a promise that is—at the very least—improbable, and more likely impossible to replicate because the conditions have to be perfectly perfect to get the same results.

In contrast, God is faithful and trustworthy. With him, we will never waste our time and energy chasing mirages. He doesn't hoodwink us with earthly bait and switch tactics that leave us feeling like failures when the promise was an illusion to begin with. And when we linger in Scripture, we gratefully find clarity and truth that settles deeply within our spirits.

We can depend upon God's unchanging character no matter the changing circumstances around us. He makes our paths straight and gives us light to see where to place our feet. He does not leave us to navigate this world in uncertainty.

Julie

Today's Act of Gratitude

How has God provided a light to guide your feet when you've had a choice to make? Write a list you can refer to when life and circumstances feel uncertain.

Family Friends

Love each other with genuine affection, and
take delight in honoring each other.

ROMANS 12:10

"Morning! Are my friends planning to go to the football game this Friday? Caden was ask-ing me if you guys were coming," my friend Christa texted early one Monday morning.

"Oh yes, it's on our calendar! Tell him we wouldn't miss it!" I responded.

"You better believe it!" Julie chimed in.

We've been friends for years, and although we don't see each other as often as we'd like, we've been intentional about staying connected as individuals and as families—participating in one another's lives and cheering on the kids in their interests as well. We cook together, throw parties, and celebrate birthdays and anniversaries, and we are always there to pray for one another through good and hard seasons.

We showed up to the game Friday night, cheering as loudly as we could for Caden and taking photos of ourselves for Christa to show him later to prove that we'd been there to watch his team land another victory.

As I went to leave after the game, I hugged my friends and felt grateful for these people who walk through life not only with me but with my family as well.

Friendship at any age is so important. We need people who are in similar stages of life to understand and sympathize with all that we are going through. But we also need people who are in different places in their lives, both older and younger, to give us different perspectives. And so do our kids. It's important for my children to know and build relationships with my friends, as I hope their kids can do with me as well. I'm grateful that the wisdom and skills our children gain from other adults supports all the things my husband and I are trying to teach them.

Scripture tells us that we are to have genuine love for each other. One way we do that is by coming alongside not only our friends but their family members as well, taking an interest and encouraging them in their lives and activities. It's so important for us to mentor and be mentored by others, at any age. Friendship is a gift meant to be shared with the young and the old.

Kendra

Today's Act of Gratitude

Be intentional about building relationships with the extended family members of your friends. Their kids, parents, or other relatives all need encouragement, too, and can offer a fresh perspective on life.

Growing Together

*Let us pursue what makes for peace
and for mutual upbuilding.*

ROMANS 14:19, esv

"What's going on with the trees? It looks like there's more than one plant growing on them?" the woman behind me on the tour bus asked.

Curious, I glanced over to the side of the Costa Rican road. Just as she said, there appeared to be entirely different species sprouting out of the vee created by the branches. Their unique shapes and contrasting colors set them apart from the tree.

"Trees in the rainforest can have many other species living on them," the tour guide said. "Many plants, animals, and invertebrates call rainforests home, and they've adapted to living alongside one another." In Borneo, you can find one thousand different insect species on a single tree.[*] One scientist found forty-three different types of ants on one tree in Peru.[**]

Epiphytes are one type of plant that grows in the rainforest. They don't require soil to grow, and they make their homes on trees or rocks. That was what the woman had seen as we drove along the winding roads.

I couldn't help but marvel at the sheer number of living creatures and plants around us and how they were able to work together. Epiphytes aren't parasitic, our guide explained. They don't steal nutrients. Instead, each species on the tree gets what it needs from its environment. That way, they all flourish.

As so often happens, the natural world mirrors the spiritual. Like plants in the rainforest, there are many different parts in the body of Christ. Each of us may have gifts such as teaching, encouraging, or praying for others, yet our individual actions support the body as a whole. Each person serves a singular purpose, and all of us contribute to the upbuilding of the community. Everything we accomplish can be used to glorify Jesus and pursue wholeness in him. That's a good reason to be grateful.

Kristin

Today's Act of Gratitude

Think of someone you work alongside. How do their
unique abilities support you in your contributions
to the body? Thank them for what they do.

---

[*] "Forests of Borneo," World Wildlife Federation, accessed November 22, 2022, https://wwfeu.awsassets.panda.org/downloads/borneo_forest_cc_final_12nov07_lr.pdf.

[**] Allan D. Watt, Nigel E. Stork, and Barry Bolton, "The Diversity and Abundance of Ants in Relation to Forest Disturbance and Plantation Establishment in Southern Cameroon," *Journal of Applied Ecology*, British Ecological Society, June 26, 2002, https://besjournals.onlinelibrary.wiley.com/doi/full/10.1046/j.1365-2664.2002.00699.x.

A Gift to Your Future Self

The world offers only a craving for physical pleasure, a craving for
everything we see, and pride in our achievements and possessions.
These are not from the Father, but are from this world. And this
world is fading away, along with everything that people crave.
But anyone who does what pleases God will live forever.

1 JOHN 2:16-17

Bending low to gather the seemingly hundreds of grape-sized tomatoes from my favorite, impossible-to-find variety ('Matt's Wild Cherry'), I thought back to our unseasonably cold spring and all of the plant pampering I undertook in a desperate bid to keep these now unruly, prolific plants alive.

Thank you, past Julie! Current Julie appreciates your (grumbling) dedication to hauling trays of seedlings in and out of the house for weeks on end so they could bask in the sun but be protected from nighttime temps. And future Julie is going to be blissed out when she gets to eat bruschetta made from these beauties long into the winter months!

I rolled my eyes at my ridiculous internal dialogue, even as I recognized the truth of it. I *did* appreciate my above-and-beyond efforts to keep these plants alive, and I *was* going to love having garden tomatoes and basil in my bruschetta mix when snow blanketed the ground. I was reaping the reward of my past gardening faithfulness.

But that's not always the case. How often do we seek temporary pleasure or convenience at the expense of our future self? How often do we chase temporal achievements and possessions that will fade away over that which has eternal value and is pleasing to God?

These are uncomfortable, convicting questions, putting us in direct conflict with cultural and societal norms. However, delayed gratification and intentionality in what we pursue are essential parts of our faith journey that build both grit and gratitude. If we live to please only our current self and pursue the fool's gold our culture deems valuable, we rob our future self and live lives that miss the most important, eternal points.

Julie

Today's Act of Gratitude

Commit to a habit your future self will thank you for,
and prayerfully recalibrate a short- and long-term
goal to align with God's plans, not society's.

Every Tribe and Nation

*After this I saw a vast crowd, too great to count, from every nation and tribe
and people and language, standing in front of the throne and before the Lamb.
They were clothed in white robes and held palm branches in their hands.*

REVELATION 7:9

"I told them if they were looking for another family to host an Amity intern one weekend a month, they should talk to you and that you would be very welcoming to all cultures," my friend commented over the phone. We were discussing the group that would soon be arriving to assist with the Spanish immersion program our kids are part of in our local school district.

"Thank you, friend. That's so kind of you to say," I responded, and we went on to talk about the student who would be staying with her family.

As I thought about her compliment later, I mentioned to my husband, "I've never told her that."

"She's just seen us welcome others in," he responded.

I nodded agreement. It was true. My husband and I live in a culturally diverse community, and we've been intentional about inviting in others who come from around the world—whether international students, Amity interns (Spanish-speaking teachers), refugees, or immigrants.

It all started years ago as we read Scripture and realized that God is building his Kingdom, and that includes people from every nation and tribe. We decided that we wanted to be part of this larger heavenly Kingdom and began to look around us for people who might need some encouragement or love. We realized there were many in our community from faraway places, missing family and the familiarity of home, and we wanted them to know that they were welcome here. Since then, we've built a diverse network of friends and "framily" whom we dearly love. I'm grateful for the way they have shown us a vision of what God's Kingdom can look like here on earth.

Isn't it exciting to think that one day people from every tribe and nation will stand before the throne, worshiping our God together? Although we long for that day, the good news is that we have an opportunity right now to join together in relationship with our brothers and sisters in Christ—both here and abroad.

Kendra

Today's Act of Gratitude

Look around you for someone new to your community and
maybe even this country and invite them to coffee or a meal.

The Power of Silence

The LORD will fight for you, and
you have only to be silent.

EXODUS 14:14, ESV

I worked at a women's clothing store in college. Although I liked my coworkers and the flexible hours, doing the same tasks over and over could be monotonous.

But there is a certain grace to being alone with your thoughts. I could spend half an hour folding shirts or hanging a new shipment of clothes but secretly dreaming up alternate lives for myself. I imagined myself as the director of a nonprofit organization that threw fancy galas, or as a travel writer who visited far-flung locations. Though these may seem like idle thoughts, that time of silence allowed me to dream and sort out what was most important to me.

I no longer have that job, but I still find myself folding shirts or hanging up items at home, the whirling washer and humming refrigerator my only companions.

Sometimes, we have an uneasy relationship with silence. On hard days, it can feel heavy; being alone with our thoughts is uncomfortable. Even when life is good, it can be all too easy to fill the quiet spaces with podcasts, music, or the buzz of the television—when what our souls need is a healthy dose of stillness.

Words have power, but so does silence. In fact, just two minutes of it can help calm our bodies more than listening to relaxing music can, thanks to the way it decreases our blood pressure, among other things.[*] Silence can help us sort through hurts or hard things, offer space for reflection, or give us room to breathe or plan or dream. It gives us the pause we need to think, lament, grieve, or identify the restlessness or discomfort inside us.

Yet silence is a gift we often overlook. We think that we must always be doing or saying something to be effective, but today's Scripture reminds us that sometimes, we simply need to be silent. It can offer a holy pause, one the Spirit can fill. It can allow God to work in our hearts or minds. In that sense, silence can provide the grace and the space we need to connect with God and lean closer to him.

Kristin

Today's Act of Gratitude

Spend five minutes sitting in silence. Reflect on this experience.
Was it hard to be still that long? How did you feel afterward?

---

[*] L. Bernardi, C. Porta, and P. Sleight, "Cardiovascular, Cerebrovascular, and Respiratory Changes Induced by Different Types of Music in Musicians and Non Musicians: The Importance of Silence," *Heart* 92, no. 4 (2006): 445–52, https://www.ncbi.nlm.nih.gov/pmc/articles/PMC1860846/.

Mentoring Prayer

Direct your children onto the right path, and
when they are older, they will not leave it.

PROVERBS 22:6

"Who's going to start prayer this morning?" After two beats of silence, Scott glances in the rearview mirror. "Hannah, why don't you get us going today?" As he backs the car down the driveway, they start their prayerful ride to middle school.

As the parent who handles school drop-off for his kids, Scott stumbled onto Family Prayer Commute (that's what he calls it) during a rough morning. In a car filled with tension, he decided to pray—out loud—a blessing over each member of their family in an attempt to reset attitudes and reboot the day. As he prayed, the atmosphere shifted from irritated to apologetic, with "love yous" and "I'm sorries" being exchanged in the drop-off lane.

Encouraged, Scott continued this new routine, broadening his prayer to include loved ones and friends and then assigning each child a turn to pray. He has two golden rules for Family Prayer Commute: (1) he does not criticize or critique anyone's prayers (which must be longer than "God bless us"), and (2) they practice the prayer time consistently (during every morning commute).

Rather than simply telling his kids how to pray, Scott shows them. He models prayer in how and who he prays for, smiling softly as his kids have—unprompted—started adopting his patterns and practices.

It's through this process that Scott modeled how to pray for an enemy. And while that is perhaps too strong a word to wield against this person, she was actively and intentionally sabotaging a loved one at work through rumor and gossip. Scott prayed God would intervene with blessing and presence in this woman's life, while also asking that her tongue would be stilled from wagging against their loved one. His kids picked up that prayer with an age-appropriate understanding of what was going on, praying most mornings for God to intersect her life with blessing while also thwarting her plans.

We want people of all ages to understand the power of prayer as well as feel comfortable praying aloud, and Scott's idea creates a safe space to practice both. I appreciate when someone freely shares a tool for developing spiritual habits, and we've adopted our own version of Family Prayer Commute.

Julie

Today's Act of Gratitude

How do you practice prayer with loved ones? Might a variation of Family Prayer Commute work for you? Be sure to include thanksgiving for the ways God has blessed you.

A Momentary Fog

How do you know what your life will be like tomorrow?
Your life is like the morning fog—it's here a little while, then it's gone.

JAMES 4:14

After a relentlessly rainy day, I was surprised to see the sun peek out of the clouds as evening approached. Driving my daughter to youth group a little later, I marveled at the low-lying fog that had silently appeared and now hovered near the earth, stealing through the woods and slipping over rain-slicked roads.

"The closer you get to it, the more it seems to disappear," my daughter observed.

Even though we know that fog is simply a collection of water droplets suspended in the atmosphere near the earth, it still feels a little mysterious. Elusive. Barring special measures, there is no way to capture it or hold it tightly. Its very nature is that of a vapor.

The epistle of James reminds us that our lives are just as transitory as that disappearing fog. Even though a single day can feel like it's dragging on with no end in sight, the years pass quickly. But the slippery nature of time and the brevity of life aren't something to mourn; instead, they are simply reminders that our time on earth is limited.

When James compares life to morning fog, it's not in the sense that it doesn't matter or won't last long. Nor is it that we shouldn't make plans for the future. He is simply offering the gentle reminder that it's arrogant for us to think that we alone are in charge of our fate. Fog is impermanent; its nature reminds us that much of life is beyond our control.

We can be thankful for today, for this moment. The present should be our focus—not because our past and future don't matter, but because this is all we truly have. We can't fix the past; we can't control tomorrow. But here—in this moment—we can soak up the joys of the day.

Kristin

Today's Act of Gratitude

First, pause and thank God for this moment. Then, focus on
being fully present in every activity throughout the day.

Just Show Up

Worry weighs a person down;
an encouraging word cheers a person up.

PROVERBS 12:25

As Terri walked into the sanctuary, I gasped, surprised to see my friend. She approached me, smiling.

"You came," I said, as we hugged.

"Of course," she said. "I wouldn't miss it."

My throat clenched with emotion as I thanked her. Just a few weeks earlier I'd mentioned to my Bible study that I was nervous for my first speaking engagement. I knew God wanted me to start ministering to other women, but I was still hesitant to do something new, especially in front of others.

"What if they hate it?" I'd asked. "Or what if I'm not any good?"

As the women encouraged me and prayed for me, I shared with them more details about where I'd be speaking and the time. Unbeknownst to me, Terri had taken note. And the morning of the event, she showed up and sat in the front row.

As I got up to speak, my knees were weak and my mouth was dry, but there sat my friend, smiling at me, letting me know she was already proud before I even spoke a word. To this day, all I can remember of the audience is her. She was the encouragement and support that I needed, and I am still so grateful that she came.

We all need people in our lives like Terri. Ones that will show up for us when we need a friend. Ones who'll listen and support us when we really need it. Worry really can weigh us down, making us feel like we are alone, but an encouraging word not only cheers us up, but reminds us that there is someone there with us.

Kendra

Today's Act of Gratitude

Who is someone that has shown up for you at a critical moment?
Send them a note of thanks. And who may need a friend to show
up for them? Take time to reach out and encourage them.

Remaining Influential

*Do all that you can to live
in peace with everyone.*

ROMANS 12:18

"Performing the wave is your favorite part of this baseball game, isn't it?"

My seat neighbor's question was in response to my giggle as everyone in our stadium section threw their hands in the air with an audible "wooooooo," while the swell passed and proceeded in its third slow circle.

Ignoring the batter swinging at pitches, I tracked the fun tradition as it moved through the crowd. Somewhere north of ten thousand people, mostly strangers, participated, working together to keep the wave circulating for several minutes.

Lord, thank you for fun moments reminding us of one another's humanity as we sit together, eat together, and cheer wildly at the swings and misses of the visiting team. Help me remember this moment as we move into election season. May I always see—first and foremost—the humanity of others, no matter what.

My silent prayer as I watched the opposing batter strike out against my Twinkies had me pondering other ways I might capture and share the simple joy and togetherness of such a tradition, looking for ways to build community and live in peace despite national schisms along any number of fault lines.

While I'm sure my work colleagues have no interest in performing the wave as an official way to end our meetings, bringing in an occasional treat to share is an easy way to stay in relationship despite differences. And inviting the neighborhood to a Sunday night bonfire with s'mores and hot cider is a simple option for building or maintaining community without worrying about whether your house is tidy.

Sometimes, being in proximity to us is the closest a person has ever been to meeting Jesus. We might be the first version of him a neighbor, colleague, or shopper standing behind us at the checkout counter has known. Striving to see the humanity in everyone and live in peace whenever possible helps keep us in relationship instead of falling into the divisive trap of "them versus us." And relational proximity allows us to remain influential rather than be immediately dismissed based on assumptions or stereotypes.

Julie

Today's Act of Gratitude

What's your version of the wave, helping you maintain proximity of relationship and community when it's tempting to disengage along divisive fault lines?

The Beautiful Truth

You are altogether beautiful,
my darling; there is no flaw in you.

SONG OF SOLOMON 4:7, NIV

When I was growing up, my mom often shopped at garage sales to find clothes for all three of us girls. One year, my sister wanted a pair of Girbaud jeans—which were all the rage at school—but they were deemed too expensive to buy at the regular price. My mom was so excited when she ran across a pair in my sister's size at a garage sale and brought them home.

While trends change throughout the years, they are a small part of the larger story we tell ourselves about beauty, image, and identity. Culture bombards us with feelings of being at once "too much" and "not enough," and we are battered by ever-shifting standards. Our clothing, body, face, age, cultural heritage, and race are constantly sized up, critiqued, or diminished, but none of these things get to decide our worth.

One way we can reset the narrative is by choosing to see ourselves—inside and out—the way that Jesus sees us. A beautiful prayer written by Macrina Wiederkehr turns our understanding of beauty on its head: "Help me believe the truth about myself, no matter how beautiful it is!"*

Our secret worry is that if people really knew us, they'd be disgusted by the ugliness inside of us. But the truth is that we are lovely and loved, just as we are. Consider, for a moment, your closest friends: Do you think they're beautiful? Would an internal struggle they face change the way you see them? If the answer to those questions is a respective yes and no, we need to reconsider how we view ourselves. If we're willing to extend grace to our friends, can we not extend that same grace to ourselves?

Song of Solomon details a romantic relationship between the king and his bride, and he tells her that she's beautiful. Flawless. Of course, as the church, we're often compared to the bride of Christ. And if that's true, then doesn't it also follow that this is the way Jesus regards us, too—as beautiful? Let's spend time in God's Word and see ourselves through the lens of his love. When we do, we'll be able to recognize the beautiful truth about ourselves.

Kristin

Today's Act of Gratitude

List three things you like about yourself.
Thank God for creating these parts of you.

Short Prayers of Strength for Women (Eugene, OR: Harvest House Publishers, 2021), 17.

Rejoicing in Repentance

The whole law can be summed up in this one command:
"Love your neighbor as yourself."

GALATIANS 5:14

It was a crisp fall afternoon as I walked up my driveway, slowly flipping through the larger-than-usual stack of mail.

Junk, junk, junk . . . wait, what's this?

The letter was from my friend's teenage son, and I had a feeling it was a request to support his football team. I tucked the envelope under my arm for safekeeping and continued my stroll as I flipped through the rest of the mail.

Caden plays football for my hometown's fierce—and sometimes bitter—rival, and while I haven't been to a hometown football game in a lot of years, my loyalties default always to the Hornets over the Bulldogs. But as I read his letter, I knew I'd be doing the once-upon-a-time unthinkable: monetarily supporting those rascally Bulldogs because I love Caden infinitely more than I love the Big Lake Hornets.

As I slipped the red flag up on my mailbox the next morning, I pondered where else I might be holding traditions, policies, or something else over love and care of people. A football rivalry is admittedly a rather silly example, but it got me thinking about other, more serious instances in which I've failed to love others as myself because I've supported a tradition, policy, or my own self-interest ahead of caring for them.

Ouch. It isn't pleasant to come face-to-face with the inconsistency between what I profess to believe and how I live my life; however, it is a necessary part of my faith journey. I cannot grow stronger and more firmly rooted if I refuse conviction followed by repentance when I've gotten it wrong.

Friend, there is nothing to fear from the conviction of the Holy Spirit. Each of us have fallen short of the life God calls us to live. Admitting, repenting, and striving to do better is a sign of active, maturing faith. The danger lies in the belief that we've arrived, that our theology is perfectly expressed in our deeds, that we have no more work to do.

Instead, let's thank God for that sick-to-our-stomach feeling when the Holy Spirit lets us know that we messed up. Let's rejoice over growth, changing behaviors, and a humble willingness to repent.

Julie

Today's Act of Gratitude

Gratefully embrace the Holy Spirit's conviction
as an opportunity to grow in your faith.

Believing the Truth

*Lead me by your truth and teach me, for you are the God
who saves me. All day long I put my hope in you.*

PSALM 25:5

"What is the matter?" my husband asked on our way home from church. "Why did we have to leave so quickly?"

"I don't want to talk about it," I answered, unsure as to why I felt the way I did, but knowing it had to do with a deep pain that had been festering for a long time.

It wouldn't be until several years later that I realized this pain came from a deep fear of being associated with failure. It wasn't so much that I was worried about failing. I was worried that I *was* a failure at the very core of my being.

And because of this, I would do anything possible just so the people around me wouldn't think that I was the failure I felt I was deep inside.

When I started meeting with a therapist, it finally became clear that some of my erratic behavior over the years—behavior I often didn't understand myself—had to do with this core belief. And once I knew what the lie was, I began to combat it with the Word of God. The truth. I would search out Scriptures that told me the truth about who I was and what God thought of me. I would write the verses on note cards and place them around my home so I could see them and be reminded. And slowly, the deceptions began to let go of their hold on my mind and heart. The truth was setting me free.

The Bible says that the enemy of our souls loves to lie to us and that he is the father of lies. And no matter who we are, we've all had lies that we've believed. That's why knowing what the Bible says is so important. It can be a process to overcome negative perceptions of ourselves, but thankfully, if we'll ask God, as the psalmist did, to lead us by his truth and teach us, he will. It's God who saves. And it's in him that we find hope.

Kendra

Today's Act of Gratitude

Think of a lie you've been believing about yourself. Search for a Scripture that combats it, then write or print it out and put it in a place you will read it often. Thank God for helping you to see the truth.

Assume the Best

Don't make judgments about anyone ahead of time—before the Lord returns. For he will bring our darkest secrets to light and will reveal our private motives. Then God will give to each one whatever praise is due.

1 CORINTHIANS 4:5

Oh no, I thought as soon as I saw that the elementary school was calling. *One of the kids must be sick.*

Full of dread, I picked up the call and heard the principal's voice.

"I've got your daughter in the office with me. Do you have time for a Good News Call?" he asked.

Caught off guard, I agreed.

"I'm calling because we had a new student yesterday, and your daughter went out of her way to show her around and introduce her to me. It made my day. She is such a caring, considerate student. I am so proud of her!"

Eyes stinging with unexpected tears, I thanked him for making such a happy call.

Afterward, I couldn't help but think about how my mind had immediately started down the path toward worst-case scenarios. A positive call hadn't even crossed my mind.

Unfortunately, that experience is common, especially in relationships. Someone makes an offhanded remark that hurts our feelings, and we assume they were purposely unkind. We find out about a gathering we weren't invited to and wonder if the host isn't as good a friend as we thought they were. A text goes unreturned, and we conclude that the other person doesn't care enough to respond.

In each of these situations, it's hard not to assume the worst, particularly if we've been hurt before.

What would happen if we chose instead to assume the best? We know that God—who could easily judge humanity based on the world's sin—instead considers our hearts. Let's do the same by overlooking minor missteps and considering motives. Is it possible that those around us are busy, overwhelmed, or exhausted rather than intentionally hurtful? Let's forgive minor slights and make grace our ready response. When we do, relationships will be repaired, forgiveness extended, and peace restored.

Our gratitude and joy in our relationships can only increase each time we consciously decide to see the best-case scenario. If we choose to look for the good, we'll find it. When we do, we can celebrate all God has done.

Kristin

Today's Act of Gratitude

Pause and reorient your thoughts each time you
are tempted to assume the worst.

The Fragrance of Christ

Our lives are a Christ-like fragrance rising up to God.

2 CORINTHIANS 2:15

I always loved visiting my uncle Mike. He had a tenderness to him that would draw you in. He listened. And although he was very wise, he was never arrogant. You got the sense that when he was with you, you were the most important person to him in that moment.

But Mike didn't become who he was instantaneously or by chance. If you heard Mike's story, you'd find it was one of heartbreak and pain, deep loss and trials. Mike hadn't had an easy life. And on the surface, it would seem like the things that had happened to him could have made him very harsh or angry. But Mike knew Jesus, and through every trial, he allowed himself to be formed more and more into his image.

Mike wasn't perfect, but he was just so approachable. He'd allowed Jesus to take experiences that could have made him a very bitter man and instead use them to make him compassionate and kind. He was easily able to listen to anyone's pain, sitting with them in their own suffering, because he knew what it was like. I remember my husband once commenting after spending a little time with Mike, "Why do I feel like I could just cry with him?"

I smiled.

"Because Mike has the spirit of Jesus like few people I have met," I responded. "He's allowed God to wear down all his rough edges, and love shines through above anything else."

We all desire to follow Mike's example, giving off a "Christ-like fragrance" that rises up to please God, but to do so, we must be willing to be formed by Christ. We must allow him to shape us in the way that we follow his commands to love God and others. We mustn't allow our circumstances to make us bitter, but instead allow God to use all things to bring him glory.

Mike would be the first to tell you he's not an exceptional person, just one who sought Jesus, however imperfectly, his whole life. We can do the same. I'm so glad God doesn't have favorites: what he offers to one, he'll give to another. We just have to seek after him.

Kendra

Today's Act of Gratitude

Ask God to show you how your life spreads the fragrance of Christ. And for the areas that it doesn't yet, ask him to show you how you can follow him even more.

Don't Be a Chicken

The tongue also is a fire, a world of evil among the parts of the body. It corrupts the whole body, sets the whole course of one's life on fire, and is itself set on fire by hell.

JAMES 3:6, NIV

"Ugh! You guys are just like chickens. You peck one another to death!" My middle school classmates and I stared wide-eyed as our teacher fumed her way from the doorway to her desk a moment before the bell rang.

Chickens? Death? Middle school me scoffed at her words. My parents had recently bought some bantam chicks, and they were the cutest little balls of downy fluff. I *loved* our chickens, and they were most decidedly not deadly. Until they grew up and pecked my brother's hen to death.

Chickens in a flock can be exceptionally cruel. If one of them has a wound, others will peck and peck and peck at it—sometimes until death—unless the farmer intervenes. Chickens are many wonderful things, but toward those they perceive as weak or vulnerable, they are vicious.

Sadly, it is often the same with human communities (including faith communities). If we are not vigilant, they can include a terrible tendency to peck at the weaknesses of less powerful members. Instead of beaks, we wield tongues. We gossip and backstab, undermine and insult, ostracize and exclude others in an attempt to secure a spot for ourselves in the "in" group. Today's verse reminds us that our tongues are a wicked fire that will corrupt and engulf our entire life in flames.

I still hear Ms. Russell's indignant voice when I encounter someone (including me) acting like a human chicken, and I've become grateful for this simple but visceral reminder of the damage we can do with an untamed tongue.

Are you being a chicken? is my shortcut gut check when I find my tongue veering toward gossipy territory.

Watch out for chickens is my internal reminder to be appropriately vulnerable rather than spilling everything everywhere in a particularly angsty moment, if I'm not in a circle of trust.

And the general *Don't be a chicken* is my overarching guardrail mantra reminding me to watch my wayward tongue, to be intentional about being inclusive, and to look for those on the outskirts of community, finding ways to draw them in.

Julie

Today's Act of Gratitude

Pick a guardrail mantra for watching your tongue and protecting your heart. You are welcome to share mine.

Identity and Purpose

The LORD will fulfill his purpose for me; your steadfast love,
O LORD, endures forever. Do not forsake the work of your hands.

PSALM 138:8, ESV

I was a little relieved to return to work after my first child was born.

It wasn't that I didn't love being a mom—I did and still do. My children have always been a delight. Yet, in some ways, I felt ill-equipped. The enormity of knowing that my newborn baby's ability to survive rested on my shoulders was a weight I took seriously. I wanted to do it right, and I was worried that I wouldn't.

Working at a job I loved, on the other hand, was a role in which I was confident. It was something I'd done for many years. When I walked through the door to work, deep inside, I felt like I could fully exhale.

With the wisdom of hindsight, I realize now that I had confused identity and purpose. I wanted to know that I was valued and valuable, that I still had an identity outside of being a mother. Even though I knew that working inside the home was just as meaningful and beneficial as working outside the home, I struggled to navigate who I was now that I'd added "parent" to the labels I wore.

I forgot the truth that our identity is found primarily and always in Jesus. All other labels come second.

The truth is, I craved a sense of purpose. But our purpose isn't tied to what we do—whether it's parenting, a career, or anything else. Instead, our purpose is intrinsic to *who we are* as God's beloved children. Our purpose is to know him and make him known—whether that's inside our homes, in a career, in our neighborhoods or communities, or in our everyday life.

Trying to tie our purpose to any single aspect of who we are (apart from being a child of God) will only frustrate us or make us question our worth. Thankfully, our gracious God is steadfast; no matter the different roles we take on throughout life, his purpose and our identity remain true. By embracing his vision for us, we can live our lives full of the purpose with which he's endowed us.

Kristin

Today's Act of Gratitude

What is your purpose? Spend time thanking God for the ways
his purpose has and will be accomplished in your life.

Learning from Others

To all who believed him and accepted him,
he gave the right to become children of God.

JOHN 1:12

Our youngest three children are in the Spanish immersion program through our school district. Every year, native Spanish-speaking teachers come from all over the world to teach our kids. It has been a rich learning experience for them to not only learn a second language but be exposed to other cultural experiences as well.

The Amity interns (the Spanish-speaking teachers) stay with host families for the school year and then once a month or so stay with another family to gain additional experience while they're here. After several years of having our children in the program, we finally decided to sign up as a weekend host family.

Sara came for the first time one cold fall day. I was a little nervous about how she would respond to our family, but she fit in perfectly. She loves our kids, and we find ourselves playing games, talking about what it was like growing up in Colombia, and making food together. Sara is teaching us things that we had not known, and we are showing her new aspects of the United States as well. She has a strong faith in God, and we have been able to connect over all the ways that he is showing up and guiding our lives. It has been a rewarding experience both for her and for my family, and I am so grateful for her presence.

It can be easy to forget that the people of God can be found all over the world, not just in our own country. It is awesome to see how God is working in lives both near and far. Scripture says that all who believe and accept Jesus have the right to become children of God. What a glorious promise this is. God loves us as his children, just as he loves people in every other place around the world. Taking the time to learn about others and their experiences is one way we can grow in our understanding of all the different people groups God loves as his own.

Kendra

Today's Act of Gratitude

Is there a people group you'd like to get to know more about?
Spend some time learning about them and then ask God to
show you one way you can show love toward them.

Good and Perfect Gifts

Whatever is good and perfect is a gift coming down to us from God our Father, who created all the lights in the heavens. He never changes or casts a shifting shadow.

JAMES 1:17

We bought Jon an adult-sized wearable blanket for Christmas a few years back. With a giant hood and oversize sleeves, it's otherwise an enormous square of fluffy, fleecy fabric. It hilariously covered Jon from head to ankle and was one part novelty and one part practical fun. After essentially living in it that winter, Jon eventually relegated it to our living room blanket basket.

And that's where I found it one especially cool autumn morning. With a chill permeating the entire house, I was looking for a way to stay warm without turning on the furnace, and its bulky warmth called to me as a possible solution.

You can now find me wearing Jon's giant blanket—with his permission—from midautumn all through the winter. It accompanies me onto the back patio as Aaron and I soak up the last lovely, cool fall evenings, and it's what I wear in lieu of a robe on brisk school mornings. It looks utterly ridiculous and yet allows me to move from task to task in cozy warmth without having to readjust or rearrange anything. I adore it, despite its fashionista shortcomings.

I'm on a hunt to identify gifts from God—small (and big) ways he shows his love for us as individuals, knowing exactly what brings us delight—and my wearable blanket has officially made the list. It never fails to bring me joy, and I send a thankful thought heavenward every time I pull it on.

Sometimes we get so focused on the big moves of God or on prayers that have yet to be answered that we can miss out on the ordinary, everyday joys he sends our way. Because I don't want to miss *anything* God would use to encourage or love me, it's become a bit of a game to specifically revel in small moments and simple pleasures, pausing to thank God for my ridiculous wearable blanket as it slips over my head, for that first sip of really good coffee, for a glorious sunset peeping through a tree canopy on fire with leaves in hues of reds, oranges, and yellows.

Julie

Today's Act of Gratitude

What good gifts has God given you recently? Spend a few moments thanking him for them.

A Friend Who Notices

Don't just listen to God's word. You must do what it says.
Otherwise, you are only fooling yourselves.

JAMES 1:22

Small rectangles popped up on the screen, tiny windows into participants' homes. Some people waved, others unmuted to say hello. In the background, family members, televisions, dinner tables, or office furniture could be seen.

Our local MOPS group was meeting virtually, and I had logged on, eagerly anticipating the time of connecting with the community of women. But my friend Erin, who was also on the call, noticed one woman in particular. She knew this mom had a newborn baby and a toddler at home, and in the dim lighting of the computer camera, the woman looked exhausted.

She looks like she could use some help, Erin thought to herself.

After the meeting, she reached out to the woman—a stranger to her—to ask about dropping off a meal. To her surprise, it turned out they lived in the same neighborhood. Erin's gift of food turned into a friendship that has since lasted well beyond those hard days of newborn babies.

If I'm honest, there have been times when I have noticed someone and thought they could use a helping hand but have forgotten to follow up. My good intentions sometimes fall flat. But James reminds us not simply to hear the Word and do nothing. Instead, we must participate. When we do, we take the same posture Jesus did of serving others; our actions bring him glory.

I'm grateful for friends like Erin who are good at noticing. Yet Erin's gift lies in the fact that she chooses to act in faith, not knowing the outcome. She doesn't just see someone else's distress; she goes further and actively does something about it. Her outward focus is a reminder and a challenge to me to be the kind of person who notices others. Her active friendship requires me to ask, *Who around me needs to be seen? Who needs a helping hand, a meal, or a word of encouragement? How can I meet that need?*

Kristin

Today's Act of Gratitude

Think of one person who is good at noticing others—
their needs, their challenges—and actively helping.
Thank them for being a good friend to others.

A Quiet Legacy

*Let's not get tired of doing what is good. At just the right time
we will reap a harvest of blessing if we don't give up.*

GALATIANS 6:9

"As a parent, I often sit back and wonder if I will be half the mother to my kids that my mom was to me," my friend Jill said over the phone one day as we chatted about our families. "She has taught me so many things throughout life that she doesn't even know she did."

"She was always doing things for others," she continued. "A couple of years back, a friend shared a story about my mom that I never knew. At the time, the friend's mother was battling cancer and not given long to live. On the way home from work, my mom would randomly stop in to see how she was doing. She would spend time with her on those days so she didn't have to be alone. No one ever asked my mom to do it, she just knew in her heart that the small gift of quality time, of friendship, was what the woman needed. It was an act that speaks volumes about who my mother is as a person."

As Jill told me this, I couldn't help but think what a great example her mother was setting for her children, even unintentionally, and how much it meant to Jill to hear what a blessing her mom had been to a friend. "Sometimes it's the small things, the little acts of love we do when we think no one is looking, that mean the most," I said.

Later on, I thought again about the quiet legacy Jill's mom was leaving through her everyday actions. She wasn't putting on a show or acting in front of others, she was just going through her day, genuinely loving those around her.

Scripture encourages us that we shouldn't get tired of doing good and that we will harvest blessings when we don't give up. Those blessings aren't limited to the love we receive in return but also come through the legacy we leave for those around us who are watching and following in our footsteps.

Kendra

Today's Act of Gratitude

Who is someone that you can show love to and do
good for? Spend a little time thinking about the many
blessings that come through your good deeds.

Seek the Original Source

*I will study your commandments
and reflect on your ways.*

PSALM 119:15

"Professor Fisk, have you been following the trial? What do you think? Don't you think he'll win after that direct exam?"

"Did you watch the actual direct exam in its entirety, or are you watching TikTok compilations of it?" My smile softened any sting my mostly rhetorical question held, the answer clear in the sheepish grins of several students as I surveyed my classroom.

I ask the same question of my parents when they give me their opinion about a televised court case, although instead of TikTok, I ask them which cable news personality they've watched.

One of my classroom goals is to teach business students to seek out the primary text (statute, case opinion, constitution) or the original, unedited version of a legal proceeding and read or listen to it for themselves. Sound bites, headlines, and compilations can be skewed—for accidental or nefarious purposes—and decisions (business and otherwise) made on twisty information are unsound and risky.

The spiritual application of my "original source" mantra is arguably even more important. Do we have enough direct knowledge of Scripture to know when a podcast, sermon, or book is getting a bit twisty in its theology? Do we know how the overall context of the chapter applies to the verse we are planning to use?

I am so grateful that you and I are living in this present moment. The Bible has been translated into over 700 languages, with the New Testament available in over 1,550 languages.* And with online resources, we can easily access scholarly work explaining important nuances of the original Hebrew and Greek. No one has been as well-resourced to study God's Word as you and I.

While sermons, podcasts, books, and other teachings can be incredibly helpful, reading the Bible for ourselves is important for our spiritual growth. Let's go straight to the source to find out what God has to say rather than relying solely on the paraphrases and thoughts of others.

Julie

Today's Act of Gratitude

Read, reread, or listen to John chapters 14–16, paying
particular attention to the words of Jesus.

---

* "How Many Different Languages Has the Bible Been Translated Into?" Biblica, accessed November 22, 2022, https://www.biblica.com/resources/bible-faqs/how-many-different-languages-has-the-bible-been-translated-into/.

The Gift of Going First

Joy is found in giving the right answer.
And how good is a word spoken at the right time!

PROVERBS 15:23, NIRv

"I've dealt with anxiety for most of my life, since my early twenties," the woman next to me said, voice wavering a little. She wiped a stray tear from the corner of her eye. "But I realized that I can do things afraid, that Jesus is beside me at every moment."

The women at the table nodded as my friend finished her story, murmuring quiet encouragement and offering sympathetic smiles. For a moment, the table was silent as we all reflected on what she'd said.

But before long, a second friend started to speak about her own recent experience—how she'd become discouraged at a dinner with high school friends.

"Everyone else seemed like they had something to brag about. But I don't have a college degree, I'm not building a business. I have little kids at home; this is my life right now," she said, shrugging her shoulders. "But even talking about kids turns into a competition. It makes me think that I don't want to hang out with them anymore."

As we talked about my two friends' experiences, I was glad that they had both felt like they could be vulnerable with the rest of us. But I was doubly grateful to the friend who had opened up first and created the space for our second friend to feel comfortable sharing her struggles. She'd given the other woman the gift of going first.

Both death and life can flow from the power of the tongue (see Proverbs 18:21), but equally important is knowing when to speak. An encouraging word can speak life into those around us, and a vulnerable one can help others to feel less alone. In both situations, our discernment about what our friends might need serves as the best litmus test for what we share.

Kristin

Today's Act of Gratitude

The next time you're in a group of close friends,
open up and give them the gift of going first.

The Blessing in Pain

When you go through deep waters, I will be with you. When you go through rivers of difficulty, you will not drown. When you walk through the fire of oppression, you will not be burned up; the flames will not consume you.

ISAIAH 43:2

"She doesn't feel pain in her hands and feet," my mother explained to me one day while we were talking about a family member who had recently been diagnosed with a debilitating condition. "It's actually kind of scary because she could hurt herself and not know it. She wouldn't know if there was something wrong that needed attention. And with everything else she has going on physically, it's really kind of dangerous."

I sighed, unsure how to respond.

"You would think that was a good thing, not to feel pain," I said, "but I can see how it's actually not."

"I know," my mom said. "Please be praying for her."

"Of course, I will," I responded before we hung up.

The rest of the day I couldn't help but think about the person and then stop and pray for her. I realized that what most of us try to avoid—pain, whether emotional or physical—can actually save our lives. Feeling pain lets us know that something is wrong and needs to be addressed. And when we acknowledge pain and focus on finding a solution for it, healing can occur. When we don't feel pain or choose to ignore it, whatever is causing the pain continues to fester and can destroy us, body and soul.

Maybe that's why God promises that he will be with us when we feel like we are in deep water and that when difficulties come at us like a relentless river, we won't drown. When oppression feels like flames around us, it won't burn us up. Because even though we will walk through seasons of pain, God will be there. Keeping us afloat. Joining in our suffering. Healing us through the pain. He won't always remove us from pain, but he will stay with us as we address it with his help and guidance.

Kendra

Today's Act of Gratitude

When have you experienced pain that you can now look back
on with gratitude that God was with you during that time?
Spend time in prayer thanking God for his faithfulness.

Old Dogs and New Tricks

Don't look out only for your own interests,
but take an interest in others, too.

PHILIPPIANS 2:4

"Good morning, friend! God gave me the best idea for a devotional this morning. I'm sending you the rough, rough draft and would love your thoughts." Texting a follow-up screenshot to my friend, I grinned. Some writing days feel exceptionally divinely inspired, and I suspected this story would be impactful.

Returning from a break to refresh my coffee, I reread the draft I'd sent her, wincing over a cliché I'd used to describe being deemed among the least powerful in a community. My fingers had been flying across the keyboard, and I hadn't stopped to think through the analogy.

"Um. That cliché has mildly racist undertones. I'm so sorry I used it. I wasn't thinking, and I won't do it again." My second text zipped off to my friend, a woman of color who has been undeniably gracious as I've worked hard to remove hurtful words and phrases from my language that, where I grew up, simply rolled off everyone's tongues.

It turns out that old dogs *can* learn new tricks, and I'm exhibit A. Rather than getting defensive, arguing that my good intentions ought to cancel out any harm the words themselves might cause, being willing to reform my vocabulary is an outward manifestation of my desire to care for all God's people.

It costs me nothing to jettison hurtful language. I simply have to listen and believe when I'm told a particular phrase or word is hurtful, even if that word or phrase doesn't cause me the same pain. When I mess up (and I do), I've learned that an immediate, sincere apology without excuses or justification is the best approach. While it is a process, I hold myself to a high standard in light of today's verse, knowing that I'm called to look out for my brothers and sisters in Christ (and others) with both my words and my deeds.

If you are looking for places to start your own journey of rethinking the language you use, I highly recommend looking into the social media postings of fellow believers from different races, nationalities, and countries. I've gratefully lurked on many of their accounts, prayerfully learning and processing and then seeking clarification from my real-life friends of color.

Julie

Today's Act of Gratitude

Prayerfully ask God if you need a language reformation.
Start by reading books or following social media accounts
of BIPOC (Black, Indigenous, People of Color) believers.

Choosing Joy amid Pain

The LORD is good, a strong refuge when trouble comes.
He is close to those who trust in him.

NAHUM 1:7

I recently read through a journal I kept in the year leading up to my sister's death. It was hard to revisit. She suffered fractures in her cancer-weakened bones, a fall while in a public setting, debilitating pain, and countless hospital stays.

I'd forgotten a lot of those details. But as I worked my way through the heartbreaking entries, I realized that I had forgotten a lot of the good stuff too.

One of the entries detailed the encouragement she received in a single week. She'd gotten a phone call from a woman at a local church who said that during the pastor's message on trust the previous Sunday, he had read Katrina's latest email as people cried for a stranger.

And at the hospital that Saturday, when the nurse in the emergency room found out who Kate was, she asked the other nurses to leave the room. She explained that her sister attended the same church my sister did.

"I've been praying for you for five years," she said. She then asked if she could pray with my sister in the ER. Together, they joined hands over her hospital bed.

The journal was full of stories of God's goodness amid difficulties: the women in Katrina's MOPS group who dropped off countless meals, the church member who offered to clean her house weekly, the friends who watched her kids—one woman even bought my niece and nephew Christmas presents—and the hundreds of people on her email list who prayed for someone they had never met. And those weren't a fraction of the stories she could have shared. Though Katrina experienced daily pain, she chose joy as often as possible. She believed that God had the strength to be her refuge, come what may.

Although not all of us receive a life-altering diagnosis, we all experience difficulties in which we find ourselves living in the tension between joy and pain. Yet we can take comfort in the knowledge that even if we don't experience healing or resolution on this earth, there is still goodness to be found. Pain exists. But so does joy. And regardless of what we face, God is still good.

Kristin

Today's Act of Gratitude

Think of a time in your life when you experienced both joy and pain. Thank God for his faithfulness during that season.

Support That's Needed

*Fools think their own way is right,
but the wise listen to others.*

PROVERBS 12:15

"I just don't know if he needs it," a friend shared over the phone as we were discussing whether or not her child should attend therapy.

As a therapist, I am aware of the struggle, so I told my friend. "I don't know if your child needs therapy or not, but here's what I do know. He's asking for it. He's asking for help, so if we step back and look at the bigger picture of his whole life, this is just one more moment where he'll be able to look back on his childhood and say, 'My parents listened to me. They helped me when I said I needed it.' And that is just as important, if not more so, as what therapy may or may not accomplish right now."

"Yeah," she responded.

"And truly, if he feels like therapy would be helpful, talking to someone about our emotions and thoughts is always good. It could help him develop better coping strategies for his life."

"That's true," she sighed. "Parenting is hard."

"It is," I agreed. "But you're doing the right thing."

We hung up with promises that I would send her some recommendations for therapists in our area who I thought would be a good fit for her son. She messaged me later that she'd set up an appointment for him the next month and thanked me for the information.

Asking for help isn't always easy. Whether it's for ourselves or someone we love, it's hard to admit we may need some outside support or input. But Scripture reminds us that fools think they are on the right track, but the wise listen to the advice of others.

Sometimes another perspective is needed for clarity. If we support our loved ones (and ourselves) by getting help when it's needed—whether from a therapist, pastor, or other trusted professional—we show that we are trustworthy and willing to seek out assistance when it's needed most.

Let's be the kind of Christians who, when someone says they need help, are ready to listen. Let's take their concerns seriously. And let's find the assistance that's needed.

Kendra

Today's Act of Gratitude

Thank someone who has listened to you and offered wise counsel,
and then support someone around you who is asking for help.

Reset the Day

*A person without self-control is like
a city with broken-down walls.*

PROVERBS 25:28

"MOMMMMMMMMM!"

Glancing at the clock, I winced. Someone had fallen back asleep after their alarm went off and was desperately late getting ready for school. I hadn't noticed that I was missing a loved one at the breakfast table, and now we were in a mad scramble with big emotions. And—as caretakers know—the frequency of missing socks is directly tied to elevated stress levels when trying to get everyone ready and out the door.

We've all been the person who misjudged time or missed an alarm. The rush of panicked adrenaline quickly morphs into intense frustration as we face disrupted expectations and plans, unexpectedly forced to choose what gets done and what is left undone. It's easy (and natural) to tip into anger at ourselves and others in our rushed recrimination. And while being momentarily angry is not sinful, Scripture cautions against stoking the flames of our out-of-control state.

As I gathered my flustered loved one into a mama-bear hug just before we jumped into the car, I whispered the same words I tell myself under similar circumstances: "Take a deep breath and reset. Do not let this set the tone for your entire day." And then I prayed, intentionally thanking God for several good things about the morning. As I stepped back, releasing my young adult, I received a tremulous smile and a whispered apology.

Our enemy wants us out of control. When our negative emotions are running high and hot, we open ourselves to bad decision-making and foolish impulses. Like a city with broken outer walls, being emotionally agitated lowers our defenses and makes us vulnerable to the enemy's attacks—whether they be lies in the form of negative thoughts or whether they be behaviors we know are not pleasing to God.

Understanding this vulnerability is powerful. When we find ourselves tipping into being emotionally out of control, our best option is a prayerful pause and intentional gratitude, asking God to help us reset as we express thankfulness. And he does. He has given us the gift of self-control. And as we exercise that gift, it becomes easier to maintain. Emotions, despite their intensity, should not dictate what children of the Most High God say or do.

Julie

Today's Act of Gratitude

Make a pact with a loved one to practice a prayerful pause
and intentional gratitude when emotions are running hot.

Nothing to Prove

I'm not trying to win the approval of people, but of God.
If pleasing people were my goal, I would not be Christ's servant.

GALATIANS 1:10

"What do you want to do next?" Kyle asked me one morning as we drank our coffee together before the busyness of the day began. I'd just finished another manuscript and was feeling relief about turning it in.

"I'm not sure," I responded. "Part of me thinks I'd enjoy working at a coffee shop."

"That doesn't sound bad," he responded. "But it would definitely be new for you."

"I don't know," I tried to explain. "It's not that I don't have more dreams, because I do. I just don't have this overwhelming desire to prove anything to anyone anymore. Not like I used to anyway. Maybe that's what happens when you get old," I said with a laugh.

My husband nodded. He's been with me long enough to know that I have people-pleasing tendencies and care (sometimes too much) about what other people think, not only of me but of my family as well.

And although there's certainly nothing wrong with desiring a good reputation—the Bible tells us we should—we can often cross a line to doing things to try to impress others or make them like us at the expense of being our true or real selves.

No matter who we are or what stage of life we are in, we are told not to seek the approval of people, but of God. If we want to be Christ's servants, we can't let pleasing those around us be our goal. Caring about what God thinks, and doing what he says, is always most important. And when we know how much we are loved and accepted by him, pleasing people takes a back seat. There is freedom in letting go of others' approval and accepting God's, which is readily available to each of us.

Kendra

Today's Act of Gratitude

Do you try too hard to win the approval of others? Spend some time thanking God that he already loves and approves of you, and ask him how you can let go of the need for others' approval.

October

Scavenger Hunt

*Let all that I am praise the LORD; may I never
forget the good things he does for me.*

PSALM 103:2

I challenge you (yes, lovely reader, I'm talking to *you*!) to a gratitude scavenger hunt. Do it on your own as an exercise in sacred, worshipful gratitude; make it a friendship or workplace challenge; or invite kids you love to join the fun—this is *your* scavenger hunt, so tweak it to fit your life and circumstances perfectly.

The rules: we will search for joy, recording our observations over the next five days. Suggested categories are as follows:

1. *Taste.* Take a sip, nibble—or more!—of what makes your taste buds sing with joy. Don't scarf your treats; savor them as they roll around your mouth. Write down three things you loved about each taste and why.

2. *Beauty.* Look for different versions of beauty, adding them to your list. What catches your eye in creation? What about an item made with human hands? Is there something fleeting (like a flower bloom) that you find pleasing? What about something enduring—like a mountain vista? Briefly explain why you picked the items you added to your list.

3. *Sound.* What sounds bring you joy? Do you have a favorite song? What about the ringtone when a cherished person calls? Birdsong? Laughter? An appealing accent from a country you long to visit? Add your favorite sounds to your list; it's okay if you have more than three!

4. *Touch.* Do you love the feel of a book in your hands? What about snuggling up with your dog or cat? A cozy soft shirt? Concentrate on all the things you touch with your hands and feet or what you brush against as you walk through the world, noting the ones that spark joy.

5. *Scent.* Walk through your day with your nose leading the way. Do you have a favorite scented lotion or perfume? A soothing candle or diffuser recipe of essential oils? What enticing smells are wafting around a bakery or coffee shop you visit regularly? What scents evoke memories of loved ones or favorite past places?

On the sixth day, sit before God as you review your lists, pairing them with today's verse.

Julie

Today's Act of Gratitude

Prayerfully consider how you could incorporate a
search for joy into your everyday life, whether with the
scavenger hunt above or in some other way.

Family of God

He replied to him, "Who is my mother, and who are my brothers?" Pointing to his disciples, he said, "Here are my mother and my brothers. For whoever does the will of my Father in heaven is my brother and sister and mother."

MATTHEW 12:48-50, NIV

One morning as I was reading my daily devotionals, I came across this Scripture in Matthew where Jesus talks about who his true family is. He said anyone who does his Father's will is his family member. And it struck me how easy it is to be included. Love God. Love others. That's the will of the Father—inclusion at its best.

This must have sounded so strange to the disciples and people listening to Jesus at a time when everyone was separated by class, religion, race, and gender. The fact that Jesus was constantly inviting outsiders in would have been a new way to live—and not just inviting them to be friends, but calling them family would have been nothing short of scandalous.

As I reread his words, my heart swelled with gratitude that we serve a God who so easily welcomes all of us to be a part of his family. And I thought about how my own family has been shaped by adoption and foster care, both biological and family members of the heart. I believe we are a mishmash of people who all found one another because God saw fit to bring us together.

No matter who we are or where we're from, our history, mistakes, or blunders, we're all invited into the family of God. No one gets left out. What a relief and joy for those who've experienced being part of an earthly family, but especially for those who haven't been part of such a loving relationship, who've felt left out or overlooked. God sees you. And he calls you brother, sister, mother. We are all welcome in the family of God.

Kendra

Today's Act of Gratitude

Thank God for the invitation into his family and
encourage someone who may feel lonely and need
the reminder that they are welcome as well.

A Love for Home

My people will live in a peaceful place,
in secure dwellings, and in quiet resting places.
ISAIAH 32:18, EHV

"Oh, wow. Minnesota," the woman said with a laugh. "Brr. Cold."

Sitting in the heat of Hawaii, I couldn't help but smile with bemusement. We had just finished a tour of a local coffee farm and were now enjoying a tasting, and even though it wasn't yet noon, it was already sweltering. As we chatted, the farm employee had asked where we were visiting from. Hearing my answer, she couldn't contain a slight grimace.

"You know," I said, feeling thoughtful. "I don't mind it. Curling up with a book in front of a fire on a cold winter's day is pretty cozy."

It was almost the end of our week on the island, and although I had enjoyed it immensely—the shimmering ocean, the lush plants and trees, the warm rain—there were things I didn't like as much. Cockroaches, for one. Though we Northerners like to complain about the cold temperatures, the truth is that there are critters we never have to deal with, thanks to our chilly climate. I also appreciate having four distinct seasons: pulling out scarves for autumn's cooler temperatures and watching the brilliant leaves fall, seeing the sparkle of snow in the winter, watching spring rains turn the grass to green, and soaking up every last bit of summer's warmth.

There are often good and bad things to every circumstance, including where we live. Every location has its own unique beauty, and the flora and fauna surrounding us serve as reminders of the grandeur of creation and the artistry of our God. And, if we live in a peaceful, secure location—free from the fear of famine or war—that freedom isn't something to take for granted. Instead, it's something to be grateful for each day, no matter how warm or cold the climate is. When we choose to find the beauty in where we live, we can let go of comparison or discontentment and enjoy the place we call home.

Kristin

Today's Act of Gratitude

List five things you like about where you live.

One-on-One with God, Your Way

Her sister, Mary, sat at the Lord's feet, listening to what he taught. But Martha was distracted by the big dinner she was preparing. She came to Jesus and said, "Lord, doesn't it seem unfair to you that my sister just sits here while I do all the work? Tell her to come and help me."

LUKE 10:39-40

"Uff," I muttered under my breath. The sermon was on Mary and Martha, and it was hitting a little too close to home.

The sisters of Lazarus are my personal litmus test, and I struggle perpetually to be less Martha, the hostess demanding Mary's help in the kitchen, and more Mary, the sister sitting at Jesus' feet, soaking in his presence and his words.

Adding to my struggle, I used to assume that spending time with Jesus meant we had to be just like Mary, literally sitting quietly before Christ. And while it is important to set aside time for focused spiritual learning, when I attempt to sit quietly in conversation with God, I sometimes find myself chasing thoughts that zigzag off in different directions. I'm left distracted, frustrated, and feeling like a failure.

Instead, I've learned to chat with Jesus as I cook, pull weeds in the garden, scrub bathrooms, and drive solo. As I putter, I find myself silently nattering to Jesus about all sorts of things before going silent, waiting for divine insight into a situation. Putting my hands to work quiets my racing thoughts and creates an undistracted space for the Holy Spirit's presence and guidance.

It took me far too long to realize that both versions of quiet time are viable and count, and I cried in gratitude and relief when I understood that my constraints around quiet time were of my own making. If we are each created uniquely, then why would God require us to meet him in exactly the same way? Oh, what a freeing realization!

How you meet with Jesus is far less important than *whether* you are meeting with him, and it's naturally going to look different for a single woman, a mom of young children, or an empty nester. Navigating life on earth requires drawing intimately close to our Savior. Find what works for you, and channel your inner Mary regularly.

Julie

Today's Act of Gratitude

If your quiet time with God has you distracted, experiment with busying your hands or changing locations.

A Firm Foundation

*Anyone who listens to my teaching and follows it is wise, like a person
who builds a house on solid rock. Though the rain comes in torrents
and the floodwaters rise and the winds beat against that house, it
won't collapse because it is built on bedrock. But anyone who hears
my teaching and doesn't obey it is foolish, like a person who builds
a house on sand. When the rains and floods come and the winds
beat against that house, it will collapse with a mighty crash.*

MATTHEW 7:24-27

A year after we'd bought our one-hundred-year-old house, we decided to finish
the basement. We hired a company that specialized in remodeling old homes and
spent the next several weeks in a construction zone. The first step was removing
old Sheetrock and flooring.

As the crew moved to work on a room toward the front of our house, they realized it had originally been a small coal room but had been dug out deeper, below
the original granite foundation, and turned into a storage room years later.

The foreman called me downstairs to show me what they'd found.

"Put your hand behind this paneling," he said. "What do you feel?"

"Uhh, it feels like dirt," I said.

"Yeah. When they dug this room out, they didn't build the foundation any
lower; they just covered the dirt with paneling."

I was shocked. "How has it stayed in place for so long?"

"Probably because the granite foundation is so large it hasn't moved, but we
really need to build a solid base now."

"Absolutely," I responded. As he told me the steps they'd need to take, I felt relief
and gratitude knowing it would be fixed quickly.

Like my house, we want our faith to be built on a solid foundation. But to have
this, we must listen to Jesus' teachings and follow what he says. If we don't, we'll
be building our lives on sand, and at the first sign of trouble, our faith will waver
because we won't know the truth and wisdom Jesus offers or how to apply it to our
circumstances. God wants us to stand firm and provides us with the wisdom to do
so if we have the ears to listen and obey.

Kendra

Today's Act of Gratitude

Is your faith built on a firm foundation? If not, plan how you will spend
more time listening to Jesus' teaching and putting it into practice.

Encouraging Others through Hardships

We know that God causes everything to work together for the good of those who love God and are called according to his purpose for them.

ROMANS 8:28

As a young woman, Megan was diagnosed with lung cancer. Shocked, she couldn't understand why she was facing such a terrible disease. How could anything good possibly come from such devastating news?

After she was discharged from the hospital and began to find a new normal, she had a conversation with an older man who had also experienced health-related challenges. He reminded her that even though we may not understand why bad things happen, God can help us to learn and grow from them. At the time, she was too angry and hurt to listen to his words, but she never forgot them.

Eighteen years later, Megan's father was diagnosed with a lung disease. Now able to see how her own health problems had prepared her to help her dad in his battle, she felt grateful. She remembered the conversation with the older man so many years earlier, and it resonated in a new way. Her dad had walked alongside her during her illness, and now she was able to do the same for him.

In Romans, the apostle Paul reminds believers that God can use all of the things we face for our good and his glory. Notice that he doesn't say everything we encounter is good or that God is the reason we experience troubles. Evil exists in the world, and bad things can and do happen to anyone. But even though we may not understand why we undergo trials, we can still choose to trust God. When we see our hardships as opportunities for personal growth or a chance to encourage someone else, we can find peace and purpose even amid painful circumstances.

Kristin

Today's Act of Gratitude

Think of a challenging experience in your own life. How can you use what you learned to encourage someone else?

The Power of Peace

I am leaving you with a gift—peace of mind and heart. And the peace I give is a gift the world cannot give. So don't be troubled or afraid.

JOHN 14:27

"I've been called back for additional screening. The radiologist wants a closer look."

My text went into further details and then confessed: *"My past experiences with loved ones and breast cancer mean fear is creeping into this process. Please pray over my mind and my emotions—that my fear would be replaced by the peace of God that surpasses all understanding."*

And with that, my text zipped off to several women who love and pray for me.

While my additional screenings were filled with good news, those days filled with waiting had me realizing that my love for Jesus doesn't mean fear never gets its insidious claws into me. And while I know *intellectually* that my anxious thoughts are not from God, and that Scriptures telling us not to be afraid are found all throughout the Old and New Testaments, sometimes fear still momentarily gets the best of me, especially when circumstances are far beyond my control.

For me, secret fears are a powerful force that push me into a spiral of paralysis and shame. I *know* I'm not *supposed* to fear, so when I do, a nasty little inner voice loves to tell me that I must be a failed Christian. The temptation is to put on a brave front, lying to myself and those around me, projecting fake confidence so that no one will see that my faith momentarily gets a bit wobbly from time to time.

When I'm in a battle against fear, I've learned to confess it to trusted loved ones, asking for prayer. And while we need to use discernment and wisdom in who we entrust with our vulnerabilities, exposing our secret worries often renders them less potent. Satan's lies cannot withstand the light of God's truth, and allowing others to stand alongside us in prayer and speak truth over the situation is a powerful weapon.

God's peace is a promise we can—and should—claim. It is a gift, freely given, no matter the circumstance.

Julie

Today's Act of Gratitude

Make a plan for combating fear: memorize a verse (John 14:27 or another), confess your concerns to someone who will pray for and with you, and thank God for his promise of peace.

Family Is What You Make It

*God decided in advance to adopt us into his own family by
bringing us to himself through Jesus Christ. This is what
he wanted to do, and it gave him great pleasure.*

EPHESIANS 1:5

My husband Kyle and I adopted three of our five kids from foster care. Before their adoptions, we'd had contact with all three of their families to varying degrees. When parental rights were terminated and we began the adoption process, we had a choice: we could open our lives and hearts to the families or we could cut them out, leaving it to our kids to decide as adults whether to pursue those relationships.

As we prayed about what would be best for our children, our answer became obvious: we wanted to keep the connection between them and their biological families. We developed and encouraged relationships with siblings, aunts, uncles, cousins, and grandparents with that in mind. And as much as we've been able (and considering what would be healthy for our kids), we've not only allowed these relatives to create connections but have also invited them into our family.

Because of this, we've celebrated birthdays and holidays with them and even taken trips together. Some of the younger relatives now call my husband and me uncle and auntie. And I couldn't be happier about it. As I sat down to look for a cabin to rent this next year, big enough to fit part of my daughter's biological family and us for a week, I was struck by the fact that of the people I call family, more of them are *not* blood-related than *are*. And I'm grateful for this reality.

Adoption is God's idea. And you don't have to formally adopt someone to invite them into your family. When we bring others in who are lonely and in need of community, we emulate what God did through Jesus. He adopted us, but he didn't do it grudgingly or out of duty. Scripture is clear; it gave God great pleasure to welcome us into his family. And as his followers, let's choose to do the same.

Kendra

Today's Act of Gratitude

Who do you know that needs some support? How could you invite them into your family, whether for a meal, an activity, or coffee?

The Faith of a Child

Let the message of Christ dwell among you richly as you teach and admonish one another with all wisdom through psalms, hymns, and songs from the Spirit, singing to God with gratitude in your hearts.

COLOSSIANS 3:16, NIV

Hands raised, the little girl danced with abandon at the front of the church. Though her younger brother ran up next to her and other kids were on the periphery, she continued, joy evident in every movement.

Watching from the section adjacent to hers, I couldn't help but smile. Though I love the occasional worship nights at our church, my singing and praising are more restrained. But seeing her unselfconscious response spurred my gratitude for the opportunity the evening presented. Together, the body of Christ was worshiping God.

Her actions also reminded me of a story my dad told me when I was a little girl.

We were in church, and Dad felt the prompting of the Holy Spirit to take off his shoes because he was standing on holy ground (see the directives to Moses in Exodus 3:5 and to Joshua in Joshua 5:15). Feeling awkward and a little embarrassed, he resisted. Not long afterward, he noticed that my toddler self kept removing her shoes. Repeatedly, I'd take them off each time I was admonished to put them on.

Convicted, my dad realized that even though he was resistant, I—a toddler—seemed to be listening to the Lord.

Though it might feel strange to take off our shoes in church, there is a beautiful lesson to be learned regarding children. Often, they are open and unashamed, unworried about what others think. When we are asked to have the faith of a child, I often wonder if it's this joyous wonder that Jesus means. You don't have to tell a child how to play, dance, or sing. Their zest for life is natural and infectious. How can we cultivate that same attitude of joy and wonder in our lives?

Kristin

Today's Act of Gratitude

Jot down three ways we can learn from childlike faith.

The Ordinary Miraculous

Now all glory to God, who is able, through his mighty power at work within us, to accomplish infinitely more than we might ask or think.

EPHESIANS 3:20

"Julie, I had to call you after the court hearing. Do you have a moment to talk?" She and I had been praying for months over a difficult circumstance. An extended family member was navigating through the legal system, and we'd been praying specifically for this morning's hearing.

As she told me what had transpired, I listened with increasing incredulity—her loved one had been divinely protected through the actions of a skilled attorney and a discerning judge. It was what I call the ordinary miraculous—God working through human institutions and knowledge to accomplish an otherwise extraordinary result.

Her recounting finished, I explained what *should* have happened under normal legal process and procedure. The outcome was such a deviation from the norm that it had to have been divine intervention. I reminded my friend of God's sovereignty over all things, including our legal system and lawsuits, regardless of whether the decision makers know God. Then we hung up, both rejoicing over the result while praying specifically over the next steps in the process.

I believe in miracles. And while I've witnessed the extraordinary kind that are bigger than any plausible, human explanation, I've most frequently experienced miracles through humans (judges, doctors, and the like) whose exceptional clarity as to motivations or root causes was—without question—divinely inspired.

Ordinary miracles are no less miraculous for how God accomplished what he intended, and I've learned to watch carefully for his quieter handiwork, that he would get the glory no matter how he accomplishes the task. Watching for and proclaiming God's work in and through ordinary means has been an ongoing source of encouragement, especially when I'm waiting on God in another area—in my own life or the life of someone I love. And noting those ordinary miracles in the lives of friends and family members has been a beautiful reminder that we are not walking through this life alone. God is moving, and he is able to "accomplish infinitely more than we might ask or think."

Julie

Today's Act of Gratitude

Make your own list of the ordinary miraculous works of God you have witnessed. As you pray for God's intervention in a new circumstance, thank him for each miracle on your list, both as encouragement (for you) and as worship to him.

Blessed Are the Peacemakers

Those who are peacemakers will plant seeds of
peace and reap a harvest of righteousness.

JAMES 3:18

One of the things Kristin, Julie, and I love to do is attend markets and fairs where we can set up a booth to sell our books. It's lovely to have the opportunity to meet and talk to all kinds of people from different ages and walks of life.

Often we'll have people stop by who've purchased one of our books in the past, and they'll share how it's affected them or helped them. These are the comments that encourage us so much.

And then, every once in a while, someone will stop and, after we explain the topics on which we write—kindness, compassion, friendship, and loving others well—they'll pause. You can see them thinking about something in particular. As we leave room for them to share, we've heard stories of hard relationships or past hurts.

This happened again at a recent event as a woman came up to our booth and we talked about friendship. She mentioned having good relationships with several women she meets with as a group. Still, one woman in particular changes the dynamic—adding anxiety and stress to any social gathering. We talked about practical ways to navigate that and how people often aren't even aware of what they may be bringing to a group.

As I thought about our conversation later, feeling grateful for good friendships, I realized that I also have people in my life who heighten the anxiety of a group or gathering. I wondered about myself: *Am I someone who brings peace into a room, or do I increase the anxiety of others?*

It's a question we would all do well to ask ourselves. Jesus said, "Blessed are the peacemakers" (Matthew 5:9, NIV), and James reminds us that those who plant peace will reap righteousness. Does that mean we'll never have conflict or struggles? No, but it does mean that God will continue to shape us into people who model Jesus more and more.

In a world that sometimes can be harsh, mean-spirited, and violent, our witness will stand in stark contrast when we walk into a room or situation with the goal of bringing peace.

Kendra

Today's Act of Gratitude

Determine to bring peace to people and groups you interact with.

Little Traditions

This is the day the LORD has made.
We will rejoice and be glad in it.

PSALM 118:24

My husband and I have a standing dinner date with another couple. Every two months—or three, or four, depending on how busy we are—the four of us try a new restaurant. Sometimes it's a casual patio, hot sun beaming down on an umbrella overhead. Other times, it's a sophisticated location that gives me a reason to wear high heels. No matter the location, it's always an enjoyable experience.

Throughout the year, I take note of restaurants mentioned in local magazines or news articles or by friends and keep a running list of new or noteworthy locations to try next.

It's a simple tradition but one of my favorites. We rarely see our friends beyond these dinners—we don't live in the same city, and our lives don't overlap as often as they once did—but we love to pick up where we left off, catching up and enjoying delicious food together.

We often think of traditions as weighty rituals tied to holidays, but we can glean just as much joy from simpler, smaller practices throughout the year. For instance, at least once a year we visit a teddy-bear-themed park in Stillwater—a beautiful town about an hour away—and walk along the riverfront with our kids, usually with dripping ice-cream cones in hand. We regularly schedule "Daddy dates" or "Mom dates" so that each of our children can have special one-on-one time with my husband or me. We grow herbs on our deck every summer, build crackling bonfires in the fall, and have a checklist of holiday movies we watch in the lead-up to Christmas. These smaller pleasures bring joy to our days, providing seasonal rhythms and helping cultivate anticipation for every new season, every new day.

This is the day the Lord has made—how can we rejoice in it? When we start to find the smallest of reasons to be grateful, we can build meaning into our everyday life.

Kristin

Today's Act of Gratitude

What simple traditions do you have in your life? How can cultivating small enjoyments add up to a life of gratitude?

Angels in Tool Belts

My God will meet all your needs according
to the riches of his glory in Christ Jesus.

PHILIPPIANS 4:19, NIV

Ding-dong.

The doorbell rang just as Minnesota's governor finished announcing an imminent stay-at-home order. Our world was headed for "unprecedented times" (oh, how I came to dislike those words), and I was praying for so many heavy things in addition to the very practical concern that we were in the midst of a massive remodeling project and had no kitchen.

No one could have known what was coming when we ripped out our kitchen and main living areas in early January. We had a microwave and toaster in the corner of our torn-apart living room and a fridge in the garage, and we had been doing dishes in our upstairs bathroom for two months. What we'd been cheerfully calling a grand temporary adventure suddenly had me praying for help as I scrambled to devise a plan in the face of massive uncertainty and chaos.

I opened the door to our contractor's crew. Upon learning of the impending lockdown, they had raced to our house to temporarily install a sink, stove, and plywood countertop. They knew the precarious position we were in and wanted to ensure that we would have the essentials, just in case construction work had to stop.

I've never thought of angels as wearing tool belts, but that's what they looked like to me as I swung open the door. And while I know they weren't actually angels, they were an answered prayer, en route before I even knew to pray for them.

During those chaotic months, I complained to God about the terrible, no-good timing of our remodel. And yet, I've changed my tune with the perspective of hindsight. I've lost count of the times I've thanked God that our project slipped through just before rampant supply chain problems, worker shortages, and cost increases.

Whenever I question God's timing or the "why" in circumstances beyond my control, I remember the sound of my doorbell ringing with God's answer to prayer. Reflecting on his past faithfulness and provision always bolsters my faith that he will meet my current needs.

Julie

Today's Act of Gratitude

List the ways God has provided for you or your loved ones
in situations beyond your control. Recite those examples
as you wait on him in your current circumstance.

Mood-Boosting Exercise

A cheerful heart is good medicine,
but a broken spirit saps a person's strength.
PROVERBS 17:22

Feeling sluggish, I sighed and leaned back in my desk chair, closing my laptop screen. Rubbing my eyes, I dreaded the next item on my list: exercise.

But, dragging myself upstairs, I went through the motions of changing into my workout clothes, putting on my shoes, and turning on the machine before getting started.

Despite my initial hesitation, I felt so much better when I was done thirty minutes later. My renewed energy reminded me of something a former colleague, Sue, had told me about her own experience with biking: "It is far easier to feel and recognize strong, genuine gratitude when doing the physical exercise that produces good chemicals in the brain. Doing and feeling go hand in hand."

I love the idea that when our heart is pumping and oxygen is flowing to our brain, releasing endorphins, we can tune in to how grateful we are for the ability to exercise, move, or adapt to our surroundings. Whenever I am sick and unable to work or care for others, I realize how much I take my overall good health for granted. Being ill reminds me to be grateful for the days I feel well. The same is true for exercise: thanks to the feel-good chemicals that are released, I often find my spirits lifted and my mood improved. Being physically active resets my body and my mind.

If a cheerful heart is a medicine that spurs us to accomplish all we need to do each day, then the quickest way to achieve that cheerfulness is by cultivating habits that spur us to gratitude. It's easy to say we're thankful, but believing it deep in our bones is something that only happens with wisdom and experience. Wisdom brings life to the body (see Proverbs 4:20-22). When we take time to move our bodies intentionally, we give our brains the boost they need to choose gratitude and cultivate a cheerful heart.

Kristin

Today's Act of Gratitude

Exercise, even if it's simply a quick walk around
the neighborhood or grocery store.

Holiday Connections

Whatever you do or say, do it as a representative of the Lord Jesus, giving thanks through him to God the Father.

COLOSSIANS 3:17

"Mom, can we look up costumes? I'm not sure what I want to be for Halloween this year," my eight-year-old said as she sat down next to me on the couch.

"Sure," I responded, moving over so there was room for her as I brought up a new search tab. "What did you have in mind?"

"I'm not sure. It was so funny when Abe was a dinosaur."

"Yeah, it was," I said as we both laughed, remembering the blow-up creature my son had worn the year before. We made sure to take a video of him in the suit and still chuckle as we watch him waddle through our neighborhood.

We spent the next half hour looking through costumes—mermaids to princesses, cowgirls to even a hamburger. The options, to her young mind, were endless. She came up with her top three, wanting to discuss them with her sister before deciding.

Halloween has become a beloved tradition in our house. We see it as a way to connect with those who live closest to us, opening up opportunity for us to meet new neighbors and grow in relationship with those we've already gotten to know.

But one of our favorite traditions is visiting our former neighbor Al. Even though we don't live in the same neighborhood anymore, the kids get dressed up every year, and our first stop is Al's senior apartment complex. We spend time in the lobby so that the other residents can enjoy the kids and their costumes as well. It's become my favorite part of the day.

Scripture says that whatever we say or do, we should do it as a representative of Jesus. Our family has decided to take the holidays and traditions of our culture and see if we can use them as an opportunity to love God and then show his love to others. Halloween has become one such occasion that we've decided to use for the glory of God. I'm grateful that it has become a beautiful way for us to connect with neighbors—old and new.

Kendra

Today's Act of Gratitude

How can you, in a loving way, represent
Jesus to others during holidays?

20,000 *Words*

*How good and pleasant it is when
God's people live together in unity!*

PSALM 133:1, NIV

"And then . . ." I trailed off as I noticed Aaron's gentle smirk. "Hey! You've been traveling, and I've been saving up my stories to tell you." My smirk matched his own. "As you know, I have twenty thousand words a day to use, and I've been saving them all for you . . .!" I trailed off with a faked wicked laugh, my eyes twinkling at our long-running inside joke.

"Well, grab your iced tea and meet me by the smoker. You can use your words while I check the steak," Aaron called over his shoulder as he headed out the door leading to our patio.

"Deal!" And off we went into the backyard, picking up my story where I left off.

Years ago, someone told us that women speak an average of twenty thousand words daily while men speak an average of seven thousand. More recent studies suggest this is a myth, but it's still our jokey acknowledgment that I feel cherished when Aaron allows me to verbally process my experiences, looking for feedback on some occasions and simple commiseration on others. At twenty-plus years into marriage, we've learned to make allowances for one another's idiosyncrasies, understanding that we have different requirements for feeling cherished. Instead of dismissing my need to chat, Aaron leans into it, just as I lean into what makes him feel loved.

Treating people in a way that makes them feel appreciated isn't reserved for spouses. Coworkers, neighbors, extended family, the cashier at the store you frequent—all represent opportunities to let people know you see them for the person they are rather than for the role they play or for what they can (or can't) do for you. It's these small moments of leaning in that build harmonious relationships and community. God built us for communal living, and we thrive when we have a network of healthy connections who care about one another.

Instead of waiting to be invited into community, those who love Jesus are often called to build it for themselves and others. Thankfully, noticing and appreciating others is a low-risk, easy way to build community, even for those of us who are not natural extroverts.

Julie

Today's Act of Gratitude

Who can you appreciate? Make it a regular habit
to express your thanks to someone.

A Little Nudge

The purpose in a man's heart is like deep water,
but a man of understanding will draw it out.

PROVERBS 20:5, ESV

Years ago, a speaker at a conference I attended told a story of harboring a vision for ministry for many years before she pursued it. The catalyst for setting her plan in motion was confessing her dream to a mentor and hearing them respond with the affirming words, "I can see that potential in you."

Our friends Andrew and Samantha are like that for my husband and me, offering encouragement and expressing their confidence that we can and should pursue God's path for our lives.

For instance, when we were thinking about ways to get involved in our local church, Andrew challenged us to consider how we could best serve the community rather than pursuing what felt easy or convenient.

"You're not going to be a greeter," he told Tim, his words frank but kind. "You need to work with kids."

More than a decade later, Tim still serves in the four-and-five-year-old room, connecting with children—including many who don't have a father figure—coloring or playing with trucks alongside them. He loves it.

Another year, when Tim said he wasn't leading a small group because it was a busy season, Andrew reminded him that as a leader, he needed to remain involved no matter the title he bore. The nudge was exactly what Tim needed to start a barbecue group that still ranks among his favorites.

What a gift it is when a friend can see our potential and takes the time to encourage us to pursue it; how grateful I am for friends who challenge us to seek out God's best. How many life-changing interactions might we have missed over the years without those nudges from our friends?

Each of us has a purpose and is uniquely positioned to fulfill the Lord's calling, but sometimes we need encouragement from someone else to see it. You and I can do the same by calling out the potential we see in others. As Romans 11:29 reminds us, the gifts and calling of God are irrevocable. We honor someone in their God-given calling when we gently encourage them in their giftings. Telling someone we see their potential may be just the boost they need to fulfill a greater purpose—God's purpose.

Kristin

Today's Act of Gratitude

Who can you encourage by seeing their potential
and gently nudging them to pursue it?

Put in the Practice

Lazy people want much but get little,
but those who work hard will prosper.

PROVERBS 13:4

She came home in tears. I waited until we'd gotten inside and the other kids had left to do other things before asking her what was wrong.

"I'm terrible, Mom," she exclaimed. "Everyone else is good at kick line, and I'm not. I'm not any good."

My daughter had just come home from her first practice with the dance team at school, and although she'd danced for several years at a studio, the school team was different.

"Wait," I said. "You aren't good at kick, or you've never done it before, so you haven't learned how to do it yet?" I asked. She paused and looked at me, pondering what I had said. "Because that's a very big difference. Not being good at something is not the same as not having had the opportunity to practice something new."

She nodded as an understanding of my words began to sink in. Over the next several weeks, she went to practice determined to learn a new skill. Each day she would come home excited about how she was progressing. I smiled as she told me, "I'm not great yet, but I'm getting there."

"That's all you can do," I said, proud of her for continuing to try.

Scripture tells us that lazy people want a lot but get very little, but those who put in the hard work will prosper. Does that mean we'll always get everything we want or be the best at something? Not at all. But many things flourish in us when we work hard—things like determination, courage, self-control, and faithfulness—just to name a few. I'm so thankful God allows us to prosper in so many ways when we're willing to put in the effort.

Kendra

Today's Act of Gratitude

Is there something you've wanted to do but you've been discouraged or afraid, unsure if you'll be any good at it? Determine to take a step, put in some hard work toward your goal, and see what prospers in you.

My Grandpa, the Cheerleader

Love is patient and kind.
1 CORINTHIANS 13:4

Growing up, my mom was more tomboy than girly girl, eschewing cute dresses for adventures around their small desert town with her best friend, Sydney. As an adult, I chuckle over stories of Sydney's pet skunk and my mom's childhood antics that resulted in tattling phone calls home from Vera at the grocery store, long before Mom walked through her front door at the end of a fun day.

My mom was a daddy's girl, and my Grandpa Meckem was a cowboy in the truest sense of the word. He worked on ranches and drove cattle before getting married and settling down later in life than most. As rough-and-tumble as he needed to be for his line of work, he had a tender heart and an artist's eye. By the time I knew Grandpa, he had taken up painting landscapes of the Arizona countryside and loved to tell stories that were approximately 25 percent true and 75 percent exaggeration in the funniest, best ways.

Grandpa spoke words of life over my mom when not many did, loving her patiently as she grew into herself, ignoring labels and expectations rather than heaping them upon her. He was an outsize presence in her life, and her strength of spirit and loving compassion come from her dad and his influence.

I've often marveled at the contradiction that was Grandpa. He was a traditionalist, but he also encouraged his daughters to be their authentic selves at a time when women had clearly defined expectations and few acceptable career options. He was an example of cheerleading his girl along her path without diminishing anyone else.

It's my grandfather's example that draws me toward the kind of cheering that embraces and encourages young people as they grow into their giftings—the kind of cheering that is filled with patience, lovingly allowing them to be wholly themselves at each stage of development.

I gratefully emulate him as I engage with those younger than me. It might be college students in my on-campus office after class, processing aloud their thoughts about next steps. Or it might be middle schoolers being quirky and goofy in the back seat of my car as I drive them to an event. There is something precious about loving people in the stage they are in, cheering them on, embracing who they are in the moment, even as you see glimpses of who they will be.

Julie

Today's Act of Gratitude

Who around you could you patiently and lovingly cheerlead?

The God of Order

God is not a God of disorder but of peace.
1 CORINTHIANS 14:33

Surveying the pantry, I couldn't help but feel excited. Loose-leaf teas in jars were lined up like tiny, rounded soldiers in orderly rows, while staples like flour and sugar had found new homes in clear, stacked containers. Everything was labeled and organized by type and purpose—a baking area, a snack area, a canned goods area.

A friend had done the bulk of the sorting—removing everything from the space, grouping it by type, and throwing out expired items—and I had finished the process. Over the next few days, I'd find myself stopping every so often to peek at the pantry and admire its clean organization.

Although I enjoyed the look of the space, I was more excited about how it felt. Because the more cluttered my home becomes, the more anxious I feel. I get stressed at the thought of clearing out items, worrying that others might see the mess and judge me as lazy. Organizing this area had lifted a burden from the mental load I'd been carrying.

As I closed the door on the pantry, I felt grateful for order and the peace it brought to my weary heart and mind. Because while I don't think my cupboards are something God is concerned about, I believe that the satisfaction that organization brings is something he understands. Our God isn't a God of chaos but of order. He created our universe, and it is full of symmetry and precision, gorgeously designed and displayed. Order brings peace and harmony rather than chaos and disorder.

This order isn't crucial just for the physical world. Though some of us—like me—can become overwhelmed by the items that stack up and take over our homes, others are wearied by a cluttered calendar, mind, or heart. Regardless of which part of your life needs a little reorganizing, God can help you tackle it today.

Kristin

Today's Act of Gratitude

Declutter or organize one area—as large as a room or as small as a drawer. Spend time thanking God for the gift of order and enjoy the fruits of your labor.

A Mentor like Carol

The words of the godly are a life-giving fountain.

PROVERBS 10:11

I walked into the clinic for an appointment. After making my way to the counter and checking in, I turned toward the waiting area and saw my dear friend and mentor, Carol.

She had a huge smile, and as she leaned in to hug me, she exclaimed, "I am just so proud of you!" Her face beamed as she let me go from her embrace, explaining that she sees all my posts on social media and enjoys hearing about all we do with our kids and their activities.

"You are such a good mom," she said.

We chatted about life for a few more minutes before she left and I went to sit down, but hours later, her affirmation was still ringing in my ears.

Carol is an encourager. A few decades my senior, she is old enough to be my mother. She is someone who mentors younger women beyond an age anyone would expect her to, stays relevant, and loves others well, inviting them into her circle of friendship and mentorship without hesitation. She is wise and loving, and I am always encouraged when I'm with her.

Everything she says is sincere, and people pay attention when she compliments or tells them what she loves about them. I messaged her later, letting her know that seeing her made my day. There are not many people like her, and I'm so grateful to know her.

Do you know a Carol? Someone who comes alongside and encourages others with their love, wisdom, and life experience? If so, you know what a treasure they are. It can often be too easy to use our comments to cut down or criticize, but a true mentor looks for ways to call out the good in those around them. Their words are like a fountain that gives life, building people up instead of tearing them down.

Kendra

Today's Act of Gratitude

Look for opportunities to let your words be a fountain of life to others by intentionally calling out the good you see in them.

Walking with Jesus

Jesus spoke to the people once more and said, "I am the light of the world. If you follow me, you won't have to walk in darkness, because you will have the light that leads to life."

JOHN 8:12

"Incredible . . ." I whispered to myself on a tired sigh. I took several additional steps onto the rocky ledge overlooking miles of birch, maple, and aspen that covered softly rolling hills sloping to the dark blue edge of Lake Superior. The views from Oberg Mountain (yes, Minnesota has mountains, albeit very old and worn into what more closely resemble large hills) are absurdly spectacular when the surrounding forest is saturated in autumnal reds, oranges, and yellows.

We'd hit the crescendo of changing leaves on a hike renowned for fall color in Northern Minnesota, and the vista stole my breath. After lingering for a long while on that ledge, we turned back onto the woodland trail, thinking we were leaving behind *the* spot for viewing as we continued the loop that would eventually take us back to our car. To our delight, the path led us to four or five additional outlooks—all slightly different but equally stunning—before it dipped back down the mountain to the trailhead.

Between vistas, we hiked mostly in silence through an aspen forest aglow with sunlit yellow leaves. The way the sunlight filtered through even the darker parts of the woods turned my thoughts toward what it's like to follow Jesus. While Oberg Mountain was not an easy trail—I wheezily watched for protruding roots and periodically tripped on rocky outcrops—my heart was filled with gratitude that I could experience it at peak fall color. It was one of the most beautiful sights I've ever encountered, and I focused on soaking it all up, savoring and storing it in my memory banks.

Following Jesus—while perhaps not as visually stunning on an ongoing basis—reminds me of Oberg Mountain and is the only way I want to live. Prayerfully looking for those who God puts in my path, asking God to show me how he is working and how I might make a difference in eternity, and actively looking for the beautiful moments in my day-to-day life is the most meaningful, exciting, beautifully *ordinary* adventure. The best part? Jesus' invitation is for you and for me, starting right now, right where we are.

Julie

Today's Act of Gratitude

Surrender your day to Jesus, asking him to help
you follow the light that leads to life.

Jesus, Our Refuge

*As for me, I will sing about your power. Each morning I will
sing with joy about your unfailing love. For you have been
my refuge, a place of safety when I am in distress.*

PSALM 59:16

After driving through the entrance, we parked and walked up to the main building at the Puʻuhonua o Hōnaunau National Historical Park. Around us, the dark lava fields looked like the surface of Mars, rocky and alien. Coconut trees waved in the breeze while gentle waves washed up to a peaceful cove.

The park—which includes the Royal Grounds and the Puʻuhonua, known as the "place of refuge" or "city of refuge"—provided a haven for long-ago Hawaiians who broke certain laws, known as Kapu. These laws were punishable by death, but if the accused managed to make it to this location, they were pardoned and could live out the rest of their days in peace.

As we watched a video about the site's history, I couldn't help but be struck by how difficult the journey was for those who needed to reach the place of refuge. To escape from their accusers, they had to run for miles and then swim in the ocean—avoiding sharks and their pursuers!—until they finally arrived, dehydrated and exhausted. Safety was available only after they had scrambled for their lives, battled the elements, and washed up on the shore.

Once they arrived, the accused would rest, recover, and find new life. Some might stay in this place of peace forever.

Similar to those who once sought safety at Puʻuhonua, we can take refuge in Jesus. Though we may fight an internal battle with ourselves, we need not wrestle with external elements or labor to reach him. Instead, he is immediately available. What's more, his power and might are balanced by his great love for us. What a privilege it is for us to turn to him, finding safety, rest, and peace. He freely forgives and provides us with all that we need for a new life in him.

Kristin

Today's Act of Gratitude

Thank God that he is a refuge we can turn to whenever we need him.

Never Alone

God has not given us a spirit of fear and timidity,
but of power, love, and self-discipline.

2 TIMOTHY 1:7

My youngest daughter had decided to join a competition dance team like her older sister and had been excited all morning about attending the first class. But as we got in the car and made our way to the studio, she became quiet.

A few blocks from our destination, she admitted, "Mom, I'm afraid."

I caught her teary eyes in the rearview mirror.

"It's okay," I affirmed to her. "It's okay to be scared. That's normal. Do you know what we do when we're afraid?"

"What?"

"We pray and remember that Jesus is with us, and then we do it anyway. It's okay to be fearful, but we don't have to let that stop us."

She nodded as we pulled into a spot. Her friend Alayna was also in the class, and as the girls headed in, I pulled them aside.

"Do you think there are some new girls in your class?"

"Yeah," they said, looking around.

"Do you think you could see if there are any that look like they might be kind of scared and go sit by them or smile and introduce yourself?" I asked. Both girls nodded. "See if there's someone you can be a friend to," I encouraged them as they walked through the door.

I watched from the window as my daughter's fear seemed to vanish. She took notice of the other girls in the room, searching for someone else who might be anxious. I smiled at her as she sat by a new girl and began talking to her.

Fear is a normal emotion at any age, especially in unfamiliar situations, but it doesn't have to stop us from stepping out in faith to try something different. God tells us over and over again in Scripture not to be afraid. I am grateful that he hasn't given us a spirit of fear; what he has given us is power, love, and self-discipline (another version says a sound mind).

This means that we can walk into a new situation and, instead of focusing on our fear, utilize that power and love he's given us, knowing that we aren't alone. God is always with us.

Kendra

Today's Act of Gratitude

Take action on something you haven't yet done or
pursued because of fear, thanking God for his promise
to be with you as you step out in faith.

Welcome Words

Gracious words are like a honeycomb,
sweetness to the soul and health to the body.

PROVERBS 16:24, ESV

When my manager walked by, I was looking over a shirt, holding it up for consideration.

"That would look great on you," she said firmly. Decisively, even.

"Really?" I asked, still in doubt. "This color?"

Pausing from her task, she looked back at me. "*Especially* that color."

At first, I felt a little stunned at how adamant her tone was, but after a moment, the kind words sank in. I could feel myself starting to glow from the inside out.

Now beaming from ear to ear, I nodded in response. As I went back to what I'd been working on, the warmth remained.

I'd been working at a new job in retail for a couple of months but had felt too shy to take advantage of the generous employee discount. As a result, I hadn't tried on or purchased anything yet. I was grateful for the manager's kind-yet-earnest tone, which did wonders for boosting my confidence. As the shift ended and we closed the store for the day, I quickly walked into the dressing room and tried on the shirt. Just as she'd predicted, it looked great on me.

Compliments can seem inconsequential in the grand scheme of things, but even our small words hold great power. I'm sure my manager thought nothing of her throwaway comments, but the surety with which she said them made an impact that I can still remember almost two decades later.

How often do you and I compliment someone else to the degree that they begin to believe it about themselves? The Bible reminds us that sincere words provide life and vitality. On good days, they give us an extra dose of confidence. But on hard days, they can feel like an infusion of living water to our thirsty hearts and souls. Each of us has the power to change what others believe about themselves with just the right remark. Words are life, and when we wield them well, we share that life-giving power with others.

Kristin

Today's Act of Gratitude

Encourage someone with a sincere compliment, and
thank someone who has complimented you.

A Good Reputation

*In the same way, let your good deeds shine out for all to see,
so that everyone will praise your heavenly Father.*

MATTHEW 5:16

It was nearing the end of the season when our son had his biggest soccer tournament of the year. Busy with kids in all different activities, we hadn't had the time to get to know other soccer team parents or families like we'd hoped.

Other moms took Abram to his games the first two days, while Kyle and I worked. As I thanked them over text, their responses were always the same: "It's no problem at all! Abram's a great kid!"

We finally made our way midweek to the first of what would be several more games over the next few days. We parked and set up chairs while Abram ran to warm up with his teammates, then we finally got to spend time with the other parents. They greeted us each day as if they already knew us, and they were warm and inviting. I was grateful for the way they accepted us with open arms.

A few days later, after the tournament ended and we were driving home, I turned to my husband. "You know, it's interesting how accepting everyone is of you and me, based on their opinion of Abram. Everyone loves him, and so they love us by default."

Kyle nodded. As we continued to drive, I thought about how this analogy could apply to our faith. *Do we have a good reputation that opens the door for others to want to know about God? Or are we harsh, cold, uninviting—making it impossible for people to want to know anything about Jesus because they don't really want to have anything to do with us?*

We don't always think about our reputation and how others might view us. But if we want to be the kind of Christian (and have the kind of witness) that makes others want to know Jesus, we've got to pay attention. We are to let our good deeds—the way we talk and act—shine for others to see so that they will praise our heavenly Father and want to get to know him too. We all need to ask ourselves: *Does the way I live make others want to know Jesus?*

Kendra

Today's Act of Gratitude

Thank God for those who have helped you feel welcome in new situations. Ask him for wisdom in how you can let your good deeds shine before others so that they will be open to hearing about God.

Love Where You Are

*Be thankful in all circumstances, for this is God's
will for you who belong to Christ Jesus.*

1 THESSALONIANS 5:18

"As soon as I can, I'm moving. I will never live in Central Minnesota when I grow up!"

I often chuckle ruefully at that angrily huffed declaration made by twelve-year-old me over something I can no longer recall.

In a funny twist, not only did I never leave Central Minnesota, but I'm the only one left here from my immediate family. And yet—despite my preteen angst—I cannot imagine God having a more perfect place for my family to be rooted at this point in our lives. We have been blessed beyond measure with deeply connected friendships, opportunities to contribute meaningfully to our community, and the intersection of our lives with people from across the globe.

Does that mean I never long to live near the ocean, in the mountains, or tucked into the rolling hills of western Ireland? Of course not! I love to daydream about what it might be like to live in the heart of Manhattan or a hill town in Northern Italy. There are so many amazing places to live; I don't have enough life left for all the options that intrigue me.

But I've learned to appreciate where God has planted me—whether for my entire life or only this season. Being obedient to God in where he sends us is always more important than the location itself, even when winter temps occasionally dip into the nostrils-freeze-shut-the-moment-you-step-outside range. And I can find reasons to be grateful, even with frozen facial features: namely, no scorpions hiding in my shoes or alligators in my lakes!

More important than the general absence of venomous critters and snappy snappers are the people God sends across my particular path. I want to be where God can best use me, which means finding and embracing with thankfulness the best parts of the place I'm planted for as long as he plants me there.

Julie

Today's Act of Gratitude

Set a timer for thirty seconds and list what you appreciate about where you live. For extra fun, play tourist and spend a day doing the local sightseeing things you've never gotten around to doing.

Grateful for Grief

Now, dear brothers and sisters, we want you to know what will happen to the believers who have died so you will not grieve like people who have no hope.

1 THESSALONIANS 4:13

Every year, I relive the day I turned twenty-two. It was a beautiful Friday in October, but I was upset because my boyfriend hadn't planned anything to celebrate my birthday. The next day, we were in the middle of breaking up when I got a call from my family.

They said that my sister Katrina, who had been in the hospital all week, had taken a turn for the worse. She'd fought breast cancer for five years, but this time was different. This time would be the last.

When I picked up that call, I didn't know she'd be gone by Sunday.

Every year, I replay those moments—the birthday, the call, the grief. I miss that twenty-two-year-old's naivete and her belief that bad things couldn't happen to good people, that healing was on the way. It was—just not in the way I expected.

I take great comfort in knowing there's more to the story. I heard a message once about how joy and grief are often intertwined and how grief reminds us that the person we mourn matters to us. Our humanity is felt in its fullest measure when we love—and when we experience loss. Grief is love.

And so, each year when my birthday arrives, I remember. Fall is my favorite season and always has been, but it's the perfect reminder to me now that death and rebirth go hand in hand. Though the seasons we experience are always temporary, I'm thankful that the arc of our life is not. Scripture assures us that as people of faith, we do not grieve like people with no hope—because we know our present reality is not the end. An eternity with Jesus is the epilogue to the story, and it's still being written.

Even though I miss my sister, I don't want to say I've "lost" her. The truth is that when someone is in your heart, they're never truly gone. Her legacies of love and joy are still with me, tempering this temporary absence. Love doesn't end with death. Our grief is but an extension of our deep love. And so we wait—and hope.

Kristin

Today's Act of Gratitude

Think of someone you've grieved, remembering how you loved that person and thanking God for the hope of eternity together.

What Defines Us?

I—yes, I alone—will blot out your sins for my own
sake and will never think of them again.

ISAIAH 43:25

My heart sank when I saw the message appear in my inbox. One of my kids had engaged in unkind behavior within a group, and we needed to address it. The note was from an adult who worked with my child, and I felt a mix of embarrassment and anger that my kid would behave in a way they knew was not okay or appropriate within our family.

I called my husband to let him know, and then I prayed. I began typing a response to the email, but I waited to complete it until I could speak with my child. When they got home from school, we sat down to talk. When I told them about the message, their head immediately dropped.

"I know it was wrong. I already apologized yesterday," they said.

I nodded. "That was so hurtful," I said.

"I know. I got caught up in what everyone else was doing. I'm sorry."

I hugged them, then turned back to finish my reply, letting all involved know of our conversation and how my child planned to change their behavior going forward. Later, my child told me that the adult who had sent the email approached them at practice, praising them for being willing to apologize even before being asked to. I was grateful for the grace extended by this person and their efforts to move beyond the incident.

One thing I love most about God is that our past poor choices or mistakes do not define us in his eyes. He reminds us over and over that he loves us. That he will blot out our sins and never think of them again. I'm so grateful that he doesn't throw them in our face when we mess up more than once. He's faithful to forgive. And because of this, we have the freedom to own our mistakes, apologize when necessary, and work to change our behavior because we know God doesn't condemn us.

Kendra

Today's Act of Gratitude

Is there someone you need to apologize to, but you've been putting it off? Or maybe you've had a hard time accepting someone else's apology. Spend time with God, remembering all he's forgiven, and then take a step to reconcile with the person.

The Only Title That Matters

"Daughter," he said to her,
"your faith has made you well. Go in peace."

LUKE 8:48

I recently read a story about how companies are getting more creative in their job titles. Some of the strangest examples included Chief Troublemaker, Galactic Viceroy of Research Excellence, Innovation Sherpa, and Wizard of Lightbulb Moments.[*]

While most of us will never add Digital Overlord or Paranoid-in-Chief to our résumé, we can find ourselves defined by other titles: Student. Neighbor. Spouse. Colleague. Parent. Sister. Friend. Though some titles can be a source of joy, others may feel constricting. We can become overwhelmed by the expectations that accompany the labels thrust upon us.

But all of those titles are simply facets of who we are. Our complete, true identity is primarily and always found in Jesus. Made in his image, we are children of God.

We are reminded of this God-given label in the Gospel of Luke. The author tells the story of a woman who has been bleeding for the past twelve years. As Jesus passes by, she touches the hem of his garment. Despite being surrounded by a crowd of people, he notices. Immediately, he stops and asks who touched him. Trembling with fear, she admits that not only is she the one who did so but that by touching his garment, she has been instantly healed.

All of that is miraculous, but what Jesus does next is equally remarkable. Speaking with kindness, he calls her "daughter"—the only time recorded in Scripture that he uses this term with an individual woman—and tells her to go in peace. At that moment, Jesus' words reveal his loving view of the woman. He is not put off by what she has faced or the desperation she reveals in touching his hem. Instead, he is moved to compassion. He sees her as a daughter, worthy of love and acceptance. His words not only offer hope and healing, they also offer an identity rooted in him.

Our ultimate identity is found in Jesus. He can and does define us through the lens of love—as his child: loved, accepted, forgiven.

Kristin

Today's Act of Gratitude

Write a list of the titles you bear. Now, cross them out and write "daughter" over them. Praise Jesus that your identity is found wholly in him, embodied by the title you bear.

---

[*]Emerald Catron, "30 Weirdest Job Titles in Corporate America," *Best Life*, May 29, 2018, https://bestlifeonline.com/weirdest-job-titles/.

Reclaiming Halloween

*We are to God the fragrance of Christ among those who
are being saved and among those who are perishing.*

2 CORINTHIANS 2:15, NKJV

"You look familiar. Do I know you?"

Pausing from cleaning up empty hot cocoa packets strewn across the long, white folding table, I reconsidered the woman stirring cups for a petite princess and a tinier Hulk amidst the Halloween chaos in our driveway.

"Well, my name is Julie Fisk . . ." I replied a bit uncertainly, trying to place how I might know her and suddenly regretting my decision to put on a giant wearable blanket that covered me from neck to knees. It was warm but looked utterly ridiculous.

"Oh! Your son is in my class. And I live two streets over." And with that slightly fumbled start, our conversation took off, revealing a million tiny connections. Aaron and I had walked past her house a hundred times, cheerfully waving to her husband as he and the kids played pickleball in the driveway. Our kids were in the same immersion program and had many of the same teachers despite the age gap. So many other small ties had me smiling long after they continued on their way—her princess was feeling slightly chilly in the cool night air and wanted to keep going.

Almost ten years ago, we decided to experiment with using Halloween to build relationships with our neighbors, near and far. We offer hot cocoa, s'mores, and full-size candy bars, and a giant bonfire lights our driveway—an invitation to warm up and linger, engaging for a few moments in conversation before continuing down the sidewalk. We want to be known as a family of warm hospitality, and we're grateful that God has taken our experiment and built it into what we'd hoped for and even gone far beyond our imaginings.

Today's verse is for me what some people call a "life verse." Being a woman who wears the "fragrance of Christ," a woman whose presence consistently (even while imperfectly) invites people toward God, is a striking visual of what it means to have your internal faith manifest externally through your actions.

Being fragrant looks different based on our stage of life, where we live, and where we work or volunteer. As long as we're willing, we can trust God to throw open the doors of opportunity.

Julie

Today's Act of Gratitude

In what ways are you fragrant? Consider one
way to increase your potency.

November

What Are You Grateful For?

*Give thanks for everything to God the Father
in the name of our Lord Jesus Christ.*

EPHESIANS 5:20

It'd become too easy in our family to overlook everything we had to be grateful for and instead notice things we didn't have. My husband and I decided it was time to change the attitude and atmosphere in our home from selfish to thankful.

"I've got an idea," I told my kids one evening around the dinner table. "This month, let's take a slip of paper each day and write down one thing we're grateful for. We'll make a chain and then read it on Thanksgiving."

The kids agreed that it was a good idea, and as I passed slips of paper to each of them, I added, "The only rule is, you can't say the same thing twice."

As the month went on, we'd pass around slips of paper each day at dinner and then tape them to our growing chain that hung in the kitchen. On the morning of Thanksgiving, while we ate breakfast, we took the chain down and began to read through them together.

What started as a simple act of hoping to create a habit of gratitude within our family became my favorite holiday memory. I was in awe of the things my kids were grateful for—the sunrise, a sibling's laugh, a shared treat, a smile someone gave them when they needed encouragement. They were the simplest of things and would have been quickly forgotten if not written down daily. It became a testament to the little joys we were grateful for each day and a tradition we've continued every year since.

We know that we are to give thanks for *everything* to God the Father, but how can we when we're rushing through our days unaware of the smallest blessings? It takes intention to stop and notice all the little (and big) things, but it doesn't take long to make it a habit. Once we do, it's easy to see simple gifts we can thank God for.

Kendra

Today's Act of Gratitude

Begin writing down one new thing you're grateful for each day between now and Thanksgiving, and then spend some time reading through all the things you've noticed this month.

Gap Fillers

The human body has many parts, but the many parts make up one whole body. So it is with the body of Christ.

1 CORINTHIANS 12:12

I volunteer alongside a man who loves numbers. Spreadsheets are his specialty, and his ability to transform numerical gibberish into tidy bar graphs and other easily digestible statistics never fails to impress me. Over the years, I've realized that he and I are both storytellers; it's just that his stories are distilled and compiled from reams of paper filled with data and numbers.

I'm grateful for his expertise and skill set, especially because his strength shores up my admitted mathematical weakness, and he's grateful for my ability to edit and rework language for clarity and consistency. Rather than competing or undermining one another's contributions, we intentionally fill one another's gaps. The result of our cooperative appreciation is a combined work product superior to what either of us could produce on our own.

While we are all created in God's likeness, we are magnificently diverse in so many ways, including interests, abilities, and skills. This wasn't by chance. We are built for community, and community naturally requires different areas of strength, aptitude, and talent. The strongest teams I know include divergent expertise and aptitudes. They are made up of people who pull out the creative best in others, acknowledging contributions and exhibiting gratitude toward one another and God for the strengths found in working together toward a common goal.

Instead of shame or resentment over skill sets that come harder to us than others, what if we simply acknowledged the difficult areas, asking God to fill in our gaps with the knowledge and expertise of those around us? What if we sought out people whose strengths balance our weaknesses in our organizations and communities, filled with gratitude for their contribution instead of feeling jealous or insecure? It's countercultural, but so much of what God calls us to do and be is the opposite of what the world says.

Julie

Today's Act of Gratitude

Who makes you better in an area of life because they fill in a gap? Thank them specifically for their skill set or knowledge and, if appropriate, do so publicly.

Stepping In

The LORD is more pleased when we do what is right
and just than when we offer him sacrifices.

PROVERBS 21:3

Sitting in Mr. Milazzo's class during my freshman year of high school, I grabbed the survey as it passed through the aisles. We were working on career development as part of our preparation for life after graduation, had taken aptitude tests, and had a folder filled with information. That day's assignment was a survey that listed job options. Our task was to check off the ones we were interested in pursuing.

Though I usually took my studies seriously, I must have been feeling a little silly that day. Instead of checking off occupations I was interested in considering after graduation, I selected the box for "sheepherding."

Days later, my heart sank when I realized that we would be job shadowing people in the local community for an entire school day based on our answers. Thankfully, some kind administrator—or possibly even my teacher—realized that I wasn't serious about sheepherding and placed me in a local childcare center instead. Though I didn't see myself pursuing a career with children, I did have fun playing with the kids that day.

Sometimes we need someone else to intervene for us when we don't have the wisdom or maturity to decide on our own. And sometimes we need to be that person for others, stepping in when we know a friend is walking down a foolish path or is unable to advocate for themselves. I'm so grateful that someone realized I was being less than authentic in my survey answers and gently steered me in another direction.

God is pleased when we advocate for others—whether it's in something small like my survey or something with more significant implications for society—and he sees our decisions to do what is right as more important than any other sacrifice. When we step in for someone, we not only show that we care for them, but we also echo the care that Jesus has for them. Though we will sometimes be the ones in need of a bit of guidance—as I was that long-ago day—we can show our gratitude to those who have assisted us by extending a helping hand to someone else in need.

Kristin

Today's Act of Gratitude

When have you helped someone? When has someone
helped you? Thank God for both situations.

Focus on Today

*Don't worry about tomorrow, for tomorrow will bring its
own worries. Today's trouble is enough for today.*

MATTHEW 6:34

"Did you read the latest headlines?"

I hadn't. It had been a busy day, and my friend's text made me certain that whatever had happened wasn't good. There was a part of me that simply didn't want to know and had me wondering if—perhaps—it was better to play ostrich and bury my head in the sand.

Lord, how do I live in this world and yet remember that this is not my home, that I belong to you?

How do I represent you well when headlines are horrific?

How do I remain compassionate and actively engage with those who hurt when I desperately want to look away and focus on something happier?

How do I keep my eyes and heart attuned to you, Lord, when everything is a dumpster fire?

Prayer is my first defense. I gratefully hand my concerns to him (sometimes hourly or even more frequently, if I'm honest), knowing nothing is too big for him to hold. He is not caught off guard, and my fretting is not helpful to anyone, especially me.

And then I ask God to use me. There is something powerful about fighting worry and fear with a simple "Here I am, Lord, send me." After all, we are the mobilized, active hands and feet of Jesus, and he will use us, even through the smallest acts of kindness. As I look for someone to bless, my fear dissipates. I can make a difference in my neighborhood, workplace, community, and—don't underestimate the one who gives us assignments—beyond.

When we exchange worry for a prayerful request to be used, we won't know this side of heaven how our simple obedience—both in not worrying and in caring for others—will amplify God's glory. Worry and fear about the future are paralyzing, but entrusting it to God while we focus on what we can do now—that is powerful, world-changing, gratifying action.

Julie

Today's Act of Gratitude

The next time you are prone to worry, thank God
as you hand him the situation, asking for a tangible
assignment to bless someone else in exchange.

We're Better Together

Moses' arms soon became so tired he could no longer hold them up. So Aaron and Hur found a stone for him to sit on. Then they stood on each side of Moses, holding up his hands. So his hands held steady until sunset.

EXODUS 17:12

Even though the little girl had received a transplant after being diagnosed with kidney disease, her kidney was once again failing. She needed a new one. As a result, she had to begin four-hour dialysis treatments at the hospital, two days a week.

Reading about the young girl's situation on a local message board, my friend Erin was moved to do something—first, to pray. Then, quietly and without fanfare, to sign up to be a donor.

Within months, she was in the hospital, recovering from surgery. Thanks to Erin donating on her behalf, the girl was placed on the living donor list, making it likely that she would receive a kidney much sooner than she would have otherwise.

After Erin's surgery, as her friends and family rallied around—her husband and mom faithfully helping each day with the kids, a round of friends dropping off meals—I couldn't help but think about the story of Moses and the battle with the Amalekites. The Israelites had the advantage in the fight as long as Moses held up his staff. But anytime his arms drooped from weariness, the Israelites' ability waned. Noticing this, his trusted friends and family members Aaron and Hur held up his arms for him. With their support, the battle was won.

What a beautiful picture of the body of Christ. We are not meant to live this life alone. We simply can't do it all on our own. Just as Erin stepped in when she saw a need, those who loved her did the same while she recuperated. I am grateful that God puts people in our lives to help us when we are struggling. When we work together, we embody the loving community we were meant to experience all along.

Kristin

Today's Act of Gratitude

Has a friend or loved one supported you when you struggled
to face something alone? If so, say thank you.

Who's Your Lindsay?

*Let us think of ways to motivate one another
to acts of love and good works.*

HEBREWS 10:24

One of the biggest blessings the three of us have found through writing together is our connections with other women.

Our friend Lindsay is at the top of the list. She is kind and gracious, encouraging and generous. We first met her through a mutual acquaintance when she was just starting a clothing store for women in our community, and we attended an event held at her house. Since then, Lindsay has grown her shop (and her following), creating a space where women are encouraged, loved, and accepted.

When we asked her one summer day if we could host the launch party for our latest devotional at her store, White Peony Boutique, she gave us a resounding yes, without hesitation. Leading up to the event, she checked in with us, ensuring we had everything we needed.

As we pulled up to unload that cool November night, her mom, Jayne, met us at the door. "How can I help?" she asked, then took an armload of items to bring in. We spent the next hour moving things around and arranging an easy flow for guests to buy books and shop in the boutique. It was a lovely evening filled with friends and acquaintances, laughter and excitement.

I'm grateful for Lindsay, Jayne, and the other women who work at the boutique for making it all possible—effortlessly inviting people in and making them feel welcome. As we packed up to leave, I couldn't stop smiling over the kindness and friendship found among such a wonderful group of women.

As much as we love writing, we love even more the community built by women who keep their circles open, love others well, and cheer each other on. And women like that? Truly, they are not hard to find (in the best of ways!). We've found them at church, in kids' activities, and in our neighborhoods. Scripture encourages us to think of ways to encourage others to do acts of love. Surround yourself with people who are like this, and you're sure to follow their example.

Kendra

Today's Act of Gratitude

Who's your Lindsay? Send them a card, text, or message telling them how much you appreciate their friendship.

Do What You Love

I recommend having fun, because there is nothing better for people in this world than to eat, drink, and enjoy life. That way they will experience some happiness along with all the hard work God gives them under the sun.

ECCLESIASTES 8:15

She was napping when I entered her room at the nursing home that afternoon but became a woman on a mission as soon as she awakened. I combed out her snowy white hair and applied a little perfume behind her ears, and together we headed toward the community room.

Though she'd just been placed on hospice, you wouldn't have known it by looking at her. My Grandma Jo—who had recently celebrated her eighty-ninth birthday—wouldn't let declining health keep her from doing what she loved. Today, that was bingo.

She beelined for what I quickly realized was her usual spot, front and center. Her reputation as an avid player—with a mile-wide competitive streak, the staff told me—meant that she had two cards she alternated, even though everyone else had one. It didn't take her long to finish lining up her bingo chips (milk caps), sorting them by color, and surreptitiously swapping them with those at the empty seat across the table. When the first round began, she was intent.

As I left for work a couple of hours later, I couldn't help the grin that slid across my face at the thought of Grandma and her love for certain games. I remembered the many rounds of Yahtzee our family had played together at her house and how, after Grandpa Hans died, she drove an hour to and from the nearest big city to play bingo once a week.

Even after she entered the nursing home and her world grew smaller, she still did things she loved.

We each have work to accomplish daily, but that doesn't mean we can't enjoy life. Let's take the time to go for an evening stroll, savor lemonade on a hot day, or eat fresh-picked strawberries still warm from the field. Let's make an effort to grab coffee with a friend, crank up the radio and belt out our favorite song, and take every opportunity to embrace our one, precious life. Let's honor the gift we've been given by doing what we love—even if it requires two bingo cards.

Kristin

Today's Act of Gratitude

What's one thing you love to do but don't often have time for?
If possible, make time to do it within the next week or two.

Wilderness Places

*"Behold, I will allure her, and bring her into
the wilderness, and speak tenderly to her."*

HOSEA 2:14, ESV

At first glance, the mountains of Colorado are paradise: snowy peaks rising above forests of conifers, crystalline blue lakes tucked into valleys, wildflowers carpeting meadows, and open places with rainbow hues. It isn't until your boots are crunching across rocks and your breath is a little harder to catch that you start to understand there is something complicated about this undeniable beauty.

Life at an altitude of ten thousand feet is challenging. Spindly evergreens stretching toward the sun are rooted in the precariously thin soil that barely covers rocky mountainsides. Delicate alpine wildflowers survive nightly temperatures hovering near freezing even in July. And those incredible clouds rolling over the peak just yonder can suddenly turn your morning romp through mountain meadows into a mad dash for the trailhead as rumbling thunder warns of life-threatening lightning strikes.

Breathtaking beauty exists—even thrives—amid difficult conditions. I pondered this dichotomy as I hiked, grieving afresh the unfairness of Katrina's death (dear friend to me, sister to Kendra and Kristin) and the ripple effects her missing presence has caused—some beautifully redemptive and some impossibly hard—in the years she has been gone. My thoughts slipped along as my feet moved, naturally shifting to women I know and their wilderness areas as they wait on God for answers, for clarity, for a miracle.

What do we do with the wilderness places in our lives when it feels like those around us are blessed beyond measure? What do we do with the waiting, the "should haves," the desperate disappointments, the unfulfilled longing in the face of seemingly unanswered prayer?

Friends, Jesus is with us in the wilderness. I am grateful that he will never leave nor forsake us (see Hebrews 13:5), and today's verse assures us that he is tender and loving toward us, drawing us near to him. Turn toward him with your heartache and sorrow, your grief and your anger. He can handle your worst parts, so dare to entrust him with your fears, your doubts, your longings. Surrender the illusion of control as you wait on him.

Julie

Today's Act of Gratitude

Take a walk, just you and Jesus, being honest with him about your wilderness areas and all the accompanying thoughts and emotions.

The Good Stuff

Go ahead. Eat your food with joy, and drink your wine
with a happy heart, for God approves of this!

ECCLESIASTES 9:7

Unscrewing the top of the small jar, I sniffed its contents appreciatively. I'd received the sugar scrub from a friend several months earlier and had put it away, waiting for just the right occasion to use it. A quiet night at home with nothing planned seemed like the perfect opportunity.

But when I tried to scoop some of the contents into my palm, nothing came out. I frowned, realizing that my fingers had hit a rock-hard surface. The scrub I'd waited so long to try was now dried out and unusable. Disappointed, I set it aside.

A few years ago, a family member's home burned down. Along with their dismay over the loss of their home and so many items tied to cherished memories was the regret that the "good stuff"—like the wine they'd saved for a special day—had burned along with everything else. With the benefit of hindsight, their advice was to stop waiting for a special occasion to arrive. Instead, they said, "Enjoy the good stuff."

Whether it's an item we receive as a gift, an object that is costly or hard to find, or something that feels too special to use, it can be a challenge to use up the good stuff. But you and I are not promised tomorrow, and when we see the things we've been given as opportunities to thank God for his blessings, our mindset changes. God wants us to enjoy what we've received.

Today is special too. Let's celebrate it. Instead of waiting, let's eat the good food. Let's use up the sugar scrub. Let's not hoard, ignore, or stow away special items for a day that never arrives. Instead, let's take the time to enjoy them, share them with others, and thank God for the gift of today.

Kristin

Today's Act of Gratitude

Use something you've been saving for a special occasion.

Let Go of Regret

I focus on this one thing: Forgetting the past and looking forward to what lies ahead, I press on to reach the end of the race and receive the heavenly prize for which God, through Christ Jesus, is calling us.

PHILIPPIANS 3:13-14

"I didn't sleep well last night, and today I am sad, sad, sad." She continued, explaining how deeply she regretted a situation from her past—pondering whether there was anything she could or should have done that would have changed her current circumstances.

I quelled my natural instinct to offer words of comfort or absolution. I simply let her share in compassionate companionship, silently inviting God into our midst to provide solace and a way forward.

Grief is a complicated, tricky beast. I've come to think of it as waves that ebb and flow over time—with unexpectedly huge waves engulfing us even decades later as new consequences from old situations play out in our lives and in the lives of those we love. And regret can be a close companion to grief, whispering could've, should've, would've in our ear as we relive our actions or inactions over and over.

Regret, if we aren't careful, will trap us in the past, rendering us ineffective for Kingdom work in the present. And the older we get, the more regrets we naturally accumulate, wishing we'd had the wisdom of experience earlier in our parenting, our relationships, our careers, and beyond.

Jesus calls us to forward living—applying the wisdom gleaned from past mistakes to break unhealthy cycles and intentionally make increasingly better choices for ourselves and those we love. But in order to move forward, we must forgive ourselves. It's tempting to repent of a past mistake, seeking forgiveness from God, but then continue to flail ourselves again and again, rejecting the gift of forgiveness and limiting how God can use us because we refuse to let go.

Instead, let's thank God for his forgiveness, asking him to use those experiences we regret redemptively—embracing what we've learned for God's glory and for use in his purpose as we move forward.

Julie

Today's Act of Gratitude

Hand Jesus your regrets, repenting of sin and thanking him for redemptive experiences to come from your newfound wisdom.

Faithful Workers

We always thank God for all of you and pray for you constantly. As we pray to our God and Father about you, we think of your faithful work, your loving deeds, and the enduring hope you have because of our Lord Jesus Christ.

1 THESSALONIANS 1:2–3

I love the library. There's something comforting about the dusty smell of the pages and row upon row of colorful books lined up and ready to be opened. I love placing holds online for new releases and picking them up when they've arrived at my local library, but simply browsing the shelves for unique finds is fun too. Taking home as many as I want feels like a sweet luxury.

Living in a rural area of Northern Minnesota, my aunt Delpha doesn't have access to the same kind of library that I do. The closest town has another type of library altogether: a bookmobile. As a child, I was delighted by the idea of a library on wheels, driving from town to town. What an ingenious way to get books to people!

But even though I appreciate the bookmobile, it's made me realize how easy it is to take for granted the many public services that help our society function. Because I live in a populated area, I've come to expect access to resources like libraries, schools, and emergency services. If an ambulance didn't arrive during an emergency or my children didn't have a school to attend, I would be concerned. Yet hundreds—if not thousands—of people work to make those services a reality for my local community.

In the New Testament, Paul, along with Silas and Timothy, writes a letter to the church in Thessalonica. Before offering advice, he begins with gratitude, thanking the believers for their faithful work. He recognizes that though the church is imperfect, what they need first is encouragement. The members have been doing the work faithfully, and Paul acknowledges their efforts.

Are we able to do the same and bite our tongue on the advice we long to give and instead focus on the faithfulness of the worker, especially those who serve a public role? We can sometimes be tempted to point out areas for improvement rather than thank them for the good in what they do. When we focus on gratitude rather than criticism, we honor others in their work for the community's good.

Kristin

Today's Act of Gratitude

Thank someone who serves the public in their role.

Speak Life

Like apples of gold in settings of silver,
is a word spoken at the proper time.

PROVERBS 25:11, NASB

"Can someone come back here? Jasmine's upset." The text came through my friend's phone, and she leaned over to show me. I nodded as I whispered that I'd go check.

We'd been watching our girls dance in their first competition of the season. They were nervous but also excited. I'd expected that my daughter would be upset—she'd just slipped and fallen during their tap routine. She quickly recovered, jumping back up on her feet, but I knew she wouldn't be happy.

As I walked into the changing room, I could see her teammates comforting her. I gave her a hug, telling her it would be okay, that she had quickly recovered and done well, but she shook her head and whispered, "I let everybody down, Mom."

Ava, a good friend and teammate of Jasmine's, overheard and quickly responded, "Not me. You didn't let me down." I smiled at Ava, grateful for her encouragement. Jasmine wiped her eyes and took a deep breath. I knew it would take a little time, but the support from her friends would help her recover.

Sometimes we can be our own worst enemies. When we mess up or make a mistake, we're often our own toughest critics, berating ourselves in our own minds or replaying how we could have done things better. But mistakes are a part of life, and we shouldn't be surprised when we aren't perfect—we weren't meant to be. This is when I'm grateful for those around us, who love us. We need them to help us see clearly what we cannot: that messing up is okay and that everyone does it.

And when we, like Ava, use our words to remind others of this truth, those words become like "apples of gold" set in silver, the perfect comment at just the right time to counteract the negative voices in our own heads.

Kendra

Today's Act of Gratitude

Pay attention to those around you and determine to use your words at the right time to build someone else up.

Fight like a Girl

If you keep quiet at a time like this, deliverance and relief for the Jews will arise from some other place, but you and your relatives will die. Who knows if perhaps you were made queen for just such a time as this?

ESTHER 4:14

As a young girl, I spilled countless tears about that very fact: I was a girl. It felt like boys had all the advantages, both physically and socially. And, of course, spending the day in the woods was no problem for them when every tree offered a potential bathroom. Yep, my younger self just knew that boys had it made.

Fast-forward several decades, and I wouldn't trade my "girl" card for the world. I see other women who love Jesus intentionally choosing collaboration and encouragement over cattiness and condemnation. They are single and married, career women and women who stay home, homeschoolers and public school advocates. They are from different generations, denominations, parts of the world, and political backgrounds.

It gives me hope that we finally realize that women in committed community are stronger than women alone, that we have voices and skills and strengths unique to us that can be used to accomplish great things for God when we fight alongside one another on common, big-picture issues instead of clashing against one another on small differences.

American women (in addition to women from many other countries) are among the freest, best educated, most resourced group of women to ever walk on earth, and I cannot help but wonder what would happen if we combined our strengths, skill sets, and intentionality toward loving God and loving others. We are part of the most amazing chapter in the history of womankind, and I draw inspiration and courage from watching how God uses us in big ways, in small ways, and a million in-between ways to change the world.

Instead of bemoaning the fact that we live in this present time with the challenges set before us, let us thank God that we were born into this age of opportunity. Let us be women who actively join forces with other women in our faith communities to bring the good news of Jesus to those around us.

Julie

Today's Act of Gratitude

Prayerfully ask God how he'd have you join forces with other women.

Beauty to Behold

The heavens proclaim the glory of God.
The skies display his craftsmanship.

PSALM 19:1

"Mom, come out here," my daughter called to me early one morning as she walked out the front door to await the school bus. The first snowfall had come, and although it wasn't more than a light dusting, the trees and ground were covered.

"It's beautiful," she said as she looked around.

I stepped out on the porch and wrapped my sweatshirt more tightly around me. I followed her gaze to see the trees that lined the boulevard, each limb glowing white against the sky just starting to lighten from the east.

"It is," I said, breathing in the cool air.

We stood together for a few moments, looking in awe at the quiet scene all around us before the bus pulled up and I kissed her goodbye for the day. As I scurried back into the warmth of my house, I realized I would have missed the beauty of that morning without my daughter's encouragement to step outside. I felt grateful to God for all the ways he shows us his love and creativity through creation.

It takes only a moment to stop and notice the splendor around us. But how many times do we miss it? So often, we can go through life, head down, thinking only of the task at hand or the to-do list for the day, but if we lift our eyes, we just might glimpse how the heavens display God's glory and craftsmanship. On any given day, we can look outside and see what God has made—every season bringing its unique loveliness to earth.

His beauty is on display for all to see. There is no denying the wonder and the glory that is available to us if only we'll take the time to stop and notice.

Kendra

Today's Act of Gratitude

Take some time to step outside, notice God's creation,
and thank him for all you see and experience.

Appreciating Opposites

*Just as our bodies have many parts and each part has a
special function, so it is with Christ's body. We are many
parts of one body, and we all belong to each other.*

ROMANS 12:4-5

The crying started as a slow whimper but escalated quickly. Blinking blearily, I flipped over and peeked at the baby monitor. *Wide awake.* Sighing, I silenced the monitor and walked to my daughter's room to feed and soothe her and get her back to sleep.

I fell back into bed but was awakened again a few hours later. Glancing at the clock, I noticed it was 4:10 a.m. *Yes!* Turning to my other side, I gently nudged my husband.

"Honey," I whispered, "it's your turn."

My husband has always been a morning person. Whereas I need a cup of coffee and a few minutes of silence to feel like myself, he practically bounces out of bed.

At times, being opposites annoyed me. Couldn't he be a little less talkative in the morning? Couldn't we have a conversation later in the evening without him falling asleep on me?

But those early morning tendencies worked in my favor when our first child was born. Between 10 a.m. and 4 a.m., I would get up with her. After 4 a.m., he would care for her until I awakened around 7 a.m., when he had to get ready for work.

No longer did our opposite schedules feel like a problem. Now, I appreciated his ready response to those early wake-up calls.

We struggle with opposites, don't we? They feel inherently problematic. Extreme heat or cold by themselves can cause death, but when used as a counterbalance to one another, they are helpful—like a blast of cool air-conditioning on a ninety-degree day or a warm bath on a snowy evening. As members of the body of Christ, each of us has a unique role. I wonder if we struggle to find balance because it's only achieved when we move closer to someone or appreciate how their differences make up for what we lack. We can work together for peace when we use our opposite natures to offset others.

Kristin

Today's Act of Gratitude

Think of a person who is your opposite in some way. How can you
appreciate a quality that counterbalances one of your own?

No Risk, No Fun

Trust in the LORD with all your heart and lean not on your own understanding; in all your ways submit to him, and he will make your paths straight.

PROVERBS 3:5-6, NIV

It was a warm, sunny day as we stood on a gently curving path leading us toward the Sedona Red Rocks. Approaching the base of Bell Rock, we spied tiny, ant-sized people standing at the tippy-top after hiking a winding, twisty path that was too near a cliff edge for my comfort. My eight-year-old daughter, Lizzie, turned to us with excitement in her voice, asking if she couldn't pretty please climb to the top. Then she ran ahead to catch up with Grandma and Grandpa as they pointed out a small lizard.

Aaron and I started quietly discussing her request. We strolled as we talked, and as I drew near to Lizzie, I heard her softly mutter the following to herself over and over:

"No risk, no fun. No risk, no fun. No risk, no fun."

My momma's heart stuttered momentarily as I realized yet again that my daughter's love of adventure colors how she sees the world in a way that sometimes makes me a little nervous. In the years since that day, I've returned to her words, processing that sentiment as it pertains to my faith journey.

Trusting God can feel risky. Jesus was countercultural, and we're to be the same. He asks us to be generous when the world tells us to cling tightly to all we can, and he requires us to love when we're encouraged to dismiss those who disagree with us.

God is good, and he sees the big picture while we see as though through a cloudy, murky mirror. And he often invites us to walk what feels like narrow, twisting paths instead of the broad avenues strolled by so many others.

I'm learning there is a joy to be found in risky obedience and that following doggedly in Jesus' steps often results in unexpected delights. Besides, who wants a boring, ordinary existence when God invites us on the grand adventure of a lifetime?

Julie

Today's Act of Gratitude

Share with a friend about two or three times Jesus asked you to step out of your comfort zone (and the results), and ask her to share a few stories of her own. Thank God even as you trust him with the next adventure he is inviting you on.

Yes and Amen

All the promises of God find their Yes in him. That is why it is through him that we utter our Amen to God for his glory.

2 CORINTHIANS 1:20, ESV

We recently had a "Yes Day" at our house. I said yes to as many things as possible for the whole day. That morning, we picked up caramel ribbon crunch Frappuccinos—minus the coffee—from Starbucks, strolled through Target, then browsed the dollar store. After that, we ate at Jimmy John's for lunch, then drove to Hyland Park, a giant playground with what felt like a million kids running around. Next, we headed to the Blue Sun Soda Shop to pick up specialty sodas for later and ended our adventures with tres leches ice cream at a local shop. When we returned home, a quiet family movie night with popcorn was the perfect ending to our fun-filled day.

I'll admit that my kids ate way too much sugar, but we had a blast.

As I reminisced about our day later, I realized that we often think of God as a cosmic killjoy, just waiting to ruin our fun—when the truth is, he often tells us yes. Yes, we can enjoy the beauty of creation. Yes, he placed us in a family. Yes, he provided the skills we need to accomplish our work. Yes, he sparked the ideas that became dreams in our hearts. So much of our enjoyment of this life directly results from a good God who tells his children yes with fondness.

The ultimate "Yes" is Christ himself, whose death and resurrection fulfilled the promises of God. He is a living "Amen" (meaning "It is so") to those promises. Yes, he loves us. Yes, he wants us to be part of his family. Yes, our purpose and meaning can be found in him. Yes, we can live for an eternity in heaven with him.

Yes and amen. What a wondrous God we serve.

Kristin

Today's Act of Gratitude

Say yes to someone's request.

NOVEMBER 18

Accepting Help

*Share each other's burdens, and
in this way obey the law of Christ.*

GALATIANS 6:2

It was going to be a busy Saturday. Kyle and I had planned to help our friends host a Thanksgiving gathering for friends and acquaintances who were new to the country and hadn't experienced the holiday before. But our kids also had activities to attend—robotics tournaments and a dance show.

As I dropped my daughter off at practice for the dance show that afternoon, I visited with my friend Staci, explaining all we had going on that day. She quickly chimed in, "I can bring Jasmine home after the show."

"No, that's fine," I said without hesitation. "I'll come get her."

"I really don't mind."

"I don't want to bother you. But thanks," I said with a smile as the girls returned from practice.

As I drove home and thought more about all the running I would have to do to get the kids and attend the party, I realized I should have taken Staci up on her offer.

When I returned home and started making food to take to the gathering, I told Kyle what Staci had said. "I don't know why I always automatically say no when people offer me help. It would be nice not to need to run back to the school to pick up Jasmine."

"Then text her back," Kyle responded. "I'm sure she wouldn't mind." And so I did. Staci immediately answered that she'd love to help. I thanked her again, grateful for a friend who would step in.

As Christians, we are supposed to support others, but what about when *we* need help? Sharing one another's burdens is a command we are to obey whether we are giving help or receiving it. God didn't want us to go through life on our own; leaning on others is part of his plan, and it's the way he wants us to give and receive love.

Kendra

Today's Act of Gratitude

Accept the help of someone else and thank
God for that person's assistance.

Sharing with the Newbie

How much better to get wisdom than gold,
and good judgment than silver!

PROVERBS 16:16

"Yikes! Look at the rain puddling in the canopy of their tent! Um . . . do you think it can hold that much water without collapsing?"

My comment was directed toward Kendra as we huddled beneath our borrowed booth tent at a late-fall outdoor market, peering through the driving rain at the booths and their inhabitants around us. Even as I spoke, we watched several tent owners (including the gentleman I'd noticed) empty pooling water from their canopies, averting imminent collapse but creating an even soggier mess on the ground around them.

A friend of a friend had loaned us her booth canopy for the summer, and we'd been hauling it with us to local fairs and markets as we experimented with selling our books at crafty, artsy venues. Surrounded by lovely neighbors, we'd picked up several tips and tricks and were no longer the newbies we'd been a few months ago.

As wet (yet still fun!) as that last market of the season was, the experience gave us a wealth of information about what to do differently next summer. We made several changes and purchased a canopy based on what we'd learned and seen and heard from the vendors around us.

I've been in situations where knowledge was hoarded and used as currency to bring value and advantage to the person with the "insider" connections. And I've been the recipient of knowledge generosity—gifted with a list of best practices and pitfalls to avoid by women who are a step or two ahead of me on the same journey.

A younger version of me might have wondered at the assertion in today's verse that wisdom and good judgment outweigh silver and gold. Still, today's version of me knows the immense heartache that can be avoided with a well-placed suggestion from someone who has been there and done that.

I owe a debt of gratitude to people who mentored me in my career, colleagues who helped me navigate those first weeks of a new job, and the friend of a friend who lent us her canopy for the summer. And I try to pay all of the good judgment and wisdom forward by doing the same for others.

Julie

Today's Act of Gratitude

Think of a time someone's suggestion helped you avoid a
pitfall or adjust to a new organization. Pay it forward.

Using Godly Wisdom

*The wisdom from above is first of all pure. It is also peace loving, gentle
at all times, and willing to yield to others. It is full of mercy and the
fruit of good deeds. It shows no favoritism and is always sincere.*

JAMES 3:17

I was angry. Someone had been saying hurtful things about my family, and it had
been going on for quite some time. Finally, when I felt it needed to be addressed,
I called the person, asking if they had time to meet.

As I made my way over to their apartment, I prayed, asking God to be in the
midst of our conversation, and then I spent some time thinking about what might
be going on in their life that could be causing them angst or hardship. I tried to
put myself in their shoes, reminding myself of their humanity and the struggles I
knew they were facing.

When I arrived and rang the doorbell, my heart was hurting but not angry.
With shaking hands and a trepidatious smile, I accepted their invitation inside and
sat down. As we talked about insignificant things, I looked for the right moment
to begin.

I started by telling the person how much they meant to me and how I valued
them as a person. And then I honestly shared how it felt to have them say hurtful
things. I explained from my perspective what I saw happening and asked them
how they saw things.

They were honest, laying out the situation from their perspective. We spent
time each saying what we thought and then made a plan for moving forward. It
wasn't perfect, but as I left, I felt a peace and gratitude that we had been able to
have an open and honest conversation.

Conflict is never easy; for many of us, it's something we try to avoid. But as
Christians who have access to godly wisdom, we don't have to shy away from
discord. Instead, we should be willing to speak with wisdom that is peace loving,
gentle, and willing to yield and consider others. We should be merciful and sincere.
It's not always easy, but I'm thankful that when we apply godly wisdom, no matter
the outcome, we can trust that God is pleased with our efforts.

Kendra

Today's Act of Gratitude

Use the godly wisdom of James 3:17 in a challenging relationship.

Highs and Lows

A good person produces good things from the treasury of a good heart, and an evil person produces evil things from the treasury of an evil heart. What you say flows from what is in your heart.

LUKE 6:45

"Okay, highs and lows," I announced, passing a plate piled high with lasagna to my oldest daughter. Next to me, my husband scooped up the salad for everyone.

"Ooh, me first," one of my daughters piped up. "My high was playing with Chloe at recess. My low was forgetting my water bottle and being thirsty at school."

We went around the table one by one, listing the best and most challenging parts of our day. Most of the lows weren't too terrible: a misunderstanding with a friend, a school assignment they didn't love working on, a rainy day, and a canceled work meeting. And while most of the highs were pretty minor, too, they were good reasons to be grateful: dinner together, something a friend said that was funny, a coffee date with a friend, and a game in gym class. Most days don't span the full range from wild successes to huge disappointments but instead involve smaller shifts between highs and lows.

Scripture reminds us that what's in our hearts will overflow in our words. Though we think of this most often in a negative sense—such as when we have an angry outburst and say something we regret—it's also revealed in the positive things we choose to focus on. Our highs-and-lows habit is a good touchstone each day because it reveals what's in our hearts. When we actively choose to name the best and the most challenging parts of our day, we have the opportunity to decide what's important to us. Our lows are often a reason for prayer, sympathy, or shared understanding. Our highs allow us to name, out loud, something that's worth celebrating. When we respond in these ways, we'll find even more reasons to show grace when someone is struggling and gratitude when we see or hear something worth praising.

Kristin

Today's Act of Gratitude

List your highs and lows for the day. How can you be grateful for the highs? How can you pray for the lows?

A Warm Welcome

Always be eager to practice hospitality.

ROMANS 12:13

"Why don't we just stay with them?" my husband asked as he peered over my shoulder at the computer screen. I'd been looking for hours at vacation rentals in Texas for an upcoming trip.

"Because—don't you think it'd be strange? We don't know them that well. Besides, they just had a baby. I really don't want to intrude."

He shrugged. "Haddie did offer for us to stay at their home. Why don't you just talk to her?"

"I'll think about it," I said, not really wanting to consider it. But as the days went on and I couldn't find a good fit for our family, I sent Haddie a text, hesitantly asking what she thought of us staying with them.

"Of course! We'd love to have you!" she quickly responded. I let out a sigh of relief as we went on to discuss food and activities for our trip.

As the weeks got closer to us leaving, I was nervous. *Will we get along? Will our kids be okay and not act too crazy? Will we have things to talk about?* I whispered my questions as prayers to God as I packed our vehicle and we made the trek to Texas.

The moment we walked in the door, all my worry was put to rest. Haddie and Leo were so kind and thoughtful, setting up bedrooms with everything we'd need, stocking foods our kids liked, and making plans to go out and enjoy activities each day.

We spent the next several days sharing stories, telling jokes, and just getting to know one another like we hadn't before. We felt so welcomed, known, and loved.

As we hugged to leave, I couldn't help but think that our proximity to one another, staying in their home, made it possible. We drove away grateful for our time but even more so for the deeper connection.

God encourages us to practice hospitality. Although there are many reasons for this, one of the most important, I believe, is that it opens us up to deeper relationships and connections with those around us, allowing us to give and receive love, kindness, and care as little else will.

Kendra

Today's Act of Gratitude

Practice hospitality by inviting someone into your home, whether for a meal, a cup of coffee, or an overnight stay, and see how your relationship deepens.

Friendsgiving

This is how God loved the world: He gave his one and only Son, so that
everyone who believes in him will not perish but have eternal life.

JOHN 3:16

"Who wants more brisket or turkey? We've got plenty!" Aaron's voice boomed through our house as he checked our slightly unorthodox Friendsgiving buffet line filled with food from around the world. A few years ago, we started hosting a pre-Thanksgiving "Friendsgiving" with friends and friends of friends—many of whom didn't grow up celebrating Thanksgiving in their culture.

As we compared notes on the cranberries and pickled herring being passed around, our rowdy, hilarious conversation about what foods were "required" for Thanksgiving to be Thanksgiving was filled with loud groans over lutefisk and questions about lefse—those with Norwegian heritage tried to convince the rest of us that both were necessary. I love exploring culture through food, and hosting a Friendsgiving is a beautiful way to celebrate those things that make us wonderfully unique and the common threads that pull us into community.

As we pulled off the cardboard hearts hanging on my makeshift Gratitude Tree (a branch cut from my lilac hedge and shoved into a large vase), a hush fell over the crowd. I read what each of us had written earlier when I'd handed out pens and hearts, tasking everyone with listing or drawing (for the young children among us) three things we were grateful for. Our lists were remarkably consistent: friends, health, a safe home, pursuit of dreams, favorite toys, freedom—it was impossible to tell our items apart, no matter how long we'd lived in this country and which country held our citizenship.

The overwhelming similarity in our lists is a lesson I've not forgotten and one I've gratefully clung to when my country feels torn apart by differences. Sometimes we can start to think that our particular group (political, denominational, cultural, regional) is a tiny bit more loved by God than other groups.

Today's verse is a beautifully convicting reminder that God sent Jesus to and for all of us. And one of the best ways to remember this truth is to intentionally seek relationships with those outside our own groups, finding ways to build on our commonalities instead of focusing intensely on our differences.

Julie

Today's Act of Gratitude

Host a Friendsgiving in your home or at a restaurant,
inviting a broad range of people to join you.

On God's Side

When Joshua was near the town of Jericho, he looked up and saw a man standing in front of him with sword in hand. Joshua went up to him and demanded, "Are you friend or foe?" "Neither one," he replied. "I am the commander of the LORD's army."

JOSHUA 5:13-14

Tensions run high when it comes to politics. I see the back-and-forth between people I know and love—Democrats, Republicans, and somewhere in between—in which Christians spew views as easily as everyone else. If I'm honest, I've had to hide some people's posts on social media, wanting to remain friends but unable to take in their rage, anger, or sarcasm.

Not long ago, I saw someone post their point of view and then say that if you disagree, you can't love God because God is on this side of the issue. I thought, *That's a dangerous statement to make—so sure that God is on your side of things and others are out.*

It grieves me. Not because I don't think people should care about politics, policies, or their country, but because I am concerned when these things overshadow our love of Jesus, when they overtake the greatest commandments: love God and love others.

It's become too easy to see people as our enemies. It reminds me of a story in Scripture where Joshua is fighting for the land God promised his people. When he comes near Jericho, he sees a man and asks if he's a friend or a foe, to which the man replies: "Neither . . . I am the commander of the Lord's army."

Joshua wisely asks what he should do, and the angel replies, "Take off your sandals, for the place where you are standing is holy" (Joshua 5:15).

I wonder how many of us are fighting battles in our belief that God must be on our side when the truth is that he is neither friend nor foe but simply the God of the universe. Ephesians 6:12 reminds us that our fight is not against flesh and blood—other people—but against mighty powers in this dark world. How easily we forget and hate, or at best dislike, people or treat them as enemies.

As Christians, this shouldn't be true of us. We are called to love God and others, including those we consider our enemies. No one is exempt. Everyone is invited to God's side. I'm so grateful to know this truth.

Kendra

Today's Act of Gratitude

Show kindness toward someone whose views
or beliefs are different from yours.

A Little Slice of Tradition

*An intelligent heart acquires knowledge, and
the ear of the wise seeks knowledge.*

PROVERBS 18:15, ESV

Dubiously, I surveyed the large pan of banana pudding with vanilla wafers. It sure didn't look like any Thanksgiving dessert I'd ever seen. And there was no pie—pumpkin, pecan, or otherwise. Shrugging, I slid a portion of the dessert on my plate anyway.

Next to me, my children lit up. "Ooh, what is that? Does it have bananas in it? I want to try it!"

Smiling at their response, I couldn't help but reflect on how our attitude toward new people, places, foods, and adventures makes a difference.

We were spending the holiday in South Carolina, and so far, it wasn't like any Thanksgiving I had experienced over the years. But I didn't mind that stuffing was called "dressing" or that there were several new dishes. And I liked that it was warm enough that we could go for a walk outside without wearing a coat. By the time we had finished watching the Thanksgiving Day Parade and the men were dozing in front of the football game on TV, I was thoroughly enjoying myself. Moreover, I loved incorporating another tradition I'd never heard of—fresh seafood the next day rather than leftover turkey. Yum.

The Bible has a lot to say about how acquiring knowledge is wise; only fools ignore instruction. We can become so used to our way of doing things that we forget to appreciate the talents and traditions of others. Yet it's only through our willingness to try new things that we can experience the fullness of life. I have to imagine that the God of the universe—who created a dizzying array of plants, animals, and organisms—wants us to celebrate the diversity of this world and its people, landscapes, and creativity. Curiosity about this wide variety is a gift that often brings us rich rewards.

And for all its minor differences, the day was still centered around food, family, and an attitude of thankfulness. I left feeling grateful that I had been welcomed in and got to try new things—including dessert. Years later, my kids still rave about that banana pudding concoction.

Kristin

Today's Act of Gratitude

Think of someone who taught you a new way of doing
something or introduced you to a new recipe. Thank
that person for expanding your knowledge.

What Forgiveness Is

If it is possible, as far as it depends on you,
live at peace with everyone.

ROMANS 12:18, NIV

"Why can't you just forgive?" The question came innocently enough from someone my husband and I were close to. As we talked later about the hard, yet necessary, conversation he'd had with the person, Kyle shrugged, expressing his misgivings about the situation and the lack of response he'd been hoping for.

Days later, he came to me. "I don't know why this still bothers me. Why can't I just forgive?"

I looked at him as I considered his question. "I think it bothers you not because you can't forgive but because the person making this request wants you to simply forget and move on. They don't really want to address their actions or any changes that might need to be made. They're dismissing your feelings. This really isn't about forgiveness." He nodded in agreement.

As we prayed together for wisdom and for God to heal our hearts and our relationship, I squeezed his hand.

"We'll get through this," I said. We determined to continue loving the person while also addressing the unhealthiness there.

Relationships can sometimes be messy. None of us gets through life unscathed. And for that reason, we're not wrong to set boundaries or lovingly address unhealthy behaviors. Sometimes people's past hurts affect how they view and respond to current relationships, making it hard to move forward in healing, especially if there's denial about what is happening.

The Bible is clear that we are to strive for peace with God and peace with others, but I'm grateful for the caveat of "as far as it depends on you"—meaning we don't have control over other people's actions or reactions. As much as we *do* have control in a situation, we are to live at peace. And although forgiveness is undoubtedly part of this, it does not mean that we must dismiss harmful actions or words. It's okay to set boundaries when we need to. So forgive. Set boundaries. Live at peace. And leave everything that is beyond your control in God's hands.

Kendra

Today's Act of Gratitude

Consider whether there is someone you need to extend
forgiveness to while also keeping healthy boundaries.
Think of some ways you could begin seeking peace.

Opportunities for Growth

Be careful how you live. Don't live like fools, but like those who are wise. Make the most of every opportunity in these evil days.

EPHESIANS 5:15-16

"I don't want to go," I groaned, burying my face in my hands. "Do I have to? There will be so many people; they won't even notice that I'm not there."

"Really?" my husband asked, disbelief written all over his face. After a moment, he sighed. "Okay. I'll tell them something came up."

Our neighbors had invited several people to their home, including the two of us. But as the time came to walk across the street, my introverted tendencies arose with a vengeance. I dreaded small talk and worried that I wouldn't know anyone. I wanted nothing more than to stay in my house and curl up with a book.

"I'm sorry," I said, sighing. My husband shrugged good-naturedly as he headed out the door.

That was the pattern for the first few years of our marriage: my husband had to coax me into any gathering at our home, and I was resistant to invitations to other people's homes. But I'm grateful that over time, his gentle nudges helped me become more and more comfortable with stepping out of my comfort zone.

Now, it's not uncommon for us to host friends or family at least once a week, and I genuinely love it. It's not because I suddenly turned into an extrovert. It's because my husband's gracious encouragement gave me the courage to try. Minor successes became larger ones.

The truth is that we learn just as much—or more—from the things that don't come to us naturally, the hardships we face, or the mistakes we make. But, as Christians, we are called to take advantage of *every* opportunity, not just the ones we like! When difficulties arise, gratefully choosing to see them as a chance to grow rather than something to avoid can make all the difference. And, over time, repetition helps us become more at ease with the things that once intimidated us.

Kristin

Today's Act of Gratitude

Consider a time when stepping out of your comfort zone led to something good. How can you build on that experience and step out of your comfort zone again?

'Tis the Season

She will give birth to a son, and you are to give him the name
Jesus, because he will save his people from their sins.
MATTHEW 1:21, NIV

"'Tis the season." That is my go-to response this time of year for all manner of things. Most often it is spoken wistfully and with a tinge of irony as I watch some of my holiday expectations implode or see a few of my best-laid plans go suddenly astray, despite all the laughter, fun, and joy we pack into the few short weeks between now and Christmas morning.

Don't get me wrong; I love Christmas. But . . .

'Tis the season for becoming overwhelmed with unattainable expectations—my own and others'.

'Tis the season for the strain of strep that took its sweet time (three consecutive weeks) to roll through my household one year, picking us off one by one.

'Tis the season for mentally counting down the days while I buy gifts, send cards, bake cookies, and attend to a myriad of traditions, hoping to get it all done in time.

And 'tis the season for becoming so consumed with the hustle and bustle that I forget to take in the wonderment of God coming to earth in the most perfectly beautiful way possible.

As much as I enjoy Christmas, I've come to appreciate the season of Advent deeply. It is an invitation to pause amid the hurry and scurry, an opportunity to breathe deeply in quiet anticipation as we await the hope that Christ Jesus fulfilled through his birth, life, and sacrificial death on the cross as an atonement for our sins, bringing us back into right standing with our heavenly Father. It's a time of reflection and repentance free from all the trappings of an overly commercialized season.

Spending a bit of time each day in Advent wonderment keeps me grounded and ensures that my heart remains soft as I check off all the necessary tasks during this busy time of the year. It helps me stay flexible as plans inevitably go awry, allowing me to keep perspective, maintain an attitude of gratitude, and hold onto my joy.

Julie

Today's Act of Gratitude

Pray that God would speak to your heart in a deeply personal way as
you wait with joyful anticipation on the cusp of this Advent season.

A Starry Night

The LORD merely spoke, and the heavens were created.
He breathed the word, and all the stars were born.

PSALM 33:6

"Okay, girls, I think I got it," I said, making a final adjustment to the lens. My daughter Elise stepped forward as I leaned away from the telescope.

"Let me see!" Ashlyn, the littlest one, piped up from the back.

"In a minute," I said cheerfully.

Our local library had recently added telescopes to their catalog of items to borrow, and after waiting for a few weeks, it was our turn. We'd picked up the telescope—housed in a padded, medium-sized garbage bin and accompanied by careful instructions—and carted it home, then waited for a clear winter's night.

Shivering, I watched as my children stepped up to see the sights. I admired the stars, pulling my coat more tightly around me. A few wispy clouds floated high above, but for the most part, our view was unimpeded. The moon was full and bright, but under the power of the lens, it was luminous.

Though astronomers aren't sure how many stars exist, they estimate that there are about 100 billion in a single galaxy (our own Milky Way). When we multiply that by the estimated 10 trillion galaxies in the universe, the result is one septillion stars: 1,000,000,000,000,000,000,000,000.*

What an incredible number! The light of the stars isn't just something to admire on a dark night but a reflection of God's vast and infinite power. He merely breathed a word, and a septillion stars were created. To count to a billion—at a rate of one number per second—would take us more than thirty-one years. Yet God not only counts them but also calls them by name (see Psalm 147:4).

Though he created a vast universe, our God cares about the details. He's named the stars, and he knows our names too. When we look at the night sky, we are reminded that God is powerful enough to bring it into existence but loves us enough to know our names. He doesn't miss a star, a person, or a detail. We can be thankful that his loving attention never wanes.

Kristin

Today's Act of Gratitude

On the next clear night, spend a few minutes stargazing.
Thank God for the reminder that he knows you by
name in the midst of the vast universe.

---

*Ailsa Harvey and Elizabeth Howell, "How Many Stars Are in the Universe?" Space.com, February 11, 2022, https://www.space.com/26078-how-many-stars-are-there.html.

There's Strength in Numbers

*As iron sharpens iron,
so a friend sharpens a friend.*

PROVERBS 27:17

"I'm wondering if I could join your group?" I started to type a message to a woman I knew only nominally. "I saw you post that you were starting one to help women with their gut health, and I'd really like to be part of it, if you don't mind." I hit send, wondering if she'd think it odd that a random person was messaging her.

A short while later, I got a reply. "Of course! I'd love to have you join us. Give me your email, and I'll send you all the information."

I whispered a prayer of thanks to God as I messaged her back. I'd been dealing with some health issues mostly on my own, and I was feeling a little overwhelmed. I knew I needed to adjust my nutrition to work with food sensitivities I have, but I just didn't know where to start.

Over the course of the next several weeks, in a group with about twenty other women, I was able to receive (and offer) encouragement and to share ideas for recipes and food options. Slowly I began to feel hopeful that I could manage the health issues I was having. Being part of a group gave me the boost in confidence that I needed and didn't have on my own.

Scripture is right, in the same way that "iron sharpens iron," so friends sharpen one another— often pushing us beyond what we're capable of doing on our own. When one friend is down, the other is there to encourage and uplift, offering perspective the other doesn't have during the hard times. God knew we'd need friends and community, and he gave us the people in our lives as a gift, a blessing here to walk with us through good and difficult days. There really is strength in numbers.

Kendra

Today's Act of Gratitude

Thank God for all the people he's placed in your life who have offered you encouragement and pushed you in areas you've needed support. Then send them a message, letting them know how much you appreciate them.

December

An Atmosphere of Love

A bowl of vegetables with someone you love is better than steak with someone you hate.

PROVERBS 15:17

Knocking on the screen door, I open it. One dog noses at me while the other lies quiescent in the corner. From the round table in the kitchen, faces turn my way.

"Hi, Krissi!" my aunt calls out, warmth in her tone. Though I've been "Kristin" to everyone else since college, my family gets a free pass, and I smile in response.

Shooing my kids inside, I take off my shoes and head to the kitchen to pour myself a cup of coffee. I lean over to hug my aunt, scooting a chair closer to the table to settle in for a visit.

For as long as I can remember, my aunt's home has been a place of comfort. The first ten years of my life were spent in this part of the state, and I have a long-standing love for the woods and pine trees that line the road.

I can't visit without recalling my uncle Jimmy's storytelling or how he'd command his enormous Belgian horses as we careened down backcountry roads on sleigh rides. Being there reminds me of horseback riding alongside gravel roads, fireworks on the Fourth of July, and the unmistakable smell of a stall that needs mucking out. It reminds me of hopping from one hay bale to the next, watching my mom and aunt quilt, or chatting with cousins and friends who visited.

I've lived in many places, but this home is among my favorites. It's not because of the setting or the memories; it's because the atmosphere is one of love. I've never worried if I fit in or wondered if my family was tired of me. I've never felt less than accepted. Love blankets my aunt's home, and it enfolds all who enter.

The Bible has a funny verse about how eating vegetables with a loved one is better than eating steak with someone you don't like. Other translations have words like "herbs" rather than vegetables and "fattened ox" rather than steak. The idea remains: even the humblest of foods taste amazing when shared with people we care about. It's not because of what's on the menu but how we make others feel. Like my aunt's family, we, too, can cultivate an atmosphere of love. When we actively choose to demonstrate love to those around us, they'll notice.

Kristin

Today's Act of Gratitude

Think of a place you've visited that radiated an atmosphere of love. Thank God for it.

Not Yet Is Not No

"My thoughts are nothing like your thoughts," says the LORD. *"And my ways are far beyond anything you could imagine. For just as the heavens are higher than the earth, so my ways are higher than your ways and my thoughts higher than your thoughts."*

ISAIAH 55:8-9

God's timing is not my timing. I am exceptionally careful to whom and when I speak those words because they can feel dismissive in the midst of a hard moment, but I whisper them over myself constantly.

I'm a doer. Once I have a plan or an idea, I want to see it implemented, pronto. That, unfortunately, isn't always how God works.

Why is there so often a delay between his putting something on our hearts and its implementation? I don't know. I've asked that question more times than I can count, standing alongside family and friends in prayer over delays and "not yets."

"Our offer fell through, again. This is the fifth house we've made an offer on and didn't get. I know God is calling us to move. I don't understand."

"I didn't get the job. Despite making it to the final rounds of interviews four times, I'm still at a company I know I'm supposed to leave."

There are no answers this side of heaven to our delays, but today's verse comforts me in those waiting seasons. It isn't that God doesn't hear us or is ignoring us; he does hear! And what feels like an unnecessary delay has a purpose. It might be that God is putting pieces into place that we cannot yet see. It might be that we need to gain a bit more of the experience and maturity necessary for handling the next step.

I know that waiting for God's timing is always better than rushing ahead of him, trying to do it on my own. God works all things on his schedule and for his glory (see Romans 8:28), and we can entrust him with our "not yet." And as I wait, I intentionally thank God for his better timing, his plan, and a partnership that will reveal his fingerprints in how everything worked out when I look back on it someday.

Julie

Today's Act of Gratitude

Memorize Isaiah 55:8-9 for when you find yourself in a "not yet" season, thanking God that he both knows more than you and has a plan.

A Mutual Understanding

O LORD, you have examined my heart and know everything about me. You know when I sit down or stand up. You know my thoughts even when I'm far away.

PSALM 139:1-2

My husband called me, excitement in his voice. He'd just dropped off Christmas gifts for foster kids at a program in the town next to ours and had a lengthy conversation with the people who run it.

"They're foster parents themselves," he explained. "They've been fostering for years and have adopted several kids."

They had shared with him about their experiences over the years, and he, in turn, got to tell them some of our stories of fostering children. "It's just nice to talk to someone else who's done it," he said as he finished.

I agreed. Over the years, we'd met a few people who have fostered or adopted kids, but not many. Our close friends and family have always supported us, but it's gratifying when we can talk with someone doing the same thing that we are, experiencing much of the joy and challenges that go along with fostering and adopting. My husband left encouraged and grateful to be able to talk with someone who had a mutual understanding of the rewards and heartaches involved.

There's just something about connecting with another person who has been on a similar journey. There's a comfort in being understood in a way that may be challenging for someone who's never walked in your shoes. No matter what we've faced, knowing that others have experienced the same thing, whether good or hard, is reassuring.

But even if we look around and can't find anyone who gets what we're going through, we can always trust that God does. The Bible tells us that he knows everything about us. He knows when we sit or stand. He knows our thoughts, even the ones we don't ever speak out loud. He knows us more intimately than anyone else could and loves us just as we are. I'm so grateful that Jesus understands every thought we have and every circumstance we face and promises to be with us through it all.

Kendra

Today's Act of Gratitude

Encourage someone walking through
an experience similar to your own.

Chain Reaction

Watch what God does, and then you do it, like children who learn proper behavior from their parents. Mostly what God does is love you. Keep company with him and learn a life of love. Observe how Christ loved us. His love was not cautious but extravagant. He didn't love in order to get something from us but to give everything of himself to us. Love like that.

EPHESIANS 5:1-2, MSG

Before he was born, an ultrasound revealed that Jenny and Brian's son John had a heart issue. Though it was labeled as mild, he was later diagnosed with Shone's syndrome. When a surgery at twelve months of age to replace a valve and correct another issue didn't go as planned, it put him in the 2 to 5 percent of children with complications.

During John's lengthy hospital stays, Jenny and Brian quickly realized that even though their son was the patient, they felt equally supported. They appreciated the skilled nurses and their ability to help the family stay positive. To lift their spirits, one nurse even dressed John in Green Bay Packers clothing, knowing full well that Jenny and Brian were avid fans of their rival, the Minnesota Vikings. The thought still makes the couple chuckle.

To give back to the staff that had treated them with such kindness, Jenny and Brian started an annual golf tournament in their son's name, with all the proceeds going to the hospital. Over the twelve years of hosting the tournament, they raised more than $160,000.

"We will never forget the gratitude we had for the nursing staff that lovingly cared for John but also showed care for us," Jenny later said. "Our gratefulness was extended for the good of many. It still warms our hearts more than twenty years later."

Generosity often starts a chain reaction. When we extend a helping hand to someone, they're more likely to do the same for someone else. The nurses' kindnesses made Jenny and Brian want to reciprocate. Their actions spilled over, benefiting the hospital and other families. Years later, John's name is still on a plaque next to a sleep room in the hospital that's available for other families to use, and the impact of Jenny and Brian's generosity lives on.

Kristin

Today's Act of Gratitude

Think of an act of generosity or kindness someone has done for you. How can you do the same to help someone else who is going through a difficult time?

The Gift of Redemption

I have swept away your offenses like a cloud, your sins like the morning mist. Return to me, for I have redeemed you.

ISAIAH 44:22, NIV

Dear Jesus, I messed up, and I'm sorry. I don't know what to do next. How do I fix this? How do I make things right? Can I have a second chance?

Even as I prayed about the mistake I'd made, apologizing to Jesus, I knew I also owed several apologies to women I'd unintentionally hurt. And I was scared. There were so many things they might say to me when I called them, and my inner dialogue was filled with the what-ifs:

What if she refuses my apology?

What if she hangs up on me?

What if she calls me names and tells the whole world that I'm an awful person?

While all those responses were certainly possible, none of them ultimately came to pass when I worked up the courage to call with a sincere apology. No excuses, no justification—simply a request for forgiveness and a chance to do better.

Each call was met with tears as women, in turn, apologized for their own role in the drama, asking forgiveness for involving others instead of connecting with me directly. As we hung up the phone, I was so grateful that we'd each received a second chance to make better choices the next time there was conflict within our community of fellow parents.

Apologizing can feel incredibly hard. It is a humbling lesson in vulnerability, especially if the other party also played a role in the situation and we are making the first move. And, in a culture that deflects blame or, at best, supports weird half-apologies without an admission of wrong, a sincere apology puts us—even momentarily—in a position of weakness rather than strength.

Do not be intimidated by fears of weakness or vulnerability: true repentance without excuse for our actions or words (regardless of what others did or said) restores us to a right relationship with Jesus. It often has the same result with those around us.

I am thankful that forgiveness followed by redemption—even if it only ever comes from Jesus—rescues us from shame, clears away our sins, and allows us to try again, to do better, and to be restored in our relationships. It is a gift worth the risk of a sincere apology.

Julie

Today's Act of Gratitude

Who deserves an apology from you?
Call (don't text) and put things right.

Small Inconveniences

*You keep him in perfect peace whose mind is
stayed on you, because he trusts in you.*

ISAIAH 26:3, ESV

"I can't find my wallet."

My husband was rummaging through the corner of the kitchen, frustration evident in his tone. He had been on his way out the door to retrieve our oldest daughter from youth group, and the pickup time was looming.

Sighing a little, I started looking around the house. It wasn't in the car, the mudroom, the kitchen, a coat pocket, or his jeans from yesterday. So where could it possibly be?

Suddenly, a thought occurred to him. Earlier in the day, while he was driving the girls to school, they had heard a sudden noise. At the time, he realized he'd forgotten to grab his coffee mug from the roof of the car, and it had fallen off. Now, he started to wonder if he'd lost his wallet the same way.

The problem was that this drive had been twelve hours earlier, and several inches of snow had fallen in the meantime. Snowplows had rumbled down the streets, and it was now nighttime. The likelihood of finding his wallet in the enormous snowbanks seemed slim. But he got into his car and started down the road to search for it. Merely two houses down, the brown dot of his leather wallet stood out in the middle of the big white snowbank.

What had felt like an inconvenience earlier in the day—forgotten coffee that had fallen off the roof with a crash—turned out to be a blessing in disguise. If he had placed only his wallet on the rooftop, the thought that he'd lost it outdoors wouldn't have occurred to him. Together, we marveled that he had been able to spot it so quickly.

It can be easy to get flustered by life. There are days when even minor inconveniences—a leaky faucet, a schedule change, a cranky coworker—seem like major problems. When things don't go our way, it's tempting to focus on and magnify the problem. Yet our mindset matters. Peace is possible when we know God and trust him to care for us. When we look for the good in the challenges we face, we can see how they play out in the larger story of our lives—even when we accidentally dump a wallet in the snowbank.

Kristin

Today's Act of Gratitude

Thank God for a time in your life when a minor inconvenience
diminished the impact of a more significant challenge.

New Traditions

A time to cry and a time to laugh.
A time to grieve and a time to dance.

ECCLESIASTES 3:4

"Why don't you guys just stay over?" my sister said as we were making our Christmas plans. "You know the kids would love a sleepover anyway."

I nodded. "Let me talk to Kyle, but that sounds fun." As I told him about our idea, he readily agreed.

A few days later, we packed our vehicle with food, games, and presents, along with our overnight bags, and made our way to my sister's house. We spent several hours preparing dinner, watching movies, and playing games. As the evening wound down and all the other family members left, Kyle and I, along with my sister and her husband, put our swimsuits on and quickly headed outside to their hot tub while the kids watched a movie. We spent the next hour alternating between jokes and laughter and dreams and goals for the coming year.

As we settled into the guest room a little while later, I whispered to Kyle, "I think we've started a new tradition." He agreed as we both drifted off to sleep.

The next day I thought about not only how much fun we'd had this year but also the hard Christmas we had walked through years earlier when our oldest sister passed away from cancer. The grief seemed, at times, to overwhelm us. I was encouraged that we could once again come together, laugh, and make new memories, even while remembering and missing our sister.

New traditions can offer us hope when we are hurting, reminding us that although we may cry and grieve for a season, there will also come a time for us to laugh and even dance again. I'm grateful that God gives us space to do both, sometimes simultaneously. No matter where you find yourself today, his promise is one of hope and joy. Don't be afraid to incorporate a new tradition into your holiday; God may just use it to bring a new season to you and your family that you haven't experienced before.

Kendra

Today's Act of Gratitude

What new tradition can you incorporate
this Christmas season, especially one that could
bring renewed hope and joy to your family?

The Power of Showing Up

Owe nothing to anyone—except for your obligation to love one another.
If you love your neighbor, you will fulfill the requirements of God's law.

ROMANS 13:8

Sitting in the semidarkness of our middle school's theater, I chatted with fellow parents I've known since our children's kindergarten years. We were waiting for the lights to dim and the play performance to begin— a murder mystery with Jon playing the twirly-mustached killer while Lizzie helped with lights and sound on the tech crew.

I couldn't help a small smile as I noticed out of the corner of my eye that a beloved, familiar woman had slipped quietly into a nearby seat. Karen Kruse, elementary music teacher, piano instructor, and second mom to thousands, had made room in her busy schedule to watch her Madison Elementary kids perform.

Karen is a world changer cleverly disguised as an ordinary woman. Because of her role as a teacher, she knows the needs her students and their families face and is constantly looking for ways to fill those gaps. She undercharges for lessons because she knows the transformative power of sitting on a piano bench alongside a loving adult week after week in relational instruction. She advocates without shaming, meeting needs with a loving hug instead of condemnation or humiliation, even before someone has their act together. Of everyone I know, it's Karen who beautifully "shows up" consistently, unfailingly.

Much of what I'm learning about being a woman who loves God and others has been gained while walking alongside Karen, and I am forever grateful. She's provided an informal apprenticeship in the day-to-day, showing up as a form of love in action. She's modeled how to love well, despite the inherent messiness of the human condition.

Showing up is different from merely dropping money into the basket passed during a Sunday service, although sharing our resources is certainly a critical part of loving God and others well. Showing up requires us to draw near with relational, tangible support while maintaining the other person's respect and dignity, which can be a tricky balance. Finding someone to walk alongside as we learn to show up with compassionate humility is a beautiful gift and never one to underestimate or take lightly.

Julie

Today's Act of Gratitude

Who "shows up" well in your circles? Let them know that you
appreciate their example, even as you build that skill set yourself.

Ripple Effects

Jesus also used this illustration: "The Kingdom of Heaven is like the yeast a woman used in making bread. Even though she put only a little yeast in three measures of flour, it permeated every part of the dough."

MATTHEW 13:33

I adore chunky handmade mugs in beautiful colors, the scent of lavender and mint emanating from my diffuser, hand embroidered dish towels, and elegant little mid-century coupe glasses. I also love the smell of the air just before it rains, jazz music from Sarah Vaughan and Billie Holiday, and the glittery sparkle of freshly fallen snow. And I can't forget to add to my list the pearlized look of milk glass, a barefoot walk on a beach, and a cozy indoor fire on a stormy night.

Each one of those favorite things is simple but brings me joy. Choosing to see value in even the smallest beauties helps us see the world around us with fresh eyes. It fosters contentment and ultimately leads to being grateful for our senses, the loveliness of creation, and the delights of human ingenuity. Over time, my ability to notice and appreciate the little things spills over and makes me even more appreciative of greater things.

Matthew 13 includes seven parables of Jesus in which he compared everyday things—a farmer scattering seed, a fishing net, a mustard seed—to the Kingdom of Heaven. In one of his parables, Jesus talks about how even a little yeast will permeate the whole batch of dough in the bread-making process.

When you and I live in a way that demonstrates the love of Jesus, it spills over into those around us, changing our neighborhoods and communities. In the same way, when we choose to be grateful for the small things, that attitude of gratitude bubbles over and impacts others. Our decision to be thankful—no matter how simple the reason—changes us, first, then it ripples outward, changing the world around us too.

Kristin

Today's Act of Gratitude

Make a list of your favorite things, being sure to thank God for even the little things that you appreciate.

Intuition

I will ask the Father, and he will give you another Advocate, who will never leave you. He is the Holy Spirit, who leads into all truth.

JOHN 14:16-17

It was a cold, wintry night, and I was returning home to my sister's house after dark. It had started snowing, adding more accumulation to the already covered streets. I pulled up and parked across from my sister's house, and as I exited my vehicle, an older gentleman pulled up and stopped, putting himself and his van between me and the house.

He leaned out his window and asked if I'd seen any kittens running in the street as he was looking for his. An odd request, I thought, since we were in a snowstorm, in the middle of winter. As he spoke, I heard a distinct voice in my head tell me not to move closer to talk to him but to back away from his vehicle and leave.

So instead of engaging him, I turned and hurried around his van, up and over the snowbanks, and into the safety of the house. As I slammed the door and locked it behind me, my dad, who had been babysitting my niece and nephew, asked what was wrong.

I told him about my interaction with the older gentleman.

"That doesn't seem right," he said. "I think you should call the police."

At his urging, I did just that.

A kind woman took my call, but as I fumbled to explain what had happened, the fear began to dissipate. I suddenly felt sheepish, second-guessing myself and wondering if maybe I was overreacting.

I started to apologize, but the police officer stopped me. "Kendra, do not apologize. Nine times out of ten, people's intuition is correct. I'm taking this seriously."

Her words were a comfort, and to this day, I think about her comment.

What that police officer called intuition, as a Christian, I would call the Holy Spirit. We can sometimes forget that the Spirit of God is with us, but Scripture is clear; he is our Advocate, and he doesn't leave us. I am grateful that if we stay attuned to him, he will lead us.

Kendra

Today's Act of Gratitude

Have you had an experience where the Holy Spirit gave insight into a situation? Thank God for his Spirit that is with us wherever we go.

Your Will Be Done

*We know that God causes everything to work together for the good of
those who love God and are called according to his purpose for them.*

ROMANS 8:28

*"My alarm didn't go off this morning! I am so, so sorry—can we reschedule our coffee
date?"*

My phone buzzed with her text just as I was reaching for my car keys. Living
three hours apart, we'd planned this get-together months ago, intending to meet
at a coffee shop roughly equidistant to our respective homes. My friend typically
doesn't run late, and she's usually up long before her morning alarm has a chance
to sound, so this was both unexpected and highly unusual.

Instead of feeling frustration or anger at the change in plans, I assured her that
we could reschedule, including her in a text prayer thanking God for his divine
ordering of my day (and hers).

As we later sat down together at our rescheduled meeting, we talked about how
we each pray for God's will over our days and in our lives. When we ask for his will
to be done, we shouldn't be upset when he upends our agenda. He may have been
diverting us from an accident. He may have been aligning a divine appointment
with someone whose path would cross ours. Or not—maybe our sudden change of
plans was simply a result of living life on an imperfect earth. We don't know—and
won't know until we are face-to-face with Jesus—all the times we've encountered
divine interference as we've gone about our daily routines.

Because of this, I've embraced viewing changed plans through a lens of
gratitude—even when the really fun stuff goes awry—thanking God for answering my prayer to order my steps, my day, and my interactions. After all, he sees
the big picture with perfect clarity when we only see glimpses of the larger plan.
His ways are always better than our own, even when it doesn't feel like that at
the moment.

Julie

Today's Act of Gratitude

When plans change, take a deep breath and thank God—out loud
when possible—for his faithfulness in ordering your steps, asking
him to reveal his plan for the day so that you might obediently
accomplish his will through the changed circumstances.

Doing What You Don't Love

*Work willingly at whatever you do, as though you
were working for the Lord rather than for people.*

COLOSSIANS 3:23

Her grades weren't good. When we confronted her about them, she exclaimed, "School's so hard! I don't like it."

"We understand," my husband, Kyle, responded calmly. "We know it's not your favorite thing to do, and it's challenging, but the truth is, you haven't really been trying very hard. That's why your grades are poor. And that's a big difference from not doing well when you've tried your best."

She stared at us, not saying anything. She knew that it was true. My daughter has many talents, and she is incredibly driven and creative. She works hard at activities she enjoys. But my husband and I want her to learn that sometimes we push through to accomplish goals in some aspect of our life, not because we enjoy it, but because it's necessary.

"Let's look at what needs to be done and make a plan," Kyle said as she pulled out her computer and we sat down to figure out how to finish her schoolwork.

We may face challenges even in activities we enjoy, but true character grows when we do the hard thing that we don't want to do but know that we need to do. With something that we're not passionate about, interested in, or engaged in, it takes a different kind of determination to stick it out when all we want to do is quit.

One way we can keep motivated is to remind ourselves that whatever work we do, we're doing it for the Lord and not for the approval of others. God knows, sees, and rewards the endeavors we put our hands to, even when they're challenging to us, even when others don't notice, and even when they're not exciting. He is pleased when we gratefully honor him with our hard work, even when it's something we do not love to do.

Kendra

Today's Act of Gratitude

What is something you have to do that you just don't love?
How would your attitude toward that task change if you
saw yourself as completing it to please the Lord?

The Hands and Feet of Jesus

My dear brothers and sisters, be strong and immovable.
Always work enthusiastically for the Lord, for you know
that nothing you do for the Lord is ever useless.

1 CORINTHIANS 15:58

Shrugging off my winter coat, I make my way to the table my mom is standing behind, lining up scissors, tags, and tape. Behind her, boxes filled with upright rolls of wrapping paper are sandwiched next to one another.

We chat idly, exchanging greetings with others stationed behind their own tables, until a slight commotion at the door signals that it's time to begin. Kids tumble into the room and are ushered over to tables.

"Hi, ladies!" one adult says brightly as she accompanies a child to our table and hands me a garbage bag filled with items. "This is Tyler."

"Hi, Tyler," I say. "Let's see what you picked out. Ooh, what a pretty bath set. Who's this one for?"

"My mom," he whispers, brown eyes raising shyly before dropping to study the floor again.

"She's going to love it," I say. We consult about the kind of paper she'd like, and as he starts carefully writing out a tag with her name on it, my mom and I get to work on wrapping it along with all of the other items in his bag.

After Tyler leaves, other children take his place in an endless round until our shift ends a couple of hours later.

I love volunteering each year for Kids Hope Shop, an event put on by our local homeless shelter that lets at-risk kids "shop" for their families for free. I love seeing the kids and their smiles, the contagious excitement of choosing items for their loved ones, and the spirit of the Christmas season that permeates the event.

By the night's end, my back aches and my feet are sore, but I always leave feeling energized and thankful. It's easy to get caught up in our day-to-day concerns, but when we step beyond our door and reach out to help others, we realize our true potential. You and I have the great privilege of being the hands and feet of Jesus in this world, and every time we do things for others, it glorifies him. No act of kindness is ever wasted when it demonstrates love to another person made in God's image.

Kristin

Today's Act of Gratitude

Schedule time to volunteer in your local
community within the next few weeks.

Loved As You Are

God showed his great love for us by sending
Christ to die for us while we were still sinners.

ROMANS 5:8

On the morning of Picture Day, I found myself standing over my preschooler, who was sprawled across the carpet in utter despair. You see, I had laid out his blue-checked button-down shirt and khaki pants only to be told on a sob that he'd already picked his outfit.

"What clothes would make you feel the most handsome today, Jon?" I asked gently, rubbing his back. His whispered response between hiccupping breaths made me cringe: "My pocketless pants and my sleeveless shirt." In other words, my son wanted to wear his ratty muscle shirt and a pair of athletic pants with a red racing stripe and a weird shimmer.

Biting back my dismay, I agreed. And with that, he scampered up the stairs and out of sight. He returned in record time dressed like a 1980s miscreant minus only the mullet, his face alight with a megawatt grin.

His school photos from that year are a bizarre juxtaposition of a dapper pose and an outfit better suited to that quintessential '80s movie, *The Breakfast Club*. But looking past the clothes and pose, you see a young man who is absolutely, unequivocally delighted. That picture has become one of my favorites because it captures perfectly the essence of Jon at age almost five.

Just as I love that picture for its authenticity, our heavenly Father loves us—the real us, the core of us, without any pretense, ruse, or mask. We are the recipients of unmerited, unconditional love. He meets us where we are, having sent his beloved Son to die for our sins, creating a way back into an intimate relationship through repentance and forgiveness.

Embracing the truth of today's verse can feel surreal. But it's as simple as a prayerful, heartfelt thank you to God that we are not the mistakes we make, and we are not the worst moment of our life. We are beloved and have intrinsic value no matter what the world would say about us or how it would calculate our value against worldly standards.

Julie

Today's Act of Gratitude

Meditate on the truth of Romans 5:8.
How does that truth change the way you see yourself?
How does it change the way you see others?

A Chilly Evening

Two people are better off than one, for they can help each other succeed. If one person falls, the other can reach out and help. But someone who falls alone is in real trouble.

ECCLESIASTES 4:9-10

It was a colder than usual winter night. We'd invited several couples over to play cards and share dinner. As the evening wore on, I noticed I was feeling a little cool. I pulled my sweater around me.

"I think something's wrong with the furnace," Kyle whispered. "It hasn't kicked on in a while, and the temperature is dropping." I looked at him and immediately felt stressed. Not only was it cold, but we were in the middle of entertaining.

Kyle got up, mentioning to the group that he was going to check the furnace as it didn't seem to be working. Our brother-in-law Rob followed him to try to help. They stayed downstairs working for the next hour or so while the rest of us continued playing cards upstairs. The temperature in our house continued to drop, but no one complained.

When Kyle and Rob finally returned from the basement, unsuccessful in fixing the problem, our friends quickly stepped in with offers to help. Each of them offered portable heaters to keep our house warm enough until the repairman could come the following day. As everyone gathered their things to leave, they again thanked us for a lovely evening. I was humbled by how flexible everyone had been in not letting the cooler temperatures ruin the night.

The next day, after the repairman had come and gone and the heat was again flowing freely from our vents, Rob made the rounds to return the assortment of heaters, for which we had been very grateful. I texted our friends, thanking them again for the enjoyable night and the heaters that got us through.

Friendships are so important. Whether they show up in big or small ways, our friends help to carry us through all the trials that life may bring our way. Scripture reminds us just how essential being in relationship with others is. It's friends who can help us succeed, and if one of us falls, the other is there to pick us up. What a gift that is.

Kendra

Today's Act of Gratitude

Thank a friend who recently supported you when you needed help.

Invited In

Welcome one another as Christ has welcomed you,
for the glory of God.

ROMANS 15:7, ESV

"Good morning!" my neighbor Polly called out as she carefully picked her way down her driveway, then stopped to wait for me.

"Good morning!" I echoed, making my way toward her. Together, we finished the walk to Debbie's home, where she opened the door and invited us in for our annual brunch.

Inside, neighbors greeted one another warmly as they chatted in the kitchen and living room.

Nearly every year since we've lived in our current home, Debbie has organized a Secret Santa gift exchange for the women in our immediate neighborhood. We spend Monday through Friday of that week surreptitiously dropping small gifts on porches and steps, sneaking over in the early morning, noon, or night—whenever we think we're least likely to get caught. Sometimes we even enlist the neighborhood kids to act as our messengers. Then, on Saturday, each of us brings a wrapped gift and a dish to share for brunch.

Although I often see my neighbors outside shoveling snow, walking their dogs, or picking up their mail, it's rare to have an in-depth visit in the winter. The Secret Santa brunch is the perfect time for us to catch up on what the last year has brought to each of us and to express gratitude for our quiet community.

Debbie's first invitation was a thoughtful, welcoming introduction to the neighborhood. Being invited in—whether into a community, church, group, or workplace—is always something to celebrate, but it's also something we can initiate. During his earthly ministry, Jesus lived alongside his disciples and constantly sought the company of others. No one was excluded from his loving, kind attention.

Sometimes we are tempted to wait for someone to invite us first because we fear rejection. The truth is that when we welcome others into our lives and homes, we demonstrate how we have been invited into fellowship with God. All are welcome; no one is left out. He invited us to be in community with him, and we are asked to extend that same invitation to others. When we find the courage to extend an invitation, we'll often discover deep, loving community on the other side.

Kristin

Today's Act of Gratitude

Invite a neighbor over for coffee or dinner.

Bittersweet

Since we are surrounded by such a huge crowd of witnesses
to the life of faith, let us strip off every weight that slows us
down, especially the sin that so easily trips us up. And let us
run with endurance the race God has set before us.

HEBREWS 12:1

As I peered into the mailbox, my eyes sought the object wedged just a little too tightly to slide out without a serious tug—a children's book.

As I wriggled it free, I tried to hold my tears at bay. It was the last book my youngest child would receive from the United Way's Imagination Library program as his fifth birthday—and all the affiliated milestones we were about to pass—loomed.

Losing the fight, I felt the tears stream as I walked up the driveway, quietly mourning the morphing of my chubby toddler into a lanky little boy, while simultaneously celebrating this new phase, grateful God chose me to be a part of his growing up journey.

Friends, our short time on this planet involves a race of faithful, spiritual endurance. Races require forward movement, even if it's only at turtle speed, and forward movement inevitably means there will be lasts as we prepare to experience new firsts. Leaving lasts and facing firsts is often bittersweet. Or, let's be honest, sometimes there is no sweet to balance the bitter when we didn't ask for and didn't want the impending change.

As we approach a new milestone—wanted or unwanted—in our children's lives, in the trajectory of our careers, in our marriages and friendships, ultimately, the direction of our gaze will set the direction of our feet. If we get too focused on looking backward, mourning our lasts, we can't properly move toward the future and the things God has waiting for us.

Today's verse reminds us that we don't run this race alone. I am so grateful for this assurance, this promise. Sisters and brothers of the faith (those listed in Hebrews and those in our present faith communities) stand along with us, cheering us forward. And our beloved Savior is with us every step of the way.

Julie

Today's Act of Gratitude

What is Jesus asking you to release so you can move
forward? Ask someone to pray for and with you as
you let go and cast your gaze ahead.

Mentoring One Another

Do not let any unwholesome talk come out of your mouths,
but only what is helpful for building others up according
to their needs, that it may benefit those who listen.

EPHESIANS 4:29, NIV

When I started shopping at a local boutique, I met a group of women ten to fifteen years younger than me. They were a diverse group, some married, others single. Some had kids, others didn't. But they all had a desire to build community, to encourage and lift one another up.

As I engaged with them, I realized how easy it was to fit into their group because of their welcoming nature. I attended events where the women shared their stories, I followed them online, and I joined groups they started.

I listened to their stories—both the hard parts and the good—and encouraged them to keep sharing and keep honestly being all that God created them to be.

It's an interesting place for me, now in my forties, having been on the side of being mentored and now also desiring to mentor women coming up behind me. I am grateful for all those who've encouraged me—who told me I was capable, worthy, or deserving—and I want so much to offer that same genuine support to younger women.

Today's Scripture offers guidance for anyone genuinely interested in mentoring others. I've read that it takes anywhere from three to five positive comments or experiences to counteract just one negative. That should make us all pause before we speak. Our verse tells us that we should avoid any "unwholesome talk" and instead offer only what is helpful for building another person up.

Does this mean we shouldn't be honest? Of course not. But even our honesty should come from a place of love and concern for the person, still using our words to build up and benefit one another, even when we have to have hard conversations. There is enough negativity in the world; let's be intentional about encouraging others.

Kendra

Today's Act of Gratitude

Use your words to build someone else up.

The Beauty of a Life Lived

Don't you realize that your body is the temple of the Holy Spirit, who lives in you and was given to you by God? You do not belong to yourself, for God bought you with a high price. So you must honor God with your body.

1 CORINTHIANS 6:19-20

"Mom, can I have some of the ornaments you made when you were first married?" I asked.

I winced a bit on my end of the phone call, certain she was going to razz me (and deservedly so) for having so often scoffed at her "ugly" hodgepodge Christmas tree in my teens and early twenties.

She chuckled a bit too gleefully before graciously telling me I could have any ornaments I wanted, as long as they didn't belong to my brothers. And so, after a few years of color-coordinated trees, I traded my trendy decorations for my mom's tradition. I was grateful to swipe a couple of memory-laden items for my own hodgepodge tree.

As I was bent over my bathroom vanity, ruefully considering a gray hair I hadn't noticed before, the Holy Spirit brought my love for those mismatched ornaments to mind as an alternative perspective on growing older. Just as my carefully trimmed tree has been replaced by one that will never win a design award but brings delight with its myriad of memories, my body is no longer that of an eighteen-year-old girl.

And while I want to look lovely, I'm learning to define loveliness as fully embracing this body that has seen me through my life thus far. That thick, double cesarean scar? It memorializes the sacred moments Aaron and I first met our babies in a sterile operating room. And the fine lines gathering in the corners of my eyes are testament to ten thousand smiles during ten thousand happy moments. Those scars or imperfections reminding me of darker moments in my story? They mark my survival, my overcoming of something difficult.

I know it's hard to go against a lifetime of the world telling us that to grow older is to grow less lovely, but consider today's verse. We are the temple of the Holy Spirit, belonging to God, bought at the highest of costs: the willing, sacrificial death of his beloved Son and our Savior, Jesus Christ. Let's honor God by seeing ourselves through his eyes, finding beauty in the wrinkles and scars as tangible reminders of cherished moments or perseverance through difficult seasons.

Julie

Today's Act of Gratitude

Stand before a mirror, thanking God for something about your reflection that you've previously criticized. Make it a habit to do this each time you look in a mirror.

Anticipation

*Hope deferred makes the heart sick, but
when the desire comes, it is a tree of life.*

PROVERBS 13:12, NKJV

"Oh, man, Christmas is almost over," my husband moaned.

I shot him an incredulous look. "It's December 20. What do you mean it's almost over? It hasn't even happened yet!"

"I know, but I'm still sad," he said with a shrug.

Every year without fail, Tim expresses disappointment when the season is almost over. He loves Christmas and all it brings—the Hallmark movies, the lights, the red and green decor, and the time spent gathering with friends and family to celebrate Jesus' birth. Though I don't share his disappointment, I understand his point of view. The end of a season, a vacation, a role in a company, or an education program— many endings bring mixed feelings even if they're something that we've anticipated.

In fact, anticipation often serves a role in motivating us to move forward in life. Looking ahead to an event stimulates the limbic cortex—where happiness and excitement are derived—and releases dopamine, a neurotransmitter that plays a role in the "reward center" of our brain. A study in 2017 showed that the brain activity of people who thought about a positive, upcoming activity indicated a greater sense of well-being.* What we think about the future impacts how we feel in the present.

We like to think that happiness is found in the fulfillment of a dream, but the truth is that even the anticipation of it—"when the desire comes," as today's verse says—brings life and renewal. This hope-filled expectation for what lies ahead isn't just true of our dreams for the future but is also a reality of what lies ahead in our Christian walk. We do not live like those who have no hope (1 Thessalonians 4:13) but instead have the confident expectation that our entire lives can be lived with anticipation for life ahead—a life with Jesus, by his side—forever. While we wait, let's find reasons to thank God for everything we have to look forward to each day—including Christmas.

Kristin

Today's Act of Gratitude

What's one thing (a vacation, a holiday, an event) you are looking forward to? Spend time thanking God for it, finding joy in the anticipation.

---

* Holly Rhue, "The Psychology of Anticipation: Why the Holidays Never Live Up to Our Expectations," Byrdie, December 1, 2021, https://www.byrdie.com/psychology-of-anticipation-expectations-5203025.

The Sun Still Rises

*Because of God's tender mercy, the morning light from heaven is
about to break upon us, to give light to those who sit in darkness and
in the shadow of death, and to guide us to the path of peace.*

LUKE 1:78-79

Minnesota, like most places, has beautiful sunrises and sunsets. But our winter sunrises are remarkable when the ground is covered in snow and the sun begins to break on the horizon. Colors of pink, purple, red, yellow, and orange swirl above the ground in stark contrast to the white that covers everything. If you step outside, there's a crispness to the morning air, especially if it's devoid of wind—a quiet like you don't experience any other time of year.

And to me, it always feels holy.

It's no secret that I love being in nature and feel most connected to God when I am out in his creation. There is something very healing and grounding about being outdoors: a stability in knowing that the sun will continue to rise and set. An assurance that seasons will continue to come and go.

This is a constant reminder of God's care and faithfulness to us, to those who have gone before us, and to our children who will carry on after we're gone. And this fills me with hope, especially when I walk through seasons of doubt, fear, or depression. The physical world reminds us of a God who is always consistent and available when we're troubled, worried, or uncertain.

And no matter what else is happening in the world, no matter how dark our circumstances get, we can trust that because of God's tender mercy, heaven's morning light will soon break upon us, bringing light to the darkness and guiding us into peace. Peace of mind. Peace of heart. Peace that we can share with others.

Kendra

Today's Act of Gratitude

Spend some time out in God's creation. If possible, watch a sunrise
or sunset and thank God for his faithfulness, mercy, and love.

Enough for Everyone

All the animals of the forest are mine, and I own the cattle on a thousand hills.

PSALM 50:10

"See the finish line just ahead? We've got this. Dig deep, and let's finish strong!" As Lizzie huffed and puffed alongside a runner from a competing team, her words of encouragement spurred her opponent to surge toward the finish line.

As Lizzie completed the race several seconds behind her competitor, she found herself engulfed in an unexpected bear hug. The young woman whispered her thanks in Lizzie's ear, telling her how much the pep talk had helped her when her energy was flagging and she'd wanted to give up.

My daughter's junior high approach to cross-country races was more than a bit unconventional. She intentionally paced girls from other schools, striking up conversations and offering words of encouragement during the most challenging portions of a course. She always crossed the finish line, but sometimes the girls she ran alongside crossed a moment or two ahead of her, and she was okay with that.

Lizzie's approach measured success in collaborative ways, which is slightly befuddling to those of us who see races through the lens of winning and losing rather than finishing or not finishing. It's a perspective shift embracing the foundational truth that there is no scarcity in the Kingdom of God. If God owns the "cattle on a thousand hills," then another woman's success does not come at my (or your) expense. Rather than dividing his blessing from an ever-dwindling resource, God has enough for everyone and infinitely beyond. When we learn to be generous, we finally shift our thinking from a scarcity win/loss mentality to a collaborative win/win mentality.* When we let go of the scarcity mindset, generosity in our resources, time, and encouragement takes on a whole new, incredibly fun dimension. We're able to cheer wildly and genuinely for one another, finding inspiration and encouragement in pursuing our own goals without worrying about the competition from another's pursuit of her goals.

I don't know about you, but I feel an immense relief as I step off the comparison merry-go-round embedded in the scarcity mindset and learn to measure success by God's standards instead of the world's.

Julie

Today's Act of Gratitude

Actively cheerlead a competitor as you
adopt God's standard of success.

---

* See Stephen R. Covey, *The 7 Habits of Highly Effective People* (New York: Simon & Schuster, 2013), 214–246.

Good News

The angel reassured them. "Don't be afraid!" he said.
"I bring you good news that will bring great joy to all people."

LUKE 2:10

Even though I'd been expecting my children to arrive home from school at any moment, the sudden noise startled me. The heavy front door swung open, then quickly shuddered to a close with one hard push. As my daughter Noelle shed her coat and shoes in the mudroom, she called out, looking for me.

"Mom? Mom! I did it. I did it! I got into the conference!" she said, excitement in every word.

"Oh, that's great!" I exclaimed, holding my arms open as she paused beside my chair for a welcome-home hug, smiling widely. She nodded in agreement, then chattered about who else was going and when the conference would take place.

A few weeks earlier, she'd painstakingly filled out the application and submitted a piece of writing in the hope of being one of the children chosen to participate. The day-long conference would feature artists and authors at a college about an hour away. Several elementary schools were participating in the event, which meant that only a small number of students would be chosen from each school.

As Noelle shared her good news, her excitement was contagious, and I couldn't help but smile along with her.

A new job, a milestone, a graduation, an achievement we've been working toward—all of these are good news and deserve to be celebrated. Sharing our achievements with the people we love only increases the joy we experience in those moments.

But the truth is that you and I have good news too. In fact, we possess the very best news! Just like the angel who appeared to the shepherds when Jesus was born, we have a message that will bring great joy to others. Because of Jesus' sacrifice and resurrection, our sins are forgiven, and we will live with him forever. Every day with Jesus is a "good news" day. When we recognize the privilege of knowing Jesus, we can reconsider our daily circumstances in light of the long scope of eternity. Friends, we have the hope of heaven! That is marvelously good news—news we should be bursting to share.

Kristin

Today's Act of Gratitude

Thank God for the good news of Jesus and
look for ways to tell it to others.

Small Traditions with a Big Impact

*Direct your children onto the right path, and
when they are older, they will not leave it.*

PROVERBS 22:6

My dad loved buying a real Christmas tree every year when I was growing up. The bigger, the better. We lived in a small house, but our favorite room was the addition the previous owners had constructed. It had a slanted ceiling and, at its peak, it was almost as tall as our second story, providing the perfect spot for a lofty tree.

We have several pictures of my dad standing proudly next to his trees. Not a small man, his six-foot-one-inch frame would be overshadowed by several feet of the tree we'd managed to erect in the highest corner of the room. (One year, the tree was so large my dad had to anchor it to the wall with wire to prevent it from toppling.) Flipping through old albums, I always stop and smile when I come across these scenes.

Memories are an interesting thing. So much of what I thought was important as a child—the gifts with my name on them under the tree, the treasures that might be in my stocking—I don't even remember. What I recall are the small things—the Christmas cookies and treats my mom would make each year, the tree we'd all help put up and decorate with ornaments and tinsel. It wasn't the material things but the consistent way my parents made the holidays special that mattered the most.

Like me, maybe you can look back and see family traditions that have impacted you. Or maybe you've started traditions in your own family that were lacking in your childhood. Either way, Scripture tells us that if we guide our children onto the right path, when they are grown, they won't step away from it. This isn't just about the things we teach our kids, but the daily habits and structures we create for them to grow up healthy and secure. Don't think that the little traditions and rhythms of life you establish now won't have an impact later; sometimes, that may be what they remember most.

Kendra

Today's Act of Gratitude

What healthy traditions are you carrying on with your family? Spend some time thinking about what new practices you'd like to start incorporating into your life.

Defiant, Gentle Hope

To us a child is born, to us a son is given, and the government
will be on his shoulders. And he will be called Wonderful
Counselor, Mighty God, Everlasting Father, Prince of Peace.

ISAIAH 9:6, NIV

"Hope is a defiant verb." Ann Voskamp's declaration about hope, spoken from a stage years and years ago, caught my attention.

Hope is most definitely a noun. I mentally argued with Ann from the bleachers, even as I wrote her statement in my cute notebook, doodling around the margins, processing her words. I'd always thought of hope as somewhat soft and gentle. If I were to assign a color to the idea of hope, it would probably be a pretty, light pink. If I were to assign feelings, they would be bubbly and happy. Ann's words had me reconsidering these ideas and wondering whether my hope and Ann's hope could both be correct.

It turns out that—officially—hope is a noun *and* a verb. And just as hope can be a soft, bubbly, baby pink, I've discovered it is also gritty, hard as granite, and a white so blindingly bright you can scarcely glance at it. Sometimes I need the comforting, softer version of hope—a compassionate reassurance that Jesus is our confidante, our Rabbi filled with encouragement, wisdom, and gentle correction as we strive to live as he did. But there are also times in which I desperately need my unwavering, unyielding Savior, the undefeated warrior who laid down his life for me, standing between me and the enemy of my soul as a fierce protector and shield.

Friends, Jesus is both. He is our greatest hope: noun and verb, gentle and unyielding, compassionate and fierce. He is the only Son of our heavenly Father, the world's Savior, sent as a babe in the humblest of beginnings to a teenage, unwed mother faced with no room at the inn, to intersect and forever alter the path of humankind. I cannot think of a Christmas gift I need more this year than the dual hopes found in Jesus Christ.

Julie

Today's Act of Gratitude

Make your own wish list of hope on this Christmas Day, thanking
God for the gift of defiant, gentle hope found in Jesus.

Trusting God's Provision

*That is why I tell you not to worry about everyday life—whether you
have enough food and drink, or enough clothes to wear. Isn't life
more than food, and your body more than clothing? Look at the birds.
They don't plant or harvest or store food in barns, for your heavenly
Father feeds them. And aren't you far more valuable to him than
they are? Can all your worries add a single moment to your life?*

MATTHEW 6:25-27

My sister-in-law April had just returned from a missions trip to Albania, and she told me about the experience that had the greatest impact on her.

"One of the most eye-opening times was when we went to a poor village with one of the local pastors to distribute food and supplies. We stopped at one older couple's place, and as they invited us into their small house with very few furnishings, they welcomed us with open arms. They didn't know us or that we were coming, but they kept saying, 'thank you for coming; we're so glad you're here.' As we gave them supplies, the wife explained how they woke up that morning with no food and had asked God to provide for them for today."

My throat clenched with emotion as I nodded in response.

"I thought, *do we ever do that?*" April said through tears. "They were so grateful, so happy; they didn't seem overly worried or stressed out. They enjoyed the moment they were in and trusted and believed that God would provide. We don't live that way. We can get so anxious about so many things."

She finished by saying, "I came home convicted about everything I worry about, when God has told us he will provide."

As I thought about April's story, I realized how easy it is in my own life to worry over the future, forgetting all the times God has made a way or provided for me in the past.

We are often told in Scripture not to fear or worry, that God will take care of us because we are valuable to him. And indeed—can all our worries add time to our lives? Not even a little bit. We can trust in God's provision for today.

Kendra

Today's Act of Gratitude

Spend time writing down the ways God has
provided for you in the past, and thank him for
the provision you know he will continue to bring.

Weathering Storms

*Devote yourselves to prayer with
an alert mind and a thankful heart.*

COLOSSIANS 4:2

Strange as it sounds, awakening to that first tiny tingling sensation in my lip, indicating an imminent cold sore, has become a welcome occurrence. Cold sores are my body's cue that an intensely stressful something has passed and that smoother emotional sailing is just ahead. As much as I dislike them, they are so accurately predictable that they've become a strange barometer measuring the passing of storms in my life.

And that's just the thing—storms happen. We watch on wobbling video as tornadoes, hurricanes, and wildfires whip through the land, and in the same way, times of trouble blow through our lives with varying levels of intensity and destruction. Some storms are creatures of our own making, but many of them strike suddenly with no warning. There is nothing that we could or should have done to avoid them or make them go away.

And while the details of my particular storms might vary wildly, how I navigate them has become unwaveringly consistent.

1. *Pray for others.* While I don't underestimate whatever I'm facing, I try to maintain an upward and outward perspective by interceding for others, even as I petition for myself. Too much navel-gazing can lead to a deep hole of self-pity, and while questions of "why me" are entirely normal, I try hard not to camp there for too long. Praying for others keeps me moving.

2. *Rally friends.* I tend to pull away from others when I'm in crisis. Don't give in to the temptation to isolate. Let your friends know what is going on and ask those you trust to pray with and for you.

3. *Count blessings.* I look for even the smallest good in each day and make it a priority to purposely pause in thanksgiving over each one of those good things.

4. *Meditate on Scripture.* Tuck the promises of God into your heart. Tape Scripture to your mirror or put it on the fridge—wherever it is that you will trip across it as you go about your daily activities. We need God's unwavering, unshakable, foundational truth in the midst of storms.

Julie

Today's Act of Gratitude

Do you have an intentional plan in place for weathering life's storms? You are welcome to adopt and tweak mine, but be sure not to neglect practicing gratitude.

The Hope of Restoration

Look! I stand at the door and knock. If you hear my voice and open the door, I will come in, and we will share a meal together as friends.

REVELATION 3:20

As I looked over the photos scattered across my living room floor, a couple of family members stood out. Despite our blood ties, I don't know them that well and haven't seen them often over the years. Seeing their faces in the photos made me mourn the time we've lost.

I felt like I had missed out.

But then I thought about other relationships that have mended over time. My husband and his brother Phil were rarely in contact for many years. Between an age gap and residing in a different location, Phil didn't know us well and didn't attend our wedding. Feeling sad over the lack of connection, my husband decided to make more effort. Years later, we have a wonderful relationship with Phil and his wife, Marlene, and see them as often as we can. We love them deeply, and the feeling is mutual.

In the same way, I rarely saw my Aunt Bernnetta as a child. She and her family lived in the southern US, so visits were few and far between. Our relationship blossomed when she moved to the area where I lived after college. I loved meeting up with her for coffee or going window-shopping together. She held my babies, listened, and loved me so well.

I'm grateful to have learned through experience that restoration is possible. Even as I organize my photos and grieve relationships that are not entirely where I'd like them to be, I know there's always the hope of tomorrow. Just as my husband did with his brother and I did with my aunt, it's possible to begin anew. You and I need look no further than our gracious God to see how to move forward. He stands at the door and knocks—waiting to be invited in, ready to receive us.

Though we may sometimes feel far from him, the truth is that restoration is possible. Our God is a God of second chances—and fourth chances, and four hundredth chances—and he longs to connect with us. By following his lead, we can find the restoration we seek, both with him and with others.

Kristin

Today's Act of Gratitude

Consider whether a relationship in your life needs to be restored. Then, prayerfully consider your next step in moving forward.

A Gracious Reply

Be kind to each other, tenderhearted, forgiving one another,
just as God through Christ has forgiven you.

EPHESIANS 4:32

My child had made a mistake. They'd hurt another person's feelings, and even though they'd apologized, I felt I should reach out to the other child's mom and clear everything up. But I was nervous. *What will her response be? Is she angry? Hurt? Will she speak poorly of my child?* All these thoughts swirled through my mind until I finally sat down and prayed.

"Lord," I said, "please help me know what to say and let her be open to my apology."

As I sent the text, apologizing on behalf of my child, I nervously watched for her response. I didn't have to wait long.

"Thank you for reaching out. I really appreciate it," her reply began. She went on to share her feelings about what had happened, being gracious toward my child. "Again, I hope you know how much it means that you reached out," she finished.

I sat stunned, with tears in my eyes. Her response was so kind and undeserved. We chatted back and forth a little bit more as I said a prayer of thanks and the burden brought by my child's behavior lifted. I knew we would get past this and keep our relationship intact.

Sometimes we need to ask forgiveness for what we ourselves have done, but other times we may seek forgiveness on behalf of another—whether that's a child, a family member, or a friend. When we see that someone has been hurt, we can offer comfort and acknowledge the pain, even if we weren't the cause of it.

Scripture tells us how we should behave as believers. We are to be kind, tenderhearted, and forgiving, remembering that it was Christ who forgave each of us. In a world that seeks to divide, we can be the peacemakers, the bridge builders, the ones who graciously forgive and seek forgiveness when necessary.

Kendra

Today's Act of Gratitude

Who have you struggled to be in a relationship with lately? What action could you display toward them that would exude Christ, whether it be kindness, forgiveness, or tenderness?

Finding Your Spot

*Search for the LORD and for his strength;
continually seek him.*

1 CHRONICLES 16:11

"Honey, can you help me move this pot? The basil isn't getting enough sunlight, and we won't have much of a crop if we don't get it moved."

Aaron isn't really a gardener, but he loves fresh basil. I only had to suggest that our harvest was in jeopardy, and there he was, ready to lift/scoot/roll my enormously heavy pot halfway across the yard.

As we settled the basil into a sunnier location, I paused to reconsider how my other plants were faring. My garden competes with a couple of nearby trees for light, and I try to plant the sun lovers in the full-sun spots while my cooler season veggies get tucked into the areas with various amounts of dappled shade. Different plants need different amounts of light to thrive, and planting in the wrong place generally results in a smaller harvest.

In the corporate world, a phrase describing the same basic concept is "putting people into the right seat on the bus."* It works the same way for us as Christians. In other words, when we're aligned with God, we're positioned for maximum personal growth and the ability to impact lives around us. This doesn't always mean we're comfortable or where we want to be; it means we're where God has planted us for his glory and purpose.

I pondered the "right seat on the bus" concept as I stood contemplating my garden plants. *Lord, am I in the right seat on your bus? Is there any seat trading or shifting I need to do? What about Aaron and the kids—are we in the right bus seats as a family? How do we increase our proverbial harvest?*

Today's verse is a wonderful reminder to keep God at the center of our decision-making as we stand on the cusp of a new year. He knows what we need before we do, and we can thank him in advance for using us to build his Kingdom—even if that is not the most outwardly comfortable, preferred spot on the bus.

Julie

Today's Act of Gratitude

Ask God to move you into the "right bus seat,"
aligning your life with his will in the big and small,
looking for opportunities to be grateful in the process.

---

* See Jim Collins, *Good to Great: Why Some Companies Make the Leap . . . and Others Don't* (New York: HarperCollins, 2001), 41–64.

Death and Life

*I am about to do something new. See, I have already
begun! Do you not see it? I will make a pathway through
the wilderness. I will create rivers in the dry wasteland.*

ISAIAH 43:19

New Year's Eve is always poignant: On one hand, the new year is on the horizon, glimmering with promise. On the other hand, another year is ending, and with it, our hopes and dreams for the last twelve months.

Maybe we've restored a relationship, accomplished a goal, taken our dream vacation.

Maybe we've experienced the loss of a loved one, the death of a dream, the end of a career.

Rarely, if ever, does life look the way we wanted or expected.

In the same way, for the first five or ten years of its life, the Joshua tree—which, despite its name, belongs to the Yucca genus and isn't truly a tree—doesn't look like much. Until it blooms it's nothing more than an upright trunk with no branches. This plant grows slowly, and it takes years to bloom. Plus, the flowering rosettes die afterwards and there will be no more growth from them. The dried stems stay on the plant though, creating a mix of dead and new growth.

Yet even when parts of the Joshua tree seem lifeless, it's still alive. It's still growing. Though one part blossoms, another part does not—death and life are intertwined, part of the same tree.

When I feel like I've experienced the death of a dream, I remember that just as with the Joshua tree, it isn't the end of the story. Life is still present. I love the promise in Isaiah: *God is about to do something new.* What's more, he's already begun. He makes pathways through the wilderness seasons of failed expectations, and he creates rivers in the wastelands of dashed hopes. He is always and already working—if only we'll have the eyes to see it. Even when we experience hardships, we can look for the good. It's still there.

Kristin

Today's Act of Gratitude

As you look back at the last year, what were the unexpected moments of sweetness and some of the things and people for which you were most grateful? How can considering those bright spots of gratitude help as you turn to the year ahead?

About the Authors

Julie Fisk left a fifteen-year legal career to become an author. Always passionate about words, she shifted her storytelling from courtrooms and boardrooms to telling stories of God's faithfulness, no matter the circumstance. Together with her cofounders of The Ruth Experience, Julie connects with an online community of women seeking and living out their faith. When she's not writing or speaking, Julie is a backyard farmer, a collector of coffee mugs, and an admitted bookworm.

Do it afraid. **Kendra Roehl** has sought to live out that advice as a social worker, foster parent, mother of five, and public speaker. She has a master's degree in social work and has naturally become a defender of those in need, serving others in hospice, low-income housing, and veterans' affairs programs. Kendra and her husband are well-known advocates for foster care, taking in more than twenty children in six years and adopting three of them. As a cofounder of The Ruth Experience, she continues to care for others as a frequent speaker and an author of several books.

A career in journalism set **Kristin Demery** up to one day publish her own stories of living this wild, precious life. She is now an author of several books and part of a trio of writers collectively known as The Ruth Experience. Kristin served as a newspaper and magazine editor, and her work has been featured in a variety of publications, including *USA Today*. She still works behind the scenes as an editor for others while writing her own series on kindness, friendship, and living with intention. An adventurer at heart, she loves checking items off the family bucket list with her husband and three daughters.